THE BOOK OF

FOOTBALL

QUOTATIONS

PHIL SHAW

TED SMART

This edition published for The Book People,
Hall Wood Avenue, Haydock

First published 2003 by Ebury Press,
An imprint of Random House,
20 Vauxhall Bridge Road, London SW1V 2SA
www.randomhouse.co.uk

Random House Australia (Pty) Limited
20 Alfred Street, Milsons Point, Sydney,
New South Wales 2061, Australia

Random House New Zealand Limited
18 Poland Road, Glenfield, Auckland 10, New Zealand

Random House South Africa (Pty) Limited
Endulini, 5a Jubilee Road, Parktown 2193, South Africa

The Random House Group Limited Reg. No. 954009

www.randomhouse.co.uk

Typeset by seagulls
Printed and bound in Great Britain
by Cox & Wyman Ltd, Reading, Berks

A CIP catalogue record for this book
is available from the British Library.

Cover designed by Keenan

ISBN 0 09188 920 0

CONTENTS

INTRODUCTION V

❶ PLAYERS: PRESENT I

❷ PLAYERS: PAST 49

❸ CLUBS 87

❹ COUNTRIES I25

❺ MANAGERS I4I

❻ MANAGING I99

❼ THE GAME 2I7

❽ THE LIFESTYLE 247

❾ PHILOSOPHERS 277

❿ FANS 293

⓫ BOARDROOM 32I

⓬ REFEREES 339

⓭ WOMEN 35I

⓮ ARTS AND MEDIA 363

⓯ FAMOUS LAST WORDS 377

INDEX 39I

Phil Shaw is a sports writer for the *Independent*. He has previously written for the *Guardian*, *Observer* and *Time Out*. Along with seven editions of *The Book of Football Quotations*, originally in collaboration with Peter Ball, he has written *Whose Game Is It Anyway?* a book about football fanzines. He lives in Staffordshire with his wife and two children.

ACKNOWLEDGEMENTS

All journalists who have stood outside a stadium in the cold and damp, be it at Old Trafford or Vale Park, waiting to elicit some precious 'nannies' (nanny goats: quotes) from reluctant players or grudging managers can take my gratitude as read. Special thanks go to Patrick Barclay, Christopher Davies, Jonathan Foster, David Instone, Tony Leighton, Grahame Lloyd, Kevin McCarra, Kenny MacDonald, Glenn Moore, Ian Ross and Henry Winter for their interest and input; to Iain Wyatt for rescuing me from megabyte meltdown; to Stuart Batsford, Will Birch, Andy Childs, Pete Frame, Mick Houghton, Jonathan Morrish, Rocky Prior, Tom Sheehan, Keith Smith and John Tobler for their friendship and for reminding me (as Shankly always knew, contrary to popular belief) that there is more to life than football; to Messrs Lennon and McCartney, Marriott and Lane, Ray Davies, Warren Zevon, Arthur Lee, the brothers and sisters of Motown, Stax and Chess, and to Tony Lawlor, among dozens of others, for providing the soundtrack to the preparation of this book; to Andrew Goodfellow for publishing it and displaying a soundness of judgement not evident in his choice of team; to my family, Julie, Ellie and Joe, for their love and support, and to my parents, Roy and Gwen, for first taking me to Elland Road too many years ago.

Phil Shaw, Staffordshire, January 2003.

INTRODUCTION

Dour Yorkshiremen. Humourless Germans. Rhythmic Jamaicans. Tight-fisted Scots. Oh, and sophisticated Swedes. To these stereotypes, trotted out daily in the media and in the 'real world', can be added The Thick Footballer.

It has long been widely accepted that the game's main practitioners, especially the players, are brainless, monosyllabic morons. Some 30 years ago there was a sketch, in 'Monty Python's Flying Circus' I believe, in which a player plainly based on George Best answered every question put to him with 'I'm opening a boutique, Brian.'

Little has changed, it seems. When the producer of the film Bend It Like Beckham announced (jokingly, it transpired) at the British Comedy Awards in 2002 that she had received a congratulatory letter from the England captain himself, a voice called out, to smug titters from the assembled scribes and comics: 'Can he write?'

Such episodes remind me of a radio interview I did in the course of publicising the first edition of *The Book of Football Quotations*, in 1984. My interrogator, a plummy BBC veteran, was incredulous that anyone should have attempted what myself and my co-compiler, Peter Ball, had done. Having clearly not taken a moment to study the erudition and wit on display within its pages, he wondered aloud how we had contrived to make such a sturdy volume out of 'sick as a parrot' and 'over the moon' utterances.

While it was never our mission to rectify the sweeping generalisation about the intelligence of football folk, it has, over the course of seven previous editions, been a pleasing by-product. There are, of course, many footballers whose brains are to be found only in their feet, which in turn are often in their mouths. But to suggest it is a defining personality trait of an entire profession betrays ignorance bordering on snobbery and is not borne out by my experiences as a sports journalist over the past 25 years.

But why has the notion arisen? One reason is that players and managers are frequently interviewed within seconds or minutes of finishing a match, when their adrenalin is still pumping furiously. Microphones are thrust in their faces and they are asked 'how it felt' to score the winner or to lose in the last minute. The question invites, nay demands, a stock answer, but if the response starts with 'obviously', whose fault is that?

That's why, incidentally, *The Book of Football Quotations* has tended to resist pressure from various publishers, not to mention reviewers, to include more Colemanballs – the slips of the tongue that have been such a source of merriment to readers of *Private Eye*. Sneering at other people's mistakes under pressure has never seemed particularly amusing to this dour Yorkshireman, unless it produces an image or wordplay that is funny in its own right.

Another factor that has led to the perception of footballers being capable only of inanities is the sheer ridiculousness of trying to capture the essence of the sport in words. The wonderfully unpredictable nature of football means that participants and watchers (among whom I include the media, however dispassionate they may strive to be) are often plunged into the depths of despair or propelled to great emotional heights in the space of seconds.

How to articulate and encapsulate such extremes is a task with which the most exceptional wordsmiths, men and women of the chattering classes, can struggle, even with the comparative luxury of an hour to go before deadline. Yet we expect a member of the clattering classes, or a manager whose job may have been on the line, to come up with bons mots.

In the circumstances, there is something brilliantly succinct and all-encompassing about a reply like Alex Ferguson's to the TV interviewer who collared him immediately after Manchester United turned defeat into victory in the European Cup final with two implausibly late goals: 'Football,' he said, shaking his head and breaking into a grin. 'Bloody hell.'

Footballers do not, it is true, tend to be well-educated, often having devoted themselves to the sport at the expense of academic learning before they reach puberty. Their intelligence develops in a different way to ordinary mortals, but it is there none the less, expressed in the humour of the dressing-room, which is often scalpel-sharp and savagely witty, rather than in correct syntax or grammar. An interview with an experienced pro with a fund of anecdotes can be as entertaining as seeing a top comedian. And managers may tell you they will let their players do the talking but cannot help filling your notebook or tape.

The book was Peter Ball's idea. Peter, who was then my sports editor at *Time Out* and later worked for *The Guardian*, *The Observer*, *The Times* and Dublin's *Sunday Tribune*, would literally surround himself with massive piles of newspapers and magazines. He particularly liked *Sports Illustrated*'s 'They Said It' section, which was the inspiration for the first-ever 'Quotes of the Week' column which I started in *The Independent* in 1986.

Every December, Peter and I trawled through this newsprint mountain and produced a quotes of the year spread. A common feature nowadays, it had previously been found solely in *The Guardian*, where my colleague Frank Keating could claim to be the father of a cottage industry.

Peter was as keen on the polished prose he found in football literature (which is often lazily or snootily dismissed as 'not as good as cricket's', despite the evidence to the contrary produced by Brian Glanville, John Moynihan, Hugh McIlvanney, Brian James, James Lawton et al) as the off-the-cuff quips by the Shanklys, Dochertys, Cloughs or Atkinsons. Anything that made 'Bally' smile or snarl, whether a bizarre verbal flight or a cold, hard put-down, would make the cut.

My more anal approach to quote-collecting, which betrayed my past incarnation as a GLC clerk and librarian, entailed clipping them throughout the year instead of the annual needle-in-haystack search. We shared equal billing in what became a solo venture after Peter died of leukemia in 1997.

The book was launched at a time when football was in decline, yet reviewers, from *The Sun* to *The Field*, were almost all positive or enthusiastic. It endured during the 'boom' years leading up to the millennium. Now, although 'bust' is rearing its head again, talking a good game is a more apt expression than ever. Speaking to the press (dailies, evenings, Sundays, local), and TV (satellite and terrestrial), and radio (local, national and commercial), and websites, and so on, is acknowledged as part of the job, be it the player, manager, chairman, groundsman, tea-lady, supporters' representative or referee. There has never been so much source material to choose from.

My role is to scan the myriad press interviews, homing in anything in inverted commas. Programme columns, letters pages and the burgeoning number of books offer rich pickings, as do press conferences, commentaries and what we still call 'terrace' humour. I also look for anything pithy said about the game by pop singers, soap actors and film stars, politicians, cricketers or vicars. Having collected great carrier-bagfuls of cuttings (my typically low-tech idea of a database) the task then is to seek out quotations that will have a life beyond the week in which they appear and to juxtapose them with remarks that provide a different, perhaps ironic twist.

My preference is for the punchy one-liner that makes me chuckle or think. Profane or profound, hilarious or humbug, the best quotations have a certain rhythm to them (it did not surprise me when a football bard approached me recently about the possibility of doing a Two Ronnies-style routine at various literary and poetry festivals, which would draw heavily on the book).

I am invariably asked which is my favourite, but that could be any one of a couple of dozen from down the decades, depending on my mood on the day in question. I have phases where neat, finely honed epigrams seem better than anything, and others where I prefer the stream of semi-consciousness (c.f. Colin Murphy).

This book tries to cover all bases. There are, however, a couple of gems that always hit the spot. One is by Joe Royle, then the manager of Oldham, after Paul Warhurst had been sent off. As we hacks clamoured for his view, which we hoped would be suitably outraged, Royle declared, without missing a beat: 'The ref says it was for foul and abusive language, but the lad swears blind he never said anything.'

I despised Margaret Thatcher's politics, and still do, but I thank her profusely for her reply when, attending the Ipswich-Arsenal FA Cup final of 1978 as leader of the opposition, she was asked who her man of the match was. Not realising that there had been a programme change which meant David Geddis had played instead of Trevor Whymark, she opined with that regal authority we came to know so well: 'I thought the Ipswich no. 10, Whymark, played particularly well.'

Even then, you see, the Iron Lady only had eyes for No. 10. But please, don't quote me on that.

1

PLAYERS: PRESENT

DARREN ANDERTON

Anderton wins England fitness fight.
'Headline you will never see',
Football365 website, 1999.

NICOLAS ANELKA

He didn't deal with the transfer business as well as he should but he was badly advised. Deep down he'll know he didn't work this one out professionally, but as the boss [Arsene Wenger] said: 'He's not bad, he's just young.'
LEE DIXON, Arsenal defender, on Anelka's exit from Highbury, 1999.

Today I am low and lots of people are torpedoing me. I know who they are and when I am back at the top, I will remember it.
NICOLAS ANELKA, after widespread criticism of his departure from Arsenal, 1999.

[David] Dein bought me for £500,000 and sold me for 44 times as much, so he has made a huge profit. And he still tried to block things.

This man thinks only about money.
ANELKA, 1999.

I'm no longer part of Arsenal. To hell with the English people.
ANELKA, 1999.

I would have sold him quicker, and though I might have had to settle for a bit less [of a transfer fee], it's swings and roundabouts. The way they got him [Arsenal allegedly poached Anelka from Paris Saint-Germain] was contentious anyway.
GEORGE GRAHAM, former Arsenal manager, 1999.

I think he is confused. He lives in a world of his own and he will have to get out of it.
VINCENTE DEL BOSQUE as Anelka's stay at Real Madrid turned sour, 2000.

PHIL BABB

Arguably the guy with the most lusted-after legs in British football.
LISA I'ANSON, compere of the TV show Dear Dilemma, *1995.*

ROBERTO BAGGIO

The Divine Pony Tail
Slogan on Italian fans' banner,
World Cup finals, 1994.

NICK BARMBY

Are we talking about a
change of religion here, or
just a change of football club?
GERARD HOULLIER,
Liverpool manager, when asked
whether Barmby 'might have to
become a recluse' after moving
from Everton, 2000.

FABIEN BARTHEZ

The man with whom most
French women would like to
spend their holidays.
Result of opinion poll in Paris
Match *magazine, 1998.*

Unconsciously, I fell in love
with the small, round sphere
with its amusing and
capricious rebounds which
sometimes play with me.
FABIEN BARTHEZ,
Manchester United's French
goalkeeper, 2000.

WARREN BARTON

The best-dressed footballer
I've ever seen. Even in training
— we're all in tracksuits and
he arrives in shirt, trousers and
shoes. And his hair's lovely. We
call him The Dog, as in the
dog's bollocks.
ROBERT LEE, Newcastle
midfielder, on his defensive
colleague, 1996.

DAVID BATTY

Batty would probably get
himself booked playing
Handel's *Largo.*
DAVID LACEY reporting in
the Guardian *on Charity Shield*
match between Leeds and
Liverpool in which Batty was
cautioned, 1992.

Batty and Le Saux there,
arguing over who has the
sillier name.
RORY BREMNER as Desmond
Lynam on his Channel 4 show,
after the two Blackburn players
had traded punches in a match
in Moscow, 1995.

I've never had a good game
in front of me dad. When
he watches me I'm always

crap. To win things with Leeds would be fantastic, but I would really like to impress him.
DAVID BATTY on rejoining Leeds, 1998.

I know people think I'm a bit of a hard man on the pitch, but I'd like the kids to see me as a bit of a softie off it.
BATTY, 1999.

DAVID BECKHAM

Beckham's silly little, smart little kick at his Argentinian opponent was what is wrong with the national character. This Gaultier-saronged, Posh-Spiced, Cooled Britannia, look-at-me, what-a-lad, loadsamoney, sex-and-shopping, fame-schooled, daytime-TV, over-coiffed twerp did not, of course, mean any harm.
Daily Telegraph *leader article after Beckham's sending-off* v. *Argentina, World Cup finals, 1998.*

The place was packed when England played. Trade went up 200 per cent. But I've never seen a pub empty so quickly. His stupid kick cost the licensed trade millions.
BILL MURRAY, London publican, on his intention to sue Beckham for loss of earnings, 1998.

Posh Spice is pregnant. At least that's one time David Beckham has stayed on long enough.
BRADLEY WALSH, host-comedian, on TV's National Lottery Show, *1998.*

I think the majority of people in Britain dislike me.
DAVID BECKHAM, interviewed by Alan Hansen on the TV documentary The Football Millionaires, *1999.*

Nobody should ever underestimate David Beckham. The lad has balls. At times I have disagreed with decisions he has taken off the field but he has a stubbornness that cannot be broken, and he will make up his own mind, whatever Alex Ferguson might think.
ALEX FERGUSON, in his autobiography, 1999.

People say you get married and spend the rest of your life in the kitchen, but my life is not like that. I'm not very domesticated — I don't even know how to turn on the washing machine and I have no intention of ever bloody learning. David does all that.
VICTORIA BECKHAM, David's pop-star wife, 1999.

We don't really have many rows. We're quite childlike.
VICTORIA, 1999.

They are precisely the kind of people that one would dread having as neighbours. They have lots of money but no class and no idea how to behave.
DAME BARBARA CARTLAND on hearing that the Beckhams planned to move near her, 1999.

Keane has said he will stay at Man United through thick and thin, or Becks and Posh as they're known.
RORY McGRATH, panelist on TV's They Think It's All Over, 1999.

David doesn't announce where and when Victoria might sing in the future, so she should stay quiet about his football.
GORDON HILL, former United winger, after Mrs Beckham reportedly suggested her husband might play abroad eventually, 1999.

The face of angel and the bum of a Greek god. Rumour has it that his tackle is enough to not only take your breath away but possibly do you serious damage.
ATTITUDE, gay magazine, naming Beckham top of its 'fantasy' players, 1999.

I saw some rock 'n' roll T-shirts in Los Angeles which had been customised with sequins. They were $250 each, which I thought was far too expensive, so I didn't buy one. The next day David was in the same shop with my sister and bought 12.
VICTORIA in OK! magazine, 1999.

Beckham can't kick with his left foot. He can't head a ball, can't tackle and doesn't score many goals. Apart from that, he's all right.
GEORGE BEST, 2000.

He's a really intelligent person. He's really deep, which I like.
VICTORIA, 2000.

I think Becks is an intelligent person. It's just that he hardly says anything.
DWIGHT YORKE, United colleague, 1999.

Whether it's men or women who fancy you, it's nice to be liked.
BECKHAM in OK! *magazine on going to gay bars with his wife, 2000.*

He walks around the kitchen going: 'I'm a gay icon, I'm a gay icon.' When I try to say, 'So am I,' he just goes: 'But they love me more.'
VICTORIA, 2000.

I'm partial to a bit of Beckham...I prefer him with his cropped hair – it makes him a little more rough and ready.
BOY GEORGE, gay pop singer and DJ, 2000.

It's a sign of the times when Beckham has to be guarded against muggers [in Rio de

Janeiro] because he's brandishing a £40,000 necklace, the big girl's blouse. I'd been in the game 20 years before I was earning that kind of dosh in a calendar year, but there he is wearing that amount around his neck.
ALAN HUDSON, former England midfielder, 2000.

Is he the guy that wears his wife's G-string? I've got a message for him: 'Get out of those G-strings as quick as you can.'
MIKE TYSON, American boxer, 2000.

It was a joke. I mean, as if he'd wear my knickers, come on.
VICTORIA, 2000.

So David Beckham was sent off playing for Manchester United against Necaxa. Clearly his wife's underwear was too tight and he was merely adjusting his tackle....Is it possible Beckham might now be suspendered? ... Blame the singer, not the thong.
Letter to the Guardian *when Beckham was dismissed soon after*

*his wife claimed he wore her
underwear, 2000.*

I feel sorry for Becks.
He must come home and
shut the door and say to
Victoria: 'What the fuck did
you say today?'
*NOEL GALLAGHER of Oasis
during the 'thong' episode, 2000.*

Posh Spice needs publicity
desperately for her career.
It is her oxygen. But for
Beckham it is cyanide.
*JOHN GILES, ex-Leeds
and Manchester United
midfielder, in his* Daily Express
column, 2000.

David is an animal in bed.
Some woman asked me in an
interview: 'Are you so thin
because you shag all day?'
And I said: 'Actually, yes.'
VICTORIA, 2000.

I've read it, cover to cover.
It's got some nice pictures.
*VICTORIA on a biography of
her husband, 2000.*

The ability to think and
focus has always been
there...it is hard to see what
could make him more

perfect...What bodes well
for David and Victoria is
that underneath the designer
labels and the style-setting
haircuts, they represent
old-fashioned family values –
what were once claimed as
the Thatcherite values of
home and hearth and
hard graft...Give the
man a medal.
HELLO! *magazine, 2000.*

I recently came across
Jonathan Lethem's new novel
Motherless Brooklyn. Surely the
ideal reconciliation gift for
Sir Alex Ferguson to send to
David Beckham.
Letter to the Guardian, *2000.*

This is what I do when I'm
bored – new tattoos, new
cars, new watches.
BECKHAM, 2000.

Football is such a male
environment, but the fact
that he is so prepared to be
involved with his baby
(Brooklyn) really matters to
all the young men who want
to be affectionate to theirs
but have had no role models.
*PROFESSOR ANTHONY
CLARE, psychiatrist, 2000.*

People like Beckham make a far better role model [than Mike Tyson]. He shops for nice clothes, has a gentle character and he loves his child.
JULIE BINDEL, Justice for Women spokesperson, 2000.

One's colleagues form their own opinion. They think: 'Why's he always at the fashion show in London?' Within the team, that can be damaging. Why are his five Ferraris always in the paper? He deserves 10 Ferraris but they shouldn't always be in the press. On the field I have no advice for him – he's a wonderful footballer.
LOTHAR MATTHAUS, former Germany captain, 2000.

I don't like Beckham because he is handsome, obviously, but also because it appears so easy for him to play and score goals.
ROBERTO CARLOS, Real Madrid and Brazil defender, 2001.

Football has become a religion and to be up to date we have to share the feelings of millions of people who admire this man.

CHAN THEERAPUNYO, Buddhist monk, after unveiling a gold statue of Beckham in a Thai temple, 2000.

I've got a little book in which I have written down the names of all those who have upset me. I know I will get them some day.
BECKHAM, 2000.

Being thick isn't an affliction if you're a footballer because your brains need to be in your feet. Beckham works hard, he's brave and he's a superb crosser. He treats a football like he does his wife –lovingly, with caresses.
BRIAN CLOUGH, 2000.

He's not going to sit down in interviews and start using really long words, because he is just not interested. Also, David is quite shy and I think people don't realise the difference between being shy and being thick.
VICTORIA, 2000.

Do you fancy me or something?
BECKHAM to male reporter who asked about his 'Mohawk' haircut, 2001.

David Beckham will not be asked to take a turn in the black chair on Mastermind, but I doubt whether I'd be wanted there either. David's not thick, just a normal guy having to put up with a lot of shit thrown at him by people who don't even know his personality.
JAAP STAM, Manchester United colleague, in Head To Head, *the book which preceded his sudden transfer to Lazio, 2001.*

[Beckham] has an almost Garbo-like frozen facial perfection.
JULIE BURCHILL in the book Burchill on Beckham, *2001.*

A man who has done nothing. Anyone can wear clothes but not quite as badly as him. He looks embarrassed about every single thing he puts on. His hairdos start out as some radical idea but end up as a horrific compromise, usually around the back.
JOHN LYDON, aka Johnny Rotten of the Sex Pistols, 2002.

Beckham is like a can of Ronseal. He is this good, honest, decent, absurdly good-looking guy.
EUGEN BEER, marketing consultant, 2002.

He's extremely good looking isn't he? And so noble. I think he's wonderful, especially when you consider what a brat he used to be.
DORIS LESSING, 83-year-old novelist, 2002.

VICTORIA: What was that film we watched last night?
DAVID: *What Lies Beneath.*
VICTORIA: Scary film. We wanted to go to the toilet but didn't have the nerve. We were so scared, weren't we?
DAVID: We was.
DIALOGUE from the TV documentary Being Victoria Beckham, *2002.*

They are Mr and Mrs Everyday who suddenly got famous.
DAVID FURNISH, Elton John's partner, 2002.

He's very good-looking and very rich, he's a fantastic footballer with an attractive

wife and a lovely child.
He has what everyone
wants, which is why everyone
hates him.
*ROBBIE WILLIAMS, pop
singer, 2002.*

He represents something
for every woman – father,
husband, footballer, icon. In a
word he's the ultimate hero.
*MARIE O'RIORDAN, editor
of* Marie Claire, *on her decision
to make Beckham the first man
ever to appear on its cover, 2002.*

The first man on the cover of
Marie Claire – I was touched.
BECKHAM, 2002.

When they picked teams at
school, I was always the last
chosen. I used to get booted
everywhere because I was
really little. I didn't have
many friends really.
BECKHAM, 2002.

Sir Alex Ferguson once
described me as a Manchester
United player in an Arsenal
shirt. I think it was a
compliment. In which case, I
look upon David Beckham as
an Arsenal player in a
Manchester United shirt.

*TONY ADAMS, Arsenal
captain, 2002.*

Don't cry for me, England!
The Empire, the Queen,
London Bridge trembles.
Once it was the hand of
Diego Armando Maradona,
now it is the foot of Aldo
Duscher. Duscher is a
national hero. If Beckham —
Sad Spice — is out [of the
World Cup] so much the
better for us!
Report in Argentina's Ole
*newspaper after Beckham
suffered a broken bone in a foot
in challenge by Deportivo La
Coruna's Argentinian defender
Duscher, 2002.*

There is nothing more
important than the state of
David Beckham's foot.
*TONY BLAIR MP, Prime
Minister, after the injury* v.
*Deportivo undermined
England's World Cup
preparations, 2002.*

Normally when you swap
shirts they are soaked in
sweat, but Beckham's smelt
only of perfume. Either he
protects himself against BO
or he sweats cologne.

RONALDO, Brazil striker, after the World Cup quarter-final win over England, 2002.

ALI BENARBIA

I was ordered to be babysitting great Ali Benarbia. It's not my ideal football experience but it is part of the job. It is so boring to follow 90 minutes just one player, especially French-speaking.
AKI RIHILAHTI, Crystal Palace and Finland midfielder, describes his role against Manchester City's Algerian playmaker on his website, 2002.

DENNIS BERGKAMP

If he thinks he's going to set the world alight he can forget it. When the fog, ice and cold arrive, he won't want to know.
ALAN SUGAR, Tottenham chairman, after the Dutchman's £7.25m move to Arsenal, 1995.

I never believed in star status. To me that means Rolex watches, gold chains and flashy cars. I hate all those.
DENNIS BERGKAMP on joining Arsenal, 1995.

Dennis is such a nice man, such a tremendous gentleman with such a lovely family. It's going to be very hard for me to kick him.
TONY ADAMS before facing Bergkamp for England v. Netherlands, European Championship finals, 1996.

I've heard it said that he is aloof, but he has a British sense of humour and gives as good as he gets. He is also a prankster and can't keep his hands off other players' laces and clothes.
STEVE BOULD, Arsenal colleague, 1997.

If he were in *Star Trek*, he'd be the best player in whatever solar system he was in.
IAN WRIGHT, Arsenal team-mate, 1997.

I'm not a player who feels he should sit on the bench. Look at my career and you'll see I'm not a substitute.
BERGKAMP, 2000.

EYAL BERKOVIC

It's a disgrace what he says because it's absolute nonsense. Eyal was a loner at the club and just didn't want to mix with anybody else. He didn't understand team spirit.
HARRY REDKNAPP, West Ham manager, hitting back at Berkovic's claims of racism at the club, 1999.

Eyal is a professional and clearly wants to earn as much money as possible. But he is Jewish and I am Scottish so it will be difficult for us to reach a financial agreement.
GRAEME SOUNESS, Blackburn manager, on the possibility of the Israeli's loan from Celtic becoming a permanent transfer, 2001.

GEORGE BOATENG

George's English is so good you forget he is Dutch. We gather round talking about foreigners in the English game and he is sitting there agreeing with us.
GARETH SOUTHGATE, Aston Villa captain, 2000.

LEE BOWYER

Q: What's the first film you remember watching?
A: *The Goonies* when I was off sick from school. These days the first video I play would be *The Krays.*
LEE BOWYER in Leeds United club magazine questionnaire, 1999.

He doesn't go into McDonald's any more, and he's hungry.
MARK LAWRENSON, TV pundit, on Bowyer's 'growing maturity', 2000. Bowyer had previously been fined after an assault in one of the burger-chain's 'restaurants'.

He's here, he's there, he's got no underwear, Lee Bowyer.
Song by Leeds fans after Bowyer admitted in court during his trial for allegedly assaulting an Asian student that he was not wearing pants, 2001.

He seemed to have lap dancing on his mind, not affray. He seemed to have girls on his mind, not grievous bodily harm.
DESMOND DE SILVA,

*Bowyer's counsel, during his
summing-up, 2001.*

Having been acquitted of
both charges, I was hoping
to put this matter behind me.
Now the club appear to be
victimising me and forcing
me out.
*BOWYER after he was
found not guilty but fined by
Leeds, 2001.*

I'm not saying that how a
man plays on a football
pitch is the best indicator
of guilt or innocence in
such a serious case. But to
me, Lee performed as if he
were innocent and the jury
found him innocent, yet the
public is critical. Why?
Because it has pre-judged
the issue.
*PETER RIDSDALE, Leeds
chairman, on Bowyer's good
playing form while in the
dock, 2002.*

That's what I like about
Bowyer – he really whacks
people.
*TERRY BUTCHER, former
England defender, working as
summariser for Radio Five
Live, 2002.*

LEE BRADBURY

I was on holiday in
Portugal when we signed
[Lee] Bradbury. But I can
tell you this, we would
definitely, definitely,
definitely, definitely not
have signed him if I'd
seen him play.
*FRANCIS LEE, former
Manchester City chairman,
three years after Alan Ball's £3m
club-record buy, 2000.*

MICHAEL BRIDGES

We call him Germ. He always
has a cold or something.
*DARREN HUCKERBY, fellow
Leeds striker, 1999.*

CRAIG BURLEY

Q: Most embarrassing
moment?
A: Trying to follow Craig
Burley's instructions on the
park when he didn't have
his teeth in, and getting it
hopelessly wrong.
*MALKY MACKAY,
Norwich and former Celtic
defender, 2001.*

NICKY BUTT

Lob a verbal bombshell at him and he will bat it back with interest.
JAAP STAM, former Manchester United colleague, in Head To Head, *2001.*

SOL CAMPBELL

Big Sol never says a word. When we play Spurs and I have a go at him, it's like talking to the deaf and dumb.
IAN WRIGHT, Arsenal striker, 1998.

People think they know me but they don't. They think: 'Oh, he's a quiet little boy.'
SOL CAMPBELL, a year after switching from Tottenham to Arsenal, 2002.

JAMIE CARRAGHER

He had a big mouth – about the only thing about him that was big.
LIZ TRAILL, nightclub stripper, after Carragher went naked at Liverpool's Christmas party, 1998.

STEVE CLARIDGE

Once I went training with £4,500 in my pocket and then ran out of petrol on the way home because I'd spent it all betting on horses. I had to hitch a lift.
STEVE CLARIDGE, Leicester striker and serial gambler, 1996.

NIGEL CLOUGH

He's not joining Pisa for the simple and most important reason that his mother decided that days ago.
BRIAN CLOUGH after speculation that his son was Italy-bound, 1988.

ANDY COLE

It always amazes me when people say: 'All he can do is score goals.' It's the most famous quote in football.
ALEX FERGUSON after Manchester United paid Newcastle £7m for Cole, 1995.

He needs too many chances to score a goal.
GLENN HODDLE, England manager, 1998.

His comments are diabolical and disrespectful. Is he a man or a mouse?
ANDY COLE replying to Hoddle, 1998.

It wasn't a criticism, but an observation.
HODDLE, by now Tottenham manager, after Cole scored Blackburn's winner against Spurs in the Worthington Cup final, 2002.

He raps the way he talks, and if you've ever heard him talk, you don't want to hear him rap.
NEIL McCORMICK, Daily Telegraph rock critic, after Cole released a single, 1999.

Andy Cole should stick to playing football and driving his Ferrari.
BOBBY ROBSON, Newcastle manager, after Cole criticised Alan Shearer, 1999.

JOE COLE

The older players all love him. When we took him to Newcastle before he broke into the side, they started singing his name as he boarded the coach.

HARRY REDKNAPP, West Ham manager, 1998.

EL HADJI DIOUF

Michael Owen has already nicknamed me Dioufy. It happened quite naturally one day in training.
EL HADJI DIOUF, Senegal striker, after joining Liverpool, 2002.

PAOLO DI CANIO

Paolo often storms off the training pitch in the middle of a game if something doesn't go right. Maybe it's the Italian way, or more likely he is a nutter.
NEIL RUDDOCK, West Ham colleague, 1999.

He's a smashing professional and a leader. He's like Bobby Moore in that respect, though he wouldn't have made it into Bobby's drinking school.
HARRY REDKNAPP, West Ham manager, 2000.

What fascinates me – and this is probably where Mussolini and I are very different – is the

way he was able to go against his morals to achieve his goals.
DI CANIO, self-confessed admirer of the late Italian fascist leader, 2000.

Does this man not know the meaning of cretin or moron? He clearly doesn't. A cretin suffers from a thyroid deficiency. It comes from an 18th-century French word and was initially directed at people living in the valleys of the Alps and the Pyrénées.
DAVID JAMES, Aston Villa goalkeeper, on criticism from Di Canio, 2000. Within a year the pair were West Ham team-mates.

There would have to be a bubonic plague for me to pick Di Canio.
GIOVANNI TRAPATTONI, Italy coach, 2000.

I want to finish each game sweating and bleeding.
DI CANIO, 2000.

I'm so exciting – every time I play, the fans want to have sex with me.
DI CANIO, 2000.

The man who comes to take care of my piranhas told me that if I left West Ham he would kill all my fish.
DI CANIO after projected move to Manchester United collapsed, 2002.

KIERON DYER

I haven't got a clue about the exact number of women I had – four or five maybe. But I regret it deeply.
KIERON DYER, Newcastle midfielder, on tabloid claims of an eventful holiday in Ayia Napa, 2000.

STEFAN EFFENBERG

He looked like a picture of an angel blowing a trumpet.
FRANZ BECKENBAUER, Bayern Munich president, on the former Bayern player's heavyweight appearance after he joined Wolfsburg, 2002.

LES FERDINAND

He loved sex but he always checked the football scores on Teletext first.
EVA DIJKSTRA, model, 1996.

RIO FERDINAND

When I hear about a defender who is good on the ball, I think: 'Oh Christ.'
JACK CHARLTON, ex-England defender, when Ferdinand left West Ham for Leeds, 2000.

No one is worth £18m for just kicking a ball around a pitch.
DAVID O'LEARY, Leeds manager, on his British-record outlay for Ferdinand, 2000.

It's an obscene amount of money and people will say nobody's worth that, but he is.
JONATHAN WOODGATE, new Leeds team-mate, 2000.

Rio has fantastic ball skills. This, of course, is fine by us. As is the sight of his sexy, sweaty body every Saturday afternoon.
ATTITUDE, gay magazine, naming the England defender one of its top 'fantasy' players, 1999.

I just can't get my head round the idea that someone has a five-year contract, and after 18 months he thinks: 'Well, that was very nice of you, thanks very much but I want to move on.'
TERRY VENABLES, Leeds manager, before Ferdinand moved to Manchester United for £29.1m, 2002.

DUNCAN FERGUSON

I stepped forward and I collided with [John] McStay. Subsequently he fell to the ground.
DUNCAN FERGUSON appealing against conviction for assault while playing for Rangers against Raith Rovers, 1995.

I can drink like a chimney.
FERGUSON, quoted by Rangers team-mate John Brown, Blue Grit, 1995.

TV just asked permission to interview Dunc. I said yes, but don't hold your breath. I'm just glad the refs can't understand a word he's saying to them.
JOE ROYLE, Ferguson's first manager at Everton, 1995.

GARRY FLITCROFT

How he was naive enough to think he could pledge eternal love to a lap dancer without having the whistle blown to his wife escapes me.
VANESSA FELTZ, television personality, after the Blackburn captain failed in a legal bid to prevent the press from reporting his allegedly serial philandering, 2002.

ROBBIE FOWLER

If Razor had hit me properly, I don't think I'd be here to talk about it.
ROBBIE FOWLER after airport fracas with Neil Ruddock following a Liverpool trip to Russia, 1995.

I never saw the incident, just a trail of blood going through the green exit at Customs.
STAN COLLYMORE, Liverpool colleague of Fowler and Ruddock, 1995.

I never do anyone any harm. Deep down I'm a quiet lad, believe it or not.
FOWLER after England colleague Graeme Le Saux

alleged he made homophobic taunts during Chelsea v. Liverpool match, 1999.

Fowler is a killer with a fantastic left foot, who always picks the shortest route to goal.
JAAP STAM, Manchester United defender, 2000.

You could run a university course on how to score goals, based on his finishing.
DAVID O'LEARY, Leeds manager, 2002.

RICHARD KEYS: Is there anything you've learned about Robbie from working with him that the rest of us wouldn't have seen?
RIO FERDINAND: Well, if you see his ears close up, they're quite small.
Exchange on Sky as Fowler's injured Leeds colleague acted as summariser, 2002.

PAUL GASCOIGNE

George Best without brains.
STAN SEYMOUR, Newcastle chairman, 1988.

He is accused of being arrogant, unable to cope with the press and a boozer. Sounds like he's got a chance to me.
GEORGE BEST, 1988.

He can be a loony with a fast mouth. He's either going to be one of the greats or finish up at 40, bitter about wasting such talent.
JOHN BAILEY, former Newcastle colleague, 1988.

Paul Gascoigne has done more for Mars bars than anyone since Marianne Faithfull.
PATRICK BARCLAY, football writer, the Independent, *1988.*

If he were a Brazilian or an Argentinian, you would kiss his shoes.
ARTHUR COX, Derby manager, after Gascoigne had inspired Tottenham to victory over his team, 1990.

Fierce and comic, formidable and vulnerable, urchin-like and waif-like, a strong head and torso with comparatively frail-looking breakable legs, strange-eyed, pink-faced, fair-haired, tense and upright, a priapic monolith in the Mediterranean sun – a marvellous equivocal sight.
KARL MILLER, writer, in London Review of Books, *1990.*

Before Paul Gascoigne, did anyone ever become a national hero and a dead-cert millionaire by crying? Fabulous. Weep and the world weeps with you.
SALMAN RUSHDIE, novelist and writer, in the Independent on Sunday, *1990.*

I'm extremely grateful to Gazza because at least now people are going to spell my name properly.
BAMBER GASCOIGNE, former University Challenge *presenter, 1990.*

Literally the most famous and probably the most popular person in Britain today.
TERRY WOGAN, introducing Gascoigne on his TV chat show, 1990.

I'm no poof, that's for sure.
PAUL GASCOIGNE on The Wogan Show, *1990.*

Comparing Gascoigne
with Pele is like comparing
Rolf Harris to Rembrandt.
*RODNEY MARSH, former
England striker, 1990.*

Always seems to be about
two stone overweight.
*Programme pen-picture of
Gascoigne, Republic of Ireland v.
England, 1990*

A dog of war with the face of
a child.
*GIANNI AGNELLI, Juventus
president, admiring Gascoigne
during England's World Cup
run, 1990.*

Sue, the tea-lady here, makes
such a good lasagne that
there's no need to go all the
way to Europe.
*GASCOIGNE on Tottenham's
canteen food as Italian clubs
stepped up their interest, in*
Gazza, Daft as a Brush, *1990.*

Sometimes I think I'm
playing in the wrong era.
*GASCOIGNE on being targeted
by opponents, 1990.*

He's still lovable, even
when he does something
diabolical.
*GARY LINEKER, Tottenham
team-mate, 1991.*

I was too scared to go in,
but he shouted: 'Come in,
darling.' He's got a lovely
hairy chest and his injured
leg was raised up on an
exercise machine. He said:
'Come and give us a kiss.'
*TINA BIRD, Gazza fan,
visiting him in hospital after he
suffered serious injury in the FA
Cup final, 1991.*

Coping with the language
shouldn't prove a problem. I
can't even speak English yet.
*GASCOIGNE after agreeing
move to Lazio, 1991.*

I'm very pleased for Paul
but it's like watching your
mother-in-law drive off a
cliff in your new car.
*TERRY VENABLES, Tottenham
manager, after Gazza finally
joined Lazio, 1992.*

You'll have to excuse Gazza.
He's got a very small
vocabulary.
*LAWRIE McMENEMY,
England assistant manager,
after the player had said, 'Fuck
off Norway,' on television, 1992.*

He wears a No. 10 jersey.
I thought it was his position,
but it turns out to be his IQ.
GEORGE BEST, 1993.

He's an intelligent boy who
likes people to think he's
stupid. He doesn't have a bad
bone in his body but he does
some stupid, ridiculous
things. That's what makes
him so interesting.
*ALLY McCOIST, Rangers
colleague, 1996.*

They (the schoolboys) asked
me things like: 'How big are
Gazza's balls?'
*VINNIE JONES after
addressing the boys of Eton
College, 1996.*

Tyneside's very own
renaissance man. A man
capable of breaking both leg
and wind at the same time.
*JIMMY GREAVES, Tottenham
and England predecessor, in his
Sun column, 1996.*

If he farts in front of the
Queen, we get blemished.
*PAUL McGAUGHEY, Adidas
spokesman, on the risks of a
sponsorship deal with Gazza,
1996.*

Gazza is no longer a fat,
drunken imbecile. He is, in
fact, a football genius.
*DAILY MIRROR editorial
headed 'Mr Paul Gascoigne:
An Apology', after his solo goal
v. Scotland, 1996.*

He's a fantastic player when
he isn't drunk.
*BRIAN LAUDRUP, Rangers
team-mate, 1997.*

I respect him. He goes up to
journalists and says: 'Fuck off!'
*DANNY BAKER, broadcaster
and writer, 1997.*

God gave him this
enormous footballing talent
but took his brains out to
even things up.
*TONY BANKS MP, Labour
Minister for Sport, 1997.*

Gazza reminds me of
Marilyn Monroe. She wasn't
the greatest actress in the
world, but she was a star
and you didn't mind if she
was late.
MICHAEL CAINE, actor, 1998.

Once you've played in the
same side as Gazza, you fall
in love with him because of

the sort of person and player he is.
DAVID BECKHAM, England colleague, 1998.

He was charming, he was funny ... literally, he was an angel.
SHERYL GASCOIGNE, ex-wife, on when she first met him, 1999.

I knew managing him would have been no joy ride, but the hazards that went with the talent would never have put me off.
SIR ALEX FERGUSON recalling a thwarted bid to sign Gazza, 1999.

Q: When do you think you peaked?
A: In two years' time.
GASCOIGNE in interview on Sky's Soccer AM, 1999.

At his peak, Gazza was phenomenal, the best player I've seen in this country. Becks is a great player but he isn't fit to lace Gazza's boots.
PAUL MERSON, Aston Villa midfielder, 1999.

Is there anything I'd like to change? Oh yes. I'd like to change the family's bank-account numbers and that tackle I did (on Nottingham Forest's Gary Charles) at Wembley in the FA Cup final.
GASCOIGNE in TV interview by ex-Rangers colleague Ally McCoist, 1999.

It's just Paul's luck. That man (George) Boateng must have an incredibly hard chin.
MEL STEIN, Gascoigne's agent, after he broke his arm playing for Middlesbrough v. Aston Villa, 2000.

I didn't play many games for Middlesbrough towards the end of the season – or at the start or in the middle.
GASCOIGNE, 2000.

If you read the papers, people think Gascoigne and I have a father-and-son relationship. Well I've got two sons and I have never felt like hitting them, but I have certainly felt like smacking Gascoigne a couple of times.
WALTER SMITH, his manager at Everton and Rangers, 2000.

I enjoy a glass of wine but I'm not a great drinker. I can't handle my drink brilliantly, that's all.
GASCOIGNE, 2000.

I was sorry to see Gazza go. He is probably the kindest man I've ever met in football. I had a golf day and he gave me his putter to auction, which he he'd had since he was in the 1990 World Cup squad. Everton won't change him – he'll do things that will wind them up, but deep down there's a heart of gold.
ROBBIE MUSTOE, Middlesbrough player, 2000.

I drank at the wrong times. I got into trouble and let myself down. Without the drinking I could have been one of the best players in the world. If I worked with kids I would tell them not to do what I did.
GASCOIGNE, 2002.

STEVEN GERRARD

People say you don't reach your peak until you're around 27. In that case Steven is going to be universe-class, never mind world-class by then.
ROBBIE FOWLER on his 21-year-old Liverpool and England colleague, 2001.

RYAN GIGGS

I admire his pace and skills. I'd only look that fast if you stuck me in the 1958 FA Cup final.
RICK HOLDEN, Manchester City winger, 1993.

Giggs was a big problem to us, but the biggest is that he does not have a German passport.
BERTI VOGTS, Germany coach, 1995.

I'd said we would win but your talent overwhelmed my mind.
URI GELLER, self-professed psychic and Reading fan, to Giggs after Manchester United's FA Cup win against his team, 1996.

I remember when I first saw him. He was 13 and he just floated over the ground like a cocker spaniel chasing a piece of silver paper in the wind.
ALEX FERGUSON, 1997.

He gives defenders twisted blood.
GARY PALLISTER, Manchester United colleague, 1997.

Teenagers probably look at Becks and other younger players. I'm the wrinklies' favourite these days.
RYAN GIGGS at 28, 2002.

DAVID GINOLA

Frog on the Tyne
Headline in Daily Star *after Newcastle signed the Frenchman, 1995.*

Men will love his skills and women his looks. He could end up being popular enough to replace Robbie Williams in Take That.
CHRIS WADDLE, former England midfielder, 1995.

I'm told he ran up the tunnel and dived into the bath.
JOE ROYLE, Everton manager, alleging Ginola went to ground too easily, 1995.

How can anyone say he's lazy? He is a sex symbol and has all that hair to blow-dry every day. That's an hour's job in itself.

SIMON MAYO, Tottenham fan and broadcaster, 1999.

It's the perfect way to pop back into France for a decent meal.
DAVID GINOLA at the London Boat Show on his intention to buy a £900,000 yacht, 2000.

It was beautiful. The sensitivity from everyone he met in Birmingham really impressed David.
CHANTEL STANLEY, Ginola's agent, on his reception after leaving Tottenham for Aston Villa, 2000.

He hasn't played many matches and he missed pre-season (training). So it's possible that he is carrying a little extra timber.
JOHN GREGORY, Villa manager, sparking a row with Ginola over his weight, 2001.

ANDY GORAM

When is Andy Goram going to piss off and stop annoying us with his bloody wonder saves? Yours in victimsation.

Letter to the Celtic fanzine Not The View, *1997.*

IAN HARTE

When it comes to the David Beckhams of this world, this guy's up there with Roberto Carlos.
DUNCAN McKENZIE, radio pundit and ex-Leeds player, 2001.

JOHN HARTSON

Before our five-a-side in training one day, John yelled: 'Let's have Wales *v.* The Rest.' Someone shouted: 'But you're the only Welshman here.' He said: 'Yeah, me against you fucking lot.' That's him.
TERRY WESTLEY, Hartson's former manager at Luton, 1997.

When I saw the pictures of what I did I was ashamed. The worst thing was when people phoned my girlfriend, who's six months pregnant, and said: 'What's it like living with a lunatic?'
JOHN HARTSON, after kicking West Ham colleague Eyal Berkovic in the head during training, 1998.

COLIN HENDRY

He's not happy unless he has been kicked in the bollocks three times during training.
GRAEME LE SAUX, Blackburn team-mate, 1997.

THIERRY HENRY

Q: How do you stop Henry?
A: With a gun?
GIANLUCA VIALLI, Watford manager, before FA Cup tie v. Arsenal, 2002.

EMILE HESKEY

Emile could probably pick up Gareth Southgate and throw him the length of the pitch, yet he has developed the art of dropping like a sack of spuds whenever he is touched.
JOHN GREGORY, Aston Villa manager, 1999.

Nobody likes to get that sort of criticism. But I'm pleased he got it because I tried all my career to get away crowds to give me stick and I was never good enough. I'd have loved to have 40,000 people baying for my blood. It was my lifetime ambition to have

an away crowd boo me like that, but generally they didn't even know I was playing.
MARTIN O'NEILL, Leicester manager, after Heskey was jeered at Leeds, 1999.

Soccer isn't ballet. If Heskey doesn't like getting kicked, he should play the piano.
JOVAN TANASIJEVIC, Yugoslavia Under-21 defender, 2000.

PAUL INCE

When a player is at his peak, he feels as if he can climb Everest in his slippers. That's what he was like.
ALEX FERGUSON, Ince's manager at Manchester United, 1997.

Paul Ince wants everyone to call him Guv'nor but we call him Incey.
LEE SHARPE, United colleague, 1995.

At Manchester United, everyone called me Guv. I hope it'll be the same here.
PAUL INCE, arriving for training at Inter Milan after leaving Old Trafford, 1995.

All this 'Guv'nor' nonsense should have been left in his toy-box.
SIR ALEX FERGUSON in his autobiography, 1999.

L'assino della Settimana [donkey of the week].
GUERIN SPORTIVO magazine, Italy, 1995.

After Bobby Moore, I'm probably the greatest player to come out of West Ham, which is to their credit.
INCE, 2001.

DAVID JAMES

It's not nice going into the supermarket and the woman at the till is thinking: 'Dodgy keeper.'
DAVID JAMES, then playing erratically with Liverpool, 1997.

NKWANKWO KANU

He's tall, he's black, he's had a heart attack, Kanu, Kanu.
Song by Arsenal fans in homage to Kanu, who had endured coronary problems, 2000.

ROBBIE KEANE

I will accept full responsibility for not signing him. If Coventry win the title and he gets Footballer of the Year I'll bare my backside in the Co-Op window.
JOHN GREGORY, Aston Villa manager, after declining to meet Wolves' valuation, 1999.

If we could have got him for £500,000 and played him in our reserves for a couple of seasons, we might have been interested.
ALEX FERGUSON after the Republic of Ireland striker joined Coventry from Wolves for £6m, 1999.

When I was a kid I always watched Italian football on TV. Playing in the back streets of Dublin, I always pretended I was playing for Inter.
ROBBIE KEANE, claiming lifelong passion for his new club, 2000.

I don't have a girlfriend at the moment. I'm engaged to Inter Milan.
KEANE shortly before being sold to Leeds, 2000.

ROY KEANE

Nicknamed Damien, after the character in *The Omen*. He's mad but he's funny too.
RYAN GIGGS, 1994.

Young Keane shouldn't screw up his privileged position at Old Trafford for the sake of a few thousand extra quid he might make abroad. It's tempting – 60 grand a week after tax, and a four-year contract. But I reckon that on top of what he has got already, he'd have to live until he's 634 to spend that lot.
BRIAN CLOUGH, who had brought Keane to England by signing him for Nottingham Forest from Cobh Ramblers, 1999.

He was very, very drunk and as aggressive as you can possibly imagine. He had evil in his eyes and he gave me a good kick – I'll have a bruise.
LEANNE CAREY, Australian tourist, alleging a wine-bar assault by Keane as United players celebrated winning the championship, 1999.

If I was in management now and had the money to take my pick of any player, anywhere, if I could have the best at Arsenal, Leeds, Chelsea or Real Madrid, I'd take Keane.
BRIAN CLOUGH, 1999.

I'd never put Keane in the real hard-man bracket. He's more of the roll-up-your-sleeves leader every team wishes they had. He doesn't care who you are or what you've done in the game or in the last five minutes. If you're not pulling your weight he'll bawl you out in front of 50,000 fans.
IAN WRIGHT, former Arsenal and England striker, 1999.

If that is not a sending-off offence, what is? What do we need to see, a leg with blood dripping off the stump?
PETER WILLIS, president of the Referees' Association, after Keane was sent off in the Charity Shield, 2000.

I'm a great admirer of Roy Keane. He has been there, done it and still wants to do it. I don't like Manchester United but to be mentioned in the same breath as him is great.
STEVEN GERRARD, Liverpool midfielder, 2000.

We all bang on about how much players earn these days but Keane is worth every penny of the £54,000 a week or whatever he gets. I know it's a few bob more than me, give or take 49 grand.
DEAN WINDASS, Bradford City midfielder, 2000.

I'm sick and tired of hearing commentators telling us how much running Keane does in a match, how he covers every blade of grass. He's entitled to be fresher than most because he has so much time off – eight red cards and that long injury lay-off, which was his fault, incidentally, and not Alf-Inge Haaland's. He's had more than enough rest through the suspensions alone. He's had more holidays than Judith Chalmers.
BRIAN CLOUGH, 2001.

As if cutting Haaland in half wasn't bad enough, Keane then swoops over him like Dracula. All he needed was the black cloak.
CLOUGH after Keane was sent off in the Manchester derby, 2001.

I believe Lennox Lewis didn't see that punch coming last Sunday and the skipper of the *Titanic* had some excuse for not spotting an iceberg if it was dark. But I couldn't believe my big ears when Fergie said he had not seen Keane's tackle on Haaland and that United's secretary thought it was a sending-off. A sending-off? It was among the worst fouls I've ever seen.
CLOUGH, 2001.

I'll have to see whether any of Keane's studs are still in there.
ALF-INGE HAALAND, Manchester City midfielder, before a scan on his knee, 2002.

Roy has nothing to worry about. I don't think there's a case to answer.
SIR ALEX FERGUSON on reports that the FA, Haaland and City might take action against Keane after he admitted deliberately injuring the Norwegian, 2002.

Aggression is what I do. I go to war...You don't contest football matches in a reasonable state of mind.
KEANE in his autobiography, 2002.

On the field he's a major asset. Off it he's quite unassuming, an ordinary lad. He'll say: 'What are you all doing tonight?' and he'll come to the pictures or whatever. What you see on the pitch is a usually extravagant character but he's not like that off it.
MICK McCARTHY, Republic of Ireland manager, on Keane before leaving for the World Cup finals, 2002.

As he waded in with one expletive after another, I asked myself if this was my captain. Was this a man who could serve Ireland as a role model for our children? The answer was no.
McCARTHY after banishing Keane from the squad in Japan, 2002.

Roy Keane has no manners. There's never any reason not to be polite, even with people you don't like.
GEORGE BEST, former Manchester United player, after the falling out between Keane and McCarthy, 2002.

Sanity is more important.
KEANE after being banished from the Irish World Cup squad in Japan after the row with McCarthy, 2002.

Oh, I'd have sent home all right, but I'd have shot him first.
BRIAN CLOUGH after Keane's expulsion by McCarthy, 2002.

The people of Ireland may forgive him but I never will. He is a disgrace to his country.
JACK CHARLTON, former Republic manager, 2002.

Roy Keane and Michael Collins: Two great Cork leaders shot in the back.
Slogan on a pro-Keane T-shirt sold in Ireland after the World Cup, 2002. Collins was an IRA leader in the first half of the 20th century.

I've made mistakes. I was naïve and probably drank too much.
KEANE in his controversial autobiography, 2002.

Maybe I've been too up front, but so what.
KEANE as criticism of his book mounted, 2002.

I'm surprised he did a book in the first place. He'd be the first to give someone stick in the dressing-room if they had done something similar.
DENIS IRWIN, former United and Ireland colleague, now with Wolves, 2002.

I'd rather buy a Bob the Builder CD for my two-year-old son.
JASON McATEER, former Ireland team-mate, on Keane's book, 2002. Within days, Keane was sent off for elbowing the Sunderland midfielder in the face.

GARY KELLY

Kells is the maddest one at Leeds. Without prompting, he was climbing head first into wheelie bins.

PAUL ROBINSON, Leeds goal-keeper, on his Irish team-mate, 2000.

MARTIN KEOWN

Martin Keown's up everybody's backside.
TREVOR BROOKING on Match of the Day, *1996.*

HARRY KEWELL

Harry's too famous up here (in Yorkshire). You can't go out for a meal without people interfering. It's better in London, where people are only bothered if you're a Hollywood star.
SHEREE MURPHY, Kewell's partner and Emmerdale actress, in Loaded *magazine interview, 2000.*

I thought he was cute but I never got any vibes. But we had a kiss and I thought: 'Oh my God!'
MURPHY on the start of her relationship with the Australian, 1999.

If Harry misses a goal, I hear: 'You're keeping him up too long. Stop shagging him.'
MURPHY, 2000.

I see people who are rated world-class and he does much more. He can do everything – run, head, shoot. And he's brave. Apart from that, he has got nothing.
GORDON STRACHAN, Coventry manager, 2001.

FRANK LEBOEUF

I am very happy at Chelsea, but I don't want to be the club cretin.
FRANK LEBOEUF, claiming he was under-paid, 1999.

The fella's got no spine, backbone, no bottle. He's a classic example of the foreign player who is ruining our game.
RON HARRIS, former Chelsea hard man, 1999.

I know they are after me. They think I am temperamental just because I am French and because I am a world champion.
LEBOEUF claiming a vendetta against him and other foreign players, 2000.

When he appeared on *They Think It's All Over* it was scripted for him to keep saying: 'I won the World Cup.' People now think he is big-headed, which is not the case. Opponents use it to wind him up and referees are aware of him.
COLIN HUTCHINSON, Chelsea managing director, 2000.

ROB LEE

I told him Newcastle was nearer to London than Middlesbrough and he believed me.
KEVIN KEEGAN, Newcastle manager, on how he lured Londoner Lee to Tyneside rather than Teesside, 1995.

NEIL LENNON

He has failed in the face of a hoax threat by some clown with a 10p piece.
KENNY McCLINTON, Protestant pastor, after the Celtic midfielder pulled out of a Northern Ireland match because of a death threat by a caller claiming to represent the Loyalist Volunteer Force, 2002.

I've a tiny wee daughter who knows nothing about this. It's time for me to say enough's enough.
NEIL LENNON after deciding not to play for Northern Ireland again, 2002.

GRAEME LE SAUX

I've been slaughtered for reading the *Guardian*. In most walks of life, that would be respected, differences valued. I took stick from the lads and often it was upsetting. But I stuck it out when I had plenty of opportunities to fit in with the sheep.
GRAEME LE SAUX, Blackburn and England defender, 1995.

No one cares whether or not Le Saux is gay. It is the fact that he openly admits to reading the *Guardian* that makes him the most reviled man in football.
PIERS MORGAN, editor of the Mirror, *after Le Saux alleged that England colleague Robbie Fowler called him a 'poof' during Chelsea v Liverpool match, 1999.*

Le Saux is vilified for a secret much more shameful than being a homosexual. For Le Saux is middle-class.
IAN HISLOP, satirical journalist, 1999.

FREDDIE LJUNGBERG

I like London because you can be yourself. There's no problem if you're a bit different in the way you look or dress.
FREDDIE LJUNGBERG, Arsenal midfielder with dyed red 'punk' hairstyle, 2002.

GARY MCALLISTER

I know there are far more important things in life than football, but if you cut me open and looked inside right now it wouldn't be a pretty sight. I don't know if I can sink any lower.
GARY McALLISTER after England's David Seaman saved the Scotland captain's penalty, European Championship finals, 1996.

STEVE MCMANAMAN

They compare Steve McManaman to Steve Heighway. He's nothing like him but I can see why – it's because he's a bit different.
KEVIN KEEGAN, England manager and former team-mate of Heighway's, 2000.

PAUL MERSON

My addictions are always there, waiting for me. They're doing press-ups outside my door.
PAUL MERSON, Aston Villa midfielder, on his fight against alcoholism, gambling addiction and drug abuse, 1999.

DANNY MILLS

The oldest 24-year-old I've ever met. He wears pyjamas, slippers, everything your grandad would wear.
RIO FERDINAND, Mills' Leeds and England colleague, 2002.

JODY MORRIS

Jody, you could become a great future Chelsea captain, but learn from your current peers. Don't let me see you eating hamburgers at Gatwick airport, forget your flash cars and nightclubs. If you really dedicate yourself, you could become one of Chelsea's greats. It's up to you – how much do you want it?
KEN BATES, Chelsea chairman, in his programme column, 1999.

CLINTON MORRISON

Sometimes you spit in the air and it comes back at you.
GERARD HOULLIER, Liverpool manager, after the Palace striker had criticised his team, who then beat the Londoners 5-0 in the Worthington Cup semi-final, 2001.

GARY NEVILLE

If he was an inch taller he'd be the best centre-half in Britain. His father is 6ft 2in. – I'd check the milkman.
ALEX FERGUSON on his 5ft 11in. defender, 1996.

MARC OVERMARS

A couple of players stood up ... and told Overmars bluntly he was not pulling his weight. More to the point, he had been jumping out of tackles for too long, as if he had a pole vault up his backside.
ALAN SMITH, former Arsenal player, revealing heated scenes in his old club's dressing-room after defeat by Coventry, 2000.

MICHAEL OWEN

REPORTER: What are your memories of the 1990 World Cup?
OWEN: I don't have any. I was sent to bed before the matches started.
Exchange at England press conference, World Cup finals, 1998.

I'm not sure whether he is a natural goalscorer.
GLENN HODDLE, England coach, 1998.

Some people think he gets away with a lot because he is the boy wonder, Mr Squeaky Clean.
JOHN GREGORY, Aston Villa manager, 1999.

In this country everyone seems to believe the Boy Wonder can do no wrong, and I find the hype that surrounds him a bit over the top. He scores a few goals and all of a sudden the newspapers scream that Milan want to buy him for £25m. That's absolute rubbish and I'm sure he knows it.
JAAP STAM, Manchester United defender, in Head To Head, *2001.*

He has got this enigma around him.
GABBY LOGAN, ITV football presenter, on Channel 4's 100 Greatest World Cup Moments, *2002.*

I'm a football fan now. In the papers this morning they said a nation's thoughts were on Michael Owen's groin. I thought: 'Me too!'
GRAHAM NORTON, gay talk-show host, during World Cup finals, 2002.

ANDREW O'BRIEN

Andrew's not got an ounce of fat on him, he's solid muscle and honest with it. He's also got a big hooter. Some of the strikers he marks go off with broken elbows.
PAUL JEWELL, Bradford City manager, 1999.

EMMANUEL PETIT

He's tall, he's quick, his name's a porno' flick, Emmanuel, Emmanuel.
Song by Arsenal fans in praise of Petit, 1999.

I was delighted to see *American Beauty* get some Oscars. At times I felt my life was being projected on the screen.
EMMANUEL PETIT, Barcelona midfielder, 2000.

KEVIN PHILLIPS

He was so keen to join us at the hotel that he almost got there early enough to meet the last squad going home.
KEVIN KEGAN, England manager, 1999.

NIALL QUINN

Anyone who uses the word 'quintessentially' during a half-time talk is talking crap.

MICK McCARTHY, Republic of Ireland manager, after Quinn made a suggestion during an international match, 1998.

In Ireland he is known as Sheikh Quinn because he's got nearly as many racehorses as the Aga Khan. I always knew he'd be rich and famous so I'm pleased he still says hello to me. When I finish in football, I can proudly boast that I've roomed with Niall Quinn!
DAVID O'LEARY, former Arsenal and Republic of Ireland team-mate, 1999.

FABRIZIO RAVANELLI

During the match he insulted me 150,000 times.
MARCEL DESAILLY, Chelsea defender, after rowing with the Italian striker during and after a match at Derby, 2001.

I started the shirt-lifting thing and I'm still the best at it.
FABRIZIO RAVANELLI struggling with colloquialisms at Derby, 2002.

AKI RIHILAHTI

Q: How was your performance in the game?
A: I was rubbish.
AKI RIHILAHTI, Crystal Palace and Finland midfielder, interviews himself on his website, 2002.

RIVALDO

How do you stop Rivaldo? You try to buy him the day before you play him.
ARSENE WENGER, Arsenal manager, 1999.

Q: Who would Rivaldo choose to be World Player of the Year for 1999?
A: Rivaldo.
Q: Why?
A: Because I'm the best player.
RIVALDO, Barcelona and Brazil, in World Soccer interview, 2000.

ROBERTO CARLOS

I studied him after the whistle in the World Cup final. Walking around the pitch like he was in his local park. He wasn't waving flags, crying or kissing his boots.

You could see what he's about. 'This is what I expect, this is what I deserve.'
ROY KEANE on the Brazil wing-back, 2002.

ROMARIO

God created me to delight people with my goals.
ROMARIO, Brazil striker, 1994.

Romario is arrogant and petty-minded, and without his football he would be a criminal.
DELMA KATZ, mother of the Brazilian striker's girlfriend, 1995.

RONALDO

I want to go down in the history of world football. I want to mark an era, to be a different player, to score special goals. Just to be a good player is not enough.
RONALDO, before becoming the top scorer in the World Cup finals, 2002.

After what happened to me in 1998, and all the injuries of the past four years, every time I step on the pitch and every time I score is a victory.
RONALDO after scoring both goals in Brazil's 2-0 defeat of Germany, World Cup final, 2002.

The wunderkind controlled the chaotic, bouncing ball with a gentle but firm touch. And, as only the best strikers can, he poked the precocious orb with pace and a pocketful of surprise past the sturdy figure of Rustu Recber.
FIFA WEBSITE describes Ronaldo's winner v. Turkey, World Cup semi-finals, 2002.

He arrived like a king and leaves like a thief.
CORRIERE DELLO SPORT, Italian sports newspaper, on Ronaldo's move from Inter Milan to Real Madrid, 2002.

WAYNE ROONEY

I did a radio interview and I tried to play down Rooney, but how can you play down the greatest thing around in football?
BILL KENWRIGHT, Everton deputy-chairman, on their 16-year-old striker, 2002.

NEIL RUDDOCK

Hearing Ruddock claiming to be a nice guy was shocking. Some people behave like monsters and the next day say they're not guilty.
ARSENE WENGER, Arsenal manager, after a clash with Patrick Vieira, 1999.

LOUIS SAHA

He's got pace and intelligence. It's like finding a beautiful woman with money.
TERRY BURTON, Wimbledon manager, on Fulham's French striker, 2001.

ROBBIE SAVAGE

He looks as if he should be surfing in California, and if there's one thing that annoys me about him, it's that tan. We haven't been to Barbados lately, so he must have been on the sun-bed. As we approach February, I like players to have that drained, pale look that I've always had at that stage of the season.
MARTIN O'NEILL, Leicester manager, 2000.

Outside Leicester, everyone hates him, but he's a folk hero here. There's more meat on a toothpick and to see him with his clothes off, you wonder where he gets all his energy from ... Even when he has had a poor game he thinks he should be man of the match. He's always saying: 'Didn't you think I was great today?' And I'm always saying: 'Well, not exactly great.'
ALAN BIRCHENALL, Leicester public-relations officer and ex-striker, 2000.

If brains were chocolate, he wouldn't have enough to fill a Smartie.
BIRCHENALL, 2000.

I'm a bit anxious. I think every other manager out there hates me.
ROBBIE SAVAGE on pleading with Leicester chairman John Elsom to give manager Peter Taylor more time to stop a bad run, 2001.

PETER SCHMEICHEL

Peter returns, but the operation has not worked

because he still won't admit it when he has made a mistake.
BRIAN McCLAIR, Manchester United colleague, in his diary in United Magazine, *1995.*

His sheer presence frightens opponents. In one match recently, Spurs hit the bar twice and I'm sure it was because they were trying to avoid him.
RUUD GULLIT, Chelsea player-manager, 1997.

He can throw the ball further than I go on holiday.
RON ATKINSON, ITV pundit, 1999.

PAUL SCHOLES

One of the best football brains this club has ever had.
ALEX FERGUSON, 1999.

DAVID SEAMAN

Q: Why is Nayim the most virile player in Europe?
A: Because he can lob Seaman from 50 yards.
Joke by Tottenham fans after the ex-Spurs player Nayim scored from long range to clinch the Cup-Winners' Cup for Zaragoza against Arsenal, 1995.

After the Nayim goal in Paris, people thought it was funny to totter backwards like I did that night and pretend to watch a ball dipping over their heads.
DAVID SEAMAN, 1997.

No, I don't think I've reached my peak. There's still more I can learn. I have to say that because I might get another contract out of it.
SEAMAN, 1997.

That David Seaman is a handsome young man but he spends too much time looking in his mirror rather than at the ball. You can't keep goal with hair like that.
BRIAN CLOUGH on the England keeper's ponytail, 2000.

I'd like to think that no professional stylist would do this for him. It's kitsch, but surely not deliberately so.
NICKY CLARKE, celebrity hairdresser, on Seaman's ponytail, 2001.

I've told him to cut off his ponytail. It makes him less aerodynamic.
ARSENE WENGER, Arsenal manager, 2002.

David Seaman looked a broken man afterwards. I told him: 'If you go on thinking about that goal, you'll break yourself down. You must stop it. It's over. You saved us in Germany and in other games here, so you shouldn't think about it any more.'
SVEN-GORAN ERIKSSON after Seaman let a long-range free-kick drift over him for Brazil's winner v. England, World Cup finals, 2002.

I haven't seen (Ronaldinho's) winner yet. It's not that I'm avoiding it, just that my little girl has been watching Teletubbies all the time.
SEAMAN after arriving home from England's World Cup exit against Brazil, 2002.

ALAN SHEARER

A person you'd be delighted to have as your son.
KENNY DALGLISH, his Blackburn manager, 1992.

Alan is old beyond his years, like 23 going on 50. His favourite record is 'Sailing' by Rod Stewart. Makes me feel like slapping him round the face and saying: 'Get a grip on yourself!'
GRAEME LE SAUX, Blackburn colleague, 1994.

Sunday 31 July: I manage to venture out of the house to turn the sprinkler on the lawn and then on to the local garden centre with [daughter] Chloe to feed the ducks.
ALAN SHEARER in Diary of a Season: The Inside Story of a Champion Year, 1995.

I don't know what I'd have done if I hadn't become a footballer. At school I put down 'dustbin man' on a careers questionnaire, but my dad made me change it to 'joiner'.
SHEARER, 1998.

Alan Shearer is boring. We call him Mary Poppins.
FREDDY SHEPHERD, Newcastle director, secretly recorded by a News of the World reporter, 1998.

I love playing against Alan. It's always a tough, fully committed, passionate, no-diving, no-cheating, English-style game between the two of us, which supporters love to watch.
TONY ADAMS, Arsenal captain, 1999.

I went on the bench and didn't moan or groan. Mind you, I did the following day.
SHEARER after Ruud Gullit relegated him to substitute v. *Sunderland, 1999.*

Shearer is a good captain when things are going well, but if he is not getting the service you can tell from his body language that he is not the most inspirational player to lead the side.
GRAHAM KELLY, former FA chief executive, in his book Sweet FA, *1999.*

When the speculation was at its height –would he join Newcastle or Man United – I thought: 'If England are to have the complete striker, he should go abroad.' It would have taken his game to another level.

GRAHAM TAYLOR, the manager who gave Shearer his England debut, 1999.

Shearer has always been the favourite, always picked, chosen son of all our national managers during the 1990s. It is an issue which bugs me. You are supposed to pick the best 11, not shape every strategy around a supposed golden boy.
ANDY COLE, fellow England striker, in his autobiography, 1999.

Shearer has a body language that sometimes riles us. But who are we at Watford to have a go at the England captain? It showed naivety.
GRAHAM TAYLOR, Watford and former England manager, 1999.

I see I've been used again to help sell somebody's book. Alex Ferguson, Graham Kelly and now Andy Cole have all had a pop in print at yours truly. Glad to have been of assistance, Andy.
SHEARER in his Newcastle programme column, 1999.

I remember Ray Harford when he was Blackburn manager telling me how Bill Nicholson, the great Spurs manager, walked his daughter down the aisle in floods of tears on her wedding day. He found himself asking: 'Where have all the years gone?' He had missed seeing her grow up because of his involvement in football. I don't want that to happen to me.
SHEARER announcing his international retirement, 2000.

The truth was that Alan's game really had fallen away. I sat him down and we had long, intense chats. I told him bluntly he had stopped doing the things that made him a genuine great. Some people told me Newcastle expected him to do too much, but I told them – and Alan – he wasn't doing half enough. His whole movement had stopped and he was just wearily going through the motions.
BOBBY ROBSON, Newcastle manager, 2000.

When I was at Liverpool and he was at Blackburn, he'd have me round every five minutes. He never did a thing for himself ... he's too lazy so he just pays people to do everything. He used to ring me to come and change the oil in his car. He can't even change a wheel. If his car broke down, he'd just leave it. These days he probably just buys a new one if he can't get it started.
NEIL RUDDOCK, former Southampton team-mate, 2000.

TEDDY SHERINGHAM

When he played for me at Nottingham Forest he was the slowest player in the squad – perhaps due to all those nightclubs he kept telling me he didn't frequent.
BRIAN CLOUGH after Sheringham was named Footballer of the Year, 2001.

Clough called me Edward. I told him I preferred to be called Teddy. He said: 'Right you are, Edward.'
TEDDY SHERINGHAM, 2001.

OLE GUNNAR SOLSKJAER

I always prepare myself with an Elvis Presley song and try to bring a liitle of his magic on to the pitch.
OLE GUNNAR SOLSKJAER, Manchester United striker, 2002.

THOMAS SORENSEN

I'm just as good as Peter Schmeichel, but I'm more modest by nature.
THOMAS SORENSEN, Sunderland and Denmark goalkeeper, 2000.

GARETH SOUTHGATE

I've only taken one penalty before, for Crystal Palace at Ipswich when it was 2-2 in the 89th minute. I hit the post and we went down that year. But I think I would be far more comfortable now than I was then.
GARETH SOUTHGATE, England defender, tempts fate before his decisive miss in the shoot-out v. Germany, European Championship semi-final, 1996.

Why didn't you just belt the ball?
BARBARA SOUTHGATE to her son after his infamous miss, 1996.

I'm sure that people will always say: 'He's the idiot who missed that penalty.'
SOUTHGATE, 1997.

You're a better writer than footballer.
VINNIE JONES during Wimbledon v. Crystal Palace match, 1995. Southgate had a column in the Croydon Advertiser.

Q: One wish?
A: Apart from world peace, a long, injury-free career.
SOUTHGATE, Aston Villa defender, in programme questionnaire, 1995.

The worst part is that Gareth is such a nice guy. You never normally hear him utter a single swear word.
DAVID JAMES, Villa goalkeeper, after Southgate was fined £5,000 by the FA for verbal abuse of referee Jeff Winter, 1999.

Known as The Ornament in our dressing-room because he adorns the opponents'

penalty area. He goes up for every free-kick and corner but never touches the ball.
JOHN GREGORY, Villa manager, after Southgate scored twice at Leeds, 2000.

I can only assume that their valuation is based on my penalty-taking ability.
SOUTHGATE after Villa rejected a £4m offer from Chelsea, 2000.

DAVOR SUKER

I want your headlines to read: 'Arsenal go from a Sulker to a Suker.'
DAVID DEIN, Arsenal vice-chairman, to reporters on signing Suker after losing Nicolas Anelka, 1999.

NEIL SULLIVAN

I haven't given up hope of keeping him, even if it means having to kiss his backside.
SAM HAMMAM, Wimbledon chairman, before the Scotland keeper joined Tottenham, 1999.

GERRY TAGGART

He likes to think he came here under the Bosman ruling. but that's just a euphemism for a free transfer.
MARTIN O'NEILL, Leicester manager, on his Northern Irish defender, 1999.

STIG TOFTING

The Danish people love Tofting's no-nonsense style. With him there's no flicks and farts.
JAN MOLBY, former Denmark player, on his country's burly midfielder, 2002.

JUAN SEBASTIAN VERON

Listen, you've all been going on about fucking (Juan Sebastian) Veron. He's a fucking great player. You are fucking idiots.
SIR ALEX FERGUSON in angry mood with reporters amid criticism of Manchester United's £28m Argentinian, 2002.

PATRICK VIEIRA

What I did was unforgivable, mainly because I'm a role model. My brother is a teacher. If one of his pupils

spits at another, he can't tell him not to do it. The kids will just turn round and say: 'Your brother does exactly the same.' But the thing that pisses me off is the £45,000 fine. Coming from where I do, I know the value of money. To my family that is a phenomenal sum.
PATRICK VIEIRA after being fined for spitting in retaliation to Neil Ruddock, 1999.

Pat's a great friend. When Everton were playing Arsenal last season, he called my wife and told her to get some ice packs ready because I would come back seriously bruised. My phone book is open on "V" and I plan to make a call on Wednesday night.
OLIVIER DACOURT, Leeds and ex-Everton midfielder, 2000.

There are players who have no interest in playing the game properly. They are just trying to upset Patrick. There are certain managers who encourage this.
ARSENE WENGER after Vieira was sent off for the second time in three days, 2000.

I'm amazed how big Patrick's elbows are. They can reach players 10 yards away. Let's just give him a 15-game ban and get it over and done with.
WENGER, 2002.

DES WALKER

Des was an outstanding player and a world-class playboy. He owned the cars, wore the clothes and pulled the girls. If Stuart Pearce was my role model in football matters, Des was the man for night-time adventures.
ROY KEANE, Walker's ex-Nottingham Forest colleague, in recalls the central defender in his autobiography, 2002.

PAULO WANCHOPE

Paulo was way out of order, but I deny that I ever called him a 'poof'. I'd never use that kind of language, even if it were justified.
JIM SMITH, Derby manager, on a heated row with the Costa Rican after he was substituted, 1997.

SANDER WESTERVELD

The goalkeeping strip is dreadful. It is a blue shirt with green shorts and green socks. I am very cocky and vain. A keeper needs charisma and that's impossible wearing green pants. I want blue pants and white socks.
SANDER WESTERVELD, Dutch keeper, on joining Liverpool, 1999.

DENNIS WISE

Monster, monster shocked.
ERIC HALL, Wise's agent, on his client's three-month jail sentence for assault, 1995.

Monster, monster happy.
ERIC HALL after Wise's sentence was suspended, 1995.

I try to learn the language, but every time I listen some place like Dennis Wise, my English go down.
GIANFRANCO ZOLA, Chelsea's Italian midfielder, 1997.

I'm not the sort of person you want around if you want peace and order in your life.
DENNIS WISE in his autobiography, 1999.

Wisey is one of those little big men in the mould of Billy Bremner. Five foot nothing off the pitch, ten feet tall on it.
VINNIE JONES, former Wimbledon team-mate, 2000.

Dennis is never involved in anything but he's always there. He's like the old lady who has been driving for 50 years and never been in an accident – but seen dozens.
GORDON STRACHAN, Coventry manager, 2000.

Whatever player he's up against, he tries to wind them up. If he fouls you he normally picks you up, but the referee doesn't see what he picks you up by.
RYAN GIGGS, Manchester United opponent, 2000.

Dennis Wise will be the captain. He is a very intelligent person. And though I don't speak English, you can talk to him with your eyes.
CLAUDIO RANIERI, Chelsea's Italian manager, 2000.

Wisey could be the next
Danny De Vito.
VINNIE JONES, 2001.

JONATHAN WOODGATE

Q: Which programme would
you bother to record if you
were going out?
A: I don't watch much TV.
Probably *Crimewatch*.
*JONATHAN WOODGATE in
Leeds programme questionnaire,
months before the incidents that
led to his trial on charges of affray
and grievous bodily harm, 1999.*

Q: Who would you definitely
not invite on a night out?
A: I know the first person I
would invite, and that's
Woody.
*HARRY KEWELL, Leeds team-
mate, in club magazine shortly
before Woodgate's arrest for
allegedly assaulting an Asian
student, 1999.*

He has a heart of gold but is
as daft as a brush.
*DAVID O'LEARY, Leeds
manager, after the defender was
charged, 2001.*

Jonathan is full of remorse
for the shame he has brought
on the club, his family and
himself. I believe he will end
up being a better person.
*PETER RIDSDALE, Leeds
chairman, after he was found
guilty of affray, 2002.*

ALAN WRIGHT

I got the ball and the crowd
started singing: 'One Ronnie
Corbett, there's only one
Ronnie Corbett!'
*ALAN WRIGHT, diminutive
Aston Villa defender, 2000.*

ABEL XAVIER

The manager (Walter Smith)
wrote to me and said: 'Hey
man, what have you done?'
*ABEL XAVIER, Everton and
Portugal defender, on going
blond at Euro 2000.*

TONY YEBOAH

The third goal was in the
net in the time it takes a
snowflake to melt on a
hot stove.
*HOWARD WILKINSON, Leeds
manager, on the Ghanaian's hat-
trick v. Ipswich, 1995.*

Sometimes, when I score,
I can't even explain to myself
how I did it.
TONY YEBOAH, 1995.

DWIGHT YORKE

I think he's an idiot ...
It's a shame I'm having his
kid really.
*JORDAN, model, accusing
Yorke of treating her 'like dirt'
during her pregnancy with their
child, 2002.*

ZINEDINE ZIDANE

When we don't know what to
do, we give it to him and he
works something out.
*BIXENTE LIZARAZU, France
defender, 2000.*

Sometimes you just want
to stop playing just to
watch him.
*CHRISTOPHE DUGARRY,
France colleague, 2000.*

GIANFRANCO ZOLA

The moment I turned up for
training and saw Zola, I
knew it was time to go.
*JOHN SPENCER, Scotland
striker, on the Italian's impact at
Chelsea, 1997.*

One hundred and sixty-eight
centimetres of sheer fantasy.
*Programme pen-picture,
England v. Italy, 1997.*

One of the strangest
requests he has ever had was
to appear on television to
appeal to kidnappers to let
the victim go free. He did
and it worked.
*FACT No. 78 in list of 'Things
you never knew about Zola',
Goal! magazine, 1999.*

②
PLAYERS: PAST

TONY ADAMS

I hear Tony Adams is appealing. Apparently he wasn't pissed. He was just trying to get the wall back 10 yards.
BOB 'THE CAT' BEVAN, after-dinner speaker, after Adams was imprisoned on a drink-driving charge following a collision with a wall, 1990.

When the Captain said there was a problem at the back, I thought he meant me and Steve Bould.
TONY ADAMS, Arsenal captain, after a delay to their flight from Copenhagen, 1994.

When he was sent to prison (for drink-driving), he whispered to me: 'I have done wrong and I'm going to take my punishment. I don't want to appeal.' That's Tony. If you're in a battle on the pitch, he's the first bloke you'd want on your side.
DAVID O'LEARY, former Arsenal colleague, 1995.

For Tony to admit he is an alcoholic took an awful lot of bottle.
IAN WRIGHT, Arsenal and England team-mate, 1996.

I have always admired Adams, always felt he was a Manchester United man playing in the wrong kit.
ALEX FERGUSON, United manager, 1998.

I was never too aware of his problems with booze, but he was still a hell of a player when he had them.
ALAN SHEARER, Newcastle opponent and England colleague, 1998.

Manager of Arsenal? Give us a break. It's very demanding being a manager. I need a life first. I fancy a bit of skiing and painting.
ADAMS, 1999.

[Adams] is getting ready for a new career as a traffic policeman. He was always ace at putting his hands up, indicating offside, even before the other team had kicked off. Now he is perfecting his pointing-hand routine, indicating where his team-mates should be for his next pass,

before he belts it into the stand.
HUNTER DAVIES, Tottenham fan, in his New Statesman *column, 1999.*

I haven't pissed the bed for two and a half years.
ADAMS on recovering from alcoholism, 1999.

An actor friend has got a big part in *Henry V*, and he said: 'Tone, I've got a block about learning all these lines.' I told him: 'Do it the way I work. Start with the first one and take it from there. Eventually you'll get to the end, just like I get to the end of the season.'
ADAMS with a new twist on taking each game as it comes, 2000.

It would be nice not having to spend Christmas Day in a hotel.
ADAMS contemplating retirement, 2002.

He is the greatest Arsenal man of all time. As a player, he goes beyond Liam Brady, Alex James, Joe Mercer or Frank McLintock. I don't think anyone has represented the club from the age of 17 to 35 and sustained all the injuries he he's had, while half the time fighting for his own soul. Only those close to him knew how bad it was.
BOB WILSON, goalkeeper with Arsenal's 1971 Double-winning side and club goalkeeping coach, after Adams led them to League and FA Cup success, 2002.

OSSIE ARDILES

I will never return to play in England, even if they gave me all the money in the world.
OSSIE ARDILES, Argentinian former Tottenham midfielder, during Falklands conflict, June 1982.

I can't wait to get back. Every night I go to bed dreaming of Wembley.
ARDILES, December 1982.

ALAN BALL

The only thing that stops me being a world-class player is that I don't score enough goals.
ALAN BALL, England midfielder, 1972.

Jim Baxter drove him mad
calling him Jimmy Clitheroe
but Bally couldn't get near
enough to him to do
anything about it.
*BILLY BREMNER, former
Scotland captain, recalling his
country's 1967 defeat of world
champions England, 1992.
Clitheroe was a high-voiced
comic actor.*

GORDON BANKS

At that moment I hated
Gordon Banks more than
any man in soccer. But when I
cooled down I had to applaud
him with my heart for the
greatest save I had ever seen.
*PELE after Banks saved his
header, Brazil v. England,
World Cup finals, 1970.*

JOHN BARNES

Coming from Jamaica,
I am blessed with rhythm.
*JOHN BARNES, The
Autobiography, 1999.*

Having a priest cane him
every weekend...I thought:
'That'll be good for him.'
*COLONEL KEN BARNES on
his son's upbringing, 1988.*

As the ball came over I
remembered what Graham
Taylor said about my
having no right foot – so I
headed it in.
*JOHN BARNES after scoring
for Liverpool v. Taylor's Villa,
FA Cup, 1988.*

Revenge does not feature in
my psyche. The black
community loves how Ian
Wright reacts, the way he
flings out a fist or mouths
off... I'm different.
*BARNES in his autobiography,
1999.*

My father could not stand or
understand footballers who
did tricks and took risks with
the ball, which clearly
undermined the team's cause.
BARNES, as above.

I've never seen a better eater:
Indian, Chinese, Mexican.
You serve it and 'Digger'
will see it off.
*PETER BEARDSLEY, Liverpool
and England colleague, 1988.*

JIM BAXTER

Scotsmen value things in this
world far above success, or

integrity or intelligence. What they value most is what Baxter had, the completely held conviction of their own superiority.
ALAN SHARP, Scottish novelist and screenwriter, in the book We'll Support You Evermore, *1976.*

Slim Jim had everything required of a great Scottish footballer. Outrageously skilled, totally irresponsible, supremely arrogant and thick as mince.
ALASTAIR MACSPORRAN, columnist, in the fanzine The Absolute Game, *1990.*

PETER BEARDSLEY

The bottom line is that Beardsley comes from God.
ANDY ROXBURGH, Scotland manager, after Beardsley's winner for England, 1988.

I often get called Quasimodo and have done for years. The way I look at it is that if I was in those fans' colours, they would be happy with me.
PETER BEARDSLEY, 1995.

He's the only player who, when he's on TV, Daleks hide behind the sofa.
NICK HANCOCK, compere, on TV's They Think It's All Over, *1995.*

Christ, he looks like a thin Ann Widdecombe.
NICKY CLARKE, hairstylist, 2001.

FRANZ BECKENBAUER

Tell the Kraut to get his ass up front. We don't pay a million for a guy to hang around on defence.
NEW YORK COSMOS executive on the former West Germany captain's deep-lying role, 1977.

COLIN BELL

He didn't seem to grasp his own freakish strength. I said to him: 'You're a great header of the ball, you have a terrific shot, and you're the best, most powerful runner in the business. Every time you walk off the pitch unable to say you were streets ahead of the other 21 players, you have failed.
MALCOLM ALLISON, ex-Manchester City manager, 1975

GEORGE BEST

There are times when you want to wring his neck. He hangs on to the ball when other players have found better positions. Then out of the blue he does something which wins the match. Then you know you're in the presence of someone special.
PADDY CRERAND, Manchester United team-mate, 1970.

Best makes a greater appeal to the senses than the other two [Stanley Matthews and Tom Finney]. His movements are quicker, lighter, more balletic...And with it all, there is his utter disregard for physical danger. ..He has ice in his veins, warmth in his heart, and timing and balance in his feet.
DANNY BLANCHFLOWER, former Northern Ireland captain, in David Meek's book Anatomy of a Football Star: George Best, *1970.*

I don't drink every day but when I do it's usually for four or five days on the trot. I've got a drink problem.
GEORGE BEST, 1979.

I might go to Alcoholics Anonymous but I think it would be difficult for me to be anonymous.
BEST, 1980.

Well, he has a drink problem, hasn't he?
DON MEGSON, Bournemouth manager, on why he left Best out of his team, 1983.

As recently as the late Seventies, to woo our top players home, the authorities introduced all-day drinking in Scottish pubs, a valiant effort that succeeded only in enticing George Best to Hibs.
ONLY AN EXCUSE, *BBC Radio Scotland spoof documentary, 1986.*

We had our problems with the wee feller, but I prefer to remember his genius.
SIR MATT BUSBY, 1988.

If you'd given me a choice between beating four defenders and smashing in a goal from 30 yards or going to bed with Miss World, it would have been difficult. Luckily, I had both. It's just that you do one of those

things in front of 50,000 people.
BEST, 1991.

One day they might even say I was another Ryan Giggs.
BEST, 1992.

I always had a reputation for going missing – Miss England, Miss United Kingdom, Miss World...
BEST, 1992.

I spent a lot of my money on booze, birds and fast cars. The rest I squandered.
BEST, 1992.

People say he wasted his career. Nonsense. He was hunted down by defenders for 11 seasons starting at 17. He paid his dues all right.
DAVID MEEK, journalist who covered Manchester United for four decades, 1995.

By today's prices I'd be worth around £15m.
BEST, 1996.

It's a pleasure for me to be standing up here. It's a

pleasure to be standing up.
BEST, accepting the Footballer of the Century award, 1999.

If I was reincarnated I'd come back as George Best, because he was a genius and had all them women and drank all that wine.
BARRY FRY, Peterborough manager and teenaged Old Trafford colleague, 1999.

He has three problems: he is famous, he is rich and he is Irish. Not a good combination.
PETER STRINGFELLOW, nightclub owner, 2000.

He was Roy of the Rovers on the field, but sadly Roy of the Ravers off it.
Description of Best on International Hall of Fame website, 2000.

It was typical of me to be finishing a long and distinguished drinking career just as the Government is planning to open pubs 24 hours a day.
BEST, 2001.

In her youth the Queen was quite a stunner. Who knows what might have happened if I'd met her in Trampp in my heyday.
BEST during the Queen's Golden Jubilee celebrations, 2002.

I celebrated my 56th birthday with a banana and honey milkshake. A new liver would have been a nice present.
BEST, 2002.

He's a totally different person now. The lovely side was always there, which is why I married him. It's just that I've got it all the time now.
ALEX BEST, Best's wife, before his liver-transplant operation, 2002.

DANNY BLANCHFLOWER

In a poor side Danny is an expensive luxury. That's why I dropped him when we had a poor team. But in a good side as Spurs are now he is a wonderful asset through his unorthodox approach and marvellous ball skill.
BILL NICHOLSON, Tottenham's Double-winning manager, on his captain in

Julian Holland's book Spurs - The Double, *1961.*

STAN BOWLES

If Stan could pass a betting shop the way he can pass a ball he'd have no worries whatsoever.
ERNIE TAGG, Crewe manager, who launched the compulsive gambler on a career which earned him England caps, 1974.

BILLY BREMNER

I'm no angel, but I've never kicked anyone deliberately.
BILLY BREMNER, Leeds captain, 1967.

10st of Barbed Wire
HEADLINE on Sunday Times *profile, 1970.*

TREVOR BROOKING

Floats like a butterfly and stings like one, too.
BRIAN CLOUGH, Nottingham Forest manager, on the eve of the FA Cup final, 1981. Brooking headed West Ham's winner v. *Arsenal.*

STEVE BULL

People say his first touch isn't good, but he usually scores with his second.
GRAHAM TURNER, Wolves manager, 1988.

Favourite food: conkers in gravy.
SPOOF PROFILE of Bull in The Memoirs of Seth Bottomley, *Port Vale fanzine, 1989.*

He's so single-minded in front of goal. I've known some greedy players – I remember wrestling for the ball with Gavin Peacock, who's in Christians In Sport for heaven's sake, when Newcastle had a penalty and I was on a hat-trick – but Bully takes the biscuit.
DAVID KELLY, Wolves striker, 1994.

TERRY BUTCHER

I haven't had the chance to kick a Celtic player for many years.
TERRY BUTCHER, former Rangers captain, on playing in the Old Firm Veterans' Challenge, 2001.

ERIC CANTONA

He gave interviews on art, philosophy and politics. A natural room-mate for David Batty, I thought immediately.
HOWARD WILKINSON, Leeds manager, in Managing to Succeed: My Life in Football Management, *with David Walker, 1992.*

Eric likes to do what he likes, when he likes, because he likes it – and then fuck off. We'd all want a bit of that.
WILKINSON after offloading the Frenchman to Manchester United, 1993.

Rimbaud wanted to write about everything, to seek flashes of inspiration, to enjoy different ideas and live with different philosophies. He had the spontaneity of a child, and I believe in that. He was a pioneer, but the torch he lit was picked up by others, like Jim Morrison. I believe that, even in football, I should live as instinctively as that.
ERIC CANTONA early in his time at Manchester United, 1993.

1966 was a great year
for English football. Eric
was born.
Nike advertising slogan, 1994.

Cantona will let you down at
the highest level. He let
Leeds down against Rangers,
twice, and in the big games,
against Inter Milan or
whoever, he will go missing.
He's a cry baby when the
going gets tough.
*GEORGE GRAHAM, Arsenal
manager, 1994.*

Just as I can bring happiness
to people with my spontaneity,
my instinctiveness, so there are
always going to be dark
shadows, black stains.
CANTONA, 1994.

The talk among your fellow
professionals is that you are
steadily becoming a nasty,
dirty bastard.
*JOHN FASHANU, Aston
Villa striker, in his newspaper
column, 1994.*

When Eric feels an injustice,
he has to prove to the whole
world that he's been wronged.
He can't control his temper.
That's just part of his game.

*ALEX FERGUSON after
Cantona was sent off* v. *Rangers
in a friendly, 1994.*

I just yelled: 'Off you go,
Cantona – it's an early
shower for you.'
*MATTHEW SIMMONS,
Crystal Palace fan, explaining
what he had said to provoke
Cantona's 'kung-fu'
assault, 1995.*

Pressure is no excuse. I would
take any amount of personal
abuse for £10,000 a week
(Cantona's reputed salary).
*SIR STANLEY MATTHEWS
after the Selhurst Park
incident, 1995.*

I'd have cut his balls off.
*BRIAN CLOUGH after
Cantona's fracas at Crystal
Palace, 1995.*

1995 was a great year for
English football. Eric was
banned.
*SLOGAN on T-shirts sold at
Manchester City, Leeds,
Liverpool etc., 1995.*

My initial feeling was to let
him go. I couldn't imagine
his playing for the club

again...My wife Cath said: 'You can't let him off. Never let it be said that you put winning the championship above doing the right thing.'
ALEX FERGUSON, in his diary A Year in the Life, *1995.*

Because he's a footballer, he's a thug and he's French.
GAVIN STAMP, art critic, on why the National Portrait Gallery would not be having a portrait of Cantona, 1997.

I'd give all the champagne I've ever drunk to have played alongside him in a big European match at Old Trafford.
GEORGE BEST, 1997.

Cantona is a great player, but only in the context of English football.
ROBERT LOUIS-DREYFUS, Marseille president, 1997.

For my next film role I would love to play a psychopath or an unpleasant person.
CANTONA, 2000.

TONY CASCARINO

When I arrived at Marseille, [the president] Bernard Tapie said to me: 'I didn't like Lee Chapman. I didn't like Mark Hateley. I like players like Chris Waddle. I thought: 'Oh shit, what am I doing here?'
TONY CASCARINO, former Republic of Ireland striker, on his spell in France, 2001.

LEE CHAPMAN

Footballers are supposed to look like Billy the Fish out of Viz, aren't they? Well I've never looked like that. I've never even had a mullet.
LEE CHAPMAN, former Leeds and Arsenal striker, 2000.

JOHN CHARLES

Everything John does is automatic. When he moves into position for a goal chance it is instinctive. Watch me and you'll see I am seconds late...But all my thinking has to be done in my head. My feet do not do my thinking for me as they do for [Charles]. That is why

I can never be as great a
footballer.
DANNY BLANCHFLOWER,
Tottenham captain, on the great
Welsh centre-forward and centre-
half, 1961.

He'd have been on
£50,000 a week now. No
one would have been
earning more.
HAROLD WILLIAMS, former
Leeds team-mate, 2001.

John was never interested in
money. He thought you lived
on fresh air.
GLENDA CHARLES, his
second wife, 2002.

BOBBY CHARLTON

The fact that they accused
Bobby Charlton of sheltering
me while I 'stole' a bracelet
proves I'm innocent. Bobby
has never done a dishonest
thing in his life.
BOBBY MOORE, England
captain and colleague, after
the 'jewel theft' incident in
Bogota, 1970.

That was a great day.
Bobby Charlton nearly
bought a drink.
EAMONN O'KEEFE recalling
his hat-trick that earned Wigan
promotion, 1982. Charlton was a
Wigan director.

Bobby deserves to keep the
record. He was a much better
player than me and scored far
better goals.
GARY LINEKER on retiring
from international football one
goal short of Charlton's England
record, 1992.

The Prince of Wales' visit is
big news here but Mr
Charlton's was even bigger.
Spokesman for the British
Embassy in Morocco, 1995.

I sent my son to one of his
schools of excellence and he
came back bald.
GEORGE BEST, former
Manchester United team-
mate, on TV's Mrs Merton
Show, *1996.*

We just don't get on. Our
kid was a much better player
than me but I'm a much
better bloke.
JACK CHARLTON, 1998.

Robert 'Bobby' Charlton was forward for the British team at the '66 and '67 World Cups.
PELE's website, 2002.

BRIAN CLOUGH

The only thing I enjoyed during my six years at Middlesbrough was scoring goals. From Saturday to Saturday I was very unhappy. My ability was never utilised, by me or the management. Only goals kept me sane. That was my only pleasure.
BRIAN CLOUGH, 1973.

GEORGE COHEN

We used to say of George Cohen: 'He's hit more photographers than Frank Sinatra.'...Usually he would hit his cross into the crowd, or into the photographers.
BOBBY ROBSON, former Fulham team-mate, in his book Time On the Grass, *1982.*

EDDIE COLMAN

When he waggled his hips he made the stanchions in the grandstand sway.

HARRY GREGG, Manchester United goalkeeper, on the colleague nicknamed 'Snakehips' who perished in the Munich disaster, 1958.

STAN COLLYMORE

I'm no angel but I think I'm more misunderstood than anything else. I think I'm a pretty interesting bloke.
STAN COLLYMORE, then with Liverpool, 1997.

I rang Alex Ferguson to see if he'd swap Collymore for Cole. He thought for a few seconds, then said: 'How many bags?'
JOHN GREGORY, Aston Villa manager, 1998.

I've ridiculed him, I've tried to love him and I've told him what a great player he is. I've said to him: 'I wish I was you, Stan. I wish I was on the money you're earning. I wish I had your lifestyle. And most of all, I wish I had your talent because with it, I'd have been the first name in the England team.'
GREGORY as Collymore suffered clinical depression, 1999.

Some days he could climb Everest, others he can't even climb out of bed.
GREGORY on his striker's continuing illness, 1999.

I find it difficult to understand how someone in Stan's position, with the talent and money he has, is stressed. I wonder how a 29-year-old at Rochdale, in the last three months of his contract, with a wife and three kids, copes with stress.
GREGORY, 1999.

You can't be sure he will ever be taken on by a club anywhere. Unless it's some Outer Mongolian outfit that has been locked away from news, television and society for 10 years.
Editorial in Nottingham Post after Collymore declined to rejoin Forest, 1999.

I don't know what medical condition Collymore has got but it's obvious that he's not quite mentally correct. It's a shame because it's a waste of talent.
COLIN LEE, Wolves manager, 1999.

At school Stan would have been the boy who ate worms. Weird but nice.
NEIL RUDDOCK, former Liverpool colleague, 2000.

At the end of the day I haven't killed anybody. A million players have done it [letting off a fire-extinguisher in a hotel lobby] and a million more will do it in the future.
COLLYMORE on hitting the headlines following a prank on a Spanish break with his new club, Leicester, 2000.

When I retire I want to work in the cinema and television. I want to be the first black James Bond.
COLLYMORE, 2001. He soon retired and became a match summariser on radio.

CHARLIE COOKE

When he sold you a dummy you had to pay to get back in the ground.
JIM BAXTER, Scotland team-mate, on the Chelsea winger, 1976.

KENNY DALGLISH

Is he better in midfield or up front? Och, just let him on the park.
JOCK STEIN, Dalglish's former Celtic manager, 1977.

He would make a perfect trades-union official.
GRAEME SOUNESS, former Liverpool colleague, in No Half Measures, *1985.*

The way he sticks out his arms and legs represents plain obstruction. He's supposed to be one of the best screeners of the ball in the game. I say that's rubbish – too many refs can't see that he's breaking the law.
CLIVE 'THE BOOK' THOMAS, Football League referee, 1984.

When he scored...he had a better smile than Clark Gable. Beautiful teeth, arms wide, that's how he celebrated. He wasn't that big but he had a huge arse. It came down below his knees, and that's where he got his strength from.
BRIAN CLOUGH, former managerial adversary, 1995.

The best player this club has signed this century.
JOHN SMITH, Liverpool chairman, 1986.

Few great players make the transition into management. The reason is that great players are normally like soloists in an orchestra. They perform alone and tend to look down on those of lesser ability. That was never Kenny. He was like a conductor who brought others into play. He understood that not everyone was blessed with the greatest skill. He had patience both as a player and a manager.
BOB PAISLEY, the manager who bought Dalglish for Liverpool, 1991.

DIXIE DEAN

He belongs in the company of the supremely great, like Shakespeare, Rembrandt and Beethoven.
BILL SHANKLY honours the legendary Everton centre-forward at a dinner, hours before Dean died at the Mersey derby, 1980.

JULIAN DICKS

Rumour has it that when Dicks moved to Liverpool he picked up the No. 23 shirt because it said Fowler on it.
KEVIN BALDWIN, author, This Supporting Life: How To Be A Real Fan, *1995.*

ALFREDO DI STEFANO

One of the greatest, if not the greatest footballer I had ever seen. At that time [the 1950s] we had forwards and defenders doing separate jobs, but he did everything.
MATT BUSBY, Manchester United manager, on the Real Madrid centre-forward, in Motson and Rowlandson, The European Cup 1955-80, *1980.*

TOMMY DOCHERTY

I once told Tommy that if we had five Bill Shanklys and five Tommy Dochertys, plus a goalkeeper, we'd beat the world. Tommy said: 'If there were five Bill Shanklys and five Tommy Dochertys, we wouldn't need a goalkeeper'.
BILL SHANKLY reminisces about his successor in the Preston team, quoted in John Keith's Shanks For the Memory, *1998.*

ROBBIE EARLE

One afternoon in hospital I was told I had picked up an infection again. By this time I had lost four stone. My breathing was irregular, I was in agony. If somebody had told me that death was the best choice, I would have accepted it –anything to take away the pain.
ROBBIE EARLE, Wimbledon and Jamaica midfielder, on the injury that eventually ended his career, 2000.

DUNCAN EDWARDS

The Kohinoor diamond among our crown jewels. Even when he'd won his first England cap, and was still eligible for our youth team, he used to love turning out at a lower level. He remained an unspoiled boy to the end, his head the same size it had been from the start.
JIMMY MURPHY, Matt Busby's No. 2 at Manchester United, after Edwards died from

injuries sustained in the Munich
air disaster, 1958.

People still haven't forgotten.
Strangers come up and tell
me: 'He were a good 'un.'
ANNE EDWARDS, mother
of Duncan, 35 years after his
death, 1993.

JOHN FASHANU

When I saw my face I felt like
the Elephant Man. Fashanu
was not playing with due care
and attention.
GARY MABBUTT, Tottenham
defender, after sustaining a
broken jaw from the Wimbledon
striker's elbow, 1993.

TOM FINNEY

Tommy was grizzly strong and
could run for a week. I'd have
played him in an overcoat.
There'd have been four men
marking him at the kick-in.
When I told people in Scotland
that England were coming up
with a winger better than Stanley
Matthews, they laughed at me.
They weren't bloody laughing
when Big Georgie Young was
running all over Hampden
looking for Tommy Finney.

BILL SHANKLY recalls his
former Preston team-mate, 1972.

TREVOR FRANCIS

He told me he had a system
for taking penalties. I don't
know what it is but it's
obviously bloody useless.
JIM SMITH, QPR manager,
after Francis' second successive
miss from the spot, 1988.

JOHN GILES

That Johnny Giles of Leeds is
a great player. Beats me why
Alf Ramsey has never picked
him for England.
WILLIE ORMOND,
Scotland manager, on the Irish
schemer, 1973.

I thought he was miles
better than [Billy] Bremner.
A better passer, shrewder,
more devious and harder
when he wanted to be.
STEVE PERRYMAN,
Tottenham captain, in A Man
For All Seasons, 1985.

Giles was the man everybody
wanted to sort out. He was
extremely adept at escaping
bookings. He would be

furthest away when anything
went off. And he was nearly
always the instigator.
*TERRY CONROY, former
Republic of Ireland team-mate
and Stoke adversary, 2002.*

ANDY GRAY

His style is more suited to
rugby union.
*UDO LATTEK, Bayern Munich
coach, on the Everton striker who
became a TV pundit, 1985.*

EDDIE GRAY

When he plays on snow, he
doesn't leave any footprints.
*DON REVIE on the Leeds and
Scotland midfielder, 1970.*

JIMMY GREAVES

He was always very calm,
very collected, and, where
scoring goals was concerned,
he was a Picasso.
*CLIVE ALLEN, Tottenham
striker, in* There's Only One
Clive Allen, *1987.*

Q: Who was the biggest
influence on your career?
A: IAN ST JOHN: Bill
Shankly.

A: JIMMY GREAVES:
Vladimir Smirnoff.
*Interview with Saint and
Greavsie in* Loaded
magazine, 1995.

HARRY GREGG

Somewhere in there, the
grace of a ballet dancer joins
with the strength of an SAS
squaddie, the dignity of an
ancient king, the nerve of a
bomb disposal officer.
*EAMON DUNPHY, journalist
and former Republic of Ireland
player, 1983.*

RUUD GULLIT

JIMMY GREAVES: 'E's a
Moroccan or something,
isn't 'e?'
IAN ST JOHN: Moluccan.
GREAVES: Yeah, Moluccan,
that's it. Well blimey 'e can't
'alf play a bit.
Exchange on ITV's Saint &
Greavsie Show, *1988*

If all else fails you could wait
for the first corner-kick and
use his dreadlocks to tie him
to a post.
*VINNIE JONES, Wimbledon
midfielder, 1988.*

Watching Ruud was like watching an 18-year-old play in a game for 12-year-olds.
GLENN HODDLE, Chelsea manager, on Gullit's English debut, 1995.

My pot-bellied pigs don't squeal as much as him.
VINNIE JONES after being sent off for fouling the Dutchman, 1995.

BRUCE GROBBELAAR

Football teams are a balance of road sweepers and violinists, Bruce is a lead violinist.
LAWRIE McMENEMY, Southampton manager, signing Grobbelaar from Liverpool, 1994.

I'd rather have Bruce Grobbelaar trying to throw a game than Dave Beasant trying to win one.
SOUTHAMPTON fan on Six-O-Six radio phone-in after Grobbelaar's arrest on match-fixing charges, 1994.

GHEORGHE HAGI

He's a brilliant player but we're no' getting all psychedelic about him.
ANDY ROXBURGH, Scotland coach, on the Romanian playmaker, 1991.

ALAN HANSEN

A good skipper, but he could have been a really great one if he had been a bit more extrovert.
BOB PAISLEY, former Liverpool manager, 1989.

I never liked pundits before I became one.
ALAN HANSEN on becoming a fixture on Match of the Day, *1994.*

He looks like a pissed vampire.
CHRIS DONALD, editor of Viz *magazine, 1994.*

RON HARRIS

I like to think that I've something else to offer apart from being a bit of a butcher.
RON HARRIS, Chelsea captain, 1979.

JIMMY HILL

I shall never forget my second match for Brentford Reserves.
JIMMY HILL in Striking For Soccer, *1961.*

If he can find a ground where he scored a League goal, I'll meet him there.
BRIAN CLOUGH replying to Hill's challenge to debate, 1979.

GLENN HODDLE

Hoddle a luxury? It's the bad players who are a luxury.
DANNY BLANCHFLOWER, predecessor in Tottenham's midfield, 1981.

I hear Glenn has found God. That must have been one hell of a pass.
JASPER CARROTT, comedian, 1988.

MARK HUGHES

A warrior you could trust with your life.
ALEX FERGUSON in the David Meek and Hughes book, Hughsie, The Red Dragon, *1994.*

ROGER HUNT

Yes, he misses a few. But he gets in the right places to miss them.
BILL SHANKLY, the England forward's manager at Liverpool, 1966.

NORMAN HUNTER

Norman bites yer legs.
Slogan on Leeds fans' banner honouring the hard-tackling defender, 1972.

GEOFF HURST

As I was running towards the German goal, Alan Ball was shouting: 'Hursty, Hursty, give me the ball!' I said to myself: 'Sod you, Bally. I'm on a hat-trick.'
SIR GEOFF HURST recalling England's 1966 triumph, 1999.

Deep down all the lads will be keeping a sort of score in their heads. Every time they jump for the ball and get it they'll be chalking it down, 'Three to me, one to Geoff Hurst' or whatever. Despite what the boss says, he is special. Nicking the ball off a

player like that, beating him in the tackle, is something you'll always remember. Magic!
PAUL PRICE, captain of Midland side Tividale, before FA Cup tie v. Telford, where Hurst was player-manager; from Journey to Wembley, *by Brian James, 1977.*

DAVID ICKE

David Icke says he is here to save the world. Well he saved bugger all when he played in goal for Coventry.
JASPER CARROTT, comedian, 1992.

LEIGHTON JAMES

Your pace is very deceptive, son – you're even slower than you look.
TOMMY DOCHERTY, Derby manager, to the Welsh winger, 1977.

MAURICE JOHNSTON

Scottish football was rocked to its pre-cast concrete foundations when Rangers finally broke with 100 years of tradition and bought a

player from FC Nantes for the first time in their history.
The Absolute Game, Scottish football fanzine, after Johnston spurned a return to Celtic and joined Rangers, 1989.

JIMMY JOHNSTONE

On my first day as Scotland manager I had to call off practice after half an hour because nobody could get the ball off wee Jinky.
TOMMY DOCHERTY, 1970.

VINNIE JONES

I like to upset anybody I play against.
VINNIE JONES, 1988.

He's incredibly loyal.
Ask him to jump off the stand roof and he'll do it. But he's as thick as two short planks. He always grabbed the quiz-book on our coach trips so he could ask the questions. That way he didn't have to answer.
ARNIE REED, physiotherapist at Jones' first club, Wealdstone, 1988.

Q: Person you would most like to meet?
A: Mike Tyson — any place, any time.
JONES in Leeds programme questionnaire, 1989.

Vinnie is a once-in-a-lifetime human being.
SAM HAMMAM, Wimbledon chairman, after selling Jones to Leeds, 1989.

In Don Revie's day he wouldn't have got through the door, let alone pulled on a Leeds shirt.
JOHN GILES, former Leeds midfielder, 1989.

I've been trying to be a footballer and that isn't me. I got a bit carried away with the Wogan show and all that.
JONES, 1990.

At half-time on my Wimbledon debut our old kit-man, Sid, came round with the tea. I asked him how I was doing and he said: 'I'm 85 and if you gave me the No. 4 shirt I'd do better.'
JONES, 1991.

There is more chance of me being involved in the Great Train Robbery than fixing a game.
JONES after Wimbledon team-mate Hans Segers was arrested for alleged match-rigging, 1995.

George Orwell said that political speech was the defence of the indefensible. Michael Heseltine is the Vinnie Jones of the indefensible.
ALLISON PEARSON, Observer *television reviewer, 1995.*

The Football Association have given me a pat on the back because I've taken violence off the terraces and on to the pitch.
JONES addressing the Oxford Union, 1995.

My career has been like the migrating woodcock. You've got all the shooters and storms trying to whack you down, but in the end you just want to get to new fields.
JONES, 1995.

I'm still on the transfer list but Alex Ferguson has yet to take the hint.
JONES, 1996.

Vinnie admits he threw a piece of toast at Gary Lineker. What he didn't say was that it was still in the toaster.
TONY BANKS MP, Labour, on Radio 4's News Quiz, 1997.

Vinnie is a natural [as an actor]. People have knocked him all his life but they are just bitter and twisted. He can do anything. If he goes on to manage England one day, I wouldn't be surprised.
JOHN HARTSON, former colleague in the Wales team, 2000.

In a couple of years' time I'd love to play 007. It would be a dream come true for me – all them shooters and stunts.
JONES, 1999.

You wouldn't know in our house whether I was a dustman or a movie star. There's no conversation about it.
JONES, 2000.

I can't keep up this hard image. I must be the nicest person I know.
JONES, 2000.

I've seen that advert with Giggsy wearing an apron and holding a feather duster and I wouldn't do that. I might have done it a few years ago for a few quid. I've been in some fucking ridiculous pictures, I can tell you.
JONES, 2002.

I like autobiographies. Sports ones are interesting. You might be surprised that I like a bit of poetry, too. I don't have any books on it, but I do like it. A lot of music is poetry really.
JONES, 2002.

KEVIN KEEGAN

Kevin Keegan is the Julie Andrews of football.
DUNCAN McKENZIE, playing contemporary of Keegan's, 1981.

To call Keegan a superstar is stretching a point. As a player he's not fit to lace my boots.
GEORGE BEST, 1982.

Keegan isn't fit to lace
Best's drinks.
JOHN ROBERTS, Daily Mail
football writer, 1982.

JURGEN KLINSMANN

Me dive? Never. I always go
straight for goal.
JURGEN KLINSMANN
rebutting charges of diving,
World Cup finals, 1994.

I was watching Germany and
got up to make a cup of tea. I
bumped into the telly and
Klinsmann fell over.
FRANK SKINNER,
comedian, 1994.

MICHAEL LAUDRUP

There's not a lot you can do
to stop him, short of sending
a couple of guys in balaclavas
with baseball bats round to
knock on his door.
JIM DUFFY, Hibernian
manager, when Laudrup was
with Rangers, 1997.

DENIS LAW

Denis was in the class of
[Alfredo] Di Stefano because
he could do everything,

organise a side and score
goals...Matt Busby knew
how important he was –
when Denis was doubtful
[due to injury] the boss
would practically be on his
hands and knees hoping he
would play.
HARRY GREGG, Manchester
United goalkeeper, in the John
Motson and John Rowlandson
book The European Cup
1955–80, *1980.*

MATTHEW LE TISSIER

You're never sure you
want him playing for
you, but you're sure you
don't want him playing
against you.
DARIO GRADI, Crewe
manager, 1995.

The one thing I'd like to
rid myself of is the word
'but'. You know, 'He's a
great player, but...' or
'So much skill, but...'
MATTHEW LE TISSIER,
1997.

GARY LINEKER

Conjugate the verb 'done
great': I done great. He done

great. We done great. They done great. The boy Lineker done great.
Letter to the Guardian *after TV pundit Mick Channon referred to the England striker as 'the boy Lineker' during the World Cup finals, 1986.*

I'm rather a boring sort of person.
GARY LINEKER on Desert Island Discs, *1990.*

My record, averaging a goal every two games, sounds good, but that's only one goal every three hours. Most of the time I'm frustrated, pissed off, waiting for the right ball.
LINEKER, 1992.

He had no feel for the game, no passion, and that's why, now that he has retired, he's best keeping out of football.
VINNIE JONES, former opponent, 1994.

After I've been in Japan for two days I start to get depressed and want to go home. The people get on my nerves. I just want to say: 'Stop bowing, will you?' There's no decent food,

the beer's dead expensive, there's no proper cigarettes, you can't get drugs and all the women are ugly. Everyone's too nice – no wonder Gary Lineker went there.
NOEL GALLAGHER of the rock group Oasis, 1995.

Too good to be true.
ALEX FERGUSON, Manchester United manager, 1996.

It's not deliberate. I don't think anyone would contrive an image as sickly sweet as mine.
LINEKER, by now presenting TV's Match of the Day, *2000.*

He's a bit of a babe.
BOY GEORGE, gay pop singer and DJ, 2000.

DIEGO MARADONA

The best one-footed player since Puskas.
SIR STANLEY MATTHEWS, 1986.

A little bit the hand of God, a little the head of Diego.
DIEGO MARADONA describing his 'volleyball' goal against England in the World Cup, 1986.

Pele had nearly everything.
Maradona has everything.
He works harder, does more
and is more skilful. Trouble
is he'll be remembered for
another reason – he bends the
rules to suit himself.
*SIR ALF RAMSEY after
Maradona's 'hand of god'
goal, 1986.*

With Maradona, even Arsenal
would have won it.
*BOBBY ROBSON, England
manager, after Argentina went
on to win the World Cup, 1986*

I was dancing in a disco
when this very small, fat man
approached and started hugging
me. I thought it was a fan, but
then his bodyguard came over.
Then I recognised him.
*RUUD GULLIT, Netherlands
captain, on meeting Maradona,
1988.*

His left foot is like a hand.
*OSSIE ARDILES, former
Argentina player, 1994.*

Fifa cut off my legs just when
I had the chance to prove to
my daughters that I could
play with 20-year-olds.
MARADONA leaving the

*World Cup finals after failing a
drugs test, 1994.*

I was, I am and I always will
be a drug addict. A person
who gets involved in drugs
has to fight it every day.
*MARADONA signing up to an
Argentinian government anti-
drugs campaign, 1996.*

For me, he was the perfect
footballer. Pele was a better
team player, but I believe
Maradona was better than
anyone who has played
football on this planet.
*GLENN HODDLE, England
coach, 1998.*

The best player I ever played
against. I see Ronaldo, and
Patrick Kluivert, and they're
both great players. But the ball
belonged to Maradona. He
always fought for his team,
too, on and off the pitch.
*LOTHAR MATTHAUS,
former Germany captain, 2000.*

LOTHAR MATTHAUS

The Germans have five
million registered footballers
and yet they select a 39-
year-old.

ARSENE WENGER, Arsenal manager, at Euro 2000.

STANLEY MATTHEWS

If I had to get 'stuck in' to get through a game I'm afraid my career would have ended long ago.
STANLEY MATTHEWS, then aged 45, in The Stanley Matthews Story, *1960.*

**Last night I had the strangest dream
I've never had before
Stan Matthews on the wing
   for Stoke
At the age of 84.**
Song on Keele University students' rag record, 1964.

Stan was unique. He never went for 50-50 balls, didn't score many goals and was not good in the air. But on his day he was unplayable. He beat fellows so easily, with such pace and balance, often taking on four or five at a time.
JOE MERCER, former England team-mate, 1970.

You usually knew how he'd beat you, but you couldn't do anything about it.

DANNY BLANCHFLOWER, former Tottenham captain, 1970.

I never gave many fouls away. The most was when I played [for Huddersfield] against Stanley Matthews in his comeback game for Stoke City. I coughed twice and the referee blew.
RAY WILSON, England's World Cup-winning left-back, in Martin Tyler, Boys of 66, *1981.*

Stan used to put the ball on my centre-parting. They don't do that any more.
TOMMY LAWTON, former England centre-forward, 1985.

He cut his partners out of the game. If you passed to him, you'd never see the ball again.
RAY BOWDEN, Matthews' first international partner in 1934, in Michael George's book Sportsmen of Cornwall, *1986.*

His name is symbolic of the beauty of the game, his fame timeless. A magical player, of the people, for the people.
Inscription on statue of Matthews in Hanley, his birthplace, 1987.

The maestro appears to be dribbling towards Millett's but could easily swerve across the street to Woolworth's.
GUINNESS FOOTBALL ENCYCLOPAEDIA, *ed. Graham Hart, describing the statue, 1991.*

I'm not a scientist. I'm not a poet. I'm not a writer. But of course I am very honoured.
MATTHEWS accepting an honorary degree from Keele University, 1987.

I don't know whether I was all that good. I never saw myself play, so how do I know?
MATTHEWS on his 80th birthday, 1995.

I'm no hero. Doctors and nurses are heroes. Surgeons, people like that. We had a real hero born right here in Stoke-on-Trent – Reginald Mitchell, who designed the Spitfire. He saved Britain. Now that's what I call a hero.
MATTHEWS , 1995.

George Best and David Beckham rolled into one.

KENNETH WOLSTENHOLME, former TV commentator, on Matthews' death, 2000.

Grabbing hold of Stan to try to stop him was fatal because he knew then that he'd got you. He'd often beat a full-back, wait for him to recover and then beat him again. It was never for show, but for the ruthlessly simple expedient of demoralising the opponent.
JIMMY ARMFIELD, former Blackpool colleague, on Matthews' death, 2000.

Stan never looked as though he was enjoying himself. He always had a serious expression on his face because he was so focused on his game.
KEN ASTON, former World Cup referee, 2000.

He never criticised the modern game, never said that the players weren't as good as in his day.
PETER COATES, Stoke City director, 2000.

ALLY MCCOIST

He's handsome, he's rich,
he's funny and he's happy –
my envy knows no bounds.
*BILLY CONNOLLY, comedian,
in foreword to* Ally McCoist:
My Story, *1992.*

He's Superman and Roy of
the Rovers rolled into one.
We call him Golden Bollocks.
*JOHN ROBERTSON, Hearts
striker and Scotland team-
mate, 1995.*

I met Michael Jackson
backstage at the Tokyo Dome
in '93, but to be honest,
meeting Ally McCoist was a
bigger buzz.
*ALAN McGEE, Creation
Records label owner, 1995.*

PAUL MCGRATH

One of the all-time greats –
someone to compare with
Bobby Moore.
*JACK CHARLTON, McGrath's
Republic of Ireland manager
and former defensive partner to
Moore with England, 1995.*

BILLY MCNEILL

Billy sets a high standard of
conduct for all of us, and this
is the main reason why you
do not see any long-haired
wonders walking through
the doors at Celtic Park...
Professional football is our
business. We feel we do not
have to look like a crowd of
discotheque drop-outs to
attract attention.
*BOBBY MURDOCH, Celtic
and Scotland colleague, in* All
The Way With Celtic, *1970.*

PAUL MCSTAY

McStay for Rangers? Sounds
a fair swap to me.
LETTER to Sunday Mail *after
reports that Rangers coveted the
Celtic captain, 1992.*

MIRANDINHA

TRAINER: How are you
feeling?
MIRANDINHA: I'm very
well thank you, how are you?
*Exchange as Newcastle's Brazilian
striker lay injured soon after his
arrival in England, 1987.*

BOBBY MOORE

There should be a law against him. He knows what's happening 20 minutes before anyone else.
JOCK STEIN, Celtic manager, 1969.

Someone would come and kick a lump out of him, and he'd play as though he hadn't noticed. But 10 minutes later, whoof! He had a great 'golden boy' image, Moore. But he was hard.
GEOFF HURST, former West Ham and England colleague, in Brian Moore's Journey to Wembley, *1977.*

STAN MORTENSEN

They'll probably call it the Matthews funeral.
GUARDIAN journalist after Mortensen's death, 1991. Mortensen scored a hat-trick in 'the Matthews final' of 1953.

REMI MOSES

Half a million for Remi Moses? You could get the original Moses and the tablets for that price.
TOMMY DOCHERTY, former Manchester United manager, after Ron Atkinson took Moses from West Bromwich to Old Trafford, 1982.

PAT NEVIN

Being a footballer is what I do. It's not what I am.
PAT NEVIN, former Scotland winger, 1997.

STEVE NICOL

The most complete player in British football, the best two-footed player in the game, but not exactly a deep thinker.
MARK LAWRENSON, former Liverpool team-mate, 1988.

CHARLIE NICHOLAS

We talked about football but all he really wanted to talk about was sex...I hear he's not been scoring many goals lately, but all I can tell you is he certainly scored a hat-trick with me that night.
THEREZA BAZAR, pop singer with Dollar, 1988.

It was like buying a Van Gogh and sticking it away in a bank vault.
BRIAN CLOUGH on Nicholas' spell in Arsenal reserves, 1987.

Stringfellow's will miss him.
JIMMY GREAVES, TV pundit, 1988.

People reckoned I spent all my time in Stringfellow's but I never went there that much. I preferred Trampp.
CHARLIE NICHOLAS on his spell with Arsenal, 1995.

STUART PEARCE

I went to have a look at him playing for Wealdstone on a stinking night at Yeovil. After eight minutes he put in a thundering tackle and the Yeovil winger landed in my wife's lap. I said to her: 'That's it. I've seen enough. We're going home.'
BOBBY GOULD recalling how he signed Pearce for Coventry, 1991.

Who needs Johnny Rotten when you can have Psycho?
STEVE DOUBLE, FA media officer, on the ovation for Pearce after he introduced the Sex Pistols' reunion show, 1996.

Two days after a hamstring strain that would have kept anyone else out for a fortnight, on a freezing day when we were all training in bobble hats and gloves, he emerged, running out of the mist, wearing nothing but a pair of underpants and a towel wrapped round his head. That's why they call him Psycho.
KEVIN KEEGAN, Manchester City manager, after Pearce's last playing season ended in promotion to the Premiership, 2002.

I'm getting to the age where a nice tea and scone are right up my street. I'll take the missus out and we'll find a quaint tearoom somewhere.
STUART PEARCE on his plans after retiring from football shortly before his 40th birthday, 2002.

PELE

How do you spell Pele? G-O-D.
Headline in the Sunday Times *after Brazil's World Cup success, 1970.*

Pele does everything superbly, with the possible exception of taking a dive in an opponent's penalty area. He has to learn about that art, though with his skills I can't think why he bothers to lower himself and start acting.
MARTIN PETERS, England midfielder, 1970.

I go much faster
Than those who run
Without thinking.
POEM by Pele, from My Life and the Beautiful Game, *1977.*

I had the pleasure of being in Pele's company more than once, and if there was ever a World Drinking XI, he would get the No. 10 shirt.
ALAN HUDSON, former England midfielder, 1996.

Football is like music, where there is Beethoven and the rest. In football, there is Pele and the rest.
PELE on the decision by Fifa, football's world governing body, to split a player-of-the-century award between himself and Diego Maradona, 2001.

MARTIN PETERS

Martin Peters is a player 10 years ahead of his time.
ALF RAMSEY, England manager, 1968.

He's the one who's 10 years ahead of his time so we've got to wait for him to come good.
MALCOLM ALLISON, Manchester City manager and TV World Cup panellist, 1970.

DAVID PLATT

Crewe to captain
Advertising slogan after Platt's appointment as England captain, 1994.

FERENC PUSKAS

His shooting was unbelievable and his left foot was like a hand. He could do anything with it. In the showers he would even juggle with the soap.
FRANCISCO GENTO, Real Madrid colleague, in Motson and Rowlandson, The European Cup 1955-80, *1980.*

CYRILLE REGIS

I know Cyrille has found God. Now I want him to find the devil.
RON ATKINSON, Aston Villa manager, 1992.

JOHN ROBERTSON

He was a very unattractive young man. If ever I felt off-colour I'd sit next to him because compared with this fat, dumpy lad I was Errol Flynn. But give him the ball and a yard of grass and he was an artist.
BRIAN CLOUGH, Robertson's former manager at Nottingham Forest, 1990.

BRYAN ROBSON

I wish I was England coach because I'd teach Bryan Robson not to kick and foul people when things go wrong.
BRIAN CLOUGH, Nottingham Forest manager, 1983.

England's Captain Marvel.
BOBBY ROBSON, England manager, 1989.

Some said his bravery bordered on stupidity, but without that courage he would have been just another good player.
BOBBY ROBSON in Against All Odds, *1990.*

IAN RUSH

Painful to watch, but beautiful.
DAVID PLEAT, Luton manager, after Rush scored five for Liverpool against his team, 1983.

If I was really unhappy I would rather go home and play for Flint Town United.
IAN RUSH, struggling to settle in Italy with Juventus, 1988.

TOMMY SMITH

With 11 Tommy Smiths you would not only win the European Cup, you would fancy your chances against the whole Russian Army.
MARTIN BUCHAN, Manchester United captain, 1977.

GRAEME SOUNESS

If he was a chocolate drop, he'd eat himself.
ARCHIE GEMMILL, Scotland team-mate, 1978.

He's the nastiest, most ruthless man in soccer. Don Revie's bunch of assassins at Leeds were bad enough, but there is a streak in Souness that puts him top of the list.
FRANK WORTHINGTON, widely travelled striker, 1984.

They serve a drink in Glasgow called the Souness – one half and you're off.
TOMMY DOCHERTY after Souness attracted red cards with Rangers, 1988.

NEVILLE SOUTHALL

I wouldn't go so far as to say he's a complete nutcase, but he comes very close.
TERRY YORATH, the Everton goalkeeper's manager with Wales, 1993.

NOBBY STILES

Andy Lochhead was streaking towards the goal when Nobby clipped him from behind. Out came my book and Stiles, full of apologies, pleaded: 'It's the floodlights, ref. They shine in my contact lenses and I can't see a thing.' As I was writing Nobby leaned over and said: 'You spell it with an 'i' not a 'y'.
PAT PARTRIDGE, Football League referee, in Oh, Ref!, *1979.*

GORDON STRACHAN

A lot of the time he was playing from memory – but my God, what a memory.
RON ATKINSON, Manchester United manager, on Strachan's comeback after injury, 1985.

He can destroy at once the big tough guys in the dressing room with one lash of his coruscating tongue. That's why he earned the nickname 'King Tongue.'
HOWARD WILKINSON, Leeds manager, in Managing to Succeed: My life in Football Management, *1992.*

There's nobody fitter at his age, except maybe Racquel Welch.
RON ATKINSON, Coventry manager, on Strachan's form at 39, 1995.

MICKEY THOMAS

I don't mind Roy Keane making £60,000 a week. I was making the same when I was playing. The only difference is that I was printing my own.
MICKEY THOMAS, former Manchester United midfielder with a conviction for counterfeiting currency, 2002.

BERT TRAUTMANN

What manner of man is Trautmann? He is of the Nordic type, with blond hair, keen grey eyes, a gentle manner, a charming smile and a deceptive air of indolence in repose. But a steely look can come into those grey eyes; the thrust of a panther's spring into those clean, straight limbs; and few can pass with such lightning rapidity from complete immobility to energetic action. In straightforwardness and clean living he is a model for any young boy.
H.D. DAVIES, Guardian football writer, on Manchester City's German goalkeeper in Boy's Own Paper, *1957.*

MARCO VAN BASTEN

Orrible Little Basten
Headline in the Sun *after van Basten's hat-trick, Netherlands v.England, European Championship finals, 1988.*

Marco played football like a ballcrina, like Rudolf Nuryev with a colossal body, but eventually his ankle wouldn't stand the strain.
RENE MARTI, Swiss surgeon who treated van Basten before his retirement, 1995.

TERRY VENABLES

A clever, cocky player – arrogant, but then he was good.
MICK PEJIC, ex-Stoke and England defender, 1989.

BERTI VOGTS

A team of 11 Berti Vogtses would be unbeatable.
KEVIN KEEGAN after playing for England against the West Germany defender, 1975.

CHRIS WADDLE

For a defender, Chris running at you is the worst sight in football.
ALAN HANSEN, 1993.

RAY WILKINS

He can't run, can't tackle and can't head a ball. The only time he gets forward is to toss the coin.
TOMMY DOCHERTY, 1987. Wilkins was nicknamed 'The Crab' by Ron Atkinson.

He played the game in the Liverpool fashion and I could never understand why he was criticised for that.
TREVOR BROOKING, former England midfielder, in his book 100 Great British Footballers, *1988.*

FRANK WORTHINGTON

The way he is losing his hair he'll be the first bald guy ever to do impressions of Elvis Presley.
GRAEME SOUNESS, Scotland midfielder, 1984.

IAN WRIGHT

On his first day at Palace he told me he wanted to play for England, a bold statement for someone who had just walked in off a building site.
STEVE COPPELL, Crystal Palace manager, 1993.

How can Arsenal be boring with players like Wright? I'd love him in my side.
HOWARD KENDALL, Everton manager, 1993.

I just wish the record was going to someone else. I don't have a very high opinion of Ian Wright.
JOAN BASTIN, widow of Cliff Bastin, before Wright broke his all-time Arsenal scoring record, 1997.

My surname's blinding for the press. Some of the headlines write themselves.
IAN WRIGHT, 1998.

To be quite honest I have always considered Wright to be a bit of an idiot.
PETER SCHMEICHEL, in his autobiography, 1999.

He would torment me the whole game. He was a right handful. Apart from being a nightmare to defend against, he gives it loads whenever he comes near you. I used to get him and Mark Bright running past me saying: 'Do you know where your missus was last night? We do – and she makes a great breakfast.'
NEIL RUDDOCK, former Liverpool and Tottenham defender, 2000.

RON YEATS

He's a colossus. Come outside and I'll give you a walk round him.
BILL SHANKLY, Liverpool manager, to reporters after signing the 6ft 2in, 14st centre-half, 1961.

With him at centre-half we could play Arthur Askey in goal.
SHANKLY, 1962. Ashley was a diminutive comedian and actor.

③

CLUBS

ARSENAL

Only people who will not spend big money on transfers need apply.
Advertisement for post of Arsenal secretary-manager in Athletic News, *1925. Herbert Chapman got the job.*

You'll have to watch these Trojans. They don't play your game – they play an attacking game.
GEORGE ALLISON, Arsenal manager, playing himself giving a team-talk in the film The Arsenal Stadium Mystery, *1939.*

He [Bill Shankly] didn't really give Arsenal any credit. He said: 'They're nothing to beat, these Cockneys from London.'
PETER THOMPSON, former Liverpool winger, on his manager's team talk before Arsenal won the FA Cup in 1971 to complete their first Double, in David Tossell's Seventy-One Guns, *2002.*

If [Osvaldo] Ardiles had gone to Arsenal they would have had him marking the opposing goalkeeper or something.
DANNY BLANCHFLOWER, former Tottenham captain, 1981.

Boring, boring Arsenal.
Chant by opposition fans, adopted with irony by Arsenal supporters as their team took the championship, 1991.

It doesn't bother me that we're not well-liked. It's part of our history.
GEORGE GRAHAM, Arsenal manager, 1994.

I didn't want to play another 300 games with mediocre players and be up against it. I wanted the ball to be up the opposing end so I could get my cigars out at the back.
TONY ADAMS, Arsenal captain, on the importance of bringing in Dennis Bergkamp and others, 1995.

When Arsenal aren't doing well in a game they turn it into a battle to try to make the opposition lose their concentration...The number of fights involving Arsenal is more than Wimbledon in their heyday.
ALEX FERGUSON,

Manchester United manager,
1999.

At some clubs success is
accidental. At Arsenal it is
compulsory.
ARSENE WENGER, manager,
on his first Premiership and FA
Cup Double, 1998.

If a player we wanted to sign
came to us and said: 'But I
can get £52,000 a week at
Manchester United', we
would say: 'Go and get it
then.' He may get it
eventually, but not from us.
PETER HILL-WOOD, Arsenal
chairman, 1999.

Arsenal want to buy success.
The manager's job is always
on the line. He needs success
now. If a few young players
come through, that's a bonus,
but they're not really
interested.
JAY BOTHROYD, teenage
striker, on leaving Arsenal for
Coventry, 2001.

We give people what they like
to see –pace, commitment,
attacking football –and
sometimes if we go

overboard, I am sorry.
WENGER on criticism of his
team's red-card tally, 2002.

Being a Gunner is a
happiness and a joy I can
hardly begin to believe.
FREDDIE LJUNGBERG,
Swedish midfielder, after Arsenal
won the League and FA Cup
Double, 2002.

ASTON VILLA

When I arrived at Villa by
way of Blackburn and
Portsmouth, it was like
joining a Guards regiment
after being with the RAOC. I
was with a great club and it's
not easy to live up to such
greatness. It wasn't until
later, after I'd left, that I
realised the peril of leaning
too much on tradition. Villa
were so mesmerised by past
glories that they couldn't see
what was happening to them
until it was too late.
Tradition was romanticised –
a fatal mistake.
DEREK DOUGAN, former
Villa and Northern Ireland
striker, 1973.

There's an aura about this club, a sense of history and tradition. Even the name is beautifully symmetrical, with five letters in each word.
JOHN GREGORY, Villa manager, 1998.

To compete week in, week out against the Man Us, Arsenals, Liverpools and Chelseas says a lot about the little team from Birmingham that plays so big!
Programme for New York City tournament featuring Villa, 1999.

Too many of us are content to play in the comfort zone. It doesn't hurt enough if we lose. I have never heard a cross word in training, let alone seen a punch-up. At Arsenal, something kicked off every week.
PAUL MERSON, Villa midfielder, 2000.

We were wimpish. And wanky, like that character says on *Men Behaving Badly*. Have you seen that?
JOHN GREGORY, Aston Villa manager, to the media after Worthington Cup semi-final defeat by Leicester, 2000.

BARCELONA

Barcelona is the best club in the world but a dreadful place to be. They never let you forget you're a South American and a spot on the face of humanity.
DIEGO MARADONA, ex-Barcelona player, 2001.

BARNET

Barnet has been a big part of my life. I took a second mortgage to save them. I gave them my testimonial money. I got arrested driving the tractor on Christmas Day to flatten the pitch, and when I told the policeman I was the manager, he said: 'Oh yeah, and I'm George Best.'
BARRY FRY after leaving the Barnet manager's job for Southend, 1993.

BILLINGHAM SYNTHONIA

Billingham Synthonia have the unique distinction of being the only club in the country named after a fertiliser (though several other possible candidates immediately spring to mind).

HARRY PEARSON, author,
The Far Corner: A Mazy
Dribble Through North-East
Football, *1994.*

BIRMINGHAM CITY

Q: What attracted you to
Birmingham City?
A: Nothing. I was told by my
boss [David Sullivan] to
come here.
*KARREN BRADY, managing
director, in interview with
King's Heath Concorde FC
fanzine, 1993.*

When I arrived there were 47
players, and it was 49 a week
later when I found two more
in a cupboard.
*TREVOR FRANCIS on taking
over as Birmingham manager
from Barry Fry, 1999.*

BLACKBURN ROVERS

All hail, ye gallant Rover lads!
Etonians thought you were
    but cads
They've found at football
    game their dads
By meeting Blackburn Rovers.
*Song by Blackburn supporters
before the FA Cup final, 1882.
Old Etonians won 1-0.*

It always seems to be pitch
dark by 3.30pm in
Blackburn. There is no
language school, no fitness
centre. And if you want to go
shopping, there is nothing to
buy. When I see the way
people live up here, I realise
how lucky I am.
*STEPHANE HENCHOZ, Swiss
defender, looking back on his spell
with Blackburn, 1999.*

Eriksson obviously fancied
the sunshine more than the
cobbled streets and flat caps.
*TONY PARKES, regular
Blackburn caretaker manager,
after Sven-Goran Eriksson
rejected Rovers to remain in
Italy, 1997.*

BURNLEY

They have the potential to be
a sleeping giant.
*CHRIS WADDLE, on becoming
player-manager, 1997.*

CARDIFF CITY

The only way you can see
Cardiff is as another
Barcelona. Yes, Barcelona is a
football club, but it is also
something that brings all the

Catalan people together.
Except Cardiff is more.
*SAM HAMMAM, Cardiff City
owner, 2002.*

CARLISLE UNITED

We have a 10-year plan to
reach the Premiership. So
now we're a year ahead of
schedule.
*MICHAEL KNIGHTON,
Carlisle United chairman,
celebrating promotion to the
Second Division, 1995. They were
relegated a year later.*

CELTIC

We don't just want to win the
European Cup. We want to
do it playing good football,
to make neutrals glad we won
it, pleased to remember how
we did it.
*JOCK STEIN, Celtic manager,
before the victory* v. *Inter Milan
in Lisbon, 1967.*

The chairman, Robert Kelly,
was the brain that fashioned
the organisation with Jock
Stein at its head. If he had a
weakness it was his obsession
with the players of the past
and especially the great Celtic

team before the First World
War. The accolade was put on
the trip [from Lisbon] when
he declared solemnly and it
seemed with some pain: 'This
was the greatest Celtic team
of all time.' He might have
expanded the adjective to
Scottish or even British and
nobody would have
questioned his judgement.
*JOHN RAFFERTY, football
writer for* The Scotsman, *on the
1967 European Cup winners in
the book* We'll Support You
Evermore, *1976.*

Winning the European Cup
might have been for Scotland
but it definitely wasn't for
Britain. It was for Celtic.
*BILLY McNEILL, captain of the
1967 'Lisbon Lions', 1995.*

I only know the first two
lines of 'The Sash' because
after that we've usually
scored.
*ROY AITKEN, Celtic
captain, on the rivalry with
Rangers, 1985.*

I am often asked how the
Rangers team of today
compares with Celtic's
Lisbon Lions of 1967. I

have to be honest and say I think it would be a draw, but then some of us are getting on for 60.
BERTIE AULD, former Celtic midfielder, as Rangers narrowly failed to reach the European Cup final, 1993.

There's nothing worse than sitting in the dressing-room at Celtic Park after a defeat, not a word being said, listening to them going mental next door.
ALLY McCOIST, Rangers striker, 1994.

Are they really any better than the Coventrys and Southamptons of this world?
MARTIN EDWARDS, Manchester United chairman, on reports that Celtic wanted to join the English Premiership, 1997.

Celtic are a big team in a crap league and understandably they want to move to a bigger stage.
XAVIER WIGGINS, Wimbledon supporters' spokesman, on speculation that the Glasgow club planned to take over the Dons, 1997.

CHARLTON ATHLETIC

Strange how a ground can catch hold of you. I came past The Valley tonight and found myself staring at it. All those memories! We had to go back, didn't we?
ROGER ALWEN, Charlton chairman, announcing their return 'home', 1989.

Unmatched by the record of any club in the British Isles, cradle of Association Football, or Soccer, the history of Charlton Athletic, one of the most sensational aggregations of the booting game ever to essay an invasion of the United States and Canada, is truly monumental in athletic annals.
Programme notes, Illinois All Stars v. Charlton, in Chicago, 1937.

CHELSEA

Chelsea are the most unusual of clubs. They have never done what every other club was doing at the same time as every other club was doing it.
RALPH FINN, author, A History of Chelsea FC, 1969.

Each season is like a woman having a baby. Winning the FA Cup was a nice baby. Right now, our baby is the stand. It's a bit of a jumbo and there's a hell of a problem with delivery.
DAVE SEXTON, Chelsea manager, as the multi-million pound West Stand went up, 1973.

Commodore already sponsors Tessa Sanderson, Chelsea FC and a football team, Bayern Munich.
COMPUTER GUARDIAN, 1988.

When I left Chelsea before, I said I would have parachuted out of a snake's backside to get away, but circumstances change.
GRAEME LE SAUX on returning to Chelsea from Blackburn, 1997.

When I first heard about Viagra I thought it was a new player Chelsea had bought.
TONY BANKS MP, Labour Minister for Sport and Chelsea fan, 1998.

I want to argue with the idea that all footballers say 'Sick as a parrot'. No Chelsea player ever says that because none of them speaks English.
ROY HATTERSLEY, journalist and former politician, on Radio 4's News Quiz, 1999.

Obviously there's a language barrier. The majority of the lads speak Italian, but there's a few who don't.
DENNIS WISE, Chelsea captain, 2000.

When the first overseas players came we produced this book of Cockney rhyming slang. Luca [Vialli] and Ruud [Gullit] were fascinated by it and took it home to study. One day we were sitting in a team meeting and Ruud suddenly said: 'I am a grave-digger...and a very rich one.'
WISE, 2000.

We're a Continental team playing in English football.
COLIN HUTCHINSON, Chelsea managing director, 2000.

Chelsea are the Foreign Legion. They may play in the English league but they are no longer an English club. Sometimes there is not one Englishman in the team. I don't like it at all. I can't understand how the fans accept that.
JOHAN CRUYFF, Dutch former Barcelona player and coach, 2000.

Chelsea is a very nice, beautiful, great club, but something is missing. Only small things need to be done to make this a top, top, top European club. It is a top club, but not a top, top, top club.
JIMMY FLOYD HASSELBAINK, Chelsea striker, 2002.

COVENTRY CITY

I've been racing Formula One in a Mini Metro.
BOBBY GOULD resigning as manager, 1995.

If the *Titanic* had been painted sky blue it would never have sunk.
BRYAN RICHARDSON, Coventry chairman, after another escape from relegation, 1997.

We should re-name ourselves Coventry Houdini.
MIKE McGINNITY, Coventry vice-chairman, 1997.

There is something curious about the relationship between Coventry and Villa. We don't particularly dislike them. But blimey, do they hate us.
JOHN GREGORY, Aston Villa manager, 2000.

COWDENBEATH

Why the nickname 'Blue Brazil'? Easy. Cowden play in blue and have the same debt as a Third World country.
BIG BOB, Cowdenbeath diehard, quoted in Ronald Ferguson's Black Diamonds and the Blue Brazil, *1993.*

CRYSTAL PALACE

It's like one of those fairytales where you see a beautiful castle but when you get inside you discover years of decay. The princess, which is the players, is asleep. I'm trying to wake her but it takes more than one kiss.
ALAN SMITH, Crystal Palace manager, 2000.

DARLINGTON

Darlington will become the most successful club in England.
GEORGE REYNOLDS, millionaire chairman, 2000.

DERBY COUNTY

Whichever teams win the League championship in the next 20 years, and I hope teams like Rochdale and Halifax will be amongst them, none of them will have as hard a job as we had. We did it with 12 players. Those London bums can't explain it.
BRIAN CLOUGH, Derby manager, after their title success, 1972.

DONCASTER BELLES

Some of them came over like lager louts. I kept wondering how they could be so unprofessional.
GILL WYLIE, Arsenal ladies' captain, on their rivals' performance in a TV documentary, 1995.

EVERTON

PRINCESS MARGARET: But Mr Labone, where is Everton?
BRIAN LABONE: In Liverpool, Ma'am.
PRINCESS MARGARET: Of course, we had your first team here last year.
BILL SHANKLY , Liverpool manager, story of FA Cup final, 1966.

If anyone ever mentions the Everton 'School of Soccer Science' to me again, well I'm sorry, I just don't see it.
ROY EVANS, Liverpool manager, after bruising derby draw, 1995.

Leeds reminded me of a very young Everton side I used to be in, who were equally precocious and just as fast, with one exception – me.
JOE ROYLE, Manchester City manager, after 5-2 FA Cup defeat by Leeds, 2000.

I was told I was going to be the first of many big-money signings. Someone was telling fibs.
JOHN COLLINS, Everton midfielder, 1999.

I soon got out of the habit of studying the top end of the League table.
WALTER SMITH, Everton manager, on the difference with his previous club, Rangers, 1999.

We're going to make sure that everybody has to have haggis and porridge in the canteen from now on.
SMITH on the club's growing Scottish enclave, 1999.

FULHAM

We've got a long-term plan for this club and apart from the results it's going well.
ERNIE CLAY, Fulham chairman, 1980.

Q: Are funds available for new signings?
A: Oh yes. About £2.54.
IAN BRANFOOT, Fulham manager, at post-match press conference during the pre-Fayed era, 1994.

I am going to make Fulham the Manchester United of the South.
MOHAMED AL FAYED, Harrods owner, on buying control of the then third-grade club, 1997.

GILLINGHAM

The possibility of a European Super League in years to come makes Gillingham a prime location for a club to play in this competition, with its proximity to the Channel Tunnel and to Europe.
PAUL SCALLY, Gillingham chairman, 2000.

GRIMSBY TOWN

It's a hard place to come for a southern team. You can dress well and have all the nice watches in the world, but that won't buy you a result at Grimsby.
ALAN SMITH, Crystal Palace manager, at Grimsby, 2000.

Last time Grimsby were top of the First Division, dinosaurs roamed the earth.
LENNIE LAWRENCE, Grimsby manager, 2001.

HARTLEPOOL UNITED

The listening bank refused to listen and the bank that likes to say yes said no.
GARRY GIBSON, Hartlepool chairman, after receiving a

winding-up petition from the Inland Revenue, 1993.

Since Hartlepool last scored you could have watched all three *Godfather* movies, waded through every technicolour moment of *Gone With the Wind*, and still had time to settle down to a two-hour episode of *Inspector Morse.*
HARTLEPOOL MAIL *on the club's record-breaking run without a goal, 1993.*

LEEDS UNITED

You get nowt for being second.
Title of Billy Bremner book, 1969. Leeds finished runners-up five times during Bremner's time as player.

I didn't used to be frightened on the football pitch. But I was always relieved to get off in one piece, particularly during those mid- and late 1960s when the likes of Leeds United were kicking anything that moved.
JIMMY GREAVES, former Tottenham striker, in This One's On Me, *1979.*

Leeds [under Don Revie] would try to win by fair means or foul…They were too good to do things like that and should have won more than they did. They were a magnificent side, a team made in heaven.
FRANK McLINTOCK, former Arsenal captain, in David Tossell's book Seventy-One Guns, *2002.*

If I try something a bit saucy, the Dutch and Belgians I play with shout 'Hard luck' or 'Try again' if it doesn't come off. At Leeds I'd turn round and there'd be someone with a fist up, threatening to chin me. One of my own team-mates!
DUNCAN McKENZIE, Leeds striker of the immediate post-Don Revie era, during his time with Anderlecht, 1976.

There's a stereotype that goes with a lot of clubs. Spurs are called stylish, West Ham is the academy, Arsenal are resilient. But Leeds are always seen as cynical and intimidating. It becomes a tired cliché.
HOWARD WILKINSON, Leeds manager, 1991.

I think this is the most wonderful place in Europe.
TONY YEBOAH, Leeds' Ghanaian striker, 1995.

Q: Do you know about Leeds' history and tradition?
A: Oh yes, I'm, very familiar with John Smith's and Tetley's.
Q: I meant the Don Revie era.
A: Yes I know. It was a joke.
ALF-INGE HAALAND, Norway midfielder, on joining Leeds, 1997.

There was a time when nobody could stand Leeds United.
DAVID O'LEARY, Leeds manager, 1999.

My babies trust me because I am their friend. They know they are safe in my hands.
O'LEARY after his youthful side won 5-1 at Portsmouth, FA Cup, 1999.

Q: Which team's results do you look for first?
A: Leeds United, Leeds reserves, Leeds youth team, Leeds Permanent Building Society pub team, Leeds & Holbeck pub team, Leeds ice hockey team, East Leeds chess under-19s, South Leeds over-19 poker team, anyone with Leeds in their name. And Middlesbrough.
JONATHAN WOODGATE, Teesside-born Leeds defender, in magazine questionnaire, 1999.

People hate Manchester United because they are so successful. People will hate us in a few years because we shall be winning everything.
WOODGATE, 1999.

Leeds reminded me of the poor Englishmen who invented football 15 centuries ago when they cut off a Viking's head, put it in a bag and started to kick it around; as awkward and primitive as that.
REPORT in Marca, Spanish newspaper, after Leeds drew 0-0 with Valencia, Champions' League semi-final, 2001.

The only people we haven't upset lately are Nato.
O'LEARY after Uefa unexpectedly suspended Lee Bowyer on the eve of a Champions' League semi-final in Valencia, 2001.

Those Leeds guys are simply out of this world. The energy just rushes through them. And their fans are just as aggressive as the team.
ROBERT PIRES, Arsenal and France midfielder, 2002.

We are a club that panics very quickly. We went to Newcastle last month and we were top of the Premiership, but the mood was as if we were bottom and looking for a win.
O'LEARY after a run of bad results saw Leeds slide, 2002.

From being the second-favourite club of many people, we seem to have become the most hated club in the country.
O'LEARY after the end of the Bowyer-Woodgate trial, 2002.

These two players let down Leeds United and the way they carried on was disgraceful. Whatever the court decided, they were guilty in my eyes of failing to exercise control, lacking responsibility and of failing to behave as professional footballers should. What did

they think they were doing, boozed up and running through the streets? Was it not inviting trouble?
O'LEARY, 2002.

It would have better for the club if they [Bowyer and Woodgate] had both gone inside. The law of the land had to sort it out, but after the courts had dealt with it, we got the backlash.
O'LEARY, 2002.

One boozy night has brought this club down.
O'LEARY as Leeds' form slumped soon after the Bowyer-Woodgate trial, 2002.

I'm still lighting my candles and my mum's in danger of burning down the church.
O'LEARY, a practising Catholic, praying for a change in Leeds' fortunes, 2002.

Leeds footballers wearing gloves isn't a fashion statement. It's so they don't leave any fingerprints.
Letter to the Daily Mail *shortly after the trial and a disciplinary crisis at the club, 2002.*

He wants to play for a bigger and better club.
PINA ZAHAVI, Rio Ferdinand's agent, on the Leeds captain's desire to move to Manchester United, 2002.

We've got to work twice as hard as other clubs to get some good news. I've never known another club that so many people have such a negative image of, for reasons that are difficult to put a finger on.
PETER RIDSDALE, Leeds chairman, on employing the PR consultant Max Clifford, 2002.

LEICESTER CITY

The players work hard in training – and so they should considering what they are paid – but then only three people and five cabbages are watching them.
DAVE BASSETT, Leicester manager, facing relegation from the Premiership, 2002.

LEYTON ORIENT

Drugs? Who needs 'em? Just come to Leyton Orient. In celebration, we're going to drink from the elixir of life, here at Brisbane Road, centre of the universe,
BARRY HEARN, Orient chairman, after his team reached Third Division play-off final (which they lost), 2001.

LIVERPOOL

Yes, there are two great teams on Merseyside. Liverpool and Liverpool reserves.
BILL SHANKLY, Liverpool manager, 1965.

I want to build a team that's invincible, so they'll have to send a team from Mars to beat us.
SHANKLY, 1971.

Liverpool are the most uncomplicated side in the world. They all drive forward when they've got the ball, and they all get behind it when they haven't.
JOE MERCER, former Manchester City manager, 1973.

My idea was to build Liverpool into a bastion of invincibility. Napoleon had that idea. He wanted to conquer the bloody world. I

wanted Liverpool to be untouchable, to build the club up and up until everyone would have to submit.
SHANKLY, a year after he retired, 1975.

Mind you, I've been here during the bad times too. One year we came second.
BOB PAISLEY, Shankly's successor as manager, 1979.

A lot of teams beat us, do a lap of honour and don't stop running. They live too long on one good result. I remember Jimmy Adamson crowing after Burnley beat us that his players were in a different league. At the end of the season they were.
PAISLEY, 1979.

We do things together. I'd walk into the toughest dockside pub in the world with this lot. Because you know that if things got tough, nobody would 'bottle' it and scoot off.
EMLYN HUGHES, Liverpool captain, in Brian James'
Journey To Wembley, *1977.*

For those of you watching in black and white, Liverpool are the team with the ball.
Joke by Liverpool fans, quoted in Brian Barwick and Gerald Sinstadt, The Great Derbies: Everton *v.* Liverpool, *1988.*

As we all knew would happen when Ian Rush went abroad, Liverpool have fallen to pieces.
TED CROKER, FA secretary, as Kenny Dalglish's side advanced to League title, 1988.

People should ask where were the wonder boys of Liverpool. Why didn't they turn it on when things started to go against them? They're good, but not that good.
LAWRIE SANCHEZ, Wimbledon match-winner, after their FA Cup final win, 1988.

I thought there might be eight goals but I never expected we'd get four of them.
DAVE LANCASTER, Chesterfield player, after 4-4 draw at Anfield during Liverpool's decline, 1992.

We're an old-fashioned football club, not a quoted plc, and we don't pay

dividends to shareholders.
We are here for one reason:
to win trophies.
PETER ROBINSON, Liverpool
chief executive, 1996.

The gaffer sent me to see
whether I could spot a
weakness and I found one.
The half-time tea is too milky.
KEVIN SUMMERFIELD,
Shrewsbury coach, after seeing his
club's next FA Cup opponents
beat Leeds 5-0, 1996.

We were playing for history
tonight. For immortality.
What these players have
achieved is unique.
GERARD HOULLIER,
Liverpool manager, after his side
beat Alaves of Spain 5-4 to win
the Uefa Cup and complete a
treble, 2001.

People say we're not pretty to
watch but I'll tell you
something: winning's pretty.
HOULLIER, 2002.

I was only a kid the last time
Liverpool won the League. In
fact I think I was still an
Everton fan.
MICHAEL OWEN, Liverpool
striker, 2002.

My greatest challenge is
not what's happening at the
moment [at Manchester
United]. It was knocking
Liverpool off their fucking
perch. And you can print that.
SIR ALEX FERGUSON after
Alan Hansen said the United
manager faced 'the biggest
challenge of his career', 2002.

MANCHESTER CITY

Check out the details
about Manchester's second-
largest club.
Blurb on the dustcover of
Manchester City FC – An A to
Z, *by Dean Hayes, 1995.*

There are three types of Oxo
cubes. Light brown for
chicken stock. Dark brown
for beef stock. And light blue
for laughing stock.
TOMMY DOCHERTY, former
manager of neighbouring
United, 1988.

1976 was a strange year for
English football – City won
a trophy.
Slogan on T-shirts sold outside
Old Trafford, 1995.

Seeing 42 players coming towards me I felt like the garrison commander at Rorke's Drift when the Zulus came pouring over the hill.
ALAN BALL, City manager, on the size of his new squad, 1995.

Watching City is probably the best laxative you can have.
PHIL NEAL, City caretaker manager, after they lost a 2-0 lead before beating Bradford, 1996.

May I wish Joe Royle well in a task equivalent to nailing jelly to a ceiling.
Letter to the Manchester Evening News Pink *after Royle became manager, 1998.*

The worse City play, the better the crowds are. It's as though the fans feel the team needs them. The other factor is that we are not United. Their fans are the most horrible in the world, as everybody knows.
DAVE WALLACE, editor of Manchester City fanzine King of the Kippax, *1999.*

I really felt things had changed for City when we beat Gillingham on penalties in the Second Division play-off final after being 2-0 down going into stoppage time. But then I'm an emotional person. I might have kicked a few full-backs in my time but I always sent them flowers afterwards.
MIKE SUMMERBEE, former City winger, on promotion to the Premiership, 2000.

To score four goals when you are playing like pigs in labour is fantastic.
JOE ROYLE, City manager, after 4-1 win at Blackburn took them into the Premiership, 2000.

They're my old club and I hate to speak badly of them, but they are crap.
RODNEY MARSH as City went straight back down, 2001.

There's only one club in Manchester and that is Manchester City. In our town, people talk only about our club. In the streets, people wear the City shirt, not United's. Manchester City are Manchester's club.

ALI BENARBIA, City's Algerian midfielder, 2002.

MANCHESTER UNITED

The road back may be long and hard, but with the memory of those who died at Munich, of their stirring achievements and wonderful sportsmanship ever with us, Manchester United will rise again.
H.P. HARDMAN, chairman, in a message headed 'United will go on' on the cover of the first match-programme after the tragedy, 1958.

If you went through the Manchester United team that won the League in 1957, you would have to look very hard to find your truly great players. Look at the whole forward line – Berry, Whelan, Taylor, Viollet, Pegg – and you will search very hard to find a truly outstanding player...But because they were playing to order and precision, with method and movement, because they were fluid and not trying to do what they could not do (which is the downfall of so many people); because they

were doing things within their limits, they were successful.
ARTHUR ROWE, former Tottenham manager, in The Enclclopaedia of Association Football, *1960.*

There's a hell of a lot of politics in football. I don't think Henry Kissinger would have lasted 48 hours at Old Trafford.
TOMMY DOCHERTY, former United manager, 1982.

It's the only stadium in the world I've ever been in that's absolutely buzzing with atmosphere when it's empty and there isn't a soul inside. It's almost like a cathedral.
DOCHERTY in Call The Doc, *1982.*

It's like being in a palace, an overwhelming and inspiring place. Even the loos have gold taps.
GARRY BIRTLES, former United striker, 1995.

This team makes you suffer. I deserve a million pounds a year for doing this job.
ALEX FERGUSON after

drawn FA Cup final v. *Crystal Palace, 1990.*

ICI is a world-class business. There's no way it would want to buy a second-class football team.
City analyst quoted in the Sunday Times *on rumours that ICI wanted to buy United, 1990.*

Manchester United plc? It means Premier League champions, of course.
TERRY CHRISTIAN, United fan and presenter of Channel 4's The Word, *1994.*

I had to get rid of this idea that Manchester United were a drinking club, rather than a football club.
FERGUSON on his problems with Paul McGrath and Norman Whiteside, in Six Years at United, *1992.*

I value truth, honesty, respect for one another, compassion and understanding. I have found these qualities in Manchester United.
ERIC CANTONA in La Philosophie de Cantona, *1995.*

This has been a love story... The love of the club is the most important weapon in the world. I just couldn't leave.
CANTONA on his decision to stay with United, 1995.

A Manchester United player has to want the ball, have the courage to want it. He's a player with imagination, someone who sees he bigger picture.
FERGUSON, 1995.

It took me an hour to get the scorch marks off the turf.
KEITH KENT, United groundsman, after dazzling display v. *Bolton, 1995.*

Less than a month after thousands of youngsters pulled on their favourite club jersey at Christmas, the men who run the club ordered the Red Devils to trot out in blue at Southampton. Loyalty doesn't seem to be enough any more; rather it is exploited to make us pay more.
TONY BLAIR MP, Labour leader, criticising United's commercialism, 1995.

I get to my feet when Chelsea fans sing: 'Stand up if you hate Man U.' But though I hate them, I have to admire them too.
KEN BATES, *Chelsea chairman, 1997.*

We are the most loved club – and the most hated.
GARY NEVILLE, United defender, 1997.

There is a terrible amount of jealousy towards this club. I don't know why.
FERGUSON, 1997.

People go on about the great skill in United's side, but the most important thing is their team spirit. They give off a warmth to each other that you can almost touch.
VINNIE JONES, Premiership opponent, 1997.

The Kings of Perseverance
Headline in the Catalan newspaper La Vanguardia *after United's two late goals in Barcelona beat Bayern Munich in the European Cup final, 1999.*

In a Cairo taxi the four words of English my driver knew were 'Thatcher', 'Blair' and 'Manchester United'.
STEPHEN BYERS MP, Labour, Trade & Industry Secretary, 1999.

We would love to have a [Luis] Figo, [Zinedine] Zidane or Rivaldo at United, but we realise those sort of players are never really going to come here. Some people think it's sad, with us being the richest club in the world, but clubs have their policies and you have to respect that.
ROY KEANE, United captain, 2000.

This team never lose games – they just run out of time occasionally.
STEVE McCLAREN, United coach, 2000.

I'll do my utmost to bridge the gap, but United have the biggest stadium, biggest crowds and most money to buy the best players. And the manager ain't too bad, either.
DAVID O'LEARY, Leeds manager, 2000.

The nation was warming to us during the build-up to last season's Champions' League final. But the warmth was only ever going to be temporary. It's the British culture of being quick to put down people at the top. We are a soft target.
FERGUSON, 2000.

You have to put all the criticism down to jealousy. United have produced more people who've played for their country, more world-class players and more who've won European Footballer of the Year than any other club in the country, so we must be doing something right.
FERGUSON after United suffered a poor run, 2000.

It was a disgrace to pull out of the FA Cup to take part in something that seems to be all about greed. Brazil is probably the only country in the world where United haven't a superstore, and the only thing they've got out of the trip is a couple of million quid which they hardly need, though I suppose Sir Alex Ferguson can now get a job with Fifa when he quits as manager.
TOMMY DOCHERTY, former United manager, after the club went to Brazil to play in the new World Club Cup, 2000.

United have got into Europe thanks to the FA Cup. Where are they going? Brazil? I hope they get bloody diarrhoea.
BRIAN CLOUGH, former Nottingham Forest manager, on United's decision not to defend the FA Cup, 1999.

They're a great team with only one thing missing – me up front.
RONALDO, Brazil striker, 2000.

Everyone knows that for us to get awarded a penalty we need a certificate from the Pope and a personal letter from the Queen.
FERGUSON after Leeds were awarded a spot-kick v. United, 2001.

To get a penalty at Old Trafford, Jaap Stam needs to take a machine-gun and riddle you full of bullets.
PAOLO DI CANIO, West Ham striker, 2001.

[The club] thought merchandising was more important than the team and players. When the business is more important than the football, I don't care. I just gave up. I don't want to be treated like a pair of socks, a shirt, like shit. I'm not shit.
ERIC CANTONA, recalling why he had suddenly retired five years earlier, 2002.

When I pull on a Manchester United shirt I still get a buzz that is impossible to describe.
DAVID BECKHAM, 2002.

Everyone thinks he has the prettiest wife at home.
ARSENE WENGER, Arsenal manager, after Ferguson claimed United had been 'the best team in the country since Christmas' at the height of their tussle for the title, 2002.

They seem to think they're entitled to everything.
TERRY VENABLES, Leeds manager, as United intensified their interest in his captain, Rio Ferdinand, 2002.

You see all the faces on the wall – George Best, Denis Law, Bobby Charlton – and you just want to be part of it.
RIO FERDINAND after his £29.1m switch from Leeds, 2002.

MIDDLESBROUGH

Our long-term aim is to make Middlesbrough synonymous with a good team rather than cooling towers and chemical plants. We're well on our way, even though Ruud Gullit had never heard of us when we contacted him last summer.
STEVE GIBSON, Middlesbrough chairman, 1995.

Bryan Robson has certainly brought in the big names. But it is like going into a nightclub and getting off with a big blonde. The lads will say: 'Phwoar!' But can you keep her?
BERNIE SLAVEN, former Boro player, as Robson made some exotic signings, 1998.

My team-mates advised me to visit the city first. I went to have a look at Middlesbrough

and decided I was better off in Parma.
ANTONIO BENARRIVO, Parma player, after rejecting a move to Teesside, 2001.

MILAN

When people think of Italy, after the Mafia and pizza, they think of AC Milan.
SILVIO BERLUSCONI, Milan president, 1997.

MILLWALL

I met a pal who'd lost track of me after Celtic and he asked what I was doing. I said I was player-manager of Millwall. His wife immediately said: 'How embarrassing.'
MICK McCARTHY, 1995.

We have played for some of the great clubs in Europe, but we regard this as the pinnacle of our careers.
SERGEI YURAN, Russian striker, on an unhappy, short-lived spell at Millwall with Vassili Kulkov, 1996.

Personally, I thrive on a hostile environment. Maybe it's because I played for Millwall.
KASEY KELLER, United States goalkeeper, anticipating a rough reception in Costa Rica, 1997.

NEWCASTLE UNITED

Newcastle have been very unlucky with injuries this season. The players keep recovering.
LEN SHACKLETON, journalist and former Newcastle and Sunderland player, 1965.

I've heard of players selling dummies, but this club keeps buying them.
SHACKLETON, 1976.

Newcastle have the potential to allow me to pick up the phone and say to someone like Alex Ferguson: 'I want to buy your best.' I believe that day will come.
JIM SMITH, Newcastle manager, 1988.

Tell Alex [Ferguson] we're coming to get him.
KEVIN KEEGAN, Newcastle manager, after winning promotion, 1993.

We're like the Basques. We are fighting for a nation, the Geordie nation. Football is tribalism and we're the Mohicans.
SIR JOHN HALL, Newcastle chairman, 1995.

It's madness – Newcastle are £40m in debt yet they are the darlings of the City.
ALAN SUGAR, Tottenham chairman, 1997.

We are only flesh and blood in the end. Sometimes can't sleep. Worry about the job. Worry about the kids. Worry about growing old. Worry about interest rates going up. Worry about Newcastle going down.
TONY BLAIR MP, Prime Minister, to Labour party conference, 1999.

People talk about Newcastle as a 'sleeping giant'. They last won the championship in 1927 and the FA Cup in 1955. They already make Rip Van Winkle look like a catnapper.
HUGH McILVANNEY, Sunday Times *writer, 1999.*

We're already bigger and more financially stable than Barcelona. We can attract any player from anywhere in the world.
DOUGLAS HALL, Newcastle vice-chairman, 2001.

NEWPORT COUNTY

And they were lucky to get nil.
LEN SHACKLETON on his six-goal Newcastle debut, a 13-0 win v. *Newport, in* Clown Prince of Soccer, *1955.*

NORWICH CITY

I'd love Norwich to become famous for its football club again, and not just for Delia Smith and Alan Partridge.
NIGEL WORTHINGTON, Norwich manager, 2002.

The last 10 years has been one long story of learning how to cope with disappointment.
DELIA SMITH, celebrity chef, on being a Norwich City director, 2002.

NOTTINGHAM FOREST

Nottingham Forest will never know how lucky they were, that day they asked me to get on with the job of rebuilding their run-down club. They didn't just need a new manager – the bloody place was so dead it needed a kiss of life.
BRIAN CLOUGH on his 18-year reign in Clough: The Autobiography, *1994.*

We won two European Cups yet we never practised a free-kick. 'Just give it to Robbo' [John Robertson] was the cry.
MARTIN O'NEILL, Forest player under Clough, in Clough: The Autobiography, *1994.*

The only person certain of boarding the bus to Wembley for the Littlewoods Cup final is Albert Kershore, and he'll be driving it.
BRIAN CLOUGH keeping his players on their toes, 1990.

NOTTS COUNTY

Most people who can remember when County were a great club are dead.
JACK DUNNETT, Notts County chairman, 1983.

PARTICK THISTLE

For years I thought their name was Partick Thistle Nil.
BILLY CONNOLLY, comedian, 1988.

If anyone thinks the Partick Thistle team of today could hold their own in the Scottish Premier League, they have been smoking dope.
ROGER MITCHELL, SPL chief executive, as Thistle closed in on promotion, 2002.

PORT VALE

The reason Samantha Fox is so big in Eastern Europe and the Third World is that they are neglected in terms of the range of talent prepared to visit them. So even a small star becomes big once they arrive. In football terms, she has been playing Port Vale instead of Arsenal.
MAX CLIFFORD, public-relations consultant, 1992.

Three years at Port Vale is enough for anybody.
LEE MILLS, Bradford City striker, after leaving the Potteries club, 1998.

PORTSMOUTH

I don't even know where Portsmouth is. All I know is a lot of sailors live there.
FRANK MALONEY, boxing promoter, denying he wanted to take over Pompey, 1995.

Pathetic, abysmal, gutless and disgraceful. If my players were bricklayers the house they built would fall down.
ALAN BALL, Portsmouth manager, shortly before his sacking, 1999.

QUEEN OF THE SOUTH

The Queen of the South shall rise up in the judgement with the men of this generation and condemn them.
Luke 11:31, New Testament. The Dumfries club are the only football club mentioned in The Bible.

QUEEN'S PARK

Surely the greatest of all clubs! I have a great admiration, a great respect, a great esteem – nay even a great affection for the Queen's Park club. What pigmies some of our strictly modern clubs seem, how thin and poor their records, when a comparison is instituted between them and Queen's Park. What a halo of romance and glory surrounds them. What a wealth of honourable tradition is theirs!
WILLIAM McGREGOR, founder of the Football League, in Association Football and the Men Who Made It, *by William Pickford and Alfred Gibson, 1906.*

RANGERS

Rangers like the big, strong, powerful fellows, with a bit of strength and solidity in the tackle, rather than the frivolous, quick-moving stylists like Jimmy Johnstone, small, tiptoe-through-the-tulips type of players who excite people.
WILLIE WADDELL, Rangers manager, 1972.

Playing Rangers tonight was like trying to carry a ton weight up the down escalator. You wonder how Scotland could ever lose a football match.
HOWARD WILKINSON, Leeds manager, after his team's European Cup defeat by the Scottish champions, 1992.

How many Scots have they got at Ibrox now? They're rushing out buying Englishmen, Italians and Chileans when every other kid in Scotland dreams of pulling on the blue jersey.
RON DIXON, former Dundee chairman, 1998.

It isn't about balance sheets. Rangers is a world brand where everything follows from what happens on the park.
DAVID MURRAY, Rangers chairman, 1998.

I only ever have a drink when we win a trophy. People are starting to think I'm an alcoholic.
IAN FERGUSON, Rangers midfielder, after his 23rd medal with the club, 1999.

REAL MADRID

To be honest I was terribly pleased I wasn't playing. I saw [Alfredo] Di Stefano and these others, and I thought: 'These people just aren't human. It's not the sort of game I've been taught.'
BOBBY CHARLTON quoted in Motson and Rowlandson's The European Cup 1955-80, *on watching Real play Manchester United, 1957.*

They could dish out the hard stuff, too, especially [Jose] Santamaria. People gloat about them and say they never kicked anybody. Well they certainly kicked me.
JOHN CHARLES, Juventus' Welsh centre-forward, in Motson and Rowlandson, as above.

The most educated person at Real Madrid is the woman who cleans the toilets.
JOAN GASPART, Barcelona vice-president, 1997.

SCARBOROUGH

If only our motto 'No Battle, No Victory' wasn't taken so literally.

MARK STANIFORTH,
Scarborough supporter, 1995.

SHEFFIELD UNITED

Sheffield Eagles [rugby league team] play the ball on the ground more than Sheffield United do.
JONATHAN FOSTER reporting on Sheffield United match in the Independent, *1990.*

When I was a lad and we played Wednesday, they wore blue-and-white stripes and we'd wear red-and-white stripes. Now they wear all sorts of stuff, like a fashion parade. Where have our stripes gone this season? Blades' strip looks look it was designed by Julian Clary when he had a migraine.
SEAN BEAN, actor and Sheffield United fan, 1996.

I remember the day when this club sold Brian Deane and Jan Aage Fjortoft. It was like when President Kennedy was shot – that's how deeply I felt.
NEIL WARNOCK, Sheffield United manager and fan, 1999.

SHEFFIELD WEDNESDAY

The big-city team with the small-town mentality.
HOWARD WILKINSON, Leeds and former Wednesday manager, 1991.

There are Wednesday players with more money than the club, which can't be right.
GARY MEGSON, Sheffield-based West Bromwich Albion manager, on his favourite club's financial difficulties, 2002.

STOKE CITY

This club is a sleeping monster.
CHRIS KAMARA, Stoke manager, 1998.

STONEWALL

I remember telling one of my previous team that I was starving and could murder a plate of sausage and chips. One player just looked at me and said: 'I should think you get enough sausage already, don't you?'
PAUL BARKER, captain of the gay London team Stonewall, 1995.

SUNDERLAND

First, Margaret Thatcher does her best to destroy the town. Now Ben Thatcher viciously elbows our best crosser of the ball to destroy the Sunderland team at Wimbledon. Just what have they got against us?
Letter to Sunderland Echo, *2000.*

TOTTENHAM HOTSPUR

Than the famous Spurs there is probably no more famous club in the whole of England. Did they not recover the Association Cup for the south? Did they not play pretty and effective football? Are they not scrupulously fair? Are they not perfectly managed?
WILLIAM PICKFORD and ALFRED GIBSON, authors, Association Football and the Men Who Made It, *1906.*

We have no desire just to be a football club. That is not the basis for success.
PAUL BOBROFF, chairman of Tottenham Hotspur plc, 1983.

INTERVIEWER: Which do you prefer, Rangers or Celtic?
ALFIE CONN: Spurs.
Exchange on It's Only A Game, *TV documentary, 1986. Conn played for all three.*

The cold and damp dressing-room is our secret weapon for Spurs. Not forgetting their lukewarm pot of tea at half-time.
PHIL SPROSON, Port Vale defender, before the Third Division side faced Spurs in the FA Cup, 1988.

Spurs were like West Ham used to be, all fancy flicks and sweet sherry.
SPROSON after scoring for Vale in their victory over Spurs, 1988.

I haven't just signed a player. I've rescued a lad from hell.
BRIAN CLOUGH after buying back Steve Hodge from Spurs, 1988.

When Ilie Dumitrescu asked me when Spurs last won the championship, I couldn't answer him. That shouldn't be the case for a club this big.
OSVALDO ARDILES, Tottenham manager, 1995.

I don't think Spurs would ever sign a superstar like [Jurgen] Klinsmann or [Dennis] Bergkamp again. Those guys are floaters. They'll go anywhere, play for anyone who pays them the most.
ALAN SUGAR, Tottenham chairman, after Arsenal paid £7.25m for Bergkamp, 1995.

Wimbledon with fans.
JIMMY GREAVES, former Tottenham star, on Gerry Francis' team, 1996.

I want a consistent team, not a flash one. When I was at Highbury, the message from White Hart Lane used to be, 'Let Arsenal win things with boring football, we'd rather play entertainingly and lose'. But to me that was just a psychological crutch. I want my team to be exciting, and to win week in, week out. I'm working on it.
GEORGE GRAHAM, Tottenham manager, 2000.

We're good enough to survive in the Premiership and maybe have a good cup run or even earn a Uefa Cup spot if things go really well. But we are never going to win the championship.
TIM SHERWOOD, Spurs midfielder and 'lifelong fan', on the 'harsh reality' of under-investment, 2002.

WATFORD

Blimey, the ground looks a bit different to Watford. Where's the dog track?
LUTHER BLISSETT after exchanging Vicarage Road for Milan's San Siro stadium, 1983.

WEST BROMWICH ALBION

That's typical of this club. For an extra £10,000 they could have got John Snow.
JEFF ASTLE, West Bromwich Albion striker, after they bought goalkeeper Jim Cumbes, a fast bowler with Lancashire, 1969.

They've made some signings, but it's like putting lipstick on a pig. It's still a pig.
RODNEY MARSH, Sky pundit and former England player, as Albion prepared for the Premiership, 2002.

We haven't got his type of player at the club, someone who can pass and score goals.
GARY MEGSON, Albion manager, on signing Jason Koumas from Tranmere, 2002.

WEST HAM UNITED

You can forget the purist stuff now. We've finished with that. When people start to compare us with West Ham, that's when we'll start to worry.
PETER TAYLOR, Brian Clough's assistant at Derby, 1973.

The crowds at West Ham haven't been rewarded by results, but they keep turning up because they see good football. Other clubs will suffer from the old bugbear that results count more than anything. This has been the ruination of English soccer.
RON GREENWOOD, England and former West Ham manager, 1977.

All that 'happy losers' stuff is a load of cobblers. I hate losing.

BILLY BONDS, West Ham manager, on claims that the club put style above winning, 1991.

West Ham's performance was obscene in terms of the effort they put into the match.
ALEX FERGUSON, Manchester United manager, on a 1-0 defeat which damaged their championship prospects, in Six Years at United, *1992.*

I understand nothing when Rio Ferdinand and Frank Lampard are talking. They speak Cocknik.
EYAL BERKOVIC, West Ham's Israeli midfielder,1999.

They can't stand foreigners.
BERKOVIC, accusing his former club of xenophobia in The Magician, *1999.*

I want the West Ham fans to know that we are going to win something before I finish my career here. Otherwise I'll kill myself.
PAOLO DI CANIO, West Ham's Italian striker, 2001.

WIMBLEDON

The borstal of football.
DAVE BASSETT, Wimbledon manager, 1987,

The only hooligans here are the players.
BASSETT after fans invaded the pitch when the Dons won promotion to the First Division, 1986.

It was just welly, welly, welly. The ball must've been screaming for mercy.
RON YEATS, Liverpool scout, after watching Wimbledon, 1988.

Wimbledon are killing the dreams that made football the world's greatest game.
TERRY VENABLES, Tottenham manager, 1988.

There is one London club that have got it right. Whatever you think of Wimbledon's style of play, you can't argue with their results.
BOB PAISLEY, former Liverpool manager, 1988.

Wimbledon will take to Wembley. Once you've tried to get a decent bath at Hartlepool, you can handle anything.
WALLY DOWNES, ex-Wimbledon stalwart, before the FA Cup final, 1988.

I've been there once before – for dog racing on my stag night.
DAVE BEASANT, Wimbledon goalkeeper, on the eve of Wembley, 1988.

The Crazy Gang have beaten the Culture Club!
JOHN MOTSON, BBC-TV commentator, as Liverpool were beaten, 1988.

Everyone was drunk the night before [the FA Cup final]. Every single one of us was down the pub. Probably what won us the Cup. That, and taking me off after an hour because I was delirious.
ALAN CORK, former Wimbledon striker, 1991.

It is indeed a pleasure and a privilege to be entertaining the team that has made the

greatest impact on British football over the past decade.
THAMESMEAD TOWN programme welcome to Wimbledon Reserves, 1988.

When Wimbledon hit long balls up to a 6ft 2in black centre-forward [John Fashanu], it's destroying the game. When Arsenal hit long balls to a 6ft 4in Irishman [Niall Quinn], it's good football.
DAVE BASSETT, Wimbledon manager, 1989.

We must remain the English bulldog SAS club; to sustain ourselves by sheer power and the attitude that we will kick ass. We are an academy – we find gems and turn them into finished articles.
SAM HAMMAM, chairman, 1992.

Before we go down, we'll leave a stream of blood from here to Timbuktoo.
HAMMAM, 1992.

The best way to watch Wimbledon is on Ceefax.
GARY LINEKER, TV pundit, 1993.

They are launching the ball 50 yards instead of 60.
MIKE WALKER, Norwich manager, on the Dons' reputed change of style, 1993.

For us to compete in the Premiership with our finances is like going into a nuclear war with bows and arrows.
JOE KINNEAR, Wimbledon manager, 1997.

Wimbledon have achieved an awful lot but all I've got is my medals from my Sunday League days, and that's it.
CHRIS PERRY, Wimbledon defender, on joining Tottenham, 1999.

It was a typical Wimbledon goal. Sad, miserable, but very effective.
BOBBY ROBSON, Newcastle manager, 2000.

There are thousands of reasons why we have gone down. But there can be no excuses. When one bubble bursts you have to blow another one.
TERRY BURTON, Wimbledon manager, on relegation from the Premiership, 2000.

Businessmen tried to take our club away from us so we decided to form our own. We'd like to pass them on the way up as they slip towards extinction. For the good of football, it's important that they fail miserably.

KRIS STEWART, chairman of AFC Wimbledon, set up after Wimbledon pursued their intention to relocate from south London to Milton Keynes, 2002.

It's the young players I feel sorry for, like Joel McAnuff. He'd be bringing the house down if there was a house to bring down.

NEIL SHIPPERLEY, Wimbledon captain, as defections to AFC Wimbledon saw crowds fall below 2,500 in the First Division, 2002.

WOLVERHAMPTON WANDERERS

Hail Wolves 'Champions of the World' Now
Headline in the Daily Mail *after they beat the Hungarian side Honved in a floodlit friendly before the launch of the European Cup, 1954.*

Wolves' success does Mr [Stan] Cullis great credit, but it has also done much harm to the game in England because so many lesser managers have attempted to ape the Wolves-Cullis technique. Artistry with the ball is not all-important with Wolverhampton Wanderers.

JIMMY McILROY, Burnley midfielder, criticising Wolves' long-ball style in Right Inside Soccer, *1960.*

I told my back four: 'I'm glad I didn't have you defending me when I had my court case. The judge would have put his black cap on.'

TOMMY DOCHERTY after becoming manager at struggling Wolves, 1984.

We don't use a stopwatch to judge our Golden Goal competition. We use a calendar.

DOCHERTY during a goal famine at Molineux, 1985.

I just opened the trophy cabinet. Two Japanese soldiers fell out.

DOCHERTY, 1985.

I tried to sign one of the Vietnamese 'boat people' and he said 'I'd love to join Wolves but I've left one sinking ship already.'
DOCHERTY, 1985.

It's a bit like joining the *Titanic* in mid-voyage.
RACHEL HEYHOE-FLINT, former England women's cricket captain, on joining the fast-declining club as PRO, 1985.

There's basically no difference between the Wolves you see now and the Wolves who enjoyed the heady days of the Fifties. They just happen to be in the Third Division.
GORDON DIMBLEBY, Wolves chief executive, 1985.

I had a book of excuses for people who rang up and said: 'Where's my money?' We couldn't even pay the milk bill.
KEITH PEARSON, Wolves secretary, on the club's 1980s brush with extinction, 1993.

The place was a health hazard before the stadium was rebuilt. The dressing-room leaked, we were always mopping up and there were coackroaches doing backstroke in the bath.
KEITH DOWNING, Wolves midfielder, 1993.

Bring back the Fifties!
Chant by Wolves' fans during protest against Graham Taylor's management, 1995.

There are only four clubs I'd have considered leaving Leicester for –Manchester United, Newcastle, Rangers and Wolves. This is the last of the sleeping giants.
MARK McGHEE, Wolves manager, 1995.

They are a big club that talk a good game.
McGHEE, by now with Millwall, after Wolves sacked his successor, Colin Lee, 2001.

When I came here I found a
lot of people living in the
past, and I upset them by
telling them so. Billy Wright
won't win me promotion.
And how is Steve Bull going
to help me? Let's put all the
great names in a museum,
treasure the memories and
move on.
*DAVE JONES, Wolves manager,
striving to lead the club to the
Premiership, 2002.*

4

COUNTRIES

AMERICAN SAMOA

Their players weren't allowed to swap shirts with us at the end. I think they got theirs from a supermarket when they first arrived in Australia.
ARCHIE THOMPSON, Australia striker, after scoring 13 goals in a world-record 31-0 defeat of the Samoans, 2001.

ARGENTINA

Malvinas 2 England 1! We blasted the English pirates with Maradona and a little hand. He who robs a thief has a thousand years of pardon.
CRONICA *newspaper of Buenos Aires, 1986.* Malvinas *is the Argentinian name for the Falkland Islands.*

Why the surprise over Argentina's elimination? When did a team with a large Scottish following ever qualify for the second round of the World Cup?
LETTER to the Guardian *during the World Cup finals, 2002. Argentina had been in the same group as England.*

There haven't been so many headbands and leather necklaces on TV since the Allman Brothers played the Old Grey Whistle Test.
WHEN SATURDAY COMES *magazine describes a 'hairy' Argentinian substitutes' bench against England, World Cup finals, 2002.*

BRAZIL

Brazil played in shoes which could only be likened to Grecian slippers. We cannot laugh even about that. After all, they won the World Cup in them [in 1958].
TOM FINNEY, England winger, in Finney on Football, *1958.*

We have nothing to learn from these people.
ALF RAMSEY, England manager, after defeat by Brazil, World Cup finals, 1970.

The Romanians were hard, but as far as I was concerned the Brazilians were harder; and if that seemed difficult to believe, I had the bruises and the soreness to prove my point. Jairzinho went right over the top of the ball and

kicked my shins; Pele had a go at me and I landed on my back, so that was twice when I lost my temper which is unusual for me.
MARTIN PETERS, England midfielder, on the World Cup winners, 1970.

Our football is like our inflation: 100 per cent
Headline in Jornal da Tarde *after Brazil beat England, 1981.*

The Pope may be Polish, but God is a Brazilian.
PELE after Brazil beat Poland 4-0 in the World Cup, 1986.

It is every footballer's dream to play against Brazil, and to tuck one of their shirts into your drawer.
BILLY HAMILTON, Northern Ireland striker, World Cup finals, 1986.

Brazil – You made me cry in 82, 86, 90. This time make me dance and I can die in peace
Banner at World Cup finals, 1994.

It feels like the magic has gone. It's as if we've been cursed.

RIVALDO, Brazil playmaker, after World Cup qualifying defeat by Paraguay, less than two years before he helped his country regain the trophy, 2000

There's no beautiful game any more. You are not going to see the Brazil of 1958, '62 or '70. This is 2001.
LUIZ FELIPE SCOLARI, Brazil coach, 2001.

We're going the wrong way down the one-way street of history. The vampires have sucked the last drops of blood and sweat from our football, leaving only tears.
LANCE, Brazilian daily sports paper, airing fears for the national side before the World Cup finals, 2002.

They are better than us, which is the difference.
SVEN-GORAN ERIKSSON, England manager, after Brazil beat his side in the World Cup quarter-finals, 2002.

CAMEROON

We didn't under-estimate them. They were a lot better than we thought.

BOBBY ROBSON, *England manager, after 3-2 win* v. *Cameroon, World Cup finals, 1990.*

DENMARK

I have told Chancellor Kohl that it is absolutely not on for the Danes to want to leave the European Community and be European champions at the same time.
BERTI VOGTS, Germany manager, after Denmark beat his team to win the European Championship, 1992.

ENGLAND

The World Cup wasn't won [in 1966] on the playing fields of England. It was won on the streets.
SIR BOBBY CHARLTON, member of the class of '66, 1995.

It never crossed our minds that we could lose. No, no never. It didn't come into it.
BOBBY MOORE, captain of the '66 side, in Ian Ridley, Season in the Cold, 1992.

You've beaten them once. Now go out and bloody beat them again.
ALF RAMSEY to the England players before extra time, World Cup final, 1966.

People say England are a physical team. They have left out a word. They should say England are a physically fit team.
HAROLD SHEPHERDSON, England trainer, after the World Cup triumph, 1966.

As we came round the corner from the 18th green, a crowd of members were at the clubhouse window, cheering and waiting to tell me that England had won the World Cup. It was the blackest day of my life.
DENIS LAW, former Scottish international, 1979.

I'd have preferred it if neither team had reached the final. I'm not a great lover of the Germans – they bombed my folks' house in Clydebank during the war.
ALLY MacLEOD, former Scotland manager, on the 25th anniversary of England's World Cup victory, 1991.

They cannae play nane.
JIM BAXTER, Scotland midfielder, after Scotland beat the world champions at Wembley, 1967.

The English team had some outstanding players. Men like [Gordon] Banks and Bobby Moore, and [Terry] Cooper and Bobby and Jack Charlton. They can play on any Brazilian team at any time – and that is no light compliment.
PELE after Brazil's defeat of England during the World Cup finals, 1970. From My Life and the Beautiful Game, *1977.*

England can't always win 6-0. Bobby Charlton has retired.
DAVE BASSETT, Sheffield United manager, after a 0-0 draw, 1995.

DES O'CONNOR: If England win the World Cup, will you come back and sing a duet with me?
ELTON JOHN: If they win, I'll come back and sleep with you.
Exchange on O'Connor's TV chat show, 1998.

I can't say England are shite because they beat us in the [Euro 2000] play-offs, and that would make us even shittier.
ALLY McCOIST, former Scotland striker, 2000.

Portugal play football as I like to see it played. As a neutral it was fantastic. Unfortunately I'm not a neutral.
KEVIN KEEGAN, England manager, after Portugal beat his team, Euro 2000.

If it'd been about endeavour and honesty, we'd have won Euro 2000. But it's not.
KEEGAN, 2000.

There is a need for honesty...the bottom line is that were inept tactically, we were exposed against teams we could have beaten. England's failings have nothing to do with technical skill because I don't agree we're not good enough as footballers.
MARTIN KEOWN, Arsenal and England defender, after Euro 2000 exit.

Tony Blair is very good looking but unfortunately he has no bravado. Same with the England football team. They play so slow.
ADRIANA SKLENARIKOVA, Slovakian Wonderbra model, 2000.

Eventually I do want an English guy in charge, but one with the demeanour and style of a Wenger or an Eriksson.
TONY ADAMS, England defender, 2001.

In Sweden we say, 'You need to have a fox behind your ear'. It means being clever and cunning, which are qualities we have to develop.
SVEN-GORAN ERIKSSON, England manager, after the team's World Cup exit, 2002.

All the European teams who have gone out have played too defensively, as if they were scared. I thought England were the worst.
GUUS HIDDINK, South Korea's Dutch coach, after his team went a stage further than England to the World Cup semi-finals, 2002.

It was obvious England were overawed by Brazil, Brazil with 10 players, men against boys. You could see England's body language at the end. 'We've done okay, haven't we? Got to the quarter-finals.' England should expect to be in the semi-finals or final every time. Come on lads, wake up!
ROY KEANE, former Republic of Ireland captain, 2002. He also claimed that 'the priority' for some England players was to swap shirts with a Brazilian.

FRANCE

Half the team are foreigners who don't even know the words to the Marseillaise.
JEAN-MARIE LE PEN, leader of the far-right National Front, on the France team at the European Championship finals, 1996.

Me, sing to satisfy Le Pen? I don't think so.
MARCEL DESAILLY, black France defender, 1996.

A tricolour orgasm!
Headline in France Soir *after France's World Cup triumph, 1998.*

I claim this victory for the National Front, which designed its framework.
JEAN-MARIE LE PEN after France's multi-racial team had won the World Cup, 1998.

According to Gary Lineker, football is a match between two teams of 11 men and Germany win in the end. Nowadays his famous comment appears to apply to France.
L'EQUIPE, French sports newspaper, after Les Bleus' triumph at Euro 2000.

What would be the most logical final at Euro 2000? France A versus France B.
L'EQUIPE after Les Bleus fielded fringe players v. the Netherlands and lost only 3-2.

The French team has been my life and has led me to do things I shouldn't have. It has been my mistress – a beautiful mistress.
LAURENT BLANC retiring from the national side after the triumph at Euro 2000.

I prefer to watch England than France. If one day France have a good national team with players who play in France then maybe I will watch them.
ERIC CANTONA, former French international, 2000.

There's a few little things we have to change. It's clear the machine has jammed.
MARCEL DESAILLY, France captain, after the holders finished bottom of their group and without a goal, World Cup finals, 2002.

GERMANY

Q: What do you admire most about Germany?
A: Their results.
TERRY VENABLES, England coach, after the Germans beat them on penalties, European Championship finals, 1996.

The Germans are very well behaved, more like a lawyers' convention than a squad of footballers.
JEFF BURNIGE, Millwall director and German team liaison officer as Germany moved towards European Championship success, 1996.

There were some strange decisions against us. Perhaps there was a secret instruction, maybe German soccer had become too successful and had to be punished.
BERTI VOGTS, Germany coach, after elimination from the World Cup finals, 1998.

The reason we Germans are so good at penalties is that we have had to rebuild our country twice.
JURGEN KLINSMANN, Germany captain, in a TV documentary, On the Spot: The 12-yard Club, *1999.*

That was tired, junk football, which at times turned into abuse of the ball.
FRANZ BECKENBAUER, former Germany captain, on his country's dismal showing at Euro 2000.

The mega blancmange!
Headline in BZ newspaper, Berlin, *after Germany's demise, 2000.*

The 5-1 defeat by England was like the explosion of a nuclear bomb. The scars will last for life.

OLIVER KAHN, Germany goalkeeper on that fateful night in Munich, 2001.

You have to, you know, to some degree, er, admire the Germans.
SIR BOBBY ROBSON, ITV pundit, leads the grudging praise for Germany's feat in reaching the World Cup final, 2002.

HUNGARY

The 1954 Hungarian soccer masters did not go into the record books as the champions of the world. But they went into my personal memory file – and that of millions of other football-lovers – as the finest team ever to sort out successfully the intricacies of the wonderful game.
TOM FINNEY, Preston and England forward, in Finney on Football, *1958.*

When I returned to the Cumberland Hotel in London, a small boy came up to me in the foyer and said: 'Please sir, take me to your country and teach me to play football.'

FERENC PUSKAS in Captain of Hungary, *1955.*

ITALY

On the pitch the Italians looked no different to us. It was like playing Bournemouth on a wet Saturday.
JASON McATEER, Republic of Ireland manager, after beating Italy in the World Cup, 1994.

The Italians still don't know how to lose. Mussolini was the same when he told the players not to return from France without the World Cup in 1938.
BYRON MORENO, Ecuadorian referee, after Italy complained they were cheated by him when South Korea knocked them out of the World Cup, 2002.

LIBERIA

The worst team to feature a European Footballer of the Year since George Best turned out for Dunstable Town.
ANDY LYONS, editor of When Saturday Comes *magazine, on George Weah and his national*

team's failure at the African Nations Cup, 1996.

NETHERLANDS

Mr Martinez [the referee] was slow to realise that the Dutch invented the clog.
DAVID LACEY, reporting in the Guardian *on the Italy* v. *Netherlands match, World Cup finals, 1978.*

During the European Championship finals we went out every night until two or three in the morning. The problem with Italians is that they don't like to go out after playing.
RUUD GULLIT, Dutch captain, after they became European champions, 1988.

NORTHERN IRELAND

Our tactic is to equalise before the others have scored.
DANNY BLANCHFLOWER, Northern Ireland captain, World Cup finals, 1958.

NORWAY

The Norwegian team's eating habits surprised me, especially

mixing jam with smoked fish and even bananas and mackerel.
GEORGES-MARIE DUFFARD, manager of the Norway squad's hotel, World Cup finals, 1998.

We love each other, on and off the field.
ERIK MYKLAND, Norway midfielder, at Euro 2000.

REPUBLIC OF IRELAND

If you have a fortnight's holiday in Dublin you qualify for an Eire cap.
MIKE ENGLAND, Wales manager, 1986.

Playing for Liverpool and playing for Ireland could hardly be more different. At Liverpool I do most of my work in the penalty area. For Ireland, when you're not closing down defenders, you're chasing long balls over the top. Much more of this and my legs will be worn down to stumps.
JOHN ALDRIDGE, Republic striker, 1989.

The Irish force an unattractive game on the opposition. No team has managed to escape this contagious crap.
AHMED EL-MOKADEM, Egyptian FA official, after 0-0 draw v. the Republic, World Cup finals, 1990.

Look at the Irish. They sing their national anthem and none of them know the words. Jack [Charlton] sings, and all he knows is 'Cushy Butterfield' and 'Blaydon Races'. But look at the pride they have in those green shirts.
LAWRIE McMENEMY, England assistant manager, calling for Graham Taylor's team to sing 'God Save the Queen' before games, 1991.

As the first bars ring out, I notice the TV camera start to zoom in. Should I move my lips and sing the two or three lines that I know?
ANDY TOWNSEND, Republic captain, on an Anglo-Irishman's problems with the Irish anthem, in Andy's Game, *1994.*

Italy turn up in Armani suits looking the dog's bollocks and we arrive in bright green blazers and dodgy brogues.
PHIL BABB, Republic defender, at the World Cup finals, 1994.

Opponents used to come up to me during games and say: 'Ireland do not play football. It is rugby.' I'd reply: 'Yeah, but we're winning 2-1.'
MICK McCARTHY, Jack Charlton's successor as manager, 1996.

All I've got to do now is get the accent right.
CLINTON MORRISON, London-born Crystal Palace striker, declaring his allegiance to the Republic of Ireland, 2001.

If I opened my mouth every time there's something wrong, I'd need my own newspaper.
ROY KEANE on the Football Association of Ireland's preparations for the World Cup finals, 2002.

Ireland are a team of impertinents and battlers led by Roy Keane.

CAMEROON TRIBUNE, state-run newspaper, on the eve of the country's World Cup clash with the Irish, who had sent home Keane more than a week earlier, 2002.

We're the team that doesn't study the opposition, that takes supporters on the team coach, is not really bothered, that likes a pint and the craic. And yet here we are in the last 16 of the World Cup again. If that scenario were true, we must be the greatest group of guys who ever played the game.
MICK McCARTHY, Republic of Ireland manager, on the team's media image, 2002.

SCOTLAND

Playing for Scotland is fantastic. You look at your dark blue shirt and the wee lion looks up at you and says: 'Get out there after those English bastards!'
BILL SHANKLY, Scotland player of the 1930s, quoted in John Keith, Shanks For the Memory, 1998.

We didn't even have Scotland tracksuits. We had to bring our own training gear. And what a peculiar lot we looked among the world's best, with the green of Celtic and the white of Preston and the blue of Dundee contrasting with the beautifully turned out teams of Europe and South America. We looked like liquorice allsorts.
WILLIE FERNIE, Celtic and Scotland player, on the first, disastrous World Cup campaign of 1954 in When Will We See Your Like Again?, *1977.*

The trouble was that they used an orange ball. Eric Caldow and me, being from Rangers, didn't want to kick it, while Billy McNeill, coming from Celtic, didn't want to touch it.
BOBBY SHEARER, Scotland defender, on the 9-3 defeat by England, 1961.

I warned it would take a great team to beat us. Let's give them their due.
ALF RAMSEY after Scotland became the first team to beat his newly crowned world champions, 1967.

If patriotism is silly, then okay we're silly. When we go on to the field for Scotland, we're ready to give blood. Of course, we'd like a lot of money, but even without it we'll play till we drop.
DAVID HAY, Scotland player, at World Cup finals, 1974.

If you keep saying: 'We'll win it, we'll win it, we'll win it', eventually they believe you.
ALLY MacLEOD, Scotland manager, before the team's ill-fated World Cup, 1978.

I am proud of my team for beating the best side in Europe. I want to congratulate Scotland for the team they presented to us.
MARCUS CALDERON, Peru manager, after they beat MacLeod's Scots 3-1, World Cup finals, 1978.

It riles me to think of all the great players Scotland have had over the years and yet they haven't won anything. It's criminal that there hasn't been a really successful Scotland team.
BILL SHANKLY after his country's World Cup exit, 1978.

A good team with strong English character.
RUUD GULLIT, Netherlands midfielder, before match v. Scotland, 1992.

We've been playing for an hour and it has just occurred to me that we're drawing 0-0 with a mountain top.
IAN ARCHER, Radio Scotland summariser, during San Marino v. Scotland match, 1993. The Scots won 2-0.

Bagpipes, war-paint and claymores won't win us games in the European Championship or World Cup.
CRAIG BROWN, manager, 1994.

Our supporters expect us to beat everybody we play. The trouble is, so do I.
BROWN after defeat by the United States, 1996.

Scotsman's desire to struggle is as if sucked in almost from mother's milk.
GUNTIS INDRIKSONS, Latvian FA president, in the programme for the meeting of their countries, 1996.

They'll be home before the postcards.
TOMMY DOCHERTY, former Scotland manager, before his country's first-round exit, World Cup finals, 1998.

We owe the English big-time. They stole our land our oil, perpetrated the Highland Clearances and now they've even pinched Billy Connolly.
GORDON STRACHAN, Coventry manager and former Scotland captain, before Euro 2000 play-off matches v. England, 1999.

Where are the Jockos to replace the likes of Jim Baxter, who played a blinder when they beat us at Wembley in 1967? The only Baxter they've got up there now is a range of soups.
JIMMY GREAVES, former England striker, in his Sun column, 1999.

Unless we batter sides we are on a hiding. The way international football is going that won't happen very often. Yet if we don't play well and win, we're rubbish, and if we

play well and don't win,
we're rubbish.
CHRISTIAN DAILLY,
Scotland defender, 2000.

I remember when every great
English club had two or three
Scots in the team. Where the
talent has gone, I don't
know. But when I go home
to Sauchie, the park I played
in as a kid – jackets down,
25-a-side – is empty now.
ALAN HANSEN, former
Scotland defender, after the draw
with the Faroe Islands, 2002.

SENEGAL

Their teamwork is a good
model for Christian-Muslim
co-existence.
FIDES, Vatican missionary
service news agency, World Cup
finals, as Senegal reached the
quarter-finals of the World
Cup, 2002.

Our team is made up of
bandits and madmen.
AMDY FAYE, Senegal player,
on their run to the World Cup
quarter-finals, 2002.

TURKEY

The Turkish people adore my
team and my team adore the
Turkish people. It will be a
meeting of lovers.
SENOL GUNES, Turkey coach,
after taking third place in the
World Cup, 2002.

UNITED STATES OF AMERICA

If we lived in another
country we would be asking
for political asylum. Since
we're American we'll stay in
New York and nobody will
recognise us.
TAB RAMOS, US midfielder,
after 5-1 defeat in the World
Cup by Czechoslovakia, 1990.

A lot of people that don't
know anything about soccer,
like me, are all excited and
pulling for you.
GEORGE W. BUSH, American
President, after the USA reached
the World Cup's last eight, 2002.

URUGUAY

Other countries have their
history. Uruguay has its
football.

ONDINA VIERA, Uruguay
coach, 1966.

WALES

They gave us a difficult game,
for five or six minutes.
GUUS HIDDINK, Netherlands
manager, after 7-1 win v.
Wales, 1996.

MRS MERTON: Is it your
ambition to play in a World
Cup final?
VINNIE JONES: I play for
Wales.
Exchange on TV's Mrs Merton
Show, 1997.

I actually want Wales to lose
every game so that [manager]
Bobby Gould might be
sacked. We're the Man City of
international football. We
rank 98th in the world,
below the Congo Republic.
NICKY WIRE of the Welsh rock
group the Manic Street
Preachers, 1998.

If you had put yellow shirts
on them, you'd have sworn
you were watching Ronaldo,
Rivaldo and Ronaldinho.
RHODRI MORGAN, First
Minister in the Welsh Assembly,
after Mark Hughes' team beat
Italy, 2002.

5

MANAGERS

MALCOLM ALLISON

On the coach back from London, Allison asked where [Francis] Lee was. 'He's hiding in case you give him a right-hander for missing that penalty,' said [Rodney] Marsh. Allison was in pensive mood. 'I never tear them off a strip when they've lost. I've done it before and it's led to bad feelings that take too long to heal.' He became absorbed in his cigar. 'This game is like being in love. You've got to suffer to enjoy it.'
TONY PAWSON, author, on the aftermath of a defeat at Crystal Palace during Allison's first reign as Manchester City manager, in The Football Managers, *1973.*

It's ridiculous. I've served more time than Ronnie Biggs did for the Great Train Robbery.
MALCOLM ALLISON, Plymouth manager, appealing against a touchline ban, 1978.

OSSIE ARDILES

I'll never compromise my ideals, whichever division I'm in. I tell the boys to try to play like Pele.
OSSIE ARDILES, Swindon manager, 1990.

REPORTER: Is Klinsmann Spurs' biggest-ever signing?
OSSIE ARDILES: No, I was.
Exchange at press conference to unveil Tottenham's German recruit, 1995.

RON ATKINSON

You're welcome to my home phone number, gentlemen. But please remember not to ring me during *The Sweeney*.
RON ATKINSON on taking over as manager at Manchester United, 1981.

It's bloody tough being a legend.
ATKINSON at Old Trafford, 1983.

As far as he's concerned, he's God. There's nobody big enough to tell him what to do.
MARGARET ATKINSON, his first wife, after news broke of Atkinson's extra-marital affair, 1984.

Half an hour? You could shoot *Ben Hur* in half an hour. You've got 15 seconds.
ATKINSON to photographer who asked for 30 minutes with him, 1984.

REPORTER: What's the John Gidman situation, Ron? Is he in plaster?
RON ATKINSON: No, he's in Marbella.
Exchange at press conference, 1985.

This person suffers from erotic fantasies. He thinks a lot about sex, though he is very devoted to his mother.
Graphologist analysing Atkinson's writing on ITV's FA Cup final coverage, 1985.

I've had to swap my Merc for a BMW, I'm down to my last 37 suits and I'm drinking non-vintage champagne.
ATKINSON on life after his sacking by United, 1987.

I believe there are only a select few managers who can handle the real giant clubs of this world. I happen to be one of them.
ATKINSON at Atletico Madrid, a month before his sacking, 1988.

He has never slagged off United or criticised anyone here since he left, and he could have made a few bob doing so.
ALEX FERGUSON, Atkinson's successor at Old Trafford, 1991.

His teams were always gifted and played some lovely football...But his legacy at Manchester United was a pool of older players. Ron always liked to buy the finished article whereas I've always preferred to watch young talent grow.
FERGUSON, 1996.

Q: What was the highlight of your World Cup?
A: Bumping into Frank Sinatra.
ATKINSON at the World Cup in the USA, 1994.

There is this champagne-and-nightclubs image he has. But above all he loves the game. He's still a child at heart. In training this season he has been everyone from Arnold Muhren to David Ginola.

GORDON STRACHAN,
Coventry player-coach, 1996.

Have you seen that scene in
the film *Kes*, where Brian
Glover thinks he's Bobby
Charlton? Ron's like that. He
thinks he's the best five-a-side
player in the club.
LIAM DAISH, Coventry
defender, 1997.

I'm still the best five-a-side
player in the club. Mind you,
that's probably why we're in
the position we're in.
ATKINSON at 56, when his
Coventry side propped up the
Premiership, 1995.

The last of the great character
managers.
GORDON STRACHAN, before
succeeding Atkinson as Coventry
manager, 1996.

The only relaxed boss is Big
Ron. He had me drinking
pink champagne – before
the match.
HARRY REDKNAPP, West
Ham manager, 1995.

The champagne-and-jewellery
image has stuck with me, but
it has been perpetuated by

people who don't know me.
When I was burgled the
thieves were gutted not to
find my place bulging with
gold watches and trinkets.
ATKINSON on retiring as a
manager at 60, 1999.

My missus reckons that if
people don't recognise me in
the street, I go back and tell
them who I am.
ATKINSON, 1995.

What do you say to a team
that's 5-0 up at half-time –
though I don't suppose
you'd know.
CLIVE TYLDESLEY, ITV
commentator, to Atkinson, his
summariser, when England
played Luxembourg, 1999.

ALAN BALL

Alan Ball and I didn't see eye
to eye, and it had nothing to
do with his being 5ft 3in and
me being 6ft 4in.
DAVE BEASANT, Southampton
goalkeeper, 1995.

Round here we threaten
young Stoke fans that Alan
Ball will come back and
manage the club if they don't

go to bed early and eat all their vegetables.
MARTIN SMITH, editor of the Stoke City fanzine The Oatcake, *on 'the bogeyman' Ball's return as Portsmouth manager, 1999.*

DAVE BASSETT

I can still see 'Harry' screaming: 'You're just a bunch of clowns and amateurs, and that's why you'll never reach the top.' Twenty minutes later, the van chugged to a halt on the M4. He had forgotten to fill it up with petrol.
WALLY DOWNES, who had been a Wimbledon player in the Fourth Division under Bassett, 1988.

I know what they are all thinking – the Elephant Man is back, stand well clear. I was once called the spiv in a £400 suit. I felt right insulted. It cost at least a grand.
DAVE BASSETT on leading Sheffield United back into the top flight, 1990.

He'd get on the team bus, walk past someone, give them slap and say: 'Do you want some?' It would end up with him rolling on the floor and the rest of the lads piling in and kicking 10 bells out of him...all in good fun, of course.
ALAN KELLY, goalkeeper, on his time at Sheffield United with Bassett, 1999.

At Forest he wasn't the manager who kicked trays of sandwiches and threw cups of tea. He was more thoughtful and what he said rang true, though his mouth sometimes loses contact with his brain.
DAVE BEASANT, Nottingham Forest goalkeeper, 1999.

I don't want my players behaving like poofters. I want them to be men.
BASSETT after Sheffield United's Tom Cowan was accused of over-reacting to a push by Roy Keane, 1993.

It's going to be my epitaph, isn't it? Deep in the shit, where he started.
BASSETT, facing relegation with Nottingham Forest, 1997.

I ran out of petrol on the motorway on my way to the game. I phoned the police and they asked my name. When I told them 'Dave Bassett', this cop said: 'What, the Leicester manager?' I said yes and he burst out laughing.
BASSETT during Leicester's slide to relegation, 2002.

One thousand games in purgatory, eh?
SIR ALEX FERGUSON presenting Bassett with an award for 1,000 matches as a manager, 2002.

JOHN BECK

Beck had gone barmy before the game. The Bristol City manager, Denis Smith, had said something on the radio, a really over-the-top comment...so he [Beck] said: 'Welsh bastards!' meaning Bristol City.
COLIN BAILLIE, who had played under Beck at Cambridge United, 1992.

JOHN BOND

Like Brian Clough, I find it impossible to keep my mouth shut.
JOHN BOND, Norwich manager, 1979.

IAN BRANFOOT

It got to the stage where I thought I was being followed in my car. There was even a threat to kidnap me and take me to a zoo, but it didn't materialise.
IAN BRANFOOT, Southampton manager, on a hostile fans' campaign to oust him, 1993.

CRAIG BROWN

Kevin [Keegan] and I have 63 international caps between us. He has 63 of them.
CRAIG BROWN, Scotland manager, before the countries' Euro 2000 play-off, 1999.

My job is my holiday. I travel all the time and see the world in this business. I take my holidays at home in Ayr.
BROWN on the Scotland managership, 1997.

If he really is a sectarian bigot then he deserves an Oscar. People can have different faces depending on the company they're in but it would be difficult to disguise true sectarian hatred for four decades.
BILLY McNEILL, former Celtic and Scotland captain, after the News of the World *called Brown a 'bigot and sex cheat' 1999.*

My brother Bob has three degrees from universities, my other brother Jock is an MA from Cambridge and I'm a BA from the Open University. As a player I was the one the manager would turn to last and say: 'Right son, nothing clever from you this week.'
BROWN, 1995.

STEVE BRUCE

The biggest mistake I made was believing a great footballer would make a great manager.
BARRY RUBERRY, Huddersfield chairman, after the former Manchester United captain's departure, 2001.

MATT BUSBY

You would go in [to Busby's office] fighting and full of demands. And he would give you nothing at all. He might even take a tenner off your wages. And you would come out thinking: 'What a great guy.' I remember going in there once, absolutely livid. And 10 minutes later I came out, no better off, walking on air.
EAMON DUNPHY, former United reserve, in Only A Game?, *1976.*

Matt was the eternal optimist. In 1968 he still hoped Glenn Miller was just missing.
PADDY CRERAND, former Manchester United player under Busby, 1997.

His greatest achievement was to create the illusion of beauty in a craft wretchedly deformed from the beginning.
EAMON DUNPHY, United reserve during the Busby era at Old Trafford, in A Strange Kind of Glory, *1991.*

He has held his magnetism right through five decades. I remember in Rotterdam for the final of the Cup-Winners' Cup, a lot of fans were gathered at the main entrance chanting the names of players like 'Hughesy' as they went in. Suddenly Sir Matt arrived and the wild cheering turned to respectful applause. It was quite touching, just like the Pope arriving.
ALEX FERGUSON in Six Years at United, *1992.*

It would have been Sir Matt Busby's 90th birthday today. All I know is that someone was doing an awful lot of kicking up there.
FERGUSON after Manchester United's last-gasp victory over Bayern Munich in the European Cup final, 1999.

JACK CHARLTON

I told him not to be such a great big baby.
STAN SEYMOUR, Newcastle chairman, after Charlton quit as manager, 1985.

I won't die at a match. I might die being dragged down the River Tweed by a giant salmon, but a football match, no.
JACK CHARLTON, Republic of Ireland manager, 1988

Jack makes out he is not really interested in football, and tells the world he's going fishing. But we know what he's thinking about when he's fishing. Football.
JOHAN CRUYFF, Barcelona coach, 1990.

Jack is not always right, but he is never wrong.
JOHN GILES, former Republic of Ireland manager and ex-Leeds colleague, 1991.

We like Jack. He's a crazy man but football needs characters. However, he must learn where to draw the line with his behaviour.
GUIDO TOGNONI, Fifa spokesman, announcing touchline ban for Charlton, World Cup finals, 1994.

Imagine what Ireland might have done if led and inspired by a man of

vision and courage. This is not hard to do: remember Giants Stadium when, with the spur of an early goal, the players overcame miserable tactics to humble Italy.
EAMON DUNPHY, journalist and ex-Republic player, before what proved to be Charlton's final match, 1995.

The honour that pleased me most of all was when the House of Commons voted me Beer Drinker of the Year.
CHARLTON, 1996.

One of his cardinals introduced us, saying: 'This is Mr Charlton.' He said: 'Ah yes, the boss.'
CHARLTON after meeting the Pope with the Irish squad, World Cup finals, 1990.

Charlton developed a style of play that suited his crude convictions rather than the gifts of his players.
ROY KEANE, Manchester United and former Ireland captain, alleging that Charlton had a 'primitive' approach, 2002.

If Jack came in here now, he wouldn't buy you a drink – he'd be hoping somebody would buy him one.
KEANE, 2002.

BRIAN CLOUGH

Age does not count. It's what you know about football that matters. I know I am better than the 500 or so managers who have been sacked since the war. If they had known anything about the game they wouldn't have lost their jobs.
BRIAN CLOUGH on taking his first managerial post, with Hartlepools, 1965.

Success? Tell me the date when my obituary is going to appear and I'll tell you whether I've been a success or not. If I get to 60 I shall have done pretty well.
CLOUGH, by now Brighton manager, 1973.

He is a kind of Rolls Royce communist.
MALCOLM ALLISON, rival manager, 1973.

He's worse than the rain in Manchester. At least God stops that occasionally.
BILL SHANKLY, former managerial adversary, on Clough's pronouncements, 1979.

Outside of family life there is nothing better than winning European Cups.
CLOUGH, Nottingham Forest manager, 1980.

A player can never feel too sure of himself with Clough. That's his secret.
PETER TAYLOR, his assistant at Derby and Nottingham Forest, in With Clough By Taylor, *1980.*

It's easy enough to get to Ireland – just a walk across the Irish Sea as far as I'm concerned.
CLOUGH confirming his application for the Republic of Ireland manager's job, 1985.

I want to be manager of Scotland.
CLOUGH, 1985.

I can't promise to give the team talks in Welsh, but from now I'll be taking my holidays in Porthcawl and I've bought a complete set of Harry Secombe albums.
CLOUGH on his hopes of becoming Wales' manager, 1988.

Resignations are for Prime Ministers and those caught with their trousers down, not for me.
CLOUGH after withdrawing his threat to quit Forest over Wales, 1988.

Their decision is as bad as those I made in sanctioning the signings of [Justin] Fashanu, [Peter] Ward and [Ian] Wallace, which could easily have sent this club to the wall.
CLOUGH after Forest's board refused to let him take on the Wales job, 1988.

I hope you were as delighted as I was last week when Nelson Mandela was freed from a South African jail. But what I hadn't bargained for was that his release was going to cut across the start of our Litlewoods Cup final.
CLOUGH, Nottingham Forest programme column, 1990.

On a Saturday he'd waltz into the dressing-room at twenty to three, put a football down and say: 'Right, this is your best friend. This is what we play with.'
DARREN WASSALL, Derby and former Forest player, 1993.

He's my idol as a manager but we don't really communicate. The closest we've come is when he tried to kiss me after a testimonial match, but I smelled the after-shave and skipped past him.
NEIL WARNOCK, Notts County manager, 1991.

I played under Bill Shankly and Bob Paisley, and Clough is a better manager than either of them. As a manager there's no limit to my respect for him, but as a man he's not my cup of tea. I once told him I'd never be caught standing at a bar having a drink with him. He said the feeling was mutual.
LARRY LLOYD, former Liverpool and Forest defender, 1991.

My wife says 'OBE' stands for Old Big 'Ead.
CLOUGH, 1991.

I'd like to retire with half of what he has achieved as a manager and a quarter of his dough.
DAVE BASSETT, Sheffield United manager, 1992.

Like all the great dictators, from de Gaulle to Thatcher, he stayed on a little too long.
GAZZETTA DELLO SPORT, Italian sports newspaper, after Clough's retirement, 1993.

He gave by far the best interview of all the candidates – confident, passionate, full of common sense and above all patriotic. If Ron Greenwood hadn't been around, he'd have clinched it.
PETER SWALES, former FA international committee chairman, on Clough's 1977 application to manage England, 1995.

They didn't want an England manager who was prepared to call the Italians cheating bastards. They failed to

understand that I would have curbed my language and revelled in the relief from the day-to-day grind of club management.
CLOUGH, 1995.

I'm ill-tempered, rude and wondering what's for tea, same as ever.
CLOUGH on what he was like at 4.45pm on Saturdays after retirement, 1994.

There was talk of a testimonial match, of a stand being named after me, but there was nothing, not even a toilet. They could have had a Brian Clough Bog.
CLOUGH alleging lack of recognition for his 17 years service to Nottingham Forest, 1997. Two years later Forest named a stand after him.

When this young man says: 'Grandad, you did not get many academic qualifications,' I get out my medals. They are my O- and A-levels.
CLOUGH on the Master of Arts degree bestowed on him by Nottingham University, 1999.

He's the best manager of all time in my book because of what he's done and where he did it.
RON ATKINSON, one of Clough's successors at Forest, 1995.

I think my knees have got worse. I'll have to order a new pair from the Co-Op for Christmas. I am all right sitting down or in bed but if I get in a car they lock. The bloke who said life begins at 40 was either blind drunk or in cloud-cuckoo land. There is only one way to go when you're 40 – down.
CLOUGH, 1999.

We only saw Brian and Peter [Taylor, assistant manager] at the end of training. They would walk around the pitch, Taylor with his dog and Clough with his squash racket.
JURGEN ROBER, Hertha Berlin coach and ex-Nottingham Forest player, 1999.

STAN CULLIS

The night Stan Cullis got the
   sack
Wolverhampton wandered
   round in circles

Like a disallowed goal
Looking for a friendly
   linesman.
*MARTIN HALL, poet and
songwriter, on the Wolves
manager of the 1950s in 'The
Stan Cullis Blues', 1974.*

KENNY DALGLISH

I know he hates me. He
walked past me on the golf
course as if I were a tree.
He's the moaningest minnie
I've ever known.
*JOHN BOND, Birmingham
manager, 1987.*

Ten Modern Labours of
Hercules: 1. Make Kenny
Dalglish laugh uncontrollably.
MAIL ON SUNDAY'S *Journo-
lists' page, 1990.*

I have no hesitation in saying
he was one of the great
players of all time, but I can't
speak of him in the same
terms as a manager. That's
not a criticism, but he didn't
begin the job at the grass
roots, start with a Second or
Third Division club or build
a side from scratch. So there
are some doubts.
HOWARD KENDALL,

*Everton manager, after Dalglish
resigned at Liverpool, 1991.*

The pressure on match-days
is making my head explode. I
can't go on.
*KENNY DALGLISH on
quitting Anfield, 1991.*

He's incredibly intense about
football. He's the only person
I've ever seen come off during
a match who is still playing
every ball. Normally when
players are substituted, you'll
see them in the dug-out,
winding down. Kenny still
kicks and heads everything.
*ALAN HANSEN, friend and
former Liverpool colleague, 1992.*

Kenny is such a football
nut that you could mention
any player in England and
he'd know who you were
talking about.
HANSEN, 1993.

I've always felt there's a
scriptwriter up on a cloud
somewhere penning Kenny's
life story.
*GORDON STRACHAN on
Dalglish's championship success
with Blackburn, 1995.*

It was very difficult for me to understand what he was saying. Which was a pity, because there were certain messages I would have liked to convey to him.
DAVID GINOLA after being sold from Newcastle to Tottenham by Dalglish, 1997.

Kenny Dalglish was my boyhood hero. I even named my goldfish after him.
RICKY GILLIES, St Mirren midfielder, 1997.

Is Kenny Dalglish a big girl's blouse?
JEREMY PAXMAN, presenter of BBC2's Newsnight *programme, introducing a feature about managers, 1998.*

I had to be very careful around him and I still am now we are together at Celtic because he's the biggest mickey-taker imaginable. Kenny is completely different from his public image, loving a laugh in private. He is very guarded with those he doesn't know so I understand why people label him as dour.
JOHN BARNES, former

Liverpool player under Dalglish, in his autobiography, 1999.

TOMMY DOCHERTY

I talk a lot. On any subject. Which is always football.
TOMMY DOCHERTY, 1967.

No one will ever equal Sir Matt Busby's achievements and influence at Old Trafford, but I'd like to go down as someone who did nearly as much.
DOCHERTY after leading Manchester United to promotion, 1974.

I have been punished for falling in love. What I have done has nothing at all to do with my track record as a manager.
DOCHERTY after his sacking by United because of an affair with the wife of the club physio, 1977.

All this talk about Tommy Docherty not being fit to run a football club is rubbish. That's exactly what he's fit for.
CLIVE JAMES, TV critic, 1979.

Preston are one of my old clubs, but then most of them are. I've had more clubs than Jack Nicklaus.
DOCHERTY, 1979.

They offered me a handshake of £10,000 to settle amicably. I told them they would have to be a lot more amicable than that.
DOCHERTY on being dismissed by Preston, 1981.

They sacked me as nicely as they could – one of the nicest sackings I've had.
DOCHERTY on leaving Preston, 1981.

There's no excitement. Tommy's just been sacked again, that's all.
MARY BROWN, Docherty's partner, to doorstepping journalists after the Preston sacking, 1981.

I've been in more courts than Bjorn Borg.
DOCHERTY, 1981.

Tommy Docherty criticising Charlie Nicholas is like Bernard Manning telling Jimmy Tarbuck to clean up his act.

GORDON TAYLOR, players' union leader, after Docherty spoke of Nicholas' 'indiscipline', 1984.

Q: You are a Catholic. Are you a good Catholic?
A: At the moment, not very good, but I intend to do something about that. One thing I do miss – the traditional Tridentine Mass.
DOCHERTY in an interview with Scotland's Sunday Mail, *1980.*

His interests are limited...At home he never read anything in the newspapers but the sports pages. His knowledge of what goes on outside football is so restricted that he couldn't understand why he kept getting into trouble for parking on double yellow lines. He thought they were a new form of street decoration.
CATHERINE LOCKLEY, Docherty's daughter by his first wife, 1981.

He has gone 200 years too late.
Anonymous manager on Docherty's move to Australia, 1981.

SVEN-GORAN ERIKSSON

I didn't take it for the money or even for the weather. I took it because it's a great challenge.
SVEN-GORAN ERIKKSON on becoming England's first foreign manager, 2000.

I'm very upset [that England have appointed a foreign manager]. The French are managed by a Frenchman, Germany by a German and the Italians have one of their own.
JACK CHARLTON, Englishman and former Republic of Ireland manager, 2000.

He doesn't know anything about English football. It's a terrible mistake and a recipe for disaster.
CHARLTON, 2000.

Q: Do you know who the Leicester goalkeeper is?
A: No.
Q: Do you know who the Sunderland left-back is?
A: No. But when I come here I will know everything.
ERIKSSON on his first meeting with the English press, 2000.

The nation which gave the game of football to the world has been forced to put a foreign coach in charge of its national team for the first time. What a climbdown. What a humiliation. What a terrible, pathetic, self-inflicted indictment. What an awful mess.
Editorial in the Sun *on Eriksson's appointment, 2000.*

England's humiliation knows no end. In their trendy eagerness to appoint a designer foreigner did the FA pause for so much as a moment to consider the depth of this insult to our national pride. We sell our birthright down the fjord to a nation of seven million skiers and hammer-throwers who spend half their year living in total darkness.
Editorial in the Daily Mail, *2000.*

By going to a foreign situation we've chosen to say we're not a power any more, but we, the FA, will show you how clever we are because we are designer people now, not old farts any more.

TERRY VENABLES, former England manager, 2001.

It [Eriksson's appointment] is a betrayal of our heritage and coaching structure. Terry Venables isn't considered because the FA has laid down criteria which maybe even the Archbishop of Canterbury wouldn't meet.
GORDON TAYLOR, players' union leader, 2001.

He's certainly different from Barry Fry.
CHRIS POWELL, Charlton defender who served Fry at Southend, before his first England appearance, 2001.

I'm nervous about meeting so many new people. It's like when you go out with a woman for the first time – you're bound to wonder how it will end up.
ERIKSSON before his first game with England, v. Spain, 2001.

Eriksson is our superhero as five-goal Lions roar
Headline in the News of the World *headline after England's 5-1 win in Germany, 2001.*

This win represents one of the greatest wins by an England team. Eriksson has done so much to establish this sense of pride and purpose, to get the best out of the outstanding individual talents at his disposal.
Report in the Daily Express *on the rout of Germany, 2001.*

So he comes from Sweden. He could come from Mars as far as I'm concerned, as long as we win the World Cup or European Championship.
RIO FERDINAND, Leeds and England defender, 2001.

I've read the book about all the other England managers [*The Second Most Important Job in the Country*]. They were more or less killed, all of them. Why should I be different?
ERIKSSON, 2001.

If he should need any acclimatising, I'm here waiting on his call.
ULRIKA JONSSON, fellow Swede, when Eriksson became England manager – more than a year before their affair, 2001.

They were actually at it, naked in the middle of the day. I don't know who got the bigger shock, them or me.
MICHELLE SMITH, Ulrika Jonsson's nanny, claiming her employer had 'sex sessions' with the England manager, 2002.

Michelle told me that Sven is quite short and wears thick-soled shoes to make himself look taller.
TONY AZZOPARDI, boyfriend of Ms Jonsson's nanny, 2002.

My son having a romance with a weather-girl? I spoke to him this week and he talked as always about the weather, but not a weather-girl.
ULLA ERIKSSON, the England manager's mother, after reports of an affair between her son and Ulrika Jonsson, the former TV weather-forecaster, 2002.

I don't think it [Eriksson's affair with Ulrika Jonsson] will affect the respect he receives from the England players. If anything it could enhance it.
ARSENE WENGER, Arsenal manager, 2002.

Sven is my inspiration. It is through him that I understand the power of football.
NANCY DELL'OLIO, Eriksson's partner, shortly after the 'Ulrika affair' ended, 2002.

The Gulf War was a cakewalk compared with Eriksson's love life.
PAUL NEWMAN, FA head of communications and former BBC war correspondent, 2002.

It's no good lying in your bed at night wondering if you have made the right choice.
ERIKSSON at height of media speculation about whether he would choose Ms Dell'Olio or Ms Jonsson, 2002. He was writing in the sleeve notes of a CD of his classical-music favourites.

He is surprisingly attractive up close and bears a passing resemblance to Kevin Costner.
CHRISTA D'SOUZA, Daily Telegraph journalist, after interviewing Eriksson, 2001.

He can't resist a bird.
*ATHOLE STILL, Eriksson's
agent, quoted in Joe Lovejoy's
biography, 2002.*

Sven is probably the most
attractive person in the world
of football today for companies
to use in advertising... He is
an actor on the world scene
and we will charge a lot of
money for those who want to
use his name.
*LARS STERNMAKER,
Scandinavian head of the sports
marketing firm IMG, who also
declared Eriksson 'more
interesting than the Queen', 2002.*

What he has done is to
re-establish the self-
confidence, self-respect and
self-esteem of English
footballers and English
football – no bad thing.
*HOWARD WILKINSON, FA
technical director, 2002.*

We needed Winston
Churchill and we got Iain
Duncan Smith.
*ENGLAND DEFENDER,
anonymously alleging Eriksson
gave an 'uninspiring' half-time
talk during England's World
Cup defeat by Brazil, 2002.*

ALEX FERGUSON

You might as well talk to my
[baby] daughter. You'll get
more sense out of her.
*KENNY DALGLISH, Liverpool
player-manager, to a reporter
interviewing Ferguson after
bitter Liverpool v. Manchester
United match, 1988.*

He could be great fun with
his little quirks...for coming
out with the strangest of
things. A couple of Fergie-
isms were: 'Have you ever
seen a Pakistani funeral?' or
'Have you ever seen an Italian
with a cold?' You would be
left to ponder what he meant.
*PAT STANTON, Ferguson's
former assistant manager at
Aberdeen, in* The Quiet Man,
1989.

I don't think I ever saw Alex
smile. Even when United had
won 4-0 he would still have a
go at someone for not
defending properly or for
missing a chance.
*NEIL WEBB, Nottingham
Forest and former United
midfielder, 1993.*

He did [at Aberdeen] what he's still doing at United. He gave us a persecution complex about Celtic and Rangers, the Scottish FA and the Glasgow media; the whole West of Scotland thing. He reckoned they were all against us, and it worked a treat.
MARK McGHEE, Leicester manager and ex-Aberdeen striker, 1995.

I can meet ministers and monarchs and my children are not much impressed. But when we met Alex Ferguson they realised there was some point.
TONY BLAIR MP, Labour leader, 1995.

ALEX FERGUSON: Five hours' sleep is all I need.
INTERVIEWER: Like Margaret Thatcher.
FERGUSON: Don't associate me with that woman.
Exchange during press interview, 1995.

Alex always did have a hot temper. He'd have caused a fight in an empty house.
MARTIN FERGUSON, younger brother, 1995.

A strange bloke, irritated by everyone.
GARY LINEKER, 1996.

In the early days we named him The Hairdryer because he would come right up to your face and scream at you.
GARY PALLISTER, Manchester United defender, 1997.

He's very understanding when it comes to fellow managers. Unless you beat him.
FRANK CLARK, Manchester City manager, who had got the better of Ferguson with Nottingham Forest, 1997.

If there is an apology, it must be coming by horseback.
ARSENE WENGER, Arsenal manager, after Ferguson said he had apologised for the publication of off-record comments about Arsenal 'turning games into battles', 1999.

When we lose, he gets very angry. I don't understand him when he is speaking normally, so when he yells it's even more difficult.
MICKAEL SILVESTRE, United's French defender, 1999.

A magical manager, the greatest motivator there has ever been.
SIR BOBBY CHARLTON, United director, 1999.

A knighthood? He should get a sainthood.
RICHARD WILSON, aka Victor Meldrew, after United won the European Cup, 1999.

Apparently I'm allowed to hang my washing on Glasgow Green, which is an interesting one. And if I ever get arrested in the city, I'm entitled to my own cell, which could come in handy at some point.
FERGUSON on being made a freeman of his native Glasgow, 1999.

Lord Fergie, the best thing since sliced bread.
Inscription on medal offered to and rejected by Ferguson by Ken Bates, Chelsea chairman, after Charity Shield, 2000.

Kevin spends every minute of every day with us. There's no getting away from him. That's not something I can imagine happening with Sir Alex Ferguson at United.
GARY NEVILLE, England defender, during Euro 2000.

Of course they should give Fergie the England job. Give the rest of us a bloomin' chance.
JOE ROYLE, Manchester City manager, after Kevin Keegan left the England managership, 2000.

This is the toughest, meanest and most cussed competitor I've met in the whole of my football life. To be any use to him, you have to win.
STEVE BRUCE, Ferguson's former captain at Old Trafford, 2000.

When I see Alex, I'm always civil, but there's no exchange of Christmas cards. His book should have been a celebration of his achievements, something positive, but he chose to use it as something else. He had a different agenda.
GORDON STRACHAN, another of Ferguson's former captains, on the United manager's criticism of him in his autobiography, 2000.

I look upon him as a father figure, just like all the young players do who have grown up under his guidance. Maybe you're afraid of him at times but the main thing is we all have great respect for him.
DAVID BECKHAM, 2000.

Sometimes I wish I'd turned 60 that night in Barcelona. That could have been the final day of my career.
FERGUSON recalling the 1999 European Cup triumph, 2001.

It has got to the stage where Ferguson has even told us: 'Don't try to stay on your feet if you are in the box and get a slight kick.' He wants us to copy other sides we face in European competition and go down to win the penalty.
JAAP STAM in his autobiography Head To Head, *2001.*

He doesn't seem to have any problem spotting an opponent offside. He can see his watch all right when he wants to check the amount of injury time. How long before fans around the country see a

foul by United and set up the chant: 'Fergie didn't see it'?
BRIAN CLOUGH, after Ferguson claimed not to have seen the foul which led to Roy Keane being sent off v. *Manchester City, 2001.*

I can't stand Alex Ferguson.
DOROTHY ELLERAY, grandmother of referee David, defending him against criticism from the United manager, 2001.

I didn't see my sons grow up. Perhaps it is one of the big reasons I am leaving. I hope I can make up for lost time.
FERGUSON on announcing his intention to quit United, 2001.

He has spent too much time being a father figure to players like me, which has meant he has had less time for other areas of his life. I just hope the success that his dedication and sacrifice have brought is some compensation.
RYAN GIGGS, 2001.

I will certainly not be team manager. I think I've picked the right moment to retire but equally I'd love to stay on in any capacity which

doesn't interfere with the football...I'm actually looking forward to watching the team play without any managerial pressures.
FERGUSON, early December, 2000.

I'm definitely going. I won't be making any comebacks like singers do. I look at Bobby Robson [still managing Newcastle at 68] and think: 'Good luck to him.' But it's a decision me and my family have made. I want to enjoy a lot of other things.
FERGUSON, late December, 2000.

The decision has been taken – I'm going to leave the club... I had hoped there would be another role, but that's gone now.
FERGUSON, May, 2001.

The way I feel I don't think I'll change my mind about going at the end of the season. At the moment my mind is fixed on retiring. But you never know what might happen.
FERGUSON, late December, 2001.

I've said before that it's my intention to give up managing at the end of the season. There are powerful reasons for the decision and those haven't changed.
FERGUSON, early January, 2002.

The board has entered into discussions with Sir Alex and his advisers on a new contract.
Statement by United after Ferguson changed his mind, February, 2002.

Maybe the timing of my announcement that I was seeking a different kind of job with United was wrong, though I don't think my motive was. I simply wanted to give the club time to find the right replacement. But it is in the past, at least for the next three seasons, and we're all united again.
FERGUSON after signing his new contract, February, 2002.

I was worrying about what I was going to do at three o'clock on Saturday afternoons. I just couldn't see myself riding off into the sunset just yet.
FERGUSON after reversing his decision to retire, 2002.

When I had played 15 first-team games, I knocked on the gaffer's door, went in and told him I thought I deserved a club car like the other guys were getting. He just looked at me for a moment before shouting: 'Club car? Club car? Club bike, more like.' I've never been in there since.
RYAN GIGGS, 2002.

The first thing he always asked was: 'How much?'... And I'd say 'Look, Alex, it's only for a couple of minutes.' And he say: 'Yeah, well, how much will I get? I get £35 from STV when I do a thing for Scotsport, so how much from you guys?'
FRANK GILFEATHER, former Grampian TV journalist, on Ferguson's response to interview requests while Aberdeen manager, in Michael Crick, The Boss: The Many Sides of Alex Ferguson, *2002.*

He can spot a player a mile off and motivate people well. But his tactical acumen is negligible. If you have a fantastic horse the jockey doesn't have to be great.

MARK BOSNICH, Chelsea and former United goalkeeper, 2002.

His weakness is that he doesn't think he has any.
ARSENE WENGER, Arsenal manager, 2002.

Sir Alex is irreplaceable. I wondered whether I could work with anyone else.
DAVID BECKHAM after Ferguson changed his mind about retiring, 2002.

Alex Ferguson is a threat to my son. Sven told me it is pointless having England games in April or May because Ferguson, one way or another, makes sure his stars aren't fit.
ULLA ERIKSSON, mother of Sven-Goran, 2002.

I'm never really happy. If a player is 5ft 10in I think he should be 5ft 11in. That's the way I am.
FERGUSON, 2002.

GERRY FRANCIS

The transfer market's completely dead out there. I've even been phoning

myself up and disguising my voice just for a little bit of interest.
GERRY FRANCIS, Queen's Park Rangers manager, 2000.

TREVOR FRANCIS

Francis could not spot a great footballer if the bloke's name had four letters, started with 'P' and ended in 'e'.
ALAN HUDSON, former England midfielder, on the new Birmingham manager, 1997.

BARRY FRY

His management style seems to be based on the chaos theory.
MARK McGHEE, Wolves manager, as Fry managed nearby Birmingham, 1996.

Q: If you won the National Lottery, what would you buy?
A: 27 new strikers.
BARRY FRY, Birmingham manager, in programme Q & A, 1996.

Kirstine's out shopping as usual. I'm down the Job Centre looking for employment. Funny old game, innit?
FRY's answerphone message after Birmingham sacked him, 1996.

Someone said you could write Barry's knowledge of tactics on a stamp. You'd need to fold the stamp in half.
STEVE CLARIDGE, Birmingham striker during Fry's reign, 1997.

These days I no longer run down the touchline when we score. I just waddle a bit.
FRY, by now Peterborough manager, 2000. Fry had suffered two heart attacks and been told a third was usually fatal.

If I got as many points for football as I do for driving offences, I'd be in the Premiership by now.
FRY, Jaguar-driver, 2001.

BOBBY GOULD

He'd make a great double-glazing salesman. We had a meeting and by the end we thought: 'When's he going to sell us a new car?'
NEVILLE SOUTHALL, Wales

goalkeeper, after Gould became national manager, 1995.

I resigned as Coventry manager in the gents' toilet at QPR. This time I sorted out the terms of my departure in the dope-test room in Bologna.
BOBBY GOULD, quitting as Wales manager after 4-0 defeat v. Italy, 1999.

GEORGE GRAHAM

I remember George. He was a bit of a poseur at first, a bit lazy when he played up front, the last one you could imagine going into management. Different now. He has poseurs for breakfast.
FRANK McLINTOCK, captain of the 1971 Arsenal 'Double' side, on Graham's methods as manager at Highbury, 1992.

If ever there was a player I felt definitely would not have what it took to be a manager it was George Graham. Running a nightclub? Yes. A football club? Absolutely not.
DON HOWE, Arsenal coach during Graham's 1970s playing days, 1999.

I admit I'm single-minded. I think all of the great football managers have been single-minded.
GEORGE GRAHAM on the Arsenal players' nicknames for him – 'Ayatollah' and 'Gadaffi', 1991.

Mr Graham did not act in the best interests of the club.
Statement by Arsenal announcing their manager's dismissal, 1995. The Premier League found him guilty of accepting a 'bung' from agent.

The meeting with [agent Rune Hauge] was all very normal but the money came as a shock. I thought: 'Jesus, what a Christmas present. Fantastic.'...The ridiculous thing is it wouldn't have changed my life. I was on a good salary, but greed got the better of me. I'm as weak as the next man when it comes to temptation.
GRAHAM after being sacked by Arsenal, 1995.

He loved a 1-0 win, he really did.
STEVE BOULD, Arsenal defender, 1997.

I will always have Arsenal-red blood running through my veins.
GRAHAM, then manager at Highbury, in his autobiography, 1996.

In six months he said just two words to me: 'You're fired.'
TOMAS BROLIN, Leeds' Swedish international, 1997.

I came back last season with blond hair, and I think that did his head in.
LEE SHARPE, Leeds midfielder, 1999.

We are good friends but I wouldn't like to play for him again. I've told him that, but I think he reckons I'm joking.
TONY ADAMS, Graham's former captain at Arsenal, 1999.

People say he is ruthlessly professional. I would say he's professionally ruthless.
JOHN LUKIC, Graham's former goalkeeper at Highbury, 1999.

At least all the aggravation will keep me slim.
GRAHAM on encountering fan hostility at Tottenham because of his Arsenal background, 1999.

He's a gutless coward who will not stand up and admit he has made mistakes. Like Spurs fans, I got mugged into believing that this Adonis of the football world was the be-all and end-all in management skill and tactics.
ALAN SUGAR, former Tottenham chairman, on the last manager he appointed, 2001.

In my time at Tottenham I made lots of mistakes. The biggest was possibly employing him.
SUGAR, 2001.

RON GREENWOOD

There's only one thing better than getting an interview with Ron Greenwood. That's not getting one.
TONY FRANCIS, ITN reporter, 1981.

JOHN GREGORY

He handled the pressure brilliantly during our poor spell, except when he smashed the physio's bag across Goodison Park.
GARETH SOUTHGATE, Aston Villa captain, 2000.

I'm a much better manager than when I started, but not half as good as I will be.
JOHN GREGORY in his autobiography, The Boss, *2000.*

RUUD GULLIT

I was just as disappointed as Mandela.
RUUD GULLIT after a meeting with South African president Nelson Mandela had to be cancelled, 1997.

Ruud said very craftily today that he had asked for £2m. That's true and I immediately said: 'Gross?' And he said: 'No, netto. I always talk netto.'
COLIN HUTCHINSON, Chelsea managing director, 1998.

If you're a playboy and you're not there, you can't win the FA Cup and be second in the Premier League. That's impossible.
GULLIT answering Chelsea's reasons for sacking him, 1998.

You don't need to be Sherlock Holmes to realise Ruud was pushing his luck.
DAVID MELLOR, former Tory MP, broadcaster and Chelsea fan, 1998.

I always found him relaxed and easy to get on with, a good winner and a good loser.
ALEX FERGUSON on Gullit's demise, 1998.

It has become one big laugh between us, because she has told me, in all seriousness: 'I thought you were a poof!' Can you imagine it – Rudi, a poof!
GULLIT, on his partner Estelle Cruyff, in My Autobioraphy, *1998.*

Gullit told me within his first week that I was a bad player and he didn't want me here. When he went I had a little party.
ALESSANDRO PISTONE, Newcastle defender, 1999.

And I want to thank all the restaurants where I have been for their marvellous food and hospitality.
GULLIT in his resignation statement, 1999.

He's certainly big in the trouser department.
LISA JENSEN, Tyneside pizza-house waitress, claiming affair with Gullit, 1999.

Ruud loved conflict. He enjoyed being at loggerheads with certain players.
And he was just so arrogant. His ego was as big as Amsterdam and he didn't even try to disguise it.
ROB LEE, Newcastle midfielder, 2000.

On meeting Gullit, I could understand the accusations of arrogance. He was always amazingly friendly for about 20 seconds, then seemed completely to lose interest.
DAVID BADDIEL, comedian and Chelsea fan, 2000.

I once spent ages in a bar talking to a chap I thought was the pop singer Seal. I later found out he was

someone called Ruud Gullit.
LAWRENCE LEWELYN BOWEN, interior designer and TV personality, 2000.

RAY HARFORD

I'm going to be as natural as I can, by that I mean a right miserable bastard.
RAY HARFORD on taking over as West Bromwich Albion manager, 1997.

GLENN HODDLE

He's got a very, very tough persona, despite the fact that they used to call him Glenda.
PETER SHREEVES, Hoddle's assistant at Chelsea and his former manager at Tottenham, 1996.

You won't be surprised to know that I have some faith in astrologers and particularly what the stars predict for Scorpios.
GLENN HODDLE, by now England manager, 1998.

You and I have been given two hands, two legs and a half-decent brain. Some people have not been born like that for a reason.

HODDLE, arguing in the Times *interview which brought him down that people born disabled were being punished for sins in a previous life, 1999.*

Hoddle's attitude betrays a disabled mind. It seems he has no compassion, no allowance for weakness.
IAN DURY, handicapped singer and actor, 1999.

Had he stuck to football rather than theology he would have been playing on a better pitch.
RAY STIRLING, Hoddle's former father-in-law, 1999.

At the end of the Argentina game I found myself asking the same question again and again: 'Why am I here?'
HODDLE, England manager, World Cup finals, 1998.

My biggest mistake of the World Cup was not taking Eileen Drewery.
HODDLE, as the controversy over his faith healer continued after England's exit from the World Cup, 1998.

REPORTER: What's happening with Stewart Houston?
GLENN HODDLE: Wakey, wakey, alarm call. He left yesterday.
REPORTER: Sorry, Glenn. I was returning from Tirana with England yesterday. Some of us are still involved at international level.
Exchange at Tottenham press conference, 2001.

ROY HODGSON

My lasting memory of him is that he always had a runny nose.
DAVE MOGG, Bath City goalkeeper, after Hodgson, once his manager at Bristol City, took charge of Inter Milan, 1995.

BRIAN HORTON

It doesn't take a scientist to work out that when a team has lost 5-0, it's a bit strange if the centre-forward takes the bulk of the criticism.
NIALL QUINN on life under Horton at Manchester City, 1995.

GERARD HOULLIER

You don't need to have been a horse to be a good jockey.
GERARD HOULLIER, Liverpool manager, on his lack of top-class playing pedigree, 1999.

I have never spoken to him and never will. I could have killed him from hate, not for what he did to me but because he made the people I love cry.
DAVID GINOLA, recalling how Houllier called him 'a criminal' for a mistake which allegedly cost France a place in the 1994 World Cup finals, 1998.

They are two-faced and treat people like dirt.
PAUL INCE, former England captain, on Houllier and his No. 2, Phil Thompson, after leaving Liverpool for Middlesbrough, 1999.

He comes from France and I can't believe he has managed a team because he certainly doesn't know how to. It's okay coming out with all this technical stuff about the game, but when it comes to managing players off the field, as people, he hasn't got a clue.
INCE, 1999.

Sometimes in the morning before training, I wouldn't know whether to tell the missus to go and iron my old school uniform or get my tracksuit. Every day the Liverpool players were treated like kids.
INCE, 1999.

I wasn't disappointed with his comments because I know the man.
HOULLIER responding to Ince, 1999.

They call Houllier the French professor. Well if he really is going to fork out millions on [Emile] Heskey, I can only say I'm glad he wasn't the professor who operated on me when I was rattling the pearly gates.
ALAN HUDSON, former England midfielder, in his column for a Midlands newspaper, 2000.

I have been described as a French revolutionary with a guillotine, but I prefer to

convince people rather than dictate to them.
HOULLIER after leading Liverpool to a cup treble, 2001.

There are those who say maybe I should forget about football. Maybe I should forget about breathing. As Arnold Schwarzenegger said: 'I'll be back.'
HOULLIER during his recovery from heart surgery, 2002.

I've changed my routine since the heart surgery. I get in to work at 8.30am instead of 8.0.
HOULLIER on resuming his duties, 2002.

He's a very intelligent, rounded person, capable of dealing with different nationalities, finance and sports medicine. He fits exactly the profile of a top modern manager. He's also very modest. It's like Mrs Thatcher said: 'To be powerful is like being a lady; if you have to tell people you are, then you aren't.'
ANDY ROXBURGH, Uefa coaching official and ex-Scotland manager, 2002.

He's the most important man in the city.
PETER SISSONS, Liverpool-born TV newsreader, 2002.

DON HOWE

It was like finding Miss World was free and asking for a date.
BOBBY GOULD, Bristol Rovers manager, after Howe agreed to coach his side, 1986.

DAVE JONES

People in football and outside have been fantastic. I don't have to decorate my kitchen because it is covered in cards.
DAVE JONES on returning to management with Wolves after clearing his name of sex crimes in court, 2001.

KEVIN KEEGAN

God on the Tyne
Headline in FHM *magazine on Keegan interview, 1993.*

If Kevin Keegan fell into the Tyne, he'd come up with a salmon in his mouth.
JACK CHARLTON, one of

Keegan's Newcastle predecessors, 1995.

For the first time since I became leader, my children were impressed by something I did. 'Did you really meet Kevin Keegan, dad?' 'Did you really do 27 consecutive headers?'
TONY BLAIR MP, Labour leader, after sharing a photo opportunity with the Newcastle manager, 1995.

People are saying that Kevin leaving is like the Queen dying, but it's worse than that.
JOHN REGAN, secretary of Newcastle Independent Supporters' Association, after Keegan's resignation, 1997.

He wasn't tactically aware. He just had a charisma and used it to hide the deficiencies.
MALCOLM MACDONALD, former Newcastle striker, after Keegan left, 1997.

When Kevin broke into the squad he used to sit on my knee when we travelled away. I would pretend to be a ventriloquist and he would let me bounce him up and down on my knee.
TOM TAYLOR, journalist and father of ex-England manager Graham, on when Keegan started his career at Scunthorpe, 1999.

I'm glad it is not Ukraine because I'm not your man for a 0-0 in Kiev.
KEVIN KEEGAN after England drew Scotland in the play-offs for Euro 2000, 1999.

I don't sit down with boards and start painting pictures all over the place, it is not my style and I think the FA knew that when they appointed me. They saw a different style of management where we get people to play by getting into their minds and improve them that way.
KEEGAN after England qualified for Euro 2000 despite home defeat by Scotland in the play-offs, 1999.

He is feeding on rocket fuel. He's perfect to work with.
WATT NICOL, Scottish 'guru of self-motivation' after Keegan asked him to help inspire the England squad, 1999.

A lot of my time is taken up with thinking adventurously.
KEEGAN before Euro 2000.

Kevin has a lot of strengths but standing up to failure isn't one of them.
NOEL WHITE, FA international committee chairman, responding to Keegan's claim that he would resign if England did not win Euro 2000 [they did not].

I've told the players that that's me finished. I just feel I fall a little short of what is required in this job. I sat there in the first half and could see things weren't right but I couldn't find it in myself to solve the problem. In my heart of hearts, I'm not up to the job.
KEEGAN on resigning as England coach after defeat by Germany at Wembley, 2000.

The last thing I want is to be known as the man who lost the last game at Wembley.
KEEGAN after Germany beat England, 2000.

Some parts of the job I did very well, but not the key part of getting players to win football matches.
KEEGAN, 2000.

If Kevin is anything like I was, his first difficulty, the first problem to overcome, will be coming out of the house and facing people.
GRAHAM TAYLOR, one of Keegan's predecessors with England, 2000.

He walked away from the Newcastle job, he walked away from the Fulham job and he walked away from the England job. We'll have to wait and see if he'll walk away from the Manchester City job.
RODNEY MARSH, former City player and TV pundit, 2001.

HOWARD KENDALL

30,000 stay-at-home fans can't be wrong. Bring back attractive, winning football. Kendall out!
slogan on Everton Action Group banner, December 1985. In May, Kendall's team won the FA Cup;

*the following season they were
champions.*

JOE KINNEAR

I'm out at the moment,
but should you be the
chairman of Barcelona, AC
Milan or Real Madrid, I'll
get straight back to you.
The rest can wait.
*JOE KINNEAR's answerphone
message, 1995.*

Me and Joe are so close that
we will carry on living in the
same underpants.
*SAM HAMAMM, Wimbledon
chairman, after Kinnear's
departure as manager, 1999.*

GORDON LEE

I don't drink, don't smoke
and I'm getting fed up with
gardening. I've no interests
at all apart from football
and family.
*GORDON LEE on life after
losing the Everton manager's
job, 1981.*

BERTIE MEE

Bertie would be perfect in
today's game. All this stuff

about foreign coaching is
nonsense. What the majority
of managers do now is hire a
coach, discuss tactics and let
them get on with it. That is
what he did 30 years ago.
*GEORGE GRAHAM, Arsenal
player in Mee's Double-winning
side and later manager at
Highbury, in David Tossell's*
Seventy-One Guns, *2002.*

GARY MEGSON

No disrespect to Gary, but
anyone who knows him
knows he is the biggest
moaner in the world.
*NEIL WARNOCK, Sheffield
United manager, after his
West Brom counterpart alleged
Warnock had withdrawn two
players due to injury after having
three sent off, causing their match
to be abandoned, 2002.*

JOE MERCER

Look, son, imagine this huge
pot of money. Franny [Lee]
has had a bit, Colin [Bell]
has dipped in and of course
Malcolm [Allison] has had a
dollop. In fact all the lads
have had a bit. So there's
none left for you.

JOE MERCER, Manchester City manager of the 1960s, to a player seeking a pay rise, quoted in Fred Eyre's Another Breath of Fred Eyre, *1982.*

MICK MCCARTHY

The ref gave Arsenal a goal and as I turned around I saw this big furry microphone so I laid into it. I kicked it and it went spinning away like a boomerang before landing 20 yards away. Then the Sky touchline reporter came up to me and said: 'So Mick, you must be disappointed.'
MICK McCARTHY, Millwall manager, 1995.

You were a crap player, you're a crap manager. The only reason I have any dealings with you is that somehow you are manager of my country and you're not even Irish, you English cunt. You can stick it up your bollocks.
ROY KEANE, Republic of Ireland captain, to McCarthy during team meeting which led to Keane's being sent home from Japan on the eve of the World Cup finals, 2002.

MARK MCGHEE

He's fat, he's round, he's taken Leicester down.
Song by Reading fans aimed at their former club's manager, 1995.

I am fat. It's difficult not to get that way with my lifestyle, but the important thing is that it doesn't affect my golf swing.
MARK McGHEE responding to the taunts, 1995.

He's covering his backside in a way that takes the biscuit.
GRAHAM TAYLOR after being criticised by McGhee, his successor at Wolves, 1997.

ALLY MACLEOD

I think Ally believes tactics are a new kind of peppermint.
Scotland defender, who asked to remain anonymous, World Cup finals, 1978.

When you talk as much as he does none of it can mean very much.
RON GREENWOOD, England manager, 1978.

With a bit of luck in the World Cup I might have been knighted. Now it looks as though I might be beheaded.
ALLY MacLEOD after Scotland's World Cup failure, 1978.

TERRY NEILL

I read in the papers that Terry Neill says he's going to put the joy back in Spurs' football. What's he going to do – give them bloody banjos?
EDDIE BAILY, Bill Nicholson's former assistant manager, 1974.

BILL NICHOLSON

I did not enjoy dancing around, waving trophies in the air. I'm sure he [Nicholson] didn't like it either. His comments regarding success were always cold...I was embarrassed by the boasting around us but I escaped it with humour. He gruffed his way out of it. Our satisfaction was in doing the job.
DANNY BLANCHFLOWER, Nicholson's Double-winning captain at Tottenham, 1961.

EGIL OLSEN

He doesn't look like an international manager, but what does an international manager look like anyway? A wee baldy man with bad knees, like me?
CRAIG BROWN, Scotland manager, on the Norway and future Wimbledon manager, 1998.

We'll pass them to death, vows Olsen
'Headline you'll never see', Football365 website, 1999.

The Norwegian FA's highest honour is their gold award, which has only gone to three or four people before Egil. In nine years he took Norway from a land of eskimos to the No. 2 international team in the world. Normally the award goes to ex-presidents who are 176 years old.
LARS TJERNAAS, Wimbledon coach, on his manager's absence for a few days during their unsuccessful struggle against relegation, 2000.

A brain surgeon shouldn't have to work with peasants.
STALE SOLBAKKEN, Norwegian ex-Wimbledon player, on the club's sacking of Olsen, 2000.

WILLIE ORMOND

Willie never gave us talks about foreign teams because he couldn't pronounce their names. But once in Scandinavia he stopped us as we went out and said: 'Watch out for the big blond boy at set-pieces.' When we got out and looked across at them, there were about six big blonds. Well, we were playing Sweden.
Scotland defender, who preferred to remain anonymous, 1974.

DAVID O'LEARY

David O'Leary was one of those players we all looked up to. We'd go to him for advice as a senior pro and he was always willing to help. I must admit, though, when Frank McLintock said George Graham was the last player he expected to go into management, I thought the same about O'Leary.
IAN WRIGHT, former Arsenal team-mate, 1999.

The fans might have said: 'Clear off back to London with your mate' but the reception was brilliant so I thought: 'Right, I'll stay if they pick me.'
DAVID O'LEARY on why he changed his mind about not wanting to succeed George Graham as Leeds manager, 1998.

He used to think I was a boring old sod.
O'LEARY, recalling how he lectured his former Arsenal colleague Tony Adams on the dangers of drink, 1998.

David knows everything that's going on in football. He's Ceefax Dave as far as I'm concerned.
GORDON STRACHAN, former Leeds team-mate, 2000.

He almost wanted to attack me and he was extremely lucky he stopped short of that. I had four or five people with me and he would have faced a very humbling experience.

SAM HAMMAM, Cardiff chairman, after a confrontation with O'Leary after the clubs' FA Cup tie, 2002. Hammam's bodyguard was a convicted hooligan.

He wasn't my cup of tea. He was the kind of guy who would call you 'Top man', then put the phone down and probably hammer you. If there was someone more important in the room he would almost certainly make a beeline for them. The sort of man who will buy the chairman's wife a bunch of flowers at Christmas.
TONY CASCARINO, former Republic of Ireland colleague, 2002.

MARTIN O'NEILL

His obsession with Grantham Town was total, even when we were going to places like Bridgnorth to play before three men and a dog. What summed him up was that he once phoned me at one o'clock in the morning after we'd lost at Spalding to ask whether I thought their third goal was offside. When I told

him the time he said: 'Gerraway.' He was always saying that.
PAT NIXON, secretary of Southern League Grantham where O'Neill cut his managerial teeth, 2000.

I looked upon O'Neill as a bit of a smart-arse.
BRIAN CLOUGH, his manager at Nottingham Forest, in Clough: The Autobiography, *1994.*

Martin runs up and down the touchline quicker and more often than his No. 2, John Robertson, used to during his playing days at Nottingham Forest.
RON ATKINSON, television pundit and former manager, 2000.

I'm not even liked in my own household, so I'll be fine.
MARTIN O'NEILL on the prospect of abuse from Rangers' fans after becoming Celtic manager, 2000.

It takes one to know one. It seems to me that Martin O'Neill is losing his 'Mr Clean' image.

KEN BATES, Chelsea chairman, responding to the Celtic manager's suggestion that he was a 'footballing cretin', 2000.

Managing the football team is hard enough without going on to the board and deciding whether to sack myself or not.
O'NEILL on declining to become a Celtic director, 2001.

I will calm down when I retire or die.
O'NEILL on his manic touchline style, 2002.

CARLTON PALMER

I told the chairman that I'll keep the club in the First Division and if I don't I will look like a complete idiot.
CARLTON PALMER on becoming Stockport player-manager, 2001. The club were the first in Britain to be relegated.

Who's to say I won't be England manager in 10 years' time?
PALMER on the eve of Stockport's 10th successive defeat, 2002.

BOB PAISLEY

His great strength was that he knew something about everything...He could watch a game, even on television, and forecast that a player was going to have an injury, and invariably he would be right.
KENNY DALGLISH, former Liverpool player under Paisley, in Manager of the Millennium, by John Keith, 1998.

His smile was as wide as Stockton High Street. He had the nicest face in football.
BRIAN CLOUGH, former managerial adversary, on Paisley's death, 1996.

He has broken this silly myth that nice guys don't win anything. He's one of the nicest you could meet in any industry or walk of life.
CLOUGH, 1978.

Sponsors! They'll be wanting to pick the team next.
BOB PAISLEY at Liverpool, 1981.

DAVID PLATT

The Nottingham Playhouse hosted a David Platt in Conversation evening on 13 September. I kid you not. Forest could make a fortune flogging the tape to insomniacs.
Letter to the Daily Express *about the-then Forest manager, 2000.*

DAVID PLEAT

As the last man in Britain still sporting a quiff, David is used to things falling a bit flat after a promising start.
JIMMY GREAVES, former playing contemporary, as Pleat's Sheffield Wednesday dropped down the Premiership, 1995.

ALF RAMSEY

He's the most patriotic man I've ever met.
GEOFF HURST, Ramsey's World Cup-winning centre-forward, 1966.

I feel like jumping over the moon.
ALF RAMSEY, Ipswich manager, in an early (the first?) example of moon-jumping,
after his team clinched the championship, 1962.

I am not one to jump over the moon or off a cliff.
RAMSEY, by now England manager, 1967.

I suppose I'll have to get used to being addressed as 'Sir', but if a player gets formal on the field I will clobber him.
RAMSEY on being knighted, 1967.

REPORTER: Welcome to Scotland.
ALF RAMSEY: You must be fucking joking.
Exchange at Prestwick Airport when Ramsey arrived with England, 1968.

He is more careful of his aspirates than his answers.
ARTHUR HOPCRAFT, author, The Football Men, *1968. Ramsey had received elocution lessons.*

Alf was never one for small talk when he was with England parties [as a player]; football was his one subject of conversation. He was always a pepper-and-salt man,

working out moves and formations with the cruets on the table.
JACKIE MILBURN, former England team-mate, 1968.

We've all followed Ramsey. The winger was dead once you played four defenders. Alf saw that in '66 and it just took the rest of us a little longer to understand.
DAVE BOWEN, Wales manager, in Tony Pawson's The Football Managers, *1973.*

Ramsey recognised that the real strengths and values of English football were embodied not by Trevor Brooking, but by Nobby Stiles. Ramsey was right.
EAMON DUNPHY, media pundit and former Republic of Ireland player, 1981.

On the one hand, Alf had Geoff Hurst and Roger Hunt who could be relied upon to sweat cobs. On the other he had Jimmy Greaves, a fantastic finisher but a moderate team player. Alf did what he thought was best for the team. Mind you, if we'd lost, he would have been condemned for the rest of his days.
BOBBY CHARLTON looking back to England's World Cup triumph, 1991.

We talked Alf into letting us have a bit of sun [by the hotel pool]. He blew a whistle and we all lay down. Ten minutes later he blew it again and we all turned over.
JACK CHARLTON, former England defender, on the 1970 World Cup finals in Mexico, in Jeff Dawson, Back Home, *2001.*

CLAUDIO RANIERI

I am a lovely man as long as everyone does what I say.
CLAUDIO RANIERI on becoming Chelsea manager, 2000.

Driving a car in England is still a problem. If I am alone on the road I begin to ask whether I am driving on the right side. And when I go back to Italy I have started to wonder the same thing. It is confusing.
RANIERI, 2001.

HARRY REDKNAPP

I told my chairman that David O'Leary spent £18m to buy Rio Ferdinand from us and Leeds have given [O'Leary] £5.5m in share options, whereas I bring in £18m and all I get is a bacon sandwich.
HARRY REDKNAPP, West Ham manager, 2000.

I can't even work my video, so it's no good to me.
REDKNAPP on the launch of a pioneering system to take football transfers on to the internet, 2000.

PETER REID

He's a Cloughie for the millennium.
BOB MURRAY, Sunderland chairman, 1999.

If I lose two games on the trot here they are calling for my head. If I did that with England I wouldn't able to go out of the house.
PETER REID, Sunderland manager, ruling himself out after Kevin Keegan's departure, 2000.

DON REVIE

An utterly brilliant manager, but knotted with fear.
GARY SPRAKE, former Leeds goalkeeper, 1980.

If he had one chink in his armour it was that he probably paid teams more respect than they deserved. He should have just told us certain points and then told us to go out and beat them. Just left it to us.
NORMAN HUNTER, ex-Leeds defender, in An Alternative History of Leeds United, *1991.*

It makes me angry to hear criticism of a man who is working himself into the ground and trying all he knows to get things right for the England team.
DICK WRAGG, chairman of the FA international committee, defending Revie days before he jumped ship to Dubai, 1977.

Don Revie's appointment as England manager was a classic example of poacher turning gamekeeper.
ALAN HARDAKER, former Football League secretary, in Hardaker of the League, *1977.*

As soon as it dawned on me that we were short of players who combined skill and commitment, I should have forgotten all about trying to play more controlled, attractive football and settled for a real bastard of a team.
DON REVIE after resigning as England manager, 1977.

He was called greedy and deceitful but anyone who knows him knows he was just the opposite.
DUNCAN REVIE on his father, 1987.

He has been out of football 10 years but he still stops the traffic.
DUNCAN REVIE, 1987.

BOBBY ROBSON

I'm fed up with him pointing to his grey hair and saying the England job has aged him 10 years. If he doesn't like it, why doesn't he go back to his orchard in Suffolk.
BRIAN CLOUGH, 1983.

If the pressure had frightened me, I'd have kept my quality of life at Ipswich. I'd have kept driving my Jag six miles to work every day and got drunk with the chairman every Saturday night.
BOBBY ROBSON on calls for his resignation after England's failure at the European Championship finals, 1988.

Eighteen years as a professional player in Framham and West Bromwitch Albion...a manager for Ibswich...and England's managing job after the World Cup finals in Spain when Mr Wood Green retired.
Egyptian Gazette profile, 1989.

The Spencer Tracy of football.
Corriere Dello Sport, Italian newspaper, 1999.

We advise people of pensionable age to have fun and do whatever they want. If they want to manage a football team, that sounds great.
Help the Aged spokesman on the 66-year-old Robson's appointment by Newcastle, 1999.

On my way here I followed a car with the number plate SOS1. Perhaps someone was trying to tell me something.
ROBSON on his first day in the Newcastle job, 1999.

I intend to be at St James' Park as long as my brain, heart and legs all work... simultaneously.
ROBSON, 1999.

I bleed black and white.
ROBSON, 1999.

This is my love, my life, my drug, my motivation. Some managers have had enough at my age, but not me.
ROBSON before his 67th birthday, 2000.

BRYAN ROBSON

He's the only man I've ever known who could drink 16 pints and still play the next day.
PAUL GASCOIGNE on his admiration for Robson, who later became his manager at Middlesbrough, 1997.

ANDY ROXBURGH

Can you believe my luck? Scotland are in the World Cup finals and the guy who's in charge wears a wig and has a nose that could cut a wedding cake.
CRAIG BROWN, Scotland assistant manager, teasing his boss, 1990.

Roxburgh's a ned. Good on preparation, crap on football.
TERRY BUTCHER, Rangers and England defender, in Pete Davies, All Played Out: The Full Story of Italia 90, *1990.*

JOE ROYLE

I may be a Scouser but I'm not stupid.
JOE ROYLE, Manchester City manager, 1999.

I might have been the captain when we went down, but not when we hit the iceberg.
ROYLE on City's relegation to the Second Division, 1999.

JOHN RUDGE

Every game I go to, he's there with his 'bonnet' on. That's dedication. Port Vale should go down on their knees and thank the Lord for having him.
ALEX FERGUSON on the long-serving Vale manager, 1995.

I've been at Port Vale 16 years. Even the Great Train Robbers didn't get that long a sentence. Here you're manager, coach, chief scout, chief cook and bottle-washer. But I've loved every minute.
JOHN RUDGE, 1996.

RON SAUNDERS

RON SAUNDERS: Giving the boys the usual old rubbish, Ron?
RON ATKINSON: Yes, Ron. I was just telling them what a good manager you are.
Exchange during Atkinson press conference after a match between their teams, 1982.

LUIZ FELIPE SCOLARI

I wouldn't accept 50 trucks full of cash if they didn't let me appoint my own coaching staff.
LUIZ FELIPE SCOLARI, coach to Cruzeiro of Brazil, on his conditions for joining Barcelona before he eventually took charge of Brazil, 2001.

I will go down as the Brazil coach that lost to Honduras. It's horrible.
SCOLARI after Brazil's defeat in Copa America, 2001. The following year he led Brazil to World Cup triumph.

BILL SHANKLY

Football's not a matter of life or death. It's much more important than that.
BILL SHANKLY, Liverpool manager, 1964.

He's got a heart the size of a caraway seed.
SHANKLY on a player he transferred, 1968.

I don't drop players, I make changes.
SHANKLY, 1973.

I'm a people's man, a player's man. You could call me a humanist.
SHANKLY, 1970.

I've been so wedded to Liverpool that I've taken Nessie [his wife] out only twice in 40 years. It's time she saw more of my old ugly mug.
SHANKLY on his retirement, 1974.

I believe Bill Shankly died of a broken heart after he stopped managing Liverpool and saw them go on to even greater success without him. Giving your whole life to a football club is a sad mistake.
JOHN GILES, former Republic of Ireland manager, 1984.

A great man, a great manager and a great psychologist. He made you feel any mountain could be climbed.
KEVIN KEEGAN, a Shankly signing for Liverpool, 1998.

I'm glad he's not here now. He would have been devastated.

NESSIE SHANKLY, Bill's widow, as Liverpool struggled, 1993.

Shankly – He Made The People Happy.
Inscription on a bronze statue of Shankly at Anfield, 1990s.

PETER SHILTON

Peter Shilton would not know a footballer if he saw one. All he has ever been interested in is getting enough players back to protect his selfish hide.
ALAN HUDSON, ex-Stoke and England midfielder, on his former club-mate's managerial ambitions, 1991.

WALTER SMITH

Smith admits he is rarely at home of an evening and that his wife and family see him mainly in transit. His idea of relaxation is to pop in to watch Dumbarton Reserves.
BRIAN MEEK, Glasgow Herald columnist, 1991.

It always gets back to the same question for me. Could a former electrician

from Carmyle win the
European Cup?
*WALTER SMITH as Rangers
failed honourably, 1993.*

I didn't know Walter
personally. But I knew he
must be Scottish because I
used to see him carrying big
discount cases of lager back
from the supermarket.
*PAUL GASCOIGNE on his
first acquaintance with his
future Rangers manager in
Florida, 1995.*

GRAEME SOUNESS

What impressed me most
was his attitude – he wanted
to bring the best out of
people...In the heat of the
moment the gaffer has
knocked containers of orange
squash flying, brought a TV
set crashing to the floor and
damaged several dressing-
room doors.
*TERRY BUTCHER, Rangers
defender, in Both Sides of the
Border, 1987.*

Anyone who plays for me
should be a bad loser.
*GRAEME SOUNESS, on
becoming Liverpool manager, 1991.*

He came in raging about a
tackle by Denis Wise on Nigel
Clough. I had to tell him:
'Calm down, you've just had
a triple heart by-pass.'
*KEITH HACKETT,
Premiership referee, 1994.*

Souness labelled me negative
but if I strung defenders
across the park, his job was
to beat me, not moan about
my team.
*TOMMY McLEAN, Dundee
United manager, on his former
Rangers counterpart, 1997.*

At Rangers it was a case of
'my way is right'. Now I'm
more prepared to listen to
players' opinions though
that's not to say I'm not
still aggressive. I know that
has upset people in the past,
but I can't help that. It was
in the gene pool when I
got mine.
*SOUNESS, after becoming
Blackburn manager, 2000.*

My health is not a problem,
although who knows what's
going on inside – but if you
want a fight we can go out
on to the car park.
SOUNESS, who had undergone

major heart surgery, on taking
over at Blackburn, 2000.

I was so excited that I wasn't
sure whether my pills were
working properly.
SOUNESS after Blackburn drew
with Manchester United, 2001.

JOCK STEIN

John, you're immortal.
BILL SHANKLY, Liverpool
manager, to Stein in the Celtic
dressing-room after the European
Cup final triumph over Inter
Milan, 1967.

The greatest manager in the
history of the game. You tell
me a manager anywhere in
the world who did something
comparable, winning the
European Cup with a
Glasgow district XI.
HUGH McILVANNEY,
journalist, in his TV
documentary Busby, Stein
and Shankly: The Football
Men, *1997.*

Jock had everything. He had
the knowledge; he had that
nasty bit that managers must
have; and he could
communicate. On top of it

all, he was six feet tall, and
sometimes he seemed to get
bigger when he was talking
to you. He was the best.
GRAEME SOUNESS, former
Scotland captain, in Jock
Stein, the Authorised
Biography, *1988.*

GORDON STRACHAN

He was good but very
aggressive. Every ball he tries
to get back, so it was nice
entertainment for me. I beat
him once and next day he told
everyone: 'Never play tennis
with George because he cheats.
Every time he hits a winner he
thanks the Lord, so it's always
two against one.' I told him it
wasn't a very good joke.
GEORGE BOATENG,
Coventry midfielder, on his
tennis partner, 1999

We're used to our manager
signing players we've never
heard of. But now he is
signing them from countries
we've never heard of.
COVENTRY FAN on local-
radio phone-in after Jairo
Martinez arrived from
Honduras, 2001.

I know how people see me, but all my life I've been a victim of self-doubt. There have been many times when I have felt despondent, when I think I'm useless. I felt it many times as a player and I've often experienced it as a manager.
GORDON STRACHAN shortly before leaving Coventry, 2001.

GRAHAM TAYLOR

Graham was never a good player. He was always trying to hit the long ball.
RON GRAY, Taylor's former manager at Lincoln, 1992.

As a vision of the future it ranks right up there alongside the SDP and the Sinclair C5.
JOE LOVEJOY, football correspondent of the Independent, *on Taylor's intention to get England playing a more direct style, 1992.*

It was nearly my finest hour, but life is made up of so-nearlies.
GRAHAM TAYLOR after his England side surrendered a 2-0 lead to draw with the Netherlands, 1993.

Napoleon wanted his generals to be lucky. I don't think he would have wanted me,
TAYLOR after England failed to reach World Cup finals, 1993.

I can live with a newspaper putting a turnip on my head, except that it encourages people to treat me like shit.
TAYLOR, former England manager, on why he no longer attended England matches at Wembley, 1998.

If a journalist wrote that about me, he'd have to go into hiding.
JACK CHARLTON on the Sun's 'turnip' jibe, 1993.

I used to quite like turnips, Now my wife refuses to serve them.
TAYLOR, between jobs, 1995.

PETER TAYLOR

I'm not equipped to manage successfully without him. I'm the shop front, he is the goods at the back.
BRIAN CLOUGH, Derby manager, when he and Taylor still worked together, 1973.

We pass each other on the A52 going to work on most days of the week. But if his car broke down and I saw him thumbing a lift, I wouldn't pick him up. I'd run him over.
CLOUGH, by now managing Nottingham Forest while Taylor was in charge at Derby, after their falling-out, 1983.

PETER TAYLOR

He's very experienced. He's done his time. He's managed Dover Athletic.
JOHN GREGORY, Aston Villa manager, on Taylor's appointment as caretaker manager of England, 2000.

I was sitting there during the game thinking to myself: 'I can't believe this – I am manager of England.'
PETER TAYLOR, Leicester manager and England caretaker manager v. Italy, 2000.

PHIL THOMPSON

All Tommo does is shout his mouth off, he doesn't coach. A few years ago Tommo was slagging off the lads at

Liverpool as a TV pundit. He should realise that coaching is not about swearing at players, and that's all he does. I'd love to hear something constructive from him, but all you get is effing this, effing that.
PAUL INCE, England midfielder, after leaving Liverpool soon after Thompson's appointment as Gerard Houllier's deputy, 1999.

TERRY VENABLES

When I arrived in the summer, one of my predecessors told the Spanish press that Meester Terry would be gone by Christmas, but he forgot to say which year.
TERRY VENABLES, Barcelona coach, 1984.

The main thing I miss about London? The sausages.
VENABLES on life in Catalonia, 1984.

A lot of people seem to think I'm just a slippery Cockney boy with a few jokes. It's taken one of the biggest clubs in the world to acknowledge what I can really do: coach.

VENABLES on his initial success with Barcelona, 1985.

I can still go out as long as it's after midnight, I'm wearing dark glasses and it's a dimly lit restaurant.
VENABLES as Barca suffered the bad run that led to his sacking, 1987.

Tottenham without Terry is like Westminster without Big Ben.
PAUL GASCOIGNE reacting to Venables' sacking by Alan Sugar, 1993.

I must be the only person who actually gets less publicity by becoming manager of England.
VENABLES, newly appointed England manager, on controversy over his business dealings, 1994.

When we're away on holiday he obviously still thinks about what he's going to do because he doodles attack plans on napkins. All our newspapers are covered in crosses and arrows.
YVETTE VENABLES, the England manager's wife, 1995.

He's a great tactician, which is something I admire because I don't do tactics.
BARRY FRY, Birmingham manager, 1995.

I do not accept his evidence as totally reliable, to put it at its most charitable.
MR RECORDER WILLIAMS, giving judgement against Venables over an unpaid bill from his nightclub, Scribes West, 1995.

I was going to ask him what he thought of my idea for an El Tel theme nightclub called Wormwood Scribes, but I chickened out.
FRANK SKINNER, comedian, on meeting Venables, 1996.

People say I should concentrate on being a football person, but what does that mean? Get home in the afternoon and go to the betting shop, the pub and the snooker hall? All I've done is try to learn how to use a typewriter, Sorry about that!
VENABLES, 1998.

His conduct in relation to the four companies has been such as to make him unfit to be connected in any way with the management of a company.
ELIZABETH GLOSTER QC, representing the Department of Trade & Industry, after Venables was banned from company directorships, 1998.

Terry gave us an extra dimension in [Euro] 96. We had always had good technique – I'll argue that endlessly because I've played with enough top players to recognise it. We've just been a little bit slow up top. We were all heart and no brains but Terry started putting that right.
TONY ADAMS, Arsenal and England defender, 1999.

If there's a better coach than Terry Venables out there, believe me, he must be bloody good.
TONY CURRIE, former QPR midfielder under Venables, after his ex-manager took charge at Leeds, 2002.

JO VENGLOS

Jo was always the favourite in the back of my mind.
DOUG ELLIS, Aston Villa chairman, after appointing the Slovak as manager, 1990.

GIANLUCA VIALLI

You wouldn't trust a learner driver with a Formula One car.
FABIO CAPELLO, coach with various Italian clubs, on Vialli's surprise promotion to succeed Ruud Gullit at Chelsea, 1998.

He'll do well because he's a perfectionist. He's so fussy. If you went to his house you'd see everything laid out neatly: cushions, books, magazines. When you room with him, he'll open his case and he's got his little shirts and socks all tidy.
DENNIS WISE, Chelsea player, 1998.

I am addicted to pressure. When there isn't any, I don't give my best.
GIANLUCA VIALLI, Chelsea manager, after three successive defeats, 1999.

BERTI VOGTS

If people saw me walking on water you can be sure someone would say: 'Look at that Berti Vogts, he can't even swim.'
BERTI VOGTS, Germany coach, on mounting criticism of his style, 1996.

One thing I can bring to the job is that I have never been beaten by England as a manager.
VOGTS, newly appointed Scotland manager, 2002.

I can't see what Berti is attempting to do. Where are the tactics? Where is the discipline?
GUNTER NETZER, former Germany team-mate, after Scotland scraped a draw with the Faroe Islands in their sixth match without a win under Vogts, 2002.

For years Berti Vogts warned German football experts that there are no small football nations any more. But he was wrong: Berti and his Scotland team are now the tiniest football country.

BILD, German newspaper, after the Faroes debacle, 2002.

JOCK WALLACE

This city needed something to believe in, so I gave it me.
JOCK WALLACE, Leicester manager, 1980.

NEIL WARNOCK

When I'm doing an in-growing toenail operation, I find my patient talking to me and I'm not listening. At the end I say: 'I'm very sorry, Mrs Kirk, I was away – I was just picking the side for Saturday.'
NEIL WARNOCK, Scarborough manager and chiropodist, 1987.

I'd love to manage Wednesday. I'd buy so many tosspots – their current squad would do – and fuck 'em up so badly. Then I'd retire to Cornwall and spend the rest of my life laughing my fucking head off.
WARNOCK, Sheffield United manager, 2002. He later claimed he had been taken 'out of context' and denied including the current squad in his remarks.

ARSENE WENGER

I've got to play for a
Frenchman? You have to be
joking.
*TONY ADAMS, Arsenal
captain, recalling his initial
reaction to Wenger's arrival,
1997.*

At first I thought: 'What
does this Frenchman know
about football? He wears
glasses and looks more like
a schoolteacher. He's not
going to be as good as
George [Graham]. Does he
even speak English properly?'
Weeks later, I was still
insisting: 'He hasn't got
a clue.'
ADAMS, 1998.

He has put me on grilled
fish, grilled broccoli, grilled
everything. Yuk!
*IAN WRIGHT, Arsenal
striker, on Wenger's dietary
regime, 1997.*

He can explode, especially at
half-time, if we've been
playing badly and making
mistakes. But he is more like
a father getting angry with
his sons.
*EMMANUEL PETIT, Arsenal's
French midfielder, 1998.*

The Sigmund Freud of
football managers.
*LAURENCE MARKS, TV
sitcom scriptwriter and Arsenal
devotee, in* A Man For All
Seasons, *1999.*

He is a diplomat, a linguist
and listening to him is like
attending a university lecture.
Yet he is obsessed with
football. He knows so much.
When he bought Patrick
Vieira, all the people around
me at Highbury were saying:
'What a bloody idiot, he
should have bought Jason
McAteer.' Now, when Wenger
buys a player, the fans don't
criticise. They know he
must be right.
MARKS, 1999.

Mr Wenger's a very clever
man, but I have to say that
what he said is crap.
*PETER REID, Sunderland
manager, after his Arsenal
counterpart claimed an
opponent had helped get Patrick
Vieira sent off, 2000.*

Those people who complain about the fixture schedule should clear off to a country where they play fewer games.
DAVID O'LEARY, Leeds manager and ex-Arsenal defender, after Wenger bemoaned fixture congestion, 2000.

Arsene Wenger disappoints me when he is reluctant to give credit to Manchester United for what we have achieved. And I don't think his carping has made a good impression on other managers in the Premiership.
SIR ALEX FERGUSON, 2000.

Wenger has an English mind but also a German mind, which is very disciplined.
GLENN HODDLE, a Monaco player under Wenger in Myles Palmer's book The Professor, *2001.*

REPORTER: What are the differences between George Graham and Arsene Wenger?
TONY ADAMS: How long have you got?
Exchange at Arsenal press conference, 2002.

I call him the miracle worker. He makes an average player into a good player, a good player into a very good player and a very good player into a world-class player.
DAVID DEIN, Arsenal vice-chairman, after the Double was won, 2002.

RAY WILKINS

Ray has been at clubs like Milan where you have to wear a suit in bed, so he's very strict about the dress code.
DANIELE DICHIO, QPR striker, 1995.

HOWARD WILKINSON

When Wilkinson said last year that Wednesday were just two players away from being a championship side, I didn't realise he meant Maradona and Gullit.
Letter to Sheffield's Green 'Un, 1989. Wilkinson had recently joined Leeds.

There are bigger heads than mine in this division – Howard Wilkinson springs to mind.
BRIAN CLOUGH, 1991. He later apologised for the remark.

He disliked personalities who had a rapport with the fans.
ERIC CANTONA in Cantona: My Story, *1994.*

If ever I am reincarnated, I'd like to return as a personality.
HOWARD WILKINSON, Leeds manager, 1995.

I know it sounds nuts but for some reason I thought I was signing for Howard Kendall. He was the only Howard I had really heard of.
VINNIE JONES in Vinnie: The Autobiography, *1998.*

At the end of Wilkinson's team talks we'd be thinking: 'Eh?'
DAVID BATTY, England midfielder, on Leeds' former manager, 1999.

I'm healthy, I've got a house, I eat well. How can I be unhappy? There's thousands out there with none of those things.
WILKINSON, during a poor run at Leeds, 1993.

I've worked for the last three England managers and seen what I did to them. I saw Ron Greenwood break out in sores, Bobby Robson go grey and poor Graham Taylor double up in anguish and stick his head so far between his legs that it nearly disappeared up his backside. If I was single, with no kids, it'd be no problem. But I've a wife and three children and I've seen how this job can affect your family. It won't happen to mine.
HOWARD WILKINSON, Leeds manager, after Graham Taylor's exit, 1994. Wilkinson later took on the job as 'caretaker' on two occasions.

WALTER WINTERBOTTOM

Just because I play for England, he thinks I understand peripheral vision and positive running.
JIMMY GREAVES, Chelsea striker, on the then-England manager, 1960.

I'm as bad a judge of strikers as Walter Winterbottom – he only gave me two caps.
BRIAN CLOUGH, Nottingham Forest manager, 1988.

⑥
MANAGING

There are only two certainties in this life. People die and football managers get the sack.
EOIN HAND, Limerick and Republic of Ireland manager, 1980.

My brother always said you would have to be mad to be a manager. What other job is there where your livelihood depends on 11 daft lads?
FRANCIS LEE, Manchester City chairman, 1996.

Management is the only job in the world where everyone knows better. I would never tell a plumber, a lawyer or a journalist how to do his job but they all know better than me every Saturday...We have the absurd situation with an England manager [Kevin Keegan] who won European Footballer of the Year yet is branded by people, some of whom have never kicked a ball, as tactically naive.
JOE ROYLE, Manchester City manager, 2001.

Who wants to be out of management? Nobody. We all want to be there, winning and losing, reading in the papers that we don't know anything about football.
SVEN-GORAN ERIKSSON before England friendly with Mexico, 2001.

The face of the manager is a mirror to the health of the team.
ARSENE WENGER, Arsenal manager, 2002.

Football management these days is like nuclear war – no winners, just survivors.
TOMMY DOCHERTY, 1992.

We all end up yesterday's men in this business. You're very quickly forgotten.
JOCK STEIN, former Celtic manager, in Archie Macpherson, The Great Derbies: Blue and Green, *1989.*

When you're a football manager you don't have fitted carpets.
JOHN BARNWELL, Walsall manager, shortly before his sacking, 1990.

My son is a surgeon and makes life-and-death decisions every day. Yet I

think of my job as the most important imaginable.
DAVID PLEAT, Sheffield Wednesday manager, 1997.

Managing is a seven-day-a-week, almost 24-hour-a-day job. There's no rest or escape but I'm hooked on it.
BARRY FRY, Peterborough manager, 1999.

I'm not a politician, a social worker or clergyman. I'm a provider of distraction, and fans want to go home happy to whatever bores the arse off them during the week.
HOWARD WILKINSON, Leeds manager, 1994.

You have to have a bit of everything these days: coach, social worker, the lot. If Claire Rayner knew soccer, she'd be a great manager.
MICK McCARTHY, Millwall manager, 1995.

Every dressing-room should have a poster that says: 'There is more to life than just football and football management.'
GERRY FRANCIS, Bristol Rovers manager, 1988.

There are too many silly, unrealistic demands on a manager, and they can take the pleasure out of this job. He's a very influential person so he can expect a certain amount of criticism and blame. But you can't expect one man to be responsible for everything.
GRAHAM TAYLOR, Watford manager, 1999.

Being a manager means responsibility. It's an awful, thankless task most of the time. The only thing you get is that adrenalin rush you had as a player.
GARY LINEKER, when his ex-Everton team-mate and Sky TV presenter Andy Gray was reputedly offered the Everton manager's job, 1997.

I still miss playing. Management offers only second-hand thrills.
JOE ROYLE, Everton manager, 1997.

Playing was great. Managing was unrewarding and stupid.
GEOFF HURST, former England World Cup player and ex-Chelsea manager, 1991.

You think you're working hard when you're a player – and to an extent you are – but you really just have to look after yourself, physically and mentally. As a manager you can multiply all that by 14, which tells you how much tougher it is.
CRAIG LEVEIN, Cowdenbeath manager and former Scotland defender, 1999.

In the public's mind, players win games and managers lose them.
BRYAN ROBSON, Middlesbrough player-manager, 1995.

Managers get too much credit when things go well and too much blame when they go badly.
GRAHAM TAYLOR, England manager, 1993.

The nice aspect of football captaincy is that the manager gets the blame if things go wrong.
GARY LINEKER, former Leicestershire schools cricket captain, on being named England football captain, 1990.

In this job you get good and bad things said about you. The trick is not to spend longer thinking about one than the other. In the end they are both bollocks.
GRAHAM TAYLOR, Aston Villa manager, 2002.

A manager's aggravation is self-made. All he has to do is keep 11 players happy – the 11 in the reserves. The first team are happy because they're in the first team.
RODNEY MARSH, Manchester City striker, 1972.

There isn't another industry in the world where the employees still call the manager 'Boss' or 'Gaffer'. It's a throwback to the days of the Victorian mill-owners.
JON HOLMES, players' agent, in Colin Malam, Gary Lineker: Strikingly Different, *1992.*

If footballers think they are above the manager's control, there is only one word to say: 'Goodbye.'
ALEX FERGUSON, 1999.

In this business you've got to be a dictator or you haven't a chance.
BRIAN CLOUGH at Hartlepools, 1965.

When you're building a team, you're looking for good players, not blokes to marry your daughters.
DAVE BASSETT, Sheffield United manager, after buying Vinnie Jones, 1990.

My youngest daughter gets married on Saturday, which is more important to me than either job.
GRAHAM TAYLOR, Aston Villa and soon-to-be England manager, 1990.

One thing I have learned about management is that you don't fall in love with players.
TAYLOR, by now England manager, 1992.

To me there's no point in having confrontation for the sake of it. Look at Ruud Gullit. Can you tell me that he was a shrewd manager in what he did to Rob Lee, who was captain of Newcastle and Alan Shearer's best mate? Why make problems for yourself?
HARRY REDKNAPP, West Ham manager, 2000.

I've told my players never to believe what I say about them in the papers.
GRAHAM TAYLOR, Aston Villa manager, 1988.

I'm like a dad to my players, mixing small tellings-off with a lot of love.
GORDON STRACHAN, Coventry manager, 1999.

Q: Who is your closest friend at the club?
A: I am the manager. I have no friends.
STRACHAN in Coventry programme Q&A, 1999.

Q: Best mates at the club?
A: Managers have very few.
JOHN RUDGE, Port Vale manager, in programme Q & A, 1993.

As a manager you're like a prostitute – you depend on other people for your living.
STEVE COPPELL, Crystal Palace manager, after

controversial refereeing decision in his club's FA Cup defeat by Hartlepool, 1993.

Being a football manager is a thankless, hopeless task. It's a dreadful job and most of them can be seen on the brink of madness or deep depression.
GARY LINEKER on why he went into the media rather than management, 1999.

My wife says: 'If you're going to get ill, get wet pyjamas in the night, then pack it in.'
DAVID PLEAT, Sheffield Wednesday manager, 1997.

There are grounds where you know you'll get covered in spittle and you wear your old clothes.
DAVE BASSETT, Sheffield United manager, after Wolves' Graham Taylor was abused at Bramall Lane, 1995.

Losing is like experiencing a death in the family. For a while there is no comfort in anything.
JOHN GREGORY, Aston Villa manager, 1999.

I always enjoy the summer. You can't lose any matches.
ROY EVANS, Liverpool manager, 1997.

It's like being in the middle of an oven.
BOB PEARSON, Millwall manager, after stepping from the post of chief scout into a long run of defeats, 1990.

It was like being in the dentist's chair for six hours.
HOWARD WILKINSON, Leeds manager, after tense match v. Leicester, 1990.

I feel raped.
RAY GRAYDON, Walsall manager, after 4-1 defeat by Crewe, 1999.

No one, unless they manage a team, can know how I feel. No one – not an assistant manager, a player, anyone. They haven't a clue.
GORDON STRACHAN, Coventry manager, after home defeat v. Middlesbrough, 2000.

If you're obsessed with winning and you don't do it, you end up a lunatic.
STRACHAN at Coventry, 1998.

When you win you feel 25 years old. When you lose you feel more like 105.
GORDON LEE, Leicester manager, after 5-2 defeat v. Swindon, 1991.

The world looks a totally different place after you've won. I can even enjoy watching *Blind Date* or laugh at *Noel's House Party*.
GORDON STRACHAN, Coventry manager, 1996.

You wait a lifetime for a feeling like tonight.
ALEX FERGUSON after Manchester United's first title success in 26 years, 1993.

It's the best day since I got married.
FERGUSON after winning at Sheffield United, 1992.

I think my team are trying to kill me.
JOE ROYLE, Oldham manager, after nerve-wracking but successful fight to stay in the Premiership, 1993.

If it meant getting three points on Saturday I would shoot my grandmother. Not nastily, I would just hurt her.
BRIAN CLOUGH on life at the foot of the Premier League with Nottingham Forest, 1992.

If I became a manager the first thing I'd do is buy a bottle of Grecian 2000.
CHRIS WADDLE, former England player, 1997.

Welcome to the Grey Hair Club.
KEVIN KEEGAN in message to John Aldridge when he became player-manager of Tranmere, 1996.

The plan is to get out of management while I've still got all my marbles and all my hair.
JOE ROYLE, Manchester City manager, 2000.

We really go through it on the bench. Last night when we were 2-1 up and Cambridge got a couple of late corners, the others were all laughing at me because I was curled up in a ball in the corner of the dug-out saying : 'I hate this job.'
BRIAN LITTLE, Leicester manager, 1993.

I love football but I positively hate being a manager.
LOU MACARI, West Ham manager, 1989.

If you don't get uptight, you're either a saint or you don't care. And there aren't many who don't care.
DON HOWE, England coach, before suffering a heart attack, 1988.

How can anybody call this work? People in the game don't realise how lucky they are. You drive to the ground, play a few five-a-sides, then have lunch. It's wonderful, enjoyable fun.
RON ATKINSON, Aston Villa manager, 1993.

No crowd, no money – sometimes I ask myself why I do the job.
JOE KINNEAR, Wimbledon manager, 1997.

It's getting to the point where I'm ready to swear.
RAY GRAYDON, Walsall manager, after defeat at Charlton, 1999.

I'm convinced a big-name manager will actually top himself soon.
PROFESSOR TOM CANNON, stress expert, 1997.

I was there the night Jock [Stein] died in Cardiff, and I know where Bobby [Robson] is coming from, but I want to go when I'm in bed with my beautiful young wife.
GRAEME SOUNESS, Blackburn manager, after Robson talked of the possibility of a manager dying from stress, 2001.

It doesn't matter whether you're successful, moderate and hopeless, whether it's Peterborough United and Manchester United, the pressure follows you around like a monkey on your back.
BARRY FRY, Peterborough manager, 1999.

You are under pressure in war zones, not in football.
ARTHUR COX, Derby manager, 1993.

Stress is when you have no money and are living on the street, or lying in hospital

fighting for your life. Stress is being bottom of the league. This is pure joy.
RUUD GULLIT on life as Chelsea player-manager, 1997.

Pressure to me is being homeless or unemployed. This isn't pressure, it's pleasure.
ANDY ROXBURGH, Scotland coach, after losing 17 players from his squad to face Germany, 1993.

Pressure goes with the job, whether you're spending £3m or £30,000.
PHIL NEAL, Bolton manager and former Liverpool team-mate of Kenny Dalglish's, 1991.

Five grand a week? That's my kind of pressure.
LOU MACARI, Birmingham manager, after Kenny Dalglish's shock departure from Liverpool, 1991.

I happen to like the aggravation that goes with football management – it seems to suit my needs.
GRAEME SOUNESS on succeeding Dalglish as manager at Anfield, 1991.

My cardiologist tells me that for some people, what I do would represent pressure. For others, pressure is going home and sitting in front of *Coronation Street* with your slippers on. I would find that very stressful.
SOUNESS, by now Blackburn manager, 2001.

I've learned how to relieve managerial stress. When the ball gets into your last third, avert your eyes. Turn to your physio, ask for chewing-gum, have a few words about the match. Anything. It stops the tension building up. You might miss a goal, but someone will always tell you how it happened.
BILLY BINGHAM, Northern Ireland manager, 1992.

I close my eyes every time the ball comes near our penalty area.
JOHN TOSHACK, Real Madrid coach, on his erratic goalkeeper Albano Bizarri, 1999.

You want to try sitting in the dug-out when it's your arse in the bacon-slicer.
MICK McCARTHY, Republic

*of Ireland manager, on being
told by a reporter that he had
'looked tense' during World Cup
game v. Saudi Arabia, 2002.*

Some do it by smoking hash,
others by making love or
racing a rally car. We managers
experience extremes all the
time. You can find yourself at
the highest point or the lowest
ebb in the same week.
*ARSENE WENGER, Arsenal
manager, 2002.*

I can feel when I'm ready to
lose it. Then I get my things
and go home. I read a book
for an hour or watch TV and
come back a different man.
It's what I call experience.
WENGER, 2002.

I always thought managers
were more involved. But
when it comes down to it, I
just sit there and watch like
everyone else.
*KEVIN KEEGAN in his early
days at Newcastle, 1993.*

We've lost seven games 1-0
and drawn another seven 0-0.
If we'd drawn the 1-0 games
we lost, we'd have another
seven points. If the seven

draws had been 1-0 to us,
we'd have 28 points more
and we'd be third in the
Premiership instead of
going down.
*ALAN SMITH, Crystal Palace
manager, sliding towards
relegation, 1995.*

As I mulled it over on the
bus, reliving every kick, I
could hear the players
laughing and playing cards.
They soon forget, but it's a
seven-day punishment for
managers.
*ANDY KING, Mansfield
manager, 1994.*

As manager, it's your head
on the block. You have to
make cold-blooded decisions
and if you can't, you
shouldn't be in the job. To
be honest, I found it difficult
to be a bastard.
*TERRY BUTCHER, former
Coventry and Sunderland
manager, 1994.*

I've heard it said that you
can't be a football manager
and tell the truth. Well I'm
going to have a go at it.
*LIAM BRADY, newly appointed
Celtic manager, 1991.*

When I was appointed manager of Stoke the first phone call I received was from Joe Mercer, then with Aston Villa, offering his congratulations. He told me: 'My advice is never to trust anyone in the game, and when I put down the phone don't trust me either.'
TONY WADDINGTON, former Stoke manager, 1990.

Lots of times managers have to be cheats and con men. We are the biggest hypocrites. We cheat. The only way to survive is by cheating.
TOMMY DOCHERTY, manager of numerous clubs, 1979.

There are two types of people who succeed in coaching: the conman and confidence trickster, or the intelligent man who builds your confidence and belief. I'm the conman.
MALCOLM ALLISON on becoming chief coach to Bristol Rovers aged 65, 1992.

You hope and you pretend that you know what you're doing.
KEVIN KEEGAN, newly appointed Newcastle manager, 1992.

The buying and selling of players sounds rather like a slave market. Moreover, the payment of large transfer fees can be the refuge of the incompetent manager.
SIR NORMAN CHESTER, chairman of committee examining English football's problems, 1968.

The power managers, like Brian Clough, Alex Ferguson and, up to a point, myself are beginning to drift out of the game. Alex can take negotiations about 85 per cent of the way, but there are very few like him. Things have changed.
GEORGE GRAHAM, Tottenham manager, 2000.

There are no bungs in football. With my so-called reputation, I would be the one they approached. I deal with most managers, most clubs and I've never been asked for or offered a bung. Fact.
ERIC HALL, players' agent, 1995.

When Leeds sacked me, all my worries about pensions and bringing up three kids were gone, and I became a better manager.
BRIAN CLOUGH on his £90,000 'golden handshake' from Leeds 16 years earlier, 1990.

The richest managers are the ones who have failed and got a pay-off.
BOBBY GOULD, Coventry manager, on why he worked without a contract, 1993.

You've never really been a manager until you've been sacked.
BRIAN HORTON on replacing Peter Reid as manager of Manchester City, 1993.

There's only two types of manager. Those who have been sacked and those who will be sacked in the future.
HOWARD WILKINSON, Leeds manager, 1995.

Every manager gets sacked, but it's better to be sacked by Real Madrid than any other club.
JOHN TOSHACK, on becoming Real's coach for a second (short-lived) spell, 1999.

Ninety-nine per cent of managers that lose their jobs deserve it.
MARK McGHEE, Wolves manager, 1996.

I told the chairman that if he ever wants to sack me, all he has to do is take me into town, buy me a meal, a few pints and a cigar, and I'll piss off.
MICK McCARTHY, Millwall manager, 1995.

The manager picks the team but invariably it's the punters who pick the manager.
ALAN BALL on the 'get rid of the manager' syndrome after leaving Manchester City, 1996.

Managers are like fish. After a while, they start to smell.
GIOVANNI TRAPATTONI, Fiorentina coach, confirming his departure, 2000.

A manager can smell the end of his time. The whole club reeks of an imminent sacking. Not that they actually say: 'You're bloody fired!' It's all innuendo and muttering – 'Things aren't going well, are they?' But you know they're

after your blood, and if truth were told you've already had your bag packed for weeks.
ROY SPROSON, former Port Vale manager, 1988.

I stood up and was counted.
ROGER HYND on being sacked as Motherwell manager, 1978.

How ironic that I should have been sacked on the anniversary of the Coventry blitz. When the chairman phoned me, I felt like my house had been bombed.
JOHN SILLETT on his dismissal by Coventry, 1991.

King Louis XVI had his head cut off in the French Revolution. It's the same for managers.
JEAN TIGANA, Fulham manager, pondering possible dismissal during a long run without a win, 2002.

You just have to wait for someone to suffer the same misfortune as you. It's the only job where you can study the vacancies on Teletext as they happen.
GRAHAM TURNER, Hereford United manager, 1995.

When the TV people asked whether I'd play a football manager in a play, I asked how long it would take. They told me 'about 10 days', and I said: 'That's about par for the course.'
TOMMY DOCHERTY, 1989.

It's me in the electric chair now.
BOBBY COLLINS on succeeding Norman Hunter as Barnsley manager, 1984.

I had to go. Towards the end I felt like a turkey waiting for Christmas.
FRANK CLARK, after leaving the Nottingham Forest manager's job, 1996.

Remember that film *A Bridge Too Far*? Well I probably came a game too far.
GERRY FRANCIS after leaving the QPR manager's job following a 5-0 defeat by Wimbledon, 2001.

Football is about now, it's about your contract...we're in the age of instant solutions and the job of being manager is set in that context. You could argue, given the

demands today, that you don't want to be at a club more than three years.
HOWARD WILKINSON, former Leeds manager, 1999.

You have to be a masochist to be an international manager.
ARSENE WENGER, 1998.

The England job should be the best in the world but it's become a horrible job. To think of my children getting hammered in the school playground because their dad is England manager. Perhaps we should be looking for a guy who's divorced with no kids.
GLENN HODDLE, then Chelsea player-manager, 1994. Within two years he had taken charge of the national team.

I wouldn't take the England job for a big gold clock.
STEVE COPPELL, former Crystal Palace manager, 1993.

The only way I'd be interested in the England job is as player-manager.
RON ATKINSON, Aston Villa manager, 1993.

As England manager you know that you're probably the most hated man in the country, apart from the Chancellor [of the Exchequer].
OSSIE ARDILES, Tottenham manager, ruling himself out of the running, 1993.

Even the Pope would think twice about taking the England job.
ROY HODGSON, Switzerland manager, 1993.

The England manager has to fight the system and fight the press from day one.
HOWARD WILKINSON, Leeds manager, 1993.

There's no difference between coaching England and coaching Newbury Town. The reason is that they're all blokes. There are England blokes, Manchester United blokes, Arsenal blokes and Newbury blokes. You are coaching men, human beings.
DON HOWE, who worked with both the England squad and his local Isthmian League part-timers, 1994.

I'm the man for the job. I can revive our World Cup hopes. I couldn't do a worse job, could I?
SCREAMING LORD SUTCH, leader of the Monster Raving Loony Party, on why he should succeed Graham Taylor as England manager, 1994.

Football managers are treated like the proverbial football. Unfortunately, instead of being passed around, they get a real good kicking.
GRAHAM TAYLOR on leaving Watford (of his own volition), 2001.

Managers are treated as public property, as if we do not have feelings or families. People feel we can cope and are impervious to hurt.
MARK McGHEE, Wolves manager, 1997.

After a few years, managing in England is like working for the weather forecast office. You know when a storm is coming.
ARSENE WENGER, Arsenal manager, 1999.

One person who thinks it is ridiculous that I earn so much money from football is my grandmother. She never understood you get so much from kicking a ball. So every time I go to see her she gives me £5 or £10.
SVEN-GORAN ERIKSSON, England manager, 2002.

Just because a coach comes from overseas, it doesn't mean he's a tactical genius.
TONY ADAMS, former England captain, cautioning against expecting too much from Sven-Goran Eriksson, World Cup finals, 2002.

We get carried away with coaching and coaches. I have my coaching badges but they came out of a Cornflakes packet.
HARRY REDKNAPP, West Ham manager, 2001.

Coaching is for kids. If a player can't pass and trap the ball by the time he's in the team, he shouldn't be there in the first place. At Derby I told Roy McFarland to go out and get his bloody hair cut. Now that's coaching at the top level.

BRIAN CLOUGH *after retiring as Nottingham Forest manager, 1994.*

Many people think a coach accounts for around 80 per cent of a team's results, but I'd say it's more like 15 per cent.
SERGIO CRAGNOTTI, *Lazio president, after Sven-Goran Eriksson's departure, 2000.*

Fulham Football Club seek a Manager/Genius.
Newspaper advert, 1991.

Charisma comes from results, and not vice-versa.
CRAIG BROWN, *Scotland manager, 1996.*

It would've taken a brave man not to wear brown pants after comparing our team-sheet with theirs.
NEIL WARNOCK, *Notts County manager, after playing Arsenal, 1991.*

I always say I'll get over it when I grow up, but there are no signs of it happening yet. I still find it impossible to drive past any sort of match. I've got to stop and watch it.

CRAIG BROWN, *Scotland Under-21 manager, 1988.*

The greatest thing about being a manager is when you're out on the training pitch with your players. No phones, agents, media or directors, just you and a group of players committed to improving themselves.
GRAHAM TAYLOR, *Watford manager, 1999.*

Players don't want to retire and be managers any more. They want to be the director of football; that's definitely the one to have. Pick your games, keep an eye on the rest, no real pressure. Come in on a Saturday, sit in the boardroom, nice cup of tea, gin and tonic. Say: 'Well this is the way I'd do it. Anyway, I'm off.' Meantime, the manager sits on the bench, screaming and shouting like an idiot. I know which I'd rather have.
HARRY REDKNAPP, *West Ham manager, 1995. In 2001 he became director of football at Portsmouth before accepting their managership a year later.*

Great teams don't need managers. Brazil won the World Cup in 1970 playing exhilarating football, with a manager they'd had for three weeks. What influence can a man have who has only been with them that length of time? What about Real Madrid at their greatest? You can't even remember who the manager was.
DANNY BLANCHFLOWER, former Tottenham captain, in his Sunday Express *column, 1972.*

The Monday after we won at West Brom I received 193 calls from assorted media and well-wishers. I even got a call from my first wife's parents, which surprised me seeing as they hadn't bothered to ring in the 15 years since our divorce.
GEOFF CHAPPLE, manager of non-League Woking, on the enduring power of the FA Cup, 1992.

It may sound selfish but I want to dedicate this triumph to my dog, who died two years ago.
CARLOS BIANCHI, Boca Juniors coach, after his team won the Treble in Argentina, 2001.

You could have Mickey Mouse in charge of the team on Saturday. You could stick a bucket out there with a mop in it or a snowman with a carrot for a nose. It wouldn't matter because no one needs motivating for a match like this.
IAN ATKINS, Carlisle manager, before the Third Division club's FA Cup tie v. Arsenal, 2001.

I've come from caviar to fish 'n' chips. At Spurs you can buy daft. At Leicester I have to buy sensibly.
DAVID PLEAT, Leicester manager, 1987.

I haven't seen the lad but he comes highly recommended by my greengrocer.
BRIAN CLOUGH on signing Nigel Jemson from Preston, 1988.

My favourite politician was Margaret Thatcher. She was a bugger but she would have made the best football manager. John Major was all right. He just had a bad team.
RON ATKINSON, former manager, 1999.

The easiest team for a manager to pick is the Hindsight XI.
CRAIG BROWN, Scotland manager, 1998.

The last manager who led this club to the FA Cup semi-finals [Archie Macauley in 1959] ended up as a traffic warden in Brighton.
DAVE STRINGER, Norwich manager, on reaching the last four, 1989.

I'm going to go out and get lambasted on wine.
MARTIN O'NEILL, Leicester manager, after his team won the Coca-Cola Cup, 1997.

We will worry about the final later. Now is the time for wine and cigarettes!
KLAUS TOPPMOLLER, Bayer Leverkusen coach, after his team reached the Champions' League final at Manchester United's expense, 2002.

Funny how other managers always want to swap one of their reserves for your best player.
MURDO MacLEOD, Partick Thistle manager, on exchange deals, 1996.

7
THE GAME

The beautiful game I love so well, the game I live to play.
PELE in his autobiography
My Life and the *Beautiful*
Game, *1977.*

Football is fashionable. Political parties jockey to enlist football men to their cause; celebrities and glamorous women speak openly and at length about their love for football; and literary critics pepper their erudition with references to 'the beautiful game'.
JOHN WILLIAMS, lecturer at the Sir Norman Chester Institute for Football Research, Leicester University, 1998.

Football is bankrupt without the TV deals. If the banks ever withdrew, you would see a bigger collapse than Black Monday.
SIR JOHN HALL, Newcastle chairman, 1995.

The great fallacy is that the game is first and foremost about winning. It's nothing of the kind. The game is about glory. It's about doing things in style, with a flourish, about going out and beating the other lot, not waiting for them to die of boredom.
DANNY BLANCHFLOWER, former Tottenham captain, in Hunter Davies' book The Glory Game, *1972.*

See the boy Rudyard Kipling, who said it wasn't whether you won or lost but how you the played the game that mattered, well he obviously never played football. Winning is the only thing that matters.
ANDY GORAM, Rangers and Scotland goalkeeper, 1996.

The fair play gave me goose pimples. Everyone respected each other. It was beautiful.
SEPP BLATTER, Fifa general-secretary, after West Germany v. *England, World Cup semi-final, 1990.*

Everything is beautiful [in English football]. The stadiums are beautiful, the atmosphere beautiful, the cops on horseback beautiful. And the crowds respect you.
ERIC CANTONA on making a strong early impact at Leeds, 1992.

The most beautiful game is winning matches.
GLENN HODDLE, Chelsea manager, 1995.

I would rather play ugly football and win than play beautifully and lose.
MARIO ZAGALLO, Brazil coach, 1997.

Thank you for letting me play in your beautiful football.
ERIC CANTONA accepting the PFA Player of the Year award, 1994.

It was beautifully done. It was wrong but it was necessary.
JACK CHARLTON, former England defender, commenting as a TV pundit on a 'professional foul' in Barcelona v. Dusseldorf game, 1979.

You feel so good, so comfortable, so powerful when you win. If you don't win, it's terrible.
MARCEL DESAILLY, Chelsea and France defender, 2000.

It's the greatest game in the world. It is also the most frustrating, exasperating, infuriating, desolating game. But there is nothing else.
KEN BATES, Chelsea chairman, 1995.

Soccer is the biggest thing that's happened in creation, bigger than any 'ism' you can name.
ALAN BROWN, Sunderland manager, 1968.

Football. Bloody hell.
ALEX FERGUSON to TV interviewer moments after Manchester United had won the European Cup with two last-gasp goals v. Bayern Munich, 1999.

There is a God up there. I love Margaret Thatcher, Ken Livingstone and everybody. It's not Rwanda, it's not Bosnia and it's not Ethiopia. It's crazy, it's wonderful. It's football.
MICHAEL KNIGHTON, Carlisle chairman, after his club again avoided relegation from the League on the season's final day, 2000.

Football is loved by everyone, everywhere, because it has no definitive truth.
MICHEL PLATINI, former France captain and manager, 1998.

People are always kicking, old or young. Even an unborn child is kicking.
SEPP BLATTER. Fifa secretary-general, 1990.

Football is a battle, a small war, and sometimes players do stupid things. You can't expect 22 players to behave like Sunday-school boys. You have to remember they are human.
SVEN-GORAN ERIKSSON, England manager, 2002.

Football became popular because it was considered an art, but now too many pitches are becoming battlefields.
SOCRATES, Brazil captain, 1981.

Football's like war. When the chips are down, you need fighters.
IAN BRANFOOT, Southampton manager, 1991.

Football doesn't matter a damn...It used to be a game, now it's a war.
ANTHONY BEAUMONT-DARK MP, Conservative, 1991.

Football is a damn sight more important than arty-farty people pushing themselves around the Royal Opera House.
TERRY DICKS MP, Conservative, 1990.

Football is the opera of the people.
STAFFORD HEGINBOTHAM, Bradford City chairman, 1985.

Football as popular culture is a space of intertextuality.
RICHARD HAYNES, author, The Football Imagination: The Rise of Fanzine Culture, *1996.*

Football is a game and people have to be cunning.
RIVALDO, Brazil midfielder, after admitting he had feigned injury to get an opponent sent off in World Cup match v. *Turkey, 2002.*

Football's a rat race – and the rats are winning.
TOMMY DOCHERTY, 1982.

League football is a rat race of the first magnitude.
BOB LORD, Burnley chairman, 1968.

Football is a much more cynical game all round than cricket.
PHIL NEALE, Lincoln defender and Worcestershire cricketer, 1982.

Football is self-expression within an organised framework.
ROGER LEMERRE, France coach, 1999.

Football is a permanent orgasm.
CLAUDE LE ROY, Cameroon coach, 1998.

Football is a pantomime of pain and disappointment.
NICK HANCOCK, Stoke City supporter and TV celebrity, 1999.

Football and cookery are the two most important subjects in the country.

DELIA SMITH, television chef, after becoming a Norwich City director, 1997.

Football has become the religion of the 20th century... its fervour, enthusiasm, battle cries, violence and flags have replaced the wars of yesteryear.
Editorial in the French newspaper Le Figaro – *by its literary critic, 1998.*

Football is like a flower. When you attack, the flower is open and in bloom. Defend and the flower closes.
TOMMY SODERBERG, Sweden coach, 2000.

Football is a simple game made complicated by people who should know better.
BILL SHANKLY, Liverpool manager, 1968.

Football is a simple game. The hard part is making it look simple.
RON GREENWOOD, England manager, 1978.

If Kurt Cobain [Nirvana singer who committed suicide] had played football,

he'd probably still be alive today...Football has given me the simplicity that I'm always trying to find...It doesn't solve anything between men and women, but I think it can solve most things between men and men.
DAMON ALBARN, Chelsea fan and singer with Blur, 1995.

What the fuck is art? A picture of a bottle of sour milk lying next to a smelly old jumper? What the fuck is that all about? And look at opera. To me it's a load of shit. But people love it. I'd say football is art. When I watched France *v.* Holland at Euro 2000, I was orgasmic.
JOHN GREGORY, Aston Villa manager, in Loaded *interview, 2000.*

Fishing and nature, especially birds, I have loved, although the one passion of my life has been football – the most exhilarating game I know, the strongest protest against selfishness, without sermonising, that was ever put before a thoughtful people.
JOHN GOODALL, England player of the late 19th century, in

Andrew Ward and Anton Rippon's book The Derby County Story, *1983.*

We've all heard that Einstein is a genius but few of us are in a position to judge. Football is one of the few areas of life where, even if you're untutored, you can go to a ground, see George Best beat three men and you can realise: 'I have seen a genius.'
SIMON KUPER, writer on world football, 1999.

No player, manager, director or fan who understands football, either through his intellect or his nerve-ends, ever repeats that piece of nonsense: 'After all, it's only a game.' It has not been a game for 80 years; not since the working-classes saw in it an escape route out of drudgery and claimed it as their own.
ARTHUR HOPCRAFT, author, The Football Man, *1968.*

Football is meant to be enjoyed and I still enjoy it, but I probably enjoyed it more at 15. The finer points disappeared when England

won the World Cup in 1966. Now the object is not to get beat at all costs.
ALAN GILZEAN, Tottenham and Scotland striker, in Hunter Davies' The Glory Game, *1972.*

Even if George Orwell's Big Brother is ruling us in 1984, people will still be talking about football.
NEIL FRANKLIN, Stoke and England defender, in Soccer At Home and Abroad, *1956.*

Football in Britain could not be in a sorrier state. Sport is dying. The future lies in culture, spirituality and religion.
ROBERT MAXWELL, millionaire publisher and chairman of various clubs, 1990.

Twenty-two grown men chasing a piece of leather round a field.
BERNARD LEVIN, English journalist, describing English football in the New York Times *after the Hillsborough disaster, 1989.*

I jolly well hoped that they would keep hold of me so I would never have to hear about the blasted game again.
TERRY WAITE, former hostage in Lebanon, on his dislike of football, 1999.

The culture of the 1990s can be summed up by *Neighbours* and football.
SPIKE MILLIGAN, comedian, 1999.

Sport is an unfailing cause of ill will, and if the visit of Moscow Dynamo had any effect at all on Anglo-Soviet relations, it could only be to make them worse.
GEORGE ORWELL, in the socialist Tribune *newspaper, 1945.*

If this is what soccer is to become, let it die.
Editorial in L'Equipe, *French sports paper, after 39 spectators died following trouble at the European Cup final, 1985.*

If somebody is celebrating it means we still have much to learn.
GIORGIO CARDETTI, Mayor of Turin, after Juventus beat Liverpool in the European Cup final, 1985.

All that I know most surely about morality and the obligations of man, I owe to football.
ALBERT CAMUS, French philosopher, novelist and goalkeeper for Oran of Algeria, 1957.

I believe that sport is on the highest possible plane...as something above real life.
DAVE SEXTON, Manchester United manager, 1980.

There were plenty of fellers [in the 1950s] who would kick your bollocks off. The difference between then and now is that they would shake your hand at the end and help you look for them.
NAT LOFTHOUSE, former Bolton and England centre-forward, 1986.

I would kick my own brother if necessary. That's what being a professional is all about.
STEVE McMAHON, Liverpool and England midfielder, 1988.

All I want you to do, son, is see how fast their centre-forward can limp.
JOHN McGRATH, Port Vale manager and former rugged centre-half, to one of his defenders, 1981.

It's the first time that we've had to replace divots in the players.
RON ATKINSON, Manchester United manager, after European match against a rugged Valencia side, 1982.

The tackling in international football is frightening. Even a nation like the Swiss, who aren't noted for their ruthlessness, have joined in.
GEOFF HURST, assistant to England manager Ron Greenwood, 1981.

Nobody ever won a tackle with a smile on his face.
BRUCE RIOCH, Bolton manager, 1994.

Men like me we're never a danger anyway. It wasn't that we were desperately late, just a little slower in getting there.
CHRIS KAMARA, Sun columnist and former midfield hard man, 1999.

Players like Barry Horne and Peter Nicholas have always knocked opponents down, but now they have learned the old Norman Hunter trick of shaking hands and helping them up. In the old days, we would knock them down and then want to fight them. In fairness I would probably be the leader of the pack.
TERRY YORATH, Wales manager, 1991.

In open play I don't think I would use gamesmanship, but if someone went through with just the goalkeeper to beat and I could catch him by bringing him down, I would bring him down. If I didn't, I'd feel I'd let my team-mates and my fans down.
BRYAN ROBSON, Manchester United and England captain, in David Hemery, The Pursuit of Sporting Excellence, *1986.*

I've played my last match, scored my last goal and elbowed my last opponent.
MARTIN DAHLIN, Swedish international striker, announcing his retirement, 1999.

When I called my midfield the 'Dogs of War', it was done half-jokingly. But the game has changed: the playmaker who stands on the ball and sprays it everywhere after five pints and a cigar in the pub simply doesn't exist any more.
JOE ROYLE, Everton manager, 1995.

Brazil don't expect Zico to tackle back. It might be worth England taking a chance on a midfield player whose principal asset is not his lungs.
PETER SHREEVES, Tottenham coach, in defence of Glenn Hoddle, 1982.

Tackling is better than sex.
PAUL INCE, England midfielder, 1998.

The only thing I miss about football is that feeling you get in the 10 seconds after you've scored, when you completely lose your head. I wouldn't say it's better than sex, but it's a close call.
LEE CHAPMAN, former striker with 10 clubs, 1999.

For me, the ball is a diamond. If you have something that precious you don't get rid of it, you offer it.
GLENN HODDLE on signing for Monaco, 1988.

People keep on about stars and flair. As far as I'm concerned you find stars in the sky and flair at the bottom of your trousers.
GORDON LEE, Everton manager, 1974.

When I was manager at Tottenham there was one player who could not pass the ball to a white shirt. It looks to you like I'm exaggerating, but in a proper game, under pressure, controlling the ball was not easy for him.
OSSIE ARDILES, former Tottenham manager, 1995.

His problem was that they kept passing the ball to his wrong feet.
LEN SHACKLETON, former England player, recalling an unidentified team-mate, 1955.

It took me 16 years to realise that football is a passing game and not a dribbling game.
JIMMY HILL, television presenter and ex-Fulham forward, 1974.

[Sven-Goran] Eriksson goes on about pace but nothing and nobody can run faster than the ball.
LUIZ FELIPE SCOLARI, Brazil coach, after his team beat England, World Cup finals, 2002.

Our game is being crippled by the law-makers. Those out-of-touch people who think players should not be allowed to tackle or talk for the period of 90 minutes.
IAN WRIGHT, former England striker, after a weekend of 15 red cards in the English league, 1999.

I start from the principle that the more you shout at each other [during a match], the better you play.
FABIEN BARTHEZ, Monaco and France goalkeeper, 2000.

Attack and be damned.
DAVID PLEAT, Luton manager, 1982.

All-out attack mixed with caution.
JIM MCLAUGHLIN,
Shamrock Rovers manager, on
his tactics for a European Cup
game, 1985.

There's no rule to say a game can't finish 9-9.
GRAHAM TAYLOR, Watford
manager, after 7-3 defeat at
Nottingham Forest, 1982.

It only takes a second to score a goal.
BRIAN CLOUGH, Nottingham
Forest manager, 1984.

If you dinnae score, ye dinnae win.
JIMMY SIRREL, Notts County
manager, 1983.

Strikers win you games, but defenders win you championships.
JOHN GREGORY, Aston Villa
manager, 1998.

The secret of winning championships? Good players working hard.
GEORGE GRAHAM after
managing Arsenal to the title, 1991.

If you don't start belting that ball out of our penalty area, I'll get some big ignorant lad who can do the job better.
BRIAN CLOUGH to defenders
Colin Todd, Roy McFarland and
David Nish after Birmingham v.
Derby game, 1973.

No footballer of talent should play in the back four.
MALCOLM ALLISON,
manager with various
clubs, 1975.

It's a lot easier to rip the picture up than to paint it. I've spent my career ripping the picture up. I can kick the ball high into the stand and people say: 'Oh, great defending.'
RICHARD GOUGH, Everton
captain, 1999.

A goalkeeper is a goalkeeper because he can't play football.
RUUD GULLIT, 1997.

I'm looking for a goalkeeper with three legs.
BOBBY ROBSON after
Newcastle goalkeeper Shay Given
was twice nutmegged by Marcus
Bent of Ipswich, 2002.

I'd be the ruination of the game if I got my way. All I want to see is goalies keeping clean sheets. And that's not what the fans want, is it?
ALAN HODGKINSON, former England keeper and Scotland goalkeeping coach, 1996.

The goalkeeper is the jewel in the crown and getting at him should be almost impossible. The biggest sin in football is to make him do any work.
GEORGE GRAHAM, Leeds manager, 1997.

The penalty is the one thing goalkeepers don't fear, because they can't lose. If it is scored, no one blames him. If he saves it, he's a hero.
DAVE SEXTON, Queen's Park Rangers manager, on the Wim Wenders film The Goalkeeper's Fear of the Penalty, *1975.*

A penalty is a cowardly way to score.
PELE, whose 1,000th goal came from the penalty spot, 1966.

I know only one way to take penalties: to score them.
ERIC CANTONA in La Philosophie de Cantona, *1995.*

I asked the players who wanted to take a penalty and there was an awful smell coming from some of them.
MICK McCARTHY, Millwall manager, after victory in a shoot-out, 1995.

It is not possible to play football with your pants full.
ERNST DOKUPIL, Rapid Vienna coach, after defeat by Manchester United, 1996.

Any player not inspired by that atmosphere should go off and play golf with his grandmother.
CLEMENS WESTERHOF, Nigeria coach, in Boston during the World Cup finals, 1994.

Angels don't win you anything except a place in heaven. Football teams need one or two vagabonds.
BILLY McNEILL, Manchester City manager, 1983.

If you threaten certain spiv players, you must carry it out and not let them get away with it. A football team only has 11 players. It just needs one bad 'un to affect the rest. In ICI, with thousands and

thousands of people, you can afford to carry scoundrels. Not in a football team.
BRIAN CLOUGH, Brighton manager, 1973.

Players are a strange breed. If everything is going smoothly they are happy to take the plaudits and rewards which come with success. But once results start going wrong they look for an excuse or someone to blame.
RON ATKINSON, TV summariser and former manager, 1999.

They're squeezing the entertainment out of football now. Footballers with no character and referees behaving like Nazis. Fucking basketball on grass now, innit?
VINNIE JONES, by now a film actor, 1999.

You ought to get a bunch of clowns if you just want entertainment.
ALAN DURBAN, Stoke City manager, answering critics of his team's negative display at Arsenal, 1980.

Over the past 10 years a myth has grown up that football should in some way strive to be entertaining. Sport is not entertainment. It's an activity for the benefit of the participants. If you run away from that fact, you risk having the wrong pipers calling the tune.
HOWARD WILKINSON, Leeds manager, 1990.

The game almost broke the health of a highly intelligent man like Joe Mercer. It cut George Best off at adolescence. It has the power to destroy because it releases unnatural forces. It creates an unreal atmosphere of excitement and it deals in elation and despair and it bestows these emotions at least once a week.
MALCOLM ALLISON, manager, in Colours Of My Life, *1975.*

When the Queen came to the Bahamas, I told her – and football is not her favourite pastime: 'Ma'am you must realise that people live for this game.'
SIR JACK HAYWARD,

*Bahamas-based owner of
Wolves, 1994.*

Acting is the easiest thing in
the world. You just do it and
do it until you get it right. It's
not like being a footballer,
where you ruin everyone's
week if you get it wrong.
GARY LINEKER, 1999.

I'm sure Sunday-morning
players get more pleasure
than professionals.
*JIMMY PEARCE, Tottenham
winger, in Hunter Davies'* The
Glory Game, *1972.*

I never say I'm going to play
football. It's work.
*MIKE ENGLAND, Tottenham
and Wales player, in* The Glory
Game, *1972.*

We looked bright all week in
training, but the problem
with football is that Saturday
always comes along.
*KEITH BURKINSHAW,
Tottenham manager, 1983.*

I asked the manager for a ball
to train with. He couldn't
have been more horrified if
I'd asked for a transfer. He
told me they never used a ball

at Barnsley. The theory was
that if we didn't see it all
week, we'd be hungry for it
on Saturday. I told him that
come Saturday, I probably
wouldn't recognise it.
*DANNY BLANCHFLOWER,
Tottenham captain, recalls his
first English club, 1961.*

I am grateful to my father for
all the coaching he did not
give me.
*FERENC PUSKAS, Hungary
captain, 1961.*

Everywhere I go there are
coaches. Schoolmasters telling
young boys not to do this
and that and generally scaring
the life out of the poor little
devils. Junior clubs playing
with sweepers and one and a
half men up front, no
wingers, four across the
middle. They are frightened
to death of losing, even at
their tender age, and it
makes me cry.
*ALEC STOCK, former manager
with several clubs, in* A Little
Thing Called Pride, *1982.*

I'm uncoachable, it's true.
That's because I know more
than the stupid coaches.

GIORGIO CHINAGLIA, New York Cosmos striker, 1979.

I don't think the average English fan knows much about coaching. I don't believe we are a coaching nation.
DARIO GRADI, Crewe Alexandra manager, 1999.

You have to coach the players' minds...get them to understand the need for sacrifice.
ALEX FERGUSON, Manchester United manager, 1999.

You just cannot tell star players how they must play and what they must do when they are on the field in an international match. You must let them play their natural game...I have noticed that in recent years these pre-match instructions have become more and more long-winded while the ability of the players has dwindled.
STANLEY MATTHEWS in The Stanley Matthews Story, *1960.*

I've given him carte blanche, as Ron Greenwood used to say, though I didn't use that phrase in the dressing-room. Told him to go where he likes.
GEOFF HURST, Telford player-manager and former England striker, in Brian James' Journey To Wembley, *1977.*

If the tacticians ever reached perfection, the result would be a 0-0 draw, and there would be no one there to see it.
PADDY CRERAND, Manchester United and Scotland midfielder, 1970.

You need an O level or a degree to understand the tactics at Old Trafford.
GORDON HILL, Derby winger, after leaving Dave Sexton's Manchester United, 1978.

Some of the jargon is frightening. They talk of 'getting round the back' and sound like burglars. They say 'You must make more positive runs' or 'You're too negative', which sounds as if you're filling the team with electricians.
BOB PAISLEY, Liverpool manager, 1980.

Another feature of England training is 'mime practice'. As you jog round you go through all the motions without the ball that you do when you have the ball. You trap, pass, volley, head for goal, head clear and weight imaginary passes. All that is missing is the ball.
PHIL NEAL, Liverpool and England defender, in Attack From the Back, *1981.*

I'm very keen on a maxim by the American Football coach Vince Lombardi: the only place where winning comes before work is in the dictionary.
HOWARD WILKINSON, FA technical director, 2000.

I sat in my car one day, first in line when the traffic lights changed. I stopped and instinctively everyone behind stopped in sequence. I realised that football was that simple. My team played a marvellous eight-man move last week and one of the kids shouted: 'Traffic lights!' I could have kissed him.
ALAN BALL, Portsmouth youth coach and former England World Cup winner, 1983.

The world's best 11 players wouldn't make a team. You must have blend.
LEN SHACKLETON, former England player, in Clown Prince of Soccer, *1955.*

Everybody likes each other. It's not like we're all friends, but it's a good team. You can have 11 enemies in a team and still win.
SANDER WESTERVELD, Netherlands goalkeeper, at Euro 2000.

Team spirit is an illusion that you glimpse only when you win.
STEVE ARCHIBALD, Barcelona and Scotland striker, 1985.

It's amazing what can be achieved when no one minds who gets the credit.
HOWARD WILKINSON, Sheffield Wednesday manager, on the value of teamwork, 1982.

If I had wanted to be an individual I would have taken up tennis.
RUUD GULLIT after the Netherlands' European Championship triumph, 1988.

But you cannot have enjoyed it. There were so many mistakes, so much unprofessional play.
SIR ALF RAMSEY, England manager, to journalist enthusing over a five-goal match between Stoke and Liverpool, quoted in The Football Managers, *1973.*

You sit there and moan at them for not having it. Then you remember that if they did have it they wouldn't be playing non-League football.
RAY WILKIE, Barrow manager, 1991.

The pitch was playable. I've been in football over 25 years and it has become a game for poofters.
JOHN BURRIDGE, veteran Manchester City goalkeeper, after his match was postponed, 1995.

Could I point out that the gay Stonewall FC's third XI played a West End League fixture on a Somme-like afternoon in Regent's Park on Sunday, thereby challenging [Burridge's] theory that sexual orientation has any connection with getting muddy knees.
Letter to the Independent, *1995.*

I always thought golf was a poof's game. Now I prefer it to football.
JULIAN DICKS, West Ham defender, 1998.

It's hard to be passionate twice a week.
GEORGE GRAHAM, Arsenal manager, on the physical demands of the English game, 1992.

Hump it, bump it, whack. That may be a recipe for a good sex life, but it won't win us the World Cup.
KEN BATES, Chelsea chairman, after England's failure to qualify for the World Cup under Graham Taylor, 1993.

Make it simple, make it accurate, make it quick.
ARTHUR ROWE, manager of Tottenham's push-and-run side of the 1950s, on his football philosophy, 1975.

The good player keeps playing even without the ball. All the time he is placing himself so that when the ball comes to him he is able to make good use of it. We improved the English saying

of 'Kick and run' to 'Pass accurately and move into a good position'.
FERENC PUSKAS, Hungary player, on his country's 6-3 win v. England at Wembley, 1953.

People who talk of short passes and on-the-ground moves as the essence of good football do not help the progress of football in Britain.
STAN CULLIS, Wolves manager, defending his 'scientific kick-and-rush football' in All For the Wolves, 1960.

Our failure has not been because we have played the British way, but because we haven't. Football should be open, honest, clean, passionate. Part of a nation's culture, its heritage. And the English way is with passion, commitment.
GRAHAM TAYLOR, manager of 'long-ball' exponents Watford, after England's World Cup exit, 1982.

Possession and patience are myths. It's anathema to people in the game to say this, but goals come

from mistakes, not from possession.
TAYLOR as Watford established themselves in the top division, 1982.

The Watford controversy is going to become the England controversy, because that is the way we are going to be instructing at coaching courses from now on.
CHARLES HUGHES, FA head of coaching, 1982.

I can't watch the long-ball teams like Wimbledon, Watford and Sheffield Wednesday. Football wasn't meant to be run by two linesmen and air-traffic control.
TOMMY DOCHERTY, 1988.

People who talk about sophisticated football don't know what they're talking about. To me, the more shots you can get, the more times you threaten the opposition keeper, the better chance you have of winning. Is that any different at international level than on a Sunday park? I happen to believe that it's not.
GRAHAM TAYLOR, by now England manager, 1991.

Because I'm a British centre-forward they expect me to be heading the ball all the time.
IAN RUSH, Welsh striker, during his season with Juventus, 1987.

A pass rising a yard above the ground should be a foul. A player receiving a pass has two feet and only one head.
WILLIE READ, St Mirren manager, 1959.

Balloon ball. The percentage game. Route one. It has crept into the First Division. We get asked to loan youngsters to these teams. We don't do it. They come back with bad habits, big legs and good eyesight.
RON ATKINSON, Manchester United manager, on the long-ball game, 1984.

If God had meant football to be played in the air, he'd have put grass in the sky.
BRIAN CLOUGH, Nottingham Forest manager, 1992.

If current trends continue, it'll be a game of 6ft 10in defenders heading the ball back and forth with 6ft 11in forwards.
JOHN CARTWRIGHT, former director of the FA National School, on his fears over the prevalence of the long-ball game, 1992.

My philosophy is to play in their half of the pitch. Get the ball in behind them. Get the buggers turning, turning, turning. When you've done that enough times, holes will open up, and one of our fellas, whoever's nearest, gets to the ball first. And then all the rest pile in.
JACK CHARLTON, Republic of Ireland manager, 1988.

We don't favour a passing game [at Crewe] because of any moral principles, but because it's the best way to play. If bashing the ball were the best way, we'd do it.
DARIO GRADI, Crewe Alexandra manager, 1999.

Most of the players are too young, too small or not giving 100 per cent.
TOMMY TAYLOR after leaving the Leyton Orient manager's job, 2001.

The first time I came to England, I said to myself: 'Without a doubt, football was created here!'
ARSENE WENGER, Arsenal's French manager, 2002.

Sometimes now, when I watch the continental matches on TV, I'm a bit bored. I'm thinking: 'Where's the intensity?'
WENGER, 1998.

I've never seen so much violence on the pitch as in England. Before certain matches, I'm scared an opponent might harm me.
FRANK LEBOEUF, Chelsea's French defender, 1999.

I spent five years playing non-League football for Wealdstone. If Frank [Leboeuf] thinks the Premiership is hard, he should see what goes on there. Referees had to protect me from the wingers I was marking.
STUART PEARCE, England defender, 1999.

It's rubbish to suggest that fair play in England is dead. I'm not siding with or against Leboeuf. But some people might question what he is about as a player.
PETER WILLIS, former president of the Referees' Association, 1999.

I have watched football all over the world and can assure you that there is more fair play and fewer stoppages in the Premiership than anywhere else.
GERARD HOULLIER, Liverpool's French manager, disagreeing with Leboeuf, 1999.

It's a bit of a nancy game now. And if Leboeuf isn't too happy, he should go home. Anyway, spitting is the vilest thing in the world, and the Vieira lad and some other foreigners have brought that with them.
TOMMY SMITH, former Liverpool defender, 1999.

Why is it that so many foreign players are queuing up to come here if our football has so many faults? I don't hear Gianfranco Zola

complaining about the English game.
GORDON TAYLOR, players' union leader, responding to Leboeuf, 2000.

I'm committing wicked fouls that would have horrified me six months ago. That's how you have to play in England...Going for a high ball I use my elbow or I'm dead.
THIERRY HENRY, Arsenal and France striker, 2000.

This is a man's game – unless the FA want us to walk out carrying handbags and wearing lipstick. 'Chopper' Harris and Tommy Smith wouldn't have lasted two minutes the way the game is run today.
PAUL INCE, Middlesbrough midfielder, 2001.

Guys like 'Chopper' Harris, Nobby Stiles, Tommy Smith, Jack Charlton and Norman Hunter would be sent off every week these days. It would be a doddle for me playing today.
GEORGE BEST on his 50th birthday, 1996.

I once described English football as the working man's ballet. It's more like a clog dance now.
TONY WADDINGTON, former Stoke manager, 1991.

English football's just like rugby. All the balls go flying through the air or you're kicked into the stand.
RICHARD WITSCHGE, Dutch midfielder, recalling a loan spell with Blackburn, 1996.

I think of myself as one of the old guard. When I started playing you could kick 'owt that moved.
DAVID BATTY, Leeds midfielder, 2000.

English football [is] running, fighting war for 90 minutes non-stop.
TONY YEBOAH, former Leeds striker, happy to be back in German football 1999.

English football is hard work. You have to run all the time.
NKWANKWO KANU, Arsenal's Nigerian striker, 1999.

I love the speed of the game here [in England]. Playing from goal to goal, keeping the momentum going at all times. There's beauty in the game here. The spontaneity is beautiful.
ERIC CANTONA, from La Philosophie de Cantona, *1995.*

In the English league you can't play at less than 100 per cent. I've had to change my mentality since joining Arsenal to become more aggressive. The English game makes that inevitable.
ROBERT PIRES, Arsenal and France midfielder, 2002.

Players with a Latin mentality need a big stage to bring forth a good performance. English players respond to every occasion.
GIOVANNI TRAPATTONI, Fiorentina coach, 1999.

The average Englishman is a very limited player.
GLENN HODDLE, England midfielder, on moving from Tottenham to Monaco, 1987.

The English prejudice against educated footballers has not only led to yobbery off the pitch but to a certain mental weakness on the pitch. The England players had plenty of heart, What they lacked was the ability to think; they were out-thought by their opponents.
Editorial headlined 'Why can't we pass?' in the Spectator, *after Euro 2000.*

The attitude in England is that tricks are okay if they work. If they don't you're a wanker. It doesn't seem to have sunk in that if you never try you'll never succeed.
DUNCAN McKENZIE, maverick striker, 1976.

The English are plagued by industrial football, yet the potential remains enormous.
MILJAN MILJANIC, Real Madrid manager, on the congested schedule of England's top clubs, 1976.

Football is like a car. You've got five gears, but the trouble with English teams is that they drive in fourth and fifth all the time...When they crash

in Europe they say it's bad luck. It isn't – it's bad driving.
RUUD GULLIT on joining Chelsea after playing in Italy and the Netherlands, 1995.

When English clubs play in Europe, their opponents know what is coming: the long ball into the penalty area, which gets nowhere; the next ball, which the opposition win; and the counter-attack, which the English cannot deal with.
ANTONIO PACHECO, Portugal player, 1995.

England will never win World Cups. We simply don't have enough people who believe in playing football.
ALEX FERGUSON, Manchester United manager, 1995.

I love watching English football but I used to love playing against English teams. They always gave you the ball back if you lost it. Still do.
JOHAN CRUYFF, former Ajax, Barcelona and Netherlands captain, 1998.

I don't want people in Spain to regard me as an English footballer in the traditional sense – an idiot with lots of money who boots long balls upfield.
STEVE McMANAMAN, Real Madrid midfielder, 2001.

I love English football, even though it strikes me sometimes as a crazy game. Where are the best playmakers? Not in England.
MICHEL PLATINI, former France captain and vice-president of the French FA, 2002.

You must take care of your own football culture. English football is world-famous, but the result of all the foreigners in the Premiership is that the national team is second-class.
JOHAN CRUYFF, former Barcelona coach, after England's failure at Euro 2000.

I love English football, but the tactics haven't changed in the past 20 years – 4-4-2 and a flat back four pushing up as far as possible makes it easier for strikers to shine than in Europe.

MICHEL PLATINI, former France captain, 2002.

Dennis Bergkamp told me they [the Dutch] always thought of the English as strong but stupid.
TONY ADAMS, Arsenal and England defender, 1997.

I admire the English mentality because they are so strong, so hard-working. But we have talent.
SVEN-GORAN ERIKSSON, then coach of Portugal's Benfica, after his side knocked Arsenal out of the European Cup, 1991.

English and British players still kick the ball while continental players prefer to pass it. And while British players want to crack the ball at goal, today's really top players want to pass it into the net.
CRAIG BROWN, Scotland manager, after watching Euro 2000.

English soccer is the best...They play for 90 minutes, they try hard and they never lie down unless they're hurt. It's the only soccer you can really watch.

IVAN LENDL, Czechoslovak tennis player, 1992.

The reason we haven't signed any English players is that there aren't enough good ones about, as the European Championship showed.
KEN BATES, Chelsea chairman, 2000.

The British don't like fancy dans or fanny merchants, as they used to call them, but different players give 100 per cent in different ways.
JOHN BARNES, former England midfielder, 2000.

I got caught up in the work-rate era at Arsenal. My own improved a lot but I lost my sharpness in the box. Finally, Bill McGarry took me to Wolves with words that were music to me: 'If I see you in our half, I'll kick your arse.'
BOBBY GOULD, striker with 10 clubs, 1978.

Passion is the most overworked word and excuse in English football. Control is the key to winning. Fire in the bellies is all very well but you need ice in the head too.

BILL BESWICK, sports psychologist, 1999.

There are too many hammer-throwers in the Scottish League. I sign a world-class player and have him put out of action after a game and a bit. This league is too tough.
GRAEME SOUNESS, Rangers manager, after injury to Oleg Kuznetsov, 1990.

I got a shock when I first saw a Scottish League match on TV. The keeper was basically elbowed off the ball at a corner-kick, but the goal was given. It was a wake-up call.
FABIEN BARTHEZ, Manchester United's French keeper, 2000.

I would hate to play that kind of football. The pleasure of playing that would be zero. As a player you want to enjoy the game. I don't think the players enjoy it there. It's no fun playing with 10 men behind the ball. I wouldn't pay to watch Liverpool, but I would to watch Arsenal or Manchester United.
FRANK DE BOER, Barcelona player, on Liverpool's 0-0 draw in the Nou Camp in 2001 before the sides were again goalless there in the Champions' League, 2002.

The leagues I like are Spain, England and Holland, where most teams try to play football. Italy is horrible. If you put a camera above an Italian stadium you just see this line of activity across midfield. Incredible! It's just fighting in the midfield and expecting to score goals from free-kicks. It's in the culture – the Italians have always played for results and that's truer now than ever.
FRANK DE BOER, 2002.

A 0-0 draw in Italy is crap. A 0-0 draw in England can be really interesting.
IAN WRIGHT, Arsenal and England striker, 1995.

Italian League football was rubbish – totally defensive. Games were either no score or 1-0...When we had lost a couple of matches, we began to feel the attitude of the directors. It was as though we had lost a war. With a reaction like that, players don't want to be adventurous.

DENIS LAW, Scottish international, on his spell with Torino, An Autobiography, 1979.

In England, soccer is a grey game played by grey people on grey days.
RODNEY MARSH, former England player, to Florida TV audience, 1979.

America is the land of opportunity for soccer.
RON NEWMAN, English coach of Fort Lauderdale Strikers, 1978.

America is an elephants' graveyard.
GIANNI RIVERA, Italian international forward, rejecting an offer from the USA, 1978.

If the US becomes enthralled by soccer it will be when every back street and stretch of urban waste ground has its teams of kids playing their makeshift matches, the players claiming the temporary identity of the world's stars...Environments like that produce those stars. Football is an inner compulsion. It cannot be settled on a people like instant coffee.
ARTHUR HOPCRAFT, author, The Football Man, 1968.

To say that American soccer is the football of the future is ludicrous. You've got to see football in the black townships of South Africa or in Rio de Janeiro before you can talk about the future of football. Who can name five top American players?
JACK TAYLOR, English World Cup referee, 1978.

Soccer is a game in which everyone does a lot of running around...Mostly, 21 guys stand around and one guy does a a tap dance with the ball. It's about as exciting as Tristan and Isolde.
JIM MURRAY, sportswriter, Louisville Courier Journal, 1967.

Those Stoker guys are so cocky. They make me mad saying our game [baseball] is dull. Boy, if ours is dull, theirs is even duller. Those nuts. Running around in shorts, chasing a big ball like a bunch of schoolboys.

JOE AZCUE, Cleveland Indians baseball coach, 1967. Cleveland Stokers were Stoke City, guesting in the US city for the summer.

In this bloody country, Americans think that any guy who runs around in shorts kicking a ball instead of catching it has to be a Commie or a fairy.
CLIVE TOYE, English general manager of New York Cosmos, 1970.

With such refinements as a 35-yard offside law, synthetic pitches which are not conducive to tackling and shoot-outs to eliminate drawn games, the country which gave the world Disneyland has provided a Mickey Mouse football industry.
JACK ROLLIN, editor, Rothmans Football Yearbook, *1979.*

Biathlon. Luge. Soccer. Three of a kind.
The Plains Dealer *newspaper, Ohio, on the prospect of the US staging the World Cup finals, 1990.*

They're going to bring this thing to the US in 1994 and charge people money to watch it? Listen, if this thing were a Broadway show it would have closed after one night.
FRANK DEPFORD, editor-columnist of the USA-based The National, *on the World Cup final, 1990.*

Soccer is cruel, fate is relentless and the most coveted championship in the world hinged on the caprice of a leather boot striking a leather ball on a chalk spot 12 yards from goal.
Report in Los Angeles Times *after goalless World Cup final was settled on penalties, 1994.*

If I could live for a thousand years I'd now set aside a decade for soccer. Before this World Cup, I'd have given it the same time slot in eternity as auto racing: maybe a week.
THOMAS BOSWELL, sportswriter and baseball afficionado, Washington Post, *1994.*

Soccer will never take over from baseball. Baseball is the only chance we blacks get to wave a bat at a white man without starting a riot.
EDDIE MURPHY, actor, during the US World Cup, 1994.

For us Americans the bottom line is to win a championship. So we invent baseball and call ourselves world champions. We invent [gridiron] football and do the same. But they're not world champions, just the best team in the US in that professional sport. Only soccer has a true world championship. Our challenge is magnified thousands of times. Our situation is so much more difficult and complicated. This is the real one.
BRUCE ARENA, US coach, World Cup finals, 2002.

The FA Cup final is better because it's honest.
VINNIE JONES, footballer turned actor, at the Oscars ceremony, 2000.

Our football comes from the heart, theirs comes from the mind.

PELE on the difference between South American and European football, 1970.

These are players – men who play with their heads and their hearts.
FERENC PUSKAS, Real Madrid player, 1961.

Lots of footballers don't have a high IQ to start with, so it would be difficult to gauge the effects of heading the ball too much.
JOHN COLQUHOUN, former Scotland striker, on research which claimed that heading led to brain damage, 1995.

What is the world coming to when you get a red card and fined two weeks' wages for calling a grown man a wanker? It's an adults' game – what's wrong with a bit of industrial language in the workplace?
PAUL GASCOIGNE after being sent off for Middlesbrough v. Chelsea, 2000.

Everyone knows I am looking for a striker but I hope that makes the players say: 'I'll show that bastard that I can do it.'

EBBE SKOVDAHL, Aberdeen manager, 2001.

These days you spend £2m before you realise the player can't even trap a ball.
GRAHAM TAYLOR, back as Watford manager, 2000.

When I was at Bournemouth I kicked a tray of cups up in the air. One hit Luther Blissett on the head. He flicked it on and it went all over my suit hanging behind him. Another time, at West Ham, I threw a plate of sandwiches at Don Hutchison. He sat there, still arguing with me, with cheese and tomato running down his face. You can't do that any more, especially with all the foreigners. They'd go home.
HARRY REDKNAPP, West Ham manager, 1999.

Let us not forget that the place of truth for an athlete is, and always will be, the stadium.
ERIC CANTONA, from La Philosophie de Cantona, *1995.*

The hardest part is what you find to replace football – because there isn't anything.
KEVIN KEEGAN, 'chief operating officer' at Fulham, 1998.

Sometimes, driving home from a game, you do wonder if you're getting a bit old. But I always remember what Kenny Dalglish once told me: 'Never forget that football made you feel knackered when you were 17.'
GORDON STRACHAN, Leeds and Scotland midfielder, in An Autobiography, *1992.*

I'm frightened to stop because there can be no life as enjoyable as this.
STRACHAN on a footballer's life at 35, 1992.

The best team always wins. The rest is only gossip.
JIMMY SIRREL, Notts County manager, 1985.

8

THE LIFESTYLE

The perception of footballers has changed a lot since I played. There used to be celebrity, showbiz and football. Now it's all one thing.
KEVIN KEEGAN, England manager, 2000.

There will never, ever be a better time to be a footballer than now.
ALAN SHEARER, England captain, 1999.

The image of the footballer as a glamorous, show-business type, surrounded by pretty girls and flash cars, is firmly implanted in most people's minds. I know him more accurately as the deeply insecure family man or the tearful, failed apprentice.
EAMON DUNPHY, Republic of Ireland player, 1973.

Take away *Match of the Day* and all the hangers-on and it's all very empty and lonely being a footballer.
RODNEY MARSH, England striker, 1971.

Footballers are only interested in drinking, clothes and the size of their willies.
KARREN BRADY, Birmingham City managing director, 1994.

I like a bit of rough – footballers, roofers, blokes who get banged up.
DANIELLA WESTBROOK, EastEnders actress, 1996.

There are too many thickos in English football.
FRANCIS MAUDE MP, Conservative shadow foreign secretary, 2000.

Footballers are dumb. They're really thick. They don't have a clue about life...They're arrogant and stupid.
EMMA PADFIELD, 'kiss-and-sell' girl on the footballers she had slept with, in TV documentary, 2000.

I prefer footballers not to be too good or clever at other things. It means they concentrate on football.
BILL NICHOLSON, Tottenham manager, 1973.

Further to your recent letter I am sorry that we cannot help you with your search for

academic footballers. In fact two of the back four cannot read.
JOE ROYLE, Oldham manager, replying to a journalist researching a feature on footballers with degrees, 1987.

Without being rude, footballers are not the best talkers in the world.
JIMMY HILL, former player, chairman and TV pundit, 1998.

What they say about soccer players being ignorant is rubbish. I spoke to a couple yesterday and they were quite intelligent.
RACQUEL WELCH, American actress, after visit to Chelsea match, 1973.

We're paid to play football, not to think.
PAUL BASTOCK, Boston United goalkeeper, when asked whether he thought an FA inquiry into the running of the club had affected their start in League football, 2002.

Excuse me, but there are footballers who think.
SOL CAMPBELL, Arsenal and England defender, rebutting the stereotype of the 'thick' footballer during a press interview, 2002.

There are only two things you can be certain of with footballers. One, they'll let you down. Two, you don't know when they'll let you down. They are flawed characters.
Secretary of a Premiership club, quoted anonymously in the press, 2000.

I never wanted to be a coach because I have a low opinion of players. Footballers are the most obnoxious, ignorant and selfish people.
EDWIN STEIN, Birmingham coach, 1993.

Professionalism in rugby union implies a soccer-style mentality; training in the morning and reading comics in the afternoon.
ED GRIFFITHS, chief executive of the South African Rugby Union, 1995.

Footballers couldn't run a fish-and-chip shop.
BOB LORD, Burnley chairman, 1961.

I would not hang a dog on the word of an ex-professional footballer.
ALAN HARDAKER, Football League secretary, 1961.

I can remember the day when, as a goalkeeper playing for Reading against Millwall at The Den in 1951, I collected ninepence in old pennies which had bounced off my skull. We needed the money in those days.
Letter to the Daily Telegraph *after coin-throwing incidents at matches, 2002.*

If Mr Football Fan went to many a car park when the players are rolling up for training he would probably be unable to restrain himself from a muttered 'Cor blimey'. For he'd see a fair number of the 'slaves' turning up for their daily stint in nice, shiny cars. At my own club, for instance, many of the lads have cars. I have myself, I'll admit.
RONNIE CLAYTON, Blackburn and England player, in A Slave To Soccer, *1960.*

Some folks tell me we professional players are soccer slaves. Well if this is slavery, give me a life sentence.
BOBBY CHARLTON, a year before the lifting of the maximum wage, 1960.

I don't hold with those who say they would play for England for nothing. I'd play for Northern Ireland for nothing if they let everybody in for nothing. If they are collecting a £50,000 gate, playing for hope and glory has nothing to do with the facts.
DANNY BLANCHFLOWER, Tottenham captain, in The Encyclopaedia of Football, *1960.*

Johnny Haynes is a top entertainer and will be paid as one from now on. I will give him £100 a week to play for Fulham.
TOMMY TRINDER, Fulham chairman and comedian, making Haynes the English game's first £100-a-week player, 1961.

Italian players wonder how on earth players like Haynes live on such a salary! If anyone suggested that the Italians should play a whole season and bank only £5,000, plus another £90 or so in expenses, there would be a nationwide strike.
JOHN CHARLES, Juventus and Wales player, in The Gentle Giant, *1962.*

You always want hungry players, but the country is getting richer and that's already been bad for boxing. I can also see it harming football.
BILL SHANKLY, Liverpool manager, 1968.

The permissive society has given us young footballers totally concerned with what they can get rather than what they ought to be giving.
BERTIE MEE, Arsenal manager, 1974.

Now, anyone who has a Premiership career lasting six years will end up a millionaire. Of course, a lot of them will blow it.
ALEX FYNN, football consultant and writer, 1999.

People say the wages are too high, but it's a short career.
SIR STANLEY MATTHEWS, whose own playing career lasted nearly 40 years, 1987.

You can't blame the players for taking advantage. If you can get £40,000 a week, you'll take it. That's human nature.
ALAN HANSEN, TV pundit and former Liverpool captain, 1999.

My first contract was bigger than my father, an electrician, had ever earned in his life. So I realise how it is. Then again it would be crazy to say: 'No, I don't want it.' It's just how it is in football. Everybody makes money. Why shouldn't we? A lot of people are there to watch.
DENNIS BERGKAMP, Arsenal striker, 1999.

Society finds it hard to accept men from the lower classes, where most footballers are recruited, being paid salaries that would normally be out of bounds to them.
Letter to The Times *amid criticism of the top Premiership players' wages, 2002.*

A successful football career used to be about winning things. Now it's about how much money you end up with.
GRAEME SOUNESS, Liverpool manager, 1993.

Too many players these days judge themselves by how good their car is and by the size of their house, rather than by the medals they've won. I see players who are rich after five years in the game but have never got close to winning anything. I can see people retiring at 25 in the future.
PAUL MERSON, Aston Villa and England midfielder, 2000.

I wince at players who cheat and foul, who abuse referees and who think only about winning and the money it will bring.
TONY BLAIR MP, Labour, on the modern game, 1995.

Some of the players think: 'I've got a million in the bank. Why work harder?'
RAY HARFORD, Blackburn manager, on the champions' poor start to the season, 1995.

Few players can play really well when they are earning lots of money. They find it harder to be motivated when the bills are being paid and they are sure of having a holiday and a new career every year.
MARK McGHEE, Wolves manager, 1995.

They are just guys who get paid ridiculous amounts of money for not doing very much.
JADE JOHNSON, international long-jumper, on modern footballers, 2002.

It's weird, isn't it? I remember when a hundred quid seemed like loads of money.
JONATHAN WOODGATE, Leeds defender, after his club paid £18m for Rio Ferdinand, 2000.

It will be a story about how young men can earn £20,000 a week and virtually own whole cities, yet somehow think that they're bullet-proof.
ALLEN JEWHURST, Granada TV producer, planning a

drama-documentary on the case that led to the trial of Leeds' Lee Bowyer and Jonathan Woodgate, 2002.

Rolex watches, garages full of flashy cars and mansions, set up for life, forgot about the game, lost the hunger that got you the watches, cars and mansions.
ROY KEANE, Manchester United captain, reacting to their Champions' League semi-final defeat by Bayer Leverkusen, 2002.

Some players are cocky gits. You see them out and about, giving it large but they haven't done anything in the game to justify it.
KEANE, 2000.

There's a great American saying: 'Why bother to get out of bed when you're wearing silk pyjamas?' I think it applies to some young players. A lot earn huge amounts before they're the finished article and undoubtedly find it hard to motivate themselves. People are often driven by knowing success will bring financial

rewards, but the potential can go unfulfilled if the money is there too early.
STEVE COPPELL, Crystal Palace manager and former players' union chairman, 1999.

Some [players] would still be world-class if you paid them £20 a week. But for others it's now all about how much you can earn. I don't begrudge them the big salaries, but how can you say that someone on £30,000 a week does a better job than a nurse or a policeman, who have to risk their lives for £14,000 a year?
NEVILLE SOUTHALL, former Everton and Wales goalkeeper, 1999.

Whenever we take our young players away they have to dress in shirt and tie. They have to learn how to eat properly in restaurants and how to make speeches of thanks to the opposition. We don't produce greedy, money-grabbing bastards.
KIT CARSONS, director of Peterborough United's youth academy, 1999.

Money brings bad habits.
The players live too easily,
JAVIER CLEMENTE, Marseille coach, 2001.

Being a footballer has its advantages. Earning £40,000 to £80,000 a month demands some sacrifice. Guys in the street work hard for eight hours a day. Players put in only one hour a day and two on Saturday.
BERNARD TAPIE on returning to Marseille as director of sport, 2001.

Money is not a criterion for some people. There are multi-millionaires who still get up at 6am to get going about their business. They are winners. For players it doesn't matter what bonus they are on, playing is the meat and drink and winning is the bonus. It's the winning that gives them the kicks.
ALEX FERGUSON, Manchester United manager, 1995.

What makes big players is their love of the game. Money should not control the game. It alienates fans. If

tomorrow there was no money in football, I would still love it.
ARSENE WENGER, Arsenal manager, on losing Nicolas Anelka to Real Madrid for 'non-footballing reasons', 1999.

I wouldn't give up football even if I won the £18m jackpot on the National Lottery. I love this job and I would even pay to play.
DEAN HOLDSWORTH, Bolton striker, 1995.

People will say I've got a screw loose, but perhaps I'm in the 0.1 per cent of footballers who don't give a toss about unlimited money.
MATTHEW LE TISSIER on why he had stayed loyal to Southampton, 1995.

I took a pay cut to come here. As long as the fridge is full, I'm happy.
GORDON STRACHAN on joining Coventry as player-coach from Leeds, 1995.

The money I make, I give it all to my mother. I don't even know where it goes.
CHRISTIAN VIERI, Inter

Milan striker, after Vatican criticism of players' wages, 1999.

You go into a shop and it's just Armani this and that, and you buy it. Clothes you don't even need. I spent a grand once. Bit of a waste.
GARY KELLY, Leeds and Republic of Ireland defender, 1995.

I earn more than all you wankers put together.
CARLTON PALMER, Leeds midfielder, to police after he was arrested during a night out in the city, 1997.

I was nearly a soccer brat, but the more I earned the louder my conscience became.
NIALL QUINN, Sunderland striker, on giving the proceeds of his testimonial match to charity, 2002.

They are rich, they've got everything, but there must be something else. Something you cannot buy: honour, morals and inner desire.
GUNTER NETZER, former Germany midfielder, after his country's exit from Euro 2000.

You can make a player fitter by giving him a pay rise. It may sound daft, but he works harder and he's happier at home.
LOU MACARI, Swindon manager, 1986.

The biggest difference between playing for Forfar and playing for Rangers? Probably about £300 a week.
STEWART KENNEDY, former Rangers and Scotland goalkeeper, 1984.

I cannot feed my child on glory.
PAOLO ROSSI, Italy striker, during pay dispute with Juventus, 1982.

Two months ago [after he helped Italy win the World Cup] Rossi was over the moon. Now he is asking for it.
JUVENTUS OFFICIAL, 1982.

It's almost theft taking money after a performance like that. I'll be using the winter break to make the players' lives as miserable as possible.
CRAIG LEVEIN, Hearts manager, after defeat at Aberdeen, 2001.

We are meant to be these hard-headed, money-obsessed professionals but we are still little boys at heart. Just ask our wives.
ROB LEE, Newcastle midfielder, before playing in the FA Cup final, 1998.

Three cheers for Fifa [Football transfers to be scrapped, 1 September]. At last the likes of Keane and Beckham will be able to receive the rewards they deserve, rather than struggling on today's paltry sums.
Letter to the Guardian, 2000.

These stories about Manchester United players with six cars worry me. I fear some young players are losing touch with reality. Because there is so much money in the game, it's only right that we get our proper share, but I'd like to see young players on big, five-year contracts being paid that money over a 10- or even 15-year period, so they didn't have so much in their pocket.
NIALL QUINN, Sunderland and Republic of Ireland striker, 2000.

Motivating players isn't easy when their first signing-on fee pays off the mortgage. There is great consolation in not playing and going home in a Porsche. In my day the car park was all Vivas and Cortinas.
JOE ROYLE, Manchester City manager, 2001.

Dwight [Yorke] is getting £100,000 for this book but it couldn't be further down his priorities. His Ferrari cost twice as much, so why bother?
HUNTER DAVIES, journalist, on collaborating on Yorke's autobiography, 2000.

We're going to burn your Ferraris.
Chant by Real Madrid fans after their 5-1 defeat by Zaragoza, 1999.

The Bosman ruling has ensured that players have much more power. Look at the car park: it used to be the directors who drove fancy motors, now it's the players.
GEORGE GRAHAM, Tottenham manager, 2000.

Q: What car do you drive?
A: Two Mercs and a Porsche.
ADE AKINBIYI, Crystal Palace striker, in programme questionnaire, 2002.

Maybe it's difficult to motivate players if they earn 40 grand a week, have three Mercs and mistresses everywhere.
JOE KINNEAR, Wimbledon manager, 1997.

Players are a club's best assets, so they must be dealt with grandly. We are not looking for a bargain but for a great player, and he deserves everything his rank and industry can get.
DON RAIMUNDO SAPORTA, vice-president of Real Madrid, 1961.

It's not the likes of me who have pushed transfer fees and wages sky high but the clubs competing for our services.
TREVOR FRANCIS, England striker, before his move into Italian football, 1982.

As a player you're nothing more than a piece of meat.

We're nothing more than cattle. I had a conversation with Roy Keane about it and he agreed. He said: 'They sold you like a cow.' The fact is he [Alex Ferguson] sold me behind my back. I don't know anything about it. He fired me because he had problems about his own reputation.
JAAP STAM on his surprising transfer from Manchester United to Lazio, 2001.

As a footballer you can be happily playing away, your children can be doing well at school and your wife settled. But if the manager wants rid of you he can make life very difficult until you agree to go.
MARK McGHEE, Wolves manager, 1995.

Greed and blackmail drive the game now. Players and agents run football, not managers and chairmen. Half the time I'm not dealing with players but with millionaires.
DAVE BASSETT, Nottingham Forest manager, 1998.

Before the year 2000 I will have 50 millionaires on my books. And that's being conservative.
JOHNNY MAC, *players' agent, 1989.*

The money coming into the game is incredible. But it's just the prune-juice effect – it comes in and goes out straight away. Agents run the sport.
ALAN SUGAR, *Tottenham chairman, 1997.*

It used to be the wives who affected players, now it's agents.
BOBBY GOULD, *Wimbledon manager, 1988.*

Agents do nothing for the good of football. I'd like to see them lined up against a wall and machine-gunned...some accountants and solicitors with them.
GRAHAM TAYLOR, *Watford manager, 1983.*

I wouldn't cross the road to talk to an agent, let alone go to Manchester.
GRAHAM KELLY, *FA chief executive, declining invitation to a meeting attended by agents, 1992.*

We have to deal with these people [agents], but Bill Shankly wouldn't have done.
BRIAN CLOUGH, 1991.

What do I think of agents? Dogs, worms, vermin.
JOE KINNEAR, *Wimbledon manager, 1995.*

There's always a tendency for players to under-price themselves. No one likes to say: 'I'm worth this or that.' It's better if someone else does the talking for you and leaves you to do the playing.
RAY WILKINS, *former England captain, 1993.*

Manchester United were bad payers in the 1970s. They had the mentality that people would play for them for nothing. People moan about agents but I wish they had been around in my day.
STUART PEARSON, *former United and England striker, 1995.*

Agents are disliked by managers and directors but this is because they give players power – through the simple device of letting them know the going rate. No one I know, in any job anywhere, wants to earn less than the going rate. Footballers are no different.
ROB LEE, *Newcastle and England midfielder, 1998.*

I am trained in economics, I have the ability to run a company and I don't see why I shouldn't put these gifts at the service of my brother. But the football scene is crawling with sharks and profiteers, and my diplomas did not prepare me for facing them.
DIDIER ANELKA, *Nicolas' brother, on acting as his agent, 1999.*

There's a definite place for agents but it is turning into a spivs' market place. There are people coming into the game who are accountants, solicitors, estate agents or whatever, telling you who these footballers are.
JIM SMITH, *Derby manager, 2000.*

Most agents wouldn't know a ball from a banana.
JOHN LAMBIE, *Partick Thistle manager, 2002.*

Q: Who's your favourite player?
A: I can't say. I don't know anything about football.
ERIC HALL, *self-styled 'monster' agent, interviewed in* Total Football *magazine, 1995.*

Don't know much about the game, don't even like it much. What's that got to do with it? My business is selling people. Makes no difference what they do.
HALL, 1990.

I now believe in Father Christmas, I really do. I owe him [Jean-Marc Bosman] a monster Christmas present.
HALL *after the European Union's highest court ruled the game's transfer system illegal, 1995.*

Eric Hall is the one behind all the problems we've had, with his snide little whispers to this player and that, saying they should get away. All that weasel sees is pound signs.

VINNIE JONES, Wimbledon captain, 1995. He later apologised to Hall.

Eric [Hall] doesn't exactly present himself as Mister Bleedin' Sensible, does he? He's a good laugh, but he doesn't exactly look the most trustworthy individual. If someone's dopey enough to have him as their agent, good luck to him.
DAVE BASSETT, Sheffield United manager, 1995.

I have no morals when it comes to dealing with my clients. I would deal with the Devil to get the best deal for them.
ERIC HALL, 1989.

If there was a really star name who was represented by the Devil, there would still be a queue of clubs wishing to negotiate with him.
ATHOLE STILL, players' agent, 1999.

I'm the best. I'm an egomaniac. If my phone doesn't ring for half an hour I phone the GPO and

demand to know what's wrong with it.
ERIC HALL, 1989.

I'm available 365 days a year. Only me and Father Christmas actually work on Christmas Day and he finishes early.
HALL, 1993.

When people ask my wife what I do, she tells them I'm a Kwik-Fit fitter rather than admit I'm an agent.
JON HOLMES, players' agent, 1996.

I realised how sinister it had become when I was manager of Peterborough and I tried to sign a lad who had played one League game. He told me to talk to his agent. There are 2,000 professionals in England, but only 20 need an agent.
MARK LAWRENSON on his stint as an 'alternative agent', backed by the players' union, 1991.

Every player needs an agent because whatever their status, they are in no position to negotiate contracts. As for

signing up young players
I see nothing wrong in that.
I also handle showbiz
people and often take on
groups before they have
made a record.
*ERIC HALL responding to
Lawrenson, 1991.*

I don't want my players
playing for England because
when they come back, all they
want is big wages, sponsored
cars, a big house, Page Three
birds, ecstasy and cocaine.
I'm happy they don't know
about all that lark.
*DAVE BASSETT, Sheffield
United manager, 1990.*

From the first time I kicked a
ball as a pro 19 years ago, I
began to learn what the game
was all about. It's about the
drunken parties that go on
for days. The orgies, the birds
and the fabulous money.
Football is just a distraction:
you're so fit that you can
carry on all the high living in
secret and still play at the
highest level.
*PETER STOREY, former
Arsenal and England player,
'telling all' in a tabloid, 1980.*

Even after a skinful, I don't
have a hangover and can still
be up with the others [in
training].
*BRYAN ROBSON, former
England captain, on reports that
he was a heavy drinker, 1990.*

The legendary drinkers at a
club are usually the best
trainers. They go out and get
into an unathletic state, but
come the next training day,
they put in more effort than
the non-drinkers because they
feel they have to.
*JOHN COLQUHOUN, Hearts
striker, 1996.*

Quite a few of them
[footballers] can knock back
a pint or two, but none are
alcoholics.
*JIMMY HILL, then a Fulham
player, in his book* Striking For
Soccer, *1961.*

Of course I'm against
Sunday soccer. It'll spoil my
Saturday nights.
*JOHN RITCHIE, Stoke City
player, as his club prepared to
play in one of the first-ever
Sunday matches, 1974.*

The young players of today drink a lot more than in my teenage-to-early-twenties period. We used to be pint sinkers but now the orders are more likely to be Bacardi-and Cokes or gin-and-tonics. I have seen them pay out for a single round what I used to earn in a week at Chelsea.
JIMMY GREAVES, recovering alcoholic and former England striker, in This One's On Me, *1979.*

When I was a young player, if I ever went into a pub or restaurant and my manager came in, I'd sneak out the back door. Nowadays a player would probably come up and ask me if I wanted a drink.
PAUL JEWELL, Bradford City manager, on the modern players' lack of fear of their manager, 2000.

All the great players I've ever known have enjoyed a good drink.
JIM BAXTER, former Scotland midfielder, 1993.

It was a big surprise to me to see how much the players drank at Ipswich. In Kiev, if you arrived for training with red eyes, smelling or without sleep, no one would speak to you because they felt you had let the side down.
SERGEI BALTACHA, former Ipswich and Dynamo Kiev midfielder, 1995.

The players can get out of their brains every night as long as they're man of the match on Saturday.
JOHN GREGORY, Aston Villa manager, 1999.

There are one or two players around who'd like it renamed the Vodka and Coca-Cola Cup.
RON ATKINSON, Aston Villa manager, 1994.

Now it's a gallon or two of cold lager, a day to recover and back to the building site at 7 o'clock on Monday morning.
CHRIS BRINDLEY, part-time player with non-League Kidderminster, after FA Cup win at Birmingham, 1994.

Some of the younger players think that lager makes you invisible.
CRAIG BROWN, Scotland manager, 1999.

I have always been against players drinking and I'm always thinking of ways of getting a team that doesn't drink.
ALEX FERGUSON, Manchester United manager, 1997.

As a team we had to give up drinking. I know it's one of my hobbyhorses these days but if you want to be the best you have to make sacrifices. The boss [John Gregory] does it. Fair play to him – he stops drinking at the start of the season and doesn't touch a drop until the end because he wants to stay clear-headed.
PAUL MERSON, Aston Villa midfielder, claiming that a failure to abstain from alcohol during 1998-99 had contributed to their slide down the Premiership, 2000.

I won't stand for booze. One player who joined the club said: 'I may as well tell you, I like a drink.' I found out he was taking others along...Instead of one lager they had three. Three becomes four and it escalates. I had to get rid of him.
LOU MACARI, Swindon manager, 1986.

If I had my time again, I wouldn't do anything different. Except that knowing what I do now, I'd never open a pub.
GERD MULLER, former West Germany striker, on his alcoholism, 1991.

Alcohol controls me. It's a disease and has nothing to do with me personally. I never go a day without thinking about drinking.
GEORGE BEST, 1990.

If I go into a bar and have a lager shandy, word goes back that I'm knocking back bottles of champagne. By the time it gets to the papers or my manager at Arsenal, it's me lying in the gutter.
CHARLIE NICHOLAS, Arsenal and Scotland striker, 1984.

Scottish players booze, smoke and eat whatever comes to hand.
JEAN LUC WETZEL, French agent, 2000.

One reason [why Portuguese clubs are doing better than English teams in Europe] is that they don't bloody drink. There are no 12-pints-a-night men here. They go straight home to their families and behave like responsible adults.
BOBBY ROBSON, Porto coach, 1995.

Alcohol isn't part of the lifestyle for Italian players. They work on the principle that your body's a machine. When you drain that machine, the one thing you don't fill it with is alcohol.
GRAEME SOUNESS, Liverpool manager and ex-Sampdoria player, 1991.

In France if you say the players can have a drink, they have two. Here they have double figures.
GERARD HOULLIER, Liverpool manager and former French FA technical director, 1999.

I compare top players to racing cars. Drinking alcohol is as silly as putting diesel in a racing car.
HOULLIER, 2000.

If left to their own devices the players would have two weeks in Tenerife, another two in Cyprus and two more in the pub.
DAVID SULLIVAN, joint owner of Birmingham City, on allegations that the club's pre-season training was too gruelling, 1995.

The Italians smoke, yet they're world-class. They even nip into the toilets at half-time for a crafty fag.
PAUL GASCOIGNE, 1998.

Drink lots of beer and smoke loads of fags.
GERRY TAGGART, Leicester and Northern Ireland player, when asked for his advice to aspiring players, 2001.

Liverpool won the FA Cup a few years ago with a team of 11 foreigners, including Scots, Welsh and Irish. Now we have Spanish, French and Italians. They speak better English, are more civilised and know how to use a knife and fork.
KEN BATES, Chelsea chairman, on the influx of players from abroad, 2000.

They've got to stop going in betting shops, going out boozing and eating McDonald's and start living how a young professional should. If not, they're going to get their P45.
DAVE ALLEN, Sheffield Wednesday director, on the club's young players, 2002.

We were encouraged to open ourselves to the Japanese cuisine on offer, but having been away from home so long I could have died for a McDonald's.
DANNY MILLS, England defender, at the end of the team's World Cup run, 2002.

The odd hamburger doesn't do you any harm but you can't live on them.
MATTHEW LE TISSIER on how he lost weight after his actress girlfriend, Emily Symons, encouraged him to eat more healthily, 2000.

I have never known a group of people like footballers for eating. A huge evening meal is digested and forgotten by 9.30pm. Then they still want endless rounds of sandwiches.

ALEC STOCK, former manager, in A Little Thing Called Pride, *1982.*

I came down to the restaurant and saw some of the lads sitting at a table eating cheese sandwiches. I couldn't believe it. We'd discussed diet. Fucking cheese sandwiches, an hour and a half before training.
ROY KEANE, former Republic of Ireland captain, recalling the Irish camp before a World Cup qualifier v. the Netherlands in his autobiography, 2002.

'A bit crude when eating' states the report of an Arsenal scout, referring to a well-known international in whom Arsenal were interested... Personal background sometimes damns a player who has the necessary football qualifications.
BERNARD JOY, journalist and ex-Arsenal player, in Forward, Arsenal!, *1952.*

Once I saw [John Charles] shift two steak pies, a heaped plate of potatoes and vegetables, two helpings

of apple tart and literally gallons of tea.
ROY PAUL, Manchester City and Wales player, in A Red Dragon of Wales, *1956.*

Chelsea were a sausage, egg and chips club before they [foreign players] arrived. That's what we had to eat before training. Andy Townsend, Vinnie Jones, Tony Cascarino and me went to the cafe for a slosh-up before training. I have even had it before games.
DENNIS WISE, Chelsea midfielder, 2000.

The diet in Britain is really dreadful. The whole day you drink tea and coffee with milk and cakes. If you had a fantasy world of what you shouldn't eat in sport, it's what you eat here.
ARSENE WENGER, Arsenal manager, 1997.

The players go on to the training pitch clutching cups of coffee. Apparently they are given bacon sandwiches with all kinds of colourful sauces.

That would be unthinkable in France.
MICKAEL SILVESTRE, Manchester United defender, 1999.

My only problem seems to be with Italian breakfasts. No matter how much money you've got, you can't seem to get any Rice Krispies.
LUTHER BLISSETT after transfer from Watford to Milan, 1983.

My team-mates at Chelsea have very funny ways of celebrating. In France, when it's your birthday, they buy you champagne and cake. Here they just shove your face in the mud. Very strange.
FRANK LEBOEUF, Chelsea defender, 1999.

They go and eat free scampi after a game while I go home with indigestion from watching them play like that and I'm up all night because I can't sleep.
ULI HOENESS, Bayern Munich commercial manager and ex-player, after defeat by lowly St Pauli, 2000.

Q: Are you romantic?
A: I'm great at romantic meals. I can only make beans on toast and pot noodles, so I buy a takeaway, pile up some dirty pans and serve it up so it looks like I've cooked it.
MATT JANSEN, Blackburn striker, in newspaper questionnaire, 2001.

Q: Girl groupies?
A: Last year I got more Valentine's cards off blokes than girls. They write love poems. It's scary.
MATT JANSEN, as above.

I would say that more than 25 per cent of football is gay. It's got to be higher than average. It's a very physical, closed world, a man's world, and you form deep bonds with people you hardly know.
JUSTIN FASHANU, self-confessed homosexual striker, 1992.

I'm just a normal boy of 19. I like going out with my mates and having a meal and a few drinks. Of course I get propositioned sometimes, and it's nice. My mates love it – they get all the cast-offs.
MARK BURCHILL, Celtic striker, 1999.

Maybe my players have a rampant sex life when they stay at home on Friday nights.
TERRY BURTON, Wimbledon manager, on his team's poor home form, 2001.

Of course a player can have sexual intercourse before a match and play a blinder. But if he did for six months he'd be a decrepit old man. It takes the strength from the body.
BILL SHANKLY, Liverpool manager, 1971.

Sex before a match? The boys can do as they please. But it's not possible at half-time.
BERTI VOGTS, Germany coach, World Cup finals, 1998.

After having sex the night before a match I lose all feelings in my feet. I'm totally empty. I can't control the ball. Instead I watch erotic movies the night

before. That doesn't affect my power.
FREDRIK LJUNGBERG, Sweden and Arsenal midfielder, 2000.

We have a match every three days. How can I be a good husband if I don't make love before each one?
FRANK LEBOEUF, Chelsea and France defender, 1998.

It's not the sex that tires out young players. It's staying up all night looking for it.
CLEMENS WESTERHOF, Dutch coach to Nigeria, 1994.

We don't want them to be monks. We want them to be football players because monks don't play football at this level.
BOBBY ROBSON, Newcastle manager, after some of his players visited nightclubs until the early hours, 2002.

FOWLER: I know someone who had a wank two hours before a game and went out and scored a hat-trick.
McMANAMAN: I know him. He captains his country. But

I think the no-sex thing is a load of shite really.
INTERVIEW with Robbie Fowler and Steve McManaman in Loaded *magazine, 1995.*

This is supposed to make us world champions. Of what? Masturbation?
LUIS PEREIRA, Brazil player, on his country's policy of no women in their camp, World Cup finals, 1974.

I've nothing against letting the wives into the team camp. Love is good for footballers, as long as it's not at half-time.
RICHARD MOLLER NIELSEN, Denmark coach, during his team's triumph in the European Championship finals, 1992.

I don't think sex could ever be as rewarding as winning the World Cup. It's not that sex isn't great, just that this tournament comes around only every four years and sex is a lot more regular than that.
RONALDO, Brazil striker, immediately after his goals won the World Cup for Brazil, 2002.

Q: What's more satisfying, scoring a hat-trick or having great sex?
A: The missus might be reading this, so I'd better say the sex.
KEVIN PHILLIPS, Sunderland striker, in Loaded *magazine interview, 1999.*

If it was a straight choice between having sex and scoring a goal, I'd go for the goal every time. I've got all my life to have sex.
ANDY GRAY, Sky TV summariser and ex-Scotland striker, 1995.

Gazza said that scoring was better than an orgasm. Lee Chapman reckoned it wasn't as good. I'll go with Pele – he thought it was about the same.
RYAN GIGGS, Manchester United winger, 1994.

Footballers come pretty high up the list now in terms of shagability. Rock stars must still be first, but then it's footballers, then actors, firemen, insurance brokers, then TV quiz show hosts.
ANGUS DEAYTON, host of TV current-affairs quiz Have I Got News For You, *1997.*

Dwight [Yorke] and Fabien [Barthez] could definitely do with some extra coaching from Angus [Deayton].
CAROLINE MARTIN, kiss-and-sell 'vice girl', claiming sexual liaisons with the TV personality as well as with the two Manchester United players, 2002.

The average English footballer could not tell the difference between an attractive woman and a corner flag.
WALTER ZENGA, Italy goalkeeper, responding to Wimbledon manager Bobby Gould's quip that his players wanted the phone numbers of the Italian players' wives while the Azzurri were away at the World Cup, 1990.

There have been a lot of rumours about players sleeping with each others' wives. But it's not true. We're all pulling together.
FABIEN WILNIS, Ipswich defender, 2001.

When I was with Norwich my wife Dawn had a baby and we called her Darby. A month later I joined Derby. The Norwich lads told me they were all trying for babies and were going to name them Lazio or Barcelona.
ASHLEY WARD, Derby striker, 1996.

With the luck we've been having, one of our players must be bonking a witch.
KEN BROWN, Norwich manager, 1987.

The young lads [at Leeds] mock me because if you phone me I'm always at home at night. If you want a long career you've got to learn to like a quiet life.
NIGEL MARTYN, Leeds and England goalkeeper, 2000.

I tend to buy family men. With a married player you generally know he is at home of an evening, watching *Coronation Street.*
BRUCE RIOCH, Arsenal manager, 1995.

When the England team was travelling you always knew which hotel room Dave Watson was in because he took with him a radio-cassette player with big speakers, and you could usually hear the music all the way down the corridor. His favourite group was Status Quo.
TREVOR BROOKING on the former England centre-half in 100 Great British Footballers, *1988.*

I don't like U2, that's rebel music. Southern Irish. And Simple Minds – I found out that Jim Kerr [the vocalist] was a Celtic supporter, so all my Simple Minds tapes, they went out of the window. Celtic, you hate 'em so much.
TERRY BUTCHER, Rangers and England defender, in Pete Davies, All Played Out: The Full Story of Italia 90, *1990.*

It's hard work trying to find someone else with my taste in music. There aren't many of us around. When I get on the team coach and play my tapes, they are howled and booed off. They [the other players] all like the middle-

of-the-road stuff, but that gives me a headache.
STUART PEARCE, England defender, on his passion for punk rock, 1992.

People say footballers have terrible taste in music but I would dispute that. In my car at the moment I've got The Corrs, Cher, Phil Collins, Shania Twain and Rod Stewart.
ANDY GRAY, Sky TV presenter and former Scotland player, 2000.

I hate golf and like architecture. I don't say much but I do think a lot. Which seems to surprise people who think all footballers are thick.
BRIAN DEANE, former England striker, 1996.

I'd definitely prefer Brooklyn to be a golfer – it's a better profession than football.
VICTORIA BECKHAM, 2000.

My golf handicap is 16. I'm the only black man who can beat them. They don't want to be beaten by me.
RUUD GULLIT on playing golf with his Chelsea colleagues, 1996.

I've learned [English] from watching cartoons. Now I've progressed to films.
GILLES GRIMANDI, Arsenal's French defender, 2000.

Q: What films do you like?
A: Quentin Tarantino and stuff like that. There's nothing better than a good bit of violence.
MARK DRAPER, Aston Villa midfielder, in BigShots *magazine questionnaire, 1995.*

I room with Robbie Keane on away trips. If we're staying in a hotel on a Friday before a game we'll watch *Trigger Happy TV* then *So Graham Norton*. After that we cuddle up together and fall asleep. There's always the temptation of pay-per-view channels in hotels, but that would be embarrassing on your room bill.
RIO FERDINAND, Leeds defender and self-confessed 'EastEnders *fanatic', 2001.*

Three or four of the Villa lads buy the quality papers. At Palace it was always eight Suns, four Mirrors.
GARETH SOUTHGATE,

Aston Villa and England defender, 1996.

Labour. Definitely. Aren't all the players Labour?
STEVE PERRYMAN, Tottenham player, in Hunter Davies' The Glory Game, 1972. Only two of the players turned out to support Labour; nine were Conservatives.

I've never voted anything but Labour in my life. And never will.
KEVIN KEEGAN, England player, 1980.

Football and politics are much the same. They're both full of people who are jealous of success.
TONY BANKS MP, Labour, former Minister of Sport, 1999.

At Burnley, no moustaches, no sideburns, long hair discouraged. But when I was with Chelsea I could go through the menu, wine and all, phone home for hours, entertain friends, all on the club. If I run up a 2p call with Burnley, I get the bill. Keeps your feet on the ground, I'm telling you.

COLIN WALDRON, Burnley defender, 1975.

Q: Have you ever used public transport?
A: Yes, I've been in a taxi.
GEORGE WEAH, former Chelsea striker, in newspaper questionnaire, 2001.

Cynics often question whether footballers from comfortable backgrounds like myself, Graeme Le Saux and Ashley Ward possess a deep, burning hunger. A crazy perception persists that a footballer must have suffered a deprived childhood, not knowing where his next meal or pair of boots was coming from, to acquire the desire to turn football into a career. That is nonsense. My passion to succeed matches anybody's. My commitment to football may be even stronger because alternative career paths would have opened up for me.
JOHN BARNES, in his autobiography, 1999.

The hardcore stereotypes are still there, but there are individuals in the game...I'm

still eyed with suspicion for being different.
GRAEME LE SAUX, Blackburn defender, shortly before his on-the-pitch fight with team-mate David Batty over a remark the latter made, 1995.

Footballers are pampered by fans, massaged by management, stroked by the media. They are so cosseted that any criticism becomes an insult to their manhood.
MICHAEL PARKINSON, columnist, Daily Telegraph, *2001.*

Professional sport is a jungle and the higher you go, the worse it gets. They should stop talking about love of the shirt and being faithful. All that no longer exists, apart from in national teams.
NICOLAS ANELKA on quitting Arsenal for Real Madrid, 1999.

They [footballers] are just like film stars. They want to withdraw inside their shells and live in a closed world. If I were boss of Paris Saint-Germain I would have put it in [Nicolas] Anelka's contract

that he had to be filmed at home, eating his lunch and talking to his girlfriend. Show it on TV and watch it get a two per cent rating. Then no one would care any more and he'd be left in peace.
JEAN-LUC GODARD, French film-maker, 2002.

The worst pressure I'm under is my baby crying at night.
ALAN SHEARER, Blackburn striker, playing down the 'pressure' of his £3.3m price tag, 1992.

Football takes all my pressures away. The police have my passport and I'm not allowed to train with the other players, but nothing bothers me out on the pitch.
MICKEY THOMAS, Wrexham captain, as his team's FA Cup run coincided with his release on bail on charges of counterfeiting currency, 1992.

Nothing scares me in football. I'm the same at home – the bills come in left, right and centre, but I never look at them until the red ones arrive.

STEVE STONE, Nottingham Forest and England midfielder, 1995.

As a player it's like living in a box. Someone takes you out of the box for training and games, and makes all the decisions for you. I have seen players – famous internationals – all stand up in an airport lounge and follow one bloke to the lav. Six of them, maybe, standing there not wanting to piss themselves but following the bloke who does. Like sheep, never asking why, because that's the way they've been trained.
GEOFF HURST, former England striker, in Brian James' Journey To Wembley, *1977.*

I used to think you had to be very selfish [to be a top footballer], but as I get older my views on life change. Generally speaking, ego isn't a good thing. Humility is the most important quality in a human being.
JOHN BARNES, former England player, 2000.

In every squad of 20 players there's going to be the one who hates blacks, foreigners.

He don't know why. He just hates 'em.
VINNIE JONES on racism in football, 1991.

The players themselves are very liberal now. They've grown up in a multi-racial country. Some might do this macho thing about 'women should only be in the kitchen', but they don't mean it. You can see players with their new babies and it's often them that's doing the cleaning and changing nappies.
RACHEL ANDERSON, players' agent, 1999.

Someone asked me last week whether I missed the Villa. I said: 'No. I live in one.'
DAVID PLATT, former Aston Villa striker, on life with Bari in Italy, 1991.

When you come to a place like Barcelona, you think: 'Bloody hell, I wish I was back in England.'
TERRY BUTCHER, Ipswich and England defender, 1979.

On my debut for Besiktas they sacrificed a lamb on the pitch. Its blood was daubed on my

forehead for good luck. They never did that at QPR.
LES FERDINAND, England striker, recalls his spell in Turkey, 1995.

Q: England's best supermarket?
A: Tesco and Harrods.
SLAVISA JOKANOVIC, Chelsea midfielder, in programme questionnaire, 2001.

Q: Last tin you opened?
A: Not tin. Bottle of wine.
MARCEL DESAILLY, Chelsea defender, in programme questionnaire, 2001.

Just when I thought it was safe to go to parties again and say I was a footballer.
GARRY NELSON, striker with numerous clubs, on Eric Cantona's leap into the crowd at Selhurst Park, in Left Foot Forward: Diary of a Journeyman Footballer, *1995.*

I'm the last old-fashioned centre-half. They're all fancy dans now, too many good-looking bastards like Rio Ferdinand who all go out with pop stars.
NEIL RUDDOCK, in interview with Loaded *magazine, 2000.*

I don't speak much after a defeat. Footballers can be murder to live with. Every one I know is grumpy.
CHRIS SUTTON, Blackburn striker, 1994.

You start hiding in your house because you feel ashamed of yourself.
MAGNUS HEDMAN, Coventry goalkeeper, after run of poor results, 2000.

Q: What's the worst thing anyone has ever said to you?
A: You're not playing.
MARK STEIN, Chelsea striker, in newspaper questionnaire, 1995.

Football has given me riches, popularity and privileges, but I want even more. I live for indescribable emotions and football can give me those.
GIANLUCA VIALLI on leaving Juventus for Chelsea, 1996.

It's like turtles in the South Seas. Thousands are hatched on the beaches, but few of them reach the water.
STEVE COPPELL, *players'
union official and England
player, on career prospects for
young players, 1983.*

Take it from me, as a failed footballer, there is no better way to earn a living, to be paid for what is a hobby and a passion.
*HOWARD WILKINSON,
Leeds manager, to graduates
from the FA National School,
1992.*

I remember knocking on the manager's door at Sheffield Wednesday. I said: 'Could I have a little of your time – I don't know whether I'm coming or going.' 'Wilkinson,' he said, 'you're definitely going.'
*HOWARD WILKINSON,
Leeds manager, on under-
achieving as a player, 1992.*

You can't accuse footballers of failing society. They are very kind, going to hospitals and seeing kids, but in the main, the press don't seem to want to write a good word about them.
*ALEX FERGUSON,
Manchester United
manager, 2000.*

Footballers are funny old buggers. As long as they've got their wage packet and car, they'll distance themselves.
*STUART PEARCE,
Nottingham Forest acting
manager, on his team-mates'
reaction to a boardroom takeover
at the club, 1997.*

If I wasn't playing, I'd be putting slates on roofs back in Ireland. Playing has got to be better than that.
*PAUL McGRATH, Aston Villa
defender, 1993.*

EDITOR: What would you be if you weren't a footballer?
MARK FLATTS: On the dole.
*Arsenal programme Q & A with
the reserve forward, 1993.*

I just wish all this [the footballer's life] could last a bit longer. Playing till you're 45, that'd suit me.
*DARREN ANDERTON,
Tottenham and England
midfielder, 1995.*

❾

PHILOSOPHERS

When the seagulls follow the trawler it is because they think sardines will be thrown into the sea.
ERIC CANTONA addressing the media after escaping jail for his 'kung fu' attack on an abusive fan during Manchester United's visit to Crystal Palace, 1995.

If a Frenchman goes on about seagulls, trawlers and sardines, he's called a philosopher. I'd just be called a short Scottish bum talking crap.
GORDON STRACHAN, former Leeds team-mate of Cantona's, 1995.

Cantona is always chasing Rimbauds. [With apologies to Dorothy Parker.]
One man's metier is another man's poisson.
Readers' responses in the Independent *to Cantona's 'seagulls' remark, 1995.*

I definitely want Brooklyn to be christened, though I don't know into which religion.
DAVID BECKHAM after the birth of his and Victoria's first child, 2000.

I'd rather be a footballer than an existentialist.
ROBERT SMITH, singer-writer with the rock group The Cure, 1991.

Like the Tibetans I have learned to understand myself, even if you never fully can.
EMMANUEL PETIT, 1999.

One minute you can be riding the crest of a wave in this game and the next minute you can be down. It's a funny old game. It's a great leveller, and you can't get too cock-a-hoop about things. I know it's an old cliché but you've got to take each game as it comes and keep working at it. Whether you're in playing or management, you're only as good as your last game.
BILLY BONDS, West Ham manager, 1990.

In terms of a 15-round boxing match, we're not getting past round one. Teams will pinch your dinner from under your noses. If you don't heed the warnings, you get nailed to the cross.
GORDON MILNE, Leicester manager, 1983.

No one wants to commit hari-kari and sell themselves down the river.
GARY LINEKER, England striker and captain, explaining the dearth of goals at the European Championship finals, 1992.

We climbed three mountains and then proceeded to throw ourselves off them.
BILLY McNEILL, Celtic manager, after beating Partizan Belgrade 5-4 but losing on aggregate, 1989.

If you can't stand the heat in the dressing-room, get out of the kitchen.
TERRY VENABLES, England coach, 1995.

The cat's among the pigeons and meanwhile we're stuck in limbo.
BERNIE SLAVEN, Middlesbrough striker, after Colin Todd's demise as manager, 1991.

Argentina are the second best team in the world and there's no higher praise than that.
KEVIN KEEGAN, England manager, 2000.

Argentina won't be at Euro 2000 because they're from South America.
KEEGAN, 2000.

At this level, if five or six players don't turn up, you'll get beat.
KEEGAN after some Manchester City players 'went missing' at Villa Park, 2002.

The big monster called relegation is there, ready to bite us on the arse.
STEVE COPPELL, Crystal Palace manager, 2000.

We can only come out of this game with egg on our faces, so it's a real banana skin.
RAY STEWART, Stirling Albion manager, on facing non-League opposition in the Scottish Cup, 2001.

If we think they'll be easy meat, we'll end up with egg on our faces.
TERRY DOLAN, Bradford City manager, 1989.

Obviously for Scunthorpe it would be a nice scalp to put Wimbledon on their bottoms.
DAVE BASSETT, Wimbledon manager, 1984.

My strikers couldn't hit
a donkey's arse with a
frying pan.
*BASSETT, by now Sheffield
United manager, 1991.*

Football is a game – the
language it don't matter as
long as you run your
bollocks off.
*DANNY BERGARA,
Stockport's Uruguayan-born,
Spanish-speaking manager,
1991.*

We had a very constructive
discussion at half time,
then decided to give it the
full bollocks.
*RON ATKINSON, Aston Villa
manager, 1993.*

If you take liberties with the
opposition they'll pull your
trousers down.
*BILLY BONDS, West Ham
manager, 1991.*

Keith Curle has an ankle
injury but we'll have to take
it on the chin.
*ALAN BALL, Manchester City
manager, 1995.*

I've got irons in the fire and
things up my sleeve.
*STEVE McMAHON, Swindon
manager, 1997.*

I have other irons in the fire,
but I'm keeping them close
to my chest.
*JOHN BOND on leaving the
Manchester City manager's job,
1983.*

John Spencer's hamstring is
making alarm bells ring in
his head.
*CRAIG BROWN, Scotland
manager, 1996.*

If someone in the crowd spits
at you, you've just got to
swallow it.
*GARY LINEKER quoting the
advice of ex-Leicester manager
Gordon Milne, 1995.*

I felt a lump in my throat as
the ball went in.
*TERRY VENABLES, England
coach, 1996.*

At the end of the day it's
all about what we do on
the night.
*BRYAN HAMILTON,
Northern Ireland manager,
before game v. Germany, 1996.*

At the end of the day it's not the end of the world.
JIM McLEAN, Dundee United manager, after Uefa Cup final defeat v. Gothenberg, 1987.

There is a rat in the camp trying to throw a spanner in the works.
CHRIS CATTLIN, Brighton manager, 1983.

In football we all know that you stand still if you go backwards.
PETER REID, Sunderland manager, 1996.

Our back four was at sixes and sevens.
RON ATKINSON, Aston Villa manager, 1992.

There are 0-0 draws and 0-0 draws, and this was a 0-0 draw.
JOHN SILLETT, Coventry manager, 1989.

It was a game of two halves, and we were rubbish in both of them.
BRIAN HORTON, Oxford United manager, 1990.

In cup competitions, Jack will always have a chance of beating Goliath.
TERY BUTCHER, Sunderland manager, in his programme column, 1993.

The FA Cup touches so many people. It's a fair bet that, by the end of today, players you have never heard of will be household names – like that fellow who scored for Sutton United against Coventry City last season.
BOBBY CAMPBELL, Chelsea manager, in his programme column, 1990.

The first goal was a foul, the second was offside, and they would never have scored the third if they hadn't got the other two.
STEVE COPPELL, Crystal Palace manager, explaining defeat by Liverpool, 1991.

If corner-kicks hadn't been invented, this would have been a very close game.
NEIL WARNOCK, Sheffield United manager, after 4-1 defeat at Newcastle, 2000.

We were in an awkward position against Yugoslavia in that in order to win we needed to score more goals than they did.
JOSE ANTONIO CAMACHO, Spain coach, 2000.

I just wonder what would have happened if the shirt had been on the other foot.
MIKE WALKER, Norwich manager, after refereeing decisions allegedly went against his side v. *Manchester United, 1994.*

My players ran their socks into the ground for Manchester United.
ALEX FERGUSON, 1997.

If we played that every week, we wouldn't be so inconsistent.
BRYAN ROBSON, Manchester United captain, 1990.

If I was still at Ipswich, I wouldn't be where I am today.
DALIAN ATKINSON, Aston Villa striker, 1992.

Germany are a very difficult team to beat. They had 11 internationals out there today.
STEVE LOMAS, Northern Ireland captain, 1999.

If I played for Scotland, my grandma would be the proudest woman in the country if she wasn't dead.
MARK CROSSLEY, English-born goalkeeper [who later represented Wales], 1995.

The World Cup is every four years so this is going to be a perennial problem.
GARY LINEKER, TV football presenter, 1998.

You never know what could happen in a couple of one-off games like these.
GRAEME SHARP, former Scotland striker, before the play-off fixtures v. *England, 1999.*

Even when you're dead, you shouldn't lie down and let yourself be buried.
GORDON LEE, Everton manager, 1981.

Football matches are like days of the week. It can't be Sunday every day. There are also Mondays and Tuesdays.
GEORGE WEAH, Milan and Liberia striker, 1995.

We had enough chances to win the game. In fact we did win it.
ALEX SMITH, Aberdeen manager, 1991.

It was a draw, so in the end we didn't win.
DAVID BECKHAM to television interviewer after Manchester United draw with Croatia Zagreb, 1999.

You can't say my team aren't winners. They've proved that by finishing fourth, third and second in the past three seasons.
GERARD HOULLIER, Liverpool manager, 2002.

When their second goal went in, I knew our pig was dead.
DANNY WILLIAMS, Swindon manager, after they lost an FA Cup tie to West Ham, 1975.

Having players you've sold come back and score against you is what football's all about.
ALEX FERGUSON, Manchester United manager, 1992.

The missing of chances is one of the mysteries of life.
SIR ALF RAMSEY, England manager, 1972.

Being given chances and not taking them, that's what life is all about.
RON GREENWOOD, England manager, 1982.

Always remember that the goal is at the end of the field and not in the middle.
SVEN-GORAN ERIKSSON to his England squad, 2002.

Too many players were trying to score or create a goal.
GERARD HOULLIER, Liverpool manager, after home defeat by Watford, 1999.

It was a Limpalong Leslie sort of match.
PETER SHREEVES, Tottenham manager, after win v. Coventry, 1985.

It was a bad day at Black Rock.
*SHREEVES after Spurs' 5-1
defeat v. Watford a fortnight
later, 1985.*

What's the bottom line in
adjectives?
*SHREEVES after home loss to
Coventry, 1985.*

We threw caution to the wind
and came back from the dead.
Well it is Easter Monday.
*GLENN HODDLE, Swindon
player-manager, after they came
from 4-1 down to win 6-4 at
Birmingham, 1993.*

He was flapping about like a
kipper.
*JOHN BARNWELL, Notts
County manager, on Nicky
Law's costly handling offences v.
Tottenham, 1989.*

We held them for 89 minutes,
then they kippered us.
*DOGON ARIF, Fisher
Athletic manager, after defeat
by Telford, 1989.*

You must kill the bull or you
haven't done nowt.
*DANNY BERGARA,
Stockport's Uruguayan
manager, 1992.*

It was a mistake as big as a
house.
*RENE HIGUITA, Colombia
goalkeeper, after his error let in
Cameroon's Roger Milla for a
goal, World Cup finals, 1990.*

This for me is without
exception possibly my last
World Cup.
*RAY WILKINS, England
midfielder, en route to Mexico,
1986.*

The unthinkable is not
something we're really
thinking about at the
moment.
*PETER KENYON, chief
executive of Manchester United,
on the possibility of being
eliminated from the European
Cup, 2000.*

The new manager has given
us unbelievable belief.
*PAUL MERSON, Arsenal
midfielder, on Arsene Wenger's
impact at Highbury, 1996.*

I'm not a believer in luck, but
I do believe you need it.
*ALAN BALL, Manchester City
manager, 1996.*

Sometimes we are predictable, but out of that predictability we are unpredictable.
JOHN BECK, *Cambridge United manager, 1991.*

He's such an honest person it's untrue.
BRIAN LITTLE, *Aston Villa manager, on midfielder Ian Taylor, 1996.*

That's understandable and I understand that.
TERRY VENABLES, *England coach, 1996.*

That is in the past, and the past has no future.
DAVID PLEAT *on losing the Sheffield Wednesday manager's job, 1997.*

The road to ruin is paved with excuses.
BOBBY GOULD, *Coventry manager, after defeat by Leeds, 1993.*

I'm told we need a big name. Engelbert Humperdinck is a big name but it doesn't mean he can play football.
RAY HARFORD, *Blackburn manager, 1996.*

We're a First Division club in every sense of the word.
NAT LOFTHOUSE, *Bolton president, when the club languished in the Third, 1992.*

We must have had 99 per cent of the match. It was the other three per cent that cost us.
RUUD GULLIT *after Chelsea lost to Coventry, 1997.*

My team won't freeze in the white-hot atmosphere of Anfield.
RON SAUNDERS, *Aston Villa manager, 1980.*

We're halfway round the Grand National course with many hurdles to clear. So let's make sure we all keep our feet firmly on the ground.
MIKE BAILEY, *Charlton manager, as his team chased promotion, 1981.*

REPORTER: What are your impressions of Africa?
GORDON LEE: Africa? We're not in bloody Africa, are we?
Exchange between journalist and the Everton manager in Morooco, 1978.

Professional and amateur football have as much in common as a strawberry milkshake and a skyscraper.
HARALD SCHUMACHER, West Germany goalkeeper, in Blowing the Whistle, *1987.*

You can't compare English and German football. They're like omelette and muesli.
ERIK MEIJER, Dutch striker, leaving Liverpool for Hamburg, 2000.

There's no question of us playing for the draw. As we say in Germany: 'We will be going for the sausages.'
JURGEN ROBER, Hertha Berlin coach before game v. *Chelsea, 1999.*

The wall we had before Bochum scored from that free-kick looked as if it was built by Andy Warhol.
ULI HOENESS, Bayern Munich general manager, 2001.

The plastic pitch is a red herring.
GRAHAM TAYLOR, Aston Villa manager, after losing FA Cup tie at Oldham, 1990.

The players still had Christmas cake in their feet.
SERGIO CRAGNOTTI, Lazio president, after defeat by Napoli, 2001.

I can see the carrot at the end of the tunnel.
STUART PEARCE, England defender, on recovering from injury, 1992.

We eat a lot of McDonald's, where you have Ronald McDonald. So we chose the name Ronald.
RONALDO, Brazil striker, on his new-born son, 2000.

No one hands you cups on a plate.
TERRY McDERMOTT, Newcastle assistant manager, 1995.

Statistics are just like mini-skirts – they give you good ideas but hide the most important things.
EBBE SKOVDAHL, Aberdeen manager, 2001.

We're now arithmetically, not mathematically, safe from relegation. There's neither algebra nor geometry

involved in the calculations.
*TOM HENDRIE, St Mirren
manager, 1999.*

Never in the history of the
FAI Cup had a team wearing
hooped jerseys lost a final in
a year ending in 5.
*Home Farm [Dublin]
programme notes, 1985.*

Which Spanish side did
John Toshack take over
after leaving Sporting
Lesbian?
*Quiz question in Leek Town
programme, 1999.*

The transfer market has
changed because of the
Bosnian ruling.
*JOE KINNEAR, Wimbledon
manager, 1998.*

I expect the Croats to come
out...oh dear, I better not say
fighting, had I?
*PETER SHREEVES, Tottenham
manager, before match v.
Hajduk Split from war-torn
Croatia, 1991.*

If players won't die for this
club, then I don't want them.
*ALEX MILLER, Hibernian
manager, 1990.*

Our guys are getting
murdered twice a week.
*ANDY ROXBURGH, Scotland
coach, on the hectic schedule in
British football, 1991.*

I'd shoot myself if I had
the bottle.
*VINNIE JONES after being
sent off for the 10th time, 1995.*

I'd hang myself but the
club can't afford the rope.
*IAIN MUNRO, Hamilton
Academical manager, 1995.*

The shoot-out is like
shooting wee ducks at a
fairground to try to win
a prize.
*ALEX SMITH, Aberdeen
manager, after winning the
Scottish Cup on penalties, 1990.*

Being top won't change
much. It'll probably rain
tomorrow and the traffic
lights will still be red.
*HOWARD WILKINSON,
Leeds manager, on leading the
league for the first time in his
career, 1991.*

I feel like Corky the Cat,
who has been run over by
a steamroller, got up and

had someone punch him
n the stomach.
WILKINSON *after Leeds' FA
Cup defeat by Arsenal, 1993.*

When one door opens, another
smashes you in the face.
TOMMY DOCHERTY *on his
dismissal as manager of Preston,
1981.*

You are always one defeat
away from a crisis. On that
basis, we're in deep shit.
JOHN GREGORY, *Aston Villa
manager, during a losing
sequence, 1999.*

Q: What would you have
done if you hadn't been a
footballer?
A: A funeral director. I like
looking at dead bodies.
CHRIS SUTTON, *Chelsea
striker, in the club magazine*
Onside, *1999.*

My ambition is to meet
Prince Charles. I call
him 'King'.
ALAN BALL, *1979.*

We're like Lady Di. She's not
the Queen yet. She's not even
married. But like us, she's
nicely placed.

JIMMY SIRREL, *Notts County
manager, on his side's promotion
prospects as royal-wedding fever
spread, 1981.*

I never heard a minute's
silence like that.
GLENN HODDLE, *England
manager, at Wembley after
Princess Diana's death, 1997.*

Football is a fertility festival.
Eleven sperm trying to get
into the egg. I feel sorry for
the goalkeeper.
BJORK, *Icelandic pop singer, 1995.*

If we beat Real [Madrid] it
will be a nationwide orgasm.
JESUS GIL, *Atletico Madrid
president, before the derby, 1995.*

Dani is so good looking that
Villa didn't know whether to
mark him or bonk him.
HARRY REDKNAPP, *West
Ham manager, on his
Portuguese signing, 1996.*

The lad was sent off for
foul and abusive language
but he swears blind he didn't
say a word.
JOE ROYLE, *Oldham manager,
after Paul Warhurst's dismissal
v. Notts County, 1990.*

Tell him he's Pele and get him back on.
JOHN LAMBIE, Partick Thistle manager, on being told that concussed striker Colin McGlashan did not know who he was, 1993.

Ruel Fox is like a bar of soap. When he's on song it's hard to nail him down.
DAVE STRINGER, Norwich manager, 1990.

We let the convict out of jail, and we know what that they are like when they get free.
HOWARD WILKINSON, Leeds manager, after 3-0 defeat by VfB Stuttgart, 1992.

Rotherham reminds me of Bermuda. It's small so you bump into the same people two or three times a day.
SHAUN GOATER, Rotherham and Bermuda striker, 1993.

Q: Which TV programme would you most like to appear in?
A: Thunderbirds. I'd like to fly in Thunderbird II.
KEVIN KEEN, West Ham midfielder, interviewed in club programme, 1992.

Claim to fame outside soccer: I once put together an MFI wardrobe in less than four days.
TERRY GIBSON, Coventry striker, 1985.

I don't think my girlfriend would be too happy to hear I've been chasing Totti round Rome.
JONATHAN WOODGATE, teenaged Leeds defender, on the prospect of facing Roma's Francesco Totti, 1998.

There is nothing going on in the world at the moment that I find distressing or have a view on.
MICHAEL OWEN, 1999.

The trouble with you, son, is that your brains are all in your head.
BILL SHANKLY to unnamed Liverpool player, 1967.

I don't like being on my own because you think a lot and I don't like to think a lot.
PAUL GASCOIGNE on the TV documentary Gazza's Coming Home, *1996.*

England have the best fans in the world, and Scotland's are second to none.
KEVIN KEEGAN, England coach, 1999.

Young Gareth Barry you know, he's young.
KEEGAN, 2000.

I'm only 33 but my hair is 83.
ANDY RITCHIE, balding Oldham striker, 1994.

I know more about football than about politics.
HAROLD WILSON MP, Labour, Prime Minister, 1974.

I thought the No. 10, Whymark, played exceptionally well.
MARGARET THATCHER MP, Conservative, after the FA Cup final, 1978. Trevor Whymark was listed in the programme but did not play.

It's like going to a different country.
IAN RUSH on life in Italy with Juventus, 1988.

What you call football is like cricket to us.
ANDY WILLIAMS, American pop singer, 2002.

I definitely think we will need the two legs. It would be taking the piss to play on one.
TONY ADAMS, England defender, when they were drawn to play off against Scotland over two legs for a place at Euro 2000.

I don't really like the North of England. It's always raining, it's very cold and I don't like all those little houses.
FREDERIC KANOUTE, West Ham's French striker, 2001.

In programme notes there is a great deal of clap trap where subconsciously people tend to be become excuse worthy. I have often said to the players that there is talking and doing. Today will be a day of doing. At least we know the macabre has a habit of flourishing in different settings.
COLIN MURPHY, Lincoln programme column, 1989.

I happen to believe no one can work miracles and it strikes me that applies even to people like Holmes and

Watson, the Marx Brothers, Bilko, Inspector Clouseau or Winston Churchill. All these had immeasurable qualities but I don't know whether any of them had the attributes to be able to win promotion for Lincoln City FC with all the injuries and suspensions we have had.
COLIN MURPHY, Lincoln manager, from his 'Murph's Message' programme column, 1988.

We are now into a new season and I have no doubt that George and Mildred are delighted to be selling their cheese rolls in the Fourth Division... If we all remember that the fires of war should have some good feelings then we shall not be far short at the finish.
COLIN MURPHY in his programme message after Lincoln won promotion back into the Football League, 1988.

Music soothes the savage breast. The cobra has been tamed. Losing. A losing sequence, namely three games, always appears to put doubts in people's minds irrespective of the club's predicament and the doubting Thomas's doubt no more and the judges become experts. The cobra has an excellent habit of wriggling free and indeed Gordon Hobson wriggled three at Burnley.
COLIN MURPHY, Lincoln programme column, 1988.

People get mad over football, people enthuse over it, people exultate and people sadly even have started fighting and destructing over it.
COLIN MURPHY, Lincoln manager, 1988.

Football is important, but life is important too.
MAXIME BOSSIS, France player, after World Cup semi-final defeat by West Germany, 1986.

REPORTER: It was a funny game, Jim.
JIMMY SIRREL: Human beings are funny people.
Exchange between journalist and Notts County manager after match at Arsenal, 1982.

Footballers are no different from human beings.
GRAHAM TAYLOR, *England manager, 1992.*

Professional football is an interval between real life and real life.
TONY AGANA, *Sheffield United striker, 1990.*

I don't make predictions and I never will.
PAUL GASCOIGNE *on being asked for his new-year predictions, 1997.*

⑩

FANS

The only loyalty in football is between the supporter and his club. That will never die.
STEVE COPPELL *after leaving the Crystal Palace managership, 2000.*

Football is the only subject that can induce a bloke to swank about his fidelity.
HARRY PEARSON, author and Middlesbrough fan, in The Far Corner: A Mazy Dribble Through North-east Football, *1994.*

I have measured out my life in Arsenal fixtures, and any event of any significance has a footballing shadow. When did my first real love affair end? The day after a disappointing 2-2 draw at home to Coventry.
NICK HORNBY, author, in Fever Pitch, *1992.*

There's often talk about supporters winning representation on the board of their clubs. What's anyone doing on the board who isn't a fan in the first place?
MATTHEW HARDING, Chelsea vice-chairman, 1996.

Every thousandth person created, God unhinges their heads, scoops out their brains and issues them to football clubs [as supporters].
MIKE BATESON, Torquay chairman, 1996.

There's a fine line between loyalty and madness, and I'm not sure which side he's on. I think it's madness.
GARY ROWELL, former Sunderland player, on a fan who changed his name to Gary Sunderland AFC Lamb (and cited Rowell as his favourite-ever player), in a TV documentary about obsession, 2002.

I heard this bloke in the stand shouting 'McGraw [Alan, manager], we're fucking sick of what you're doing to Morton, buying bastards like Gahagan.' Two minutes later I scored the winner and as I ran back I heard the same guy shouting: "Yesssss, Johnny boy, gies another one!'
JOHN GAHAGAN, Morton player, 1990.

Things worth knowing:
That Association Football
is becoming notorious for
disgraceful exhibitions of
ruffianism. That the rabble
will soon make it impossible
for law-abiding citizens to
attend matches.
Scottish Athletic Journal, *1887.*

A northern horde of uncouth
garb and strange oaths.
Pall Mall Gazette *describing*
Blackburn Rovers' fans in
London for the FA Cup
final, 1884.

There is no real local interest
to excuse the frenzy of the
mob, since the players come
from all over the kingdom
and may change their clubs
each season.
C.B. Fry's magazine on crowd
trouble, 1906.

Miserable specimens...
learning to be hysterical as
they groan or cheer in panic
unison with their neighbours,
the worst sound of all being
the hysterical scream of
laughter that greets any trip
or fall by a player.
LORD BADEN POWELL,
founder of the Boy Scouts,

describing football spectators in
Scouting For Boys, 1908.

If they knew more about
football than we do, there
would be 50,000 players and
22 spectators.
BILL McCRACKEN, Newcastle
and Northern Ireland player, on
being barracked, 1911.

Generally he is short of
stature, anaemic looking,
with a head too big to
suggest it contains only
brains, a high shrieking voice,
reminiscent of a rusty saw in
quick staccato action. He is
blind to every move initiated
by the Swansea Town players,
but his attention to a faulty
clearance or badly placed pass
is microscopic.
Cygnet, columnist in Swansea's
Sporting News, *on barracking*
at Vetch Field, 1921.

Why not covered
accommodation for spectators,
dry ground to stand on and a
reduced admission if possible?
Many a wreath has been
purchased by standing on wet
ground on Saturday afternoons.
Letter to the Birmingham
Mail, *1905.*

A policeman called me at home. Friday night again. He'd caught a dozen courting couples in the stand and asked me what to do with them. I told him to fix the bloody fence and board 'em in. Best gate of the season it would've been.
FRED WESTGARTH, Hartlepools manager, 1957.

Q: What will you do when Christ comes to lead us again? A: Move St John to inside-right.
Church sign and answering graffito on Merseyside, 1965.

Football crowds are never going to sound like the hat parade on the club lawns of Cheltenham racecourse. They are always going to have more vinegar than Chanel.
ARTHUR HOPCRAFT, author, The Football Man, *1968.*

They tend to start off with things like 'Dear Stupid' or 'Dear Big Head'. One man wrote to me, beginning: 'Dear Alfie Boy.'
SIR ALF RAMSEY on his postbag, in Arthur Hopcraft's The Football Man, *1968.*

My favourite [letter received] is one which said: 'You, Smith, Jones and Heighway had better keep looking over your shoulder. You are all going to get your dews.'
EMLYN HUGHES, Liverpool captain, 1977.

The only point worth remembering about Port Vale's match with Hereford on Monday was the fact that the attendance figure, 2,744, was a perfect cube, 14 x 14 x 14.
Letter from 'Disillusioned Supporter' to Stoke-on-Trent's Sentinel *newspaper, 1979.*

I got some girl's knickers through the post the other day but I didn't like them. To be honest, they didn't fit.
JAMIE REDKNAPP, Liverpool midfielder, on his fan mail, 1995.

I got the ball in the middle of the field and a voice in the centre stand shouted out: 'Give it to Taylor.' So I gave it to Taylor. Five minutes later, I got the ball again and the same voice shouted: 'Give it to Matthews.' So I gave it to Matthews. A couple of

minutes later, I got the ball again, but this time there were three Arsenal players around me. So I looked up at the stand and the voice came back: 'Use your own discretion.'
STAN MORTENSEN, Blackpool and England player, in Robin Daniels' Blackpool Football, 1972.

It's gone now, mainly because of hooliganism. I wouldn't dare walk about now, in my old outfit, in another town. They'd be after me, wouldn't they? Around 1963, I could feel some spectators were getting out of hand.
SYD BEVERS, leader of the 'Atomic Boys', a group of Blackpool fans who attended games in fancy dress, 1972.

Five Newport County supporters were arrested after they turned up at a Kidderminster Harriers match in drag. About 150 visiting fans arrived in the town but 40 went to the Oxfam shop and bought women's clothes. 'I don't know whether this is a new style, or what it is,' said Superintendent Peter Picken.
Report in the Worcester Evening News, 1989.

There was this male MP who was found dead in stockings and suspenders. He was also wearing a Manchester City scarf but the police kept that bit quiet so as not to embarrass the relatives.
BERNARD MANNING, comedian and City supporter, 2000.

The Spurs fans, marching and shouting their way back to the station, banged on the windows of the [team] coach as it threaded its way through the crowds. 'Go on, smash the town up,' said Cyril [Knowles], encouraging them.
HUNTER DAVIES, The Glory Game, 1972.

The club call us hooligans, but who'd cheer them if we didn't come? You have to stand there and take it when Spurs are losing and the others are jeering at you. It's not easy. We support them everywhere and get no thanks.
Tottenham fan quoted in The Glory Game, 1972.

I'd like to kill all the Arsenal players and then burn the stand down.
Tottenham fan quoted in The Glory Game, *1972.*

The only answer is for decent supporters – and they are in the majority – to become terrace vigilantes. A few thumps on the nose would soon stop these silly youngsters.
ALEC STOCK, Fulham manager, 1975.

No one likes us, we don't care.
Song by Millwall fans to the tune of 'Sailing', 1980s.

Apparently they couldn't find one decent Millwall supporter.
DENIS HOWELL MP, Labour, Minister for Sport, complaining about an 'unbalanced' investigation into hooliganism by TV's Panorama, *1977.*

Really good Millwall supporters, right, they can't stand their club being slagged down you know, and it all wells up, you know, and you just feel like hitting someone.
Millwall fan quoted in Roger

Ingham et al, Football Hooliganism: The Wider Context, *1978.*

We don't normally have any police at our matches, unless one happens to wander up on his bike.
Salisbury Town secretary after the non-League club drew Millwall in the FA Cup, 1979.

He told me I was a dead man and that I wouldn't get out of The Den alive. Then he said I was fat. I said: 'Have you looked at yourself lately?'
KEVIN PRESSMAN, Sheffield Wednesday goalkeeper, on being confronted by a pitch invader at Millwall, 1995.

If Cantona had jumped into our crowd he'd never have come out alive.
ALEX RAE, Millwall midfielder, after the Frenchman's Selhurst Park fracas, 1995.

I must have done all right for them to gob all over me.
STEVE JONES, Bournemouth striker, after running a gauntlet of Birmingham fans, 1994.

The most violent offenders should be flogged in front of the main stand before home games. I feel so strongly on this that I'd volunteer to do the whipping myself.
ALLAN CLARKE, Leeds manager, 1980.

I know it sounds drastic but the only way to deal with hooligans is to shoot them. That'll stop them.
BOBBY ROBERTS, Colchester manager, 1980.

There are more hooligans in the House of Commons than at a football match.
BRIAN CLOUGH, Nottingham Forest manager, 1980.

I met these football fans smoking in a non-smoker on the railway, so I said: 'Put it out...put it out.' And they did. I think they're far less dangerous than dogs.
BARABARA WOODHOUSE, dog trainer and TV personality, 1980.

What comes next – water cannon, guards, tanks and consultant undertakers to ferry away the dead?

SIMON TURNEY, Greater London Council official, on Chelsea's proposed electric fence, 1985.

You can't turn a fire-extinguisher on fans. It'll only inflame the situation.
JOHN BALL, West Ham safety officer, after their followers were doused at French club Metz, 1999.

There have always been hooligans. In Germany they were in the Gestapo and in Russia they were in the KGB.
HOWARD WILKINSON, Leeds manager, after violence by his club's fans at Bournemouth, 1990.

What's the first word to come into your head when I say 'British soccer fan'? It was 'subhuman' wasn't it? I rest my case.
Philadelphia Inquirer, *doubting the wisdom of the United States staging the World Cup, 1990.*

There were three countries in the world whose presence would have created logistical and security problems, so we're very pleased they won't

be coming: Iraq, Iran and England.
ALAN ROTHENBERG, chairman of the US World Cup committee, 1994.

Every British male, at some time or other, goes to his last football match. It may very well be his first football match.
MARTIN AMIS, novelist, reviewing a book on 'football' hooliganism, 1991.

The fans all had the complexion and body-scent of a cheese-and-onion crisp, and the eyes of pit-bulls.
AMIS on his experience of watching Queen's Park Rangers, 1991.

English fans are brilliant. In England, when you ask someone which club he supports, it means something. The guy supports a club for his whole life, whatever the ups and downs. In France, there's no loyalty. If you're not top of the League, the fans go to another club.
ERIC CANTONA, newly signed to Leeds, on hearing that England fans had rioted in Sweden, 1992.

Football matches are now the substitute for the old medieval tournaments. They are aggressive and confrontational by their nature. It's perfectly natural for some of the fans to be obstreperous.
ALAN CLARK MP, Conservative, defending rioting England fans, World Cup finals, 1998.

Now that we don't have war, what's wrong with a good punch-up? We're a nation of yobs. Without that characteristic, how did we colonise the world? With so many milksops, left-wing liberals and wetties around, I rejoice that some people keep up our historic spirit.
DOWAGER MARCHIONESS OF READING, aged 79, after hooliganism by England fans, World Cup finals, 1998.

The people kicking up a fuss in Marseilles are true fans. They feel passionate enough about the England team to go out and fight for them.
ELLIS CASHMORE, sociology professor, 1998.

It's not surprising some fans behave badly when you realise how little consideration they receive from the clubs.
COLIN SMITH, Chief Constable, Thames Valley Police, 1990.

Football violence is like smoking. If you try it once and hate it, you don't do it again. But if you try it once and like it, it's bloody hard to give up.
DOUGIE & EDDY BRIMSON, self-confessed Watford hooligans, in their joint book Everywhere We Go, *1996.*

The terraces are the very last bastion of our once male-dominated culture, where boys can grow up and act like men...scream, shout, abuse, swear, even cry if we like without feeling like some effeminate twat.
DOUGIE BRIMSON, Watford fan and author of A Geezer's Guide to Football: A Lifetime of Lads and Lager, *1998.*

I think going to football and fighting is an illness. I don't think you can just stop.
DANNY WALFORD, 21-year-old Chelsea 'hooligan', in the Donal McIntyre TV programme Under Cover, *1999.*

Like other infections, new strains of football hooliganism are developing that are clever, resilient and increasingly resistant.
BRYAN DREW, National Criminal Intelligence Service spokesman, 2001.

Football is not about people setting out to watch a match and never returning home.
PETER RIDSDALE, Leeds chairman, after two of the club's fans were stabbed to death in Istanbul, 2000.

Even the hooligans had a good time and enjoyed the party. Maybe the cannabis relaxed them.
JOHAN BEELAN, Dutch police chief, on the behaviour of England fans in Eindhoven, 2000.

We don't welcome yobs in any form, but that isn't to say we're against tribal loyalty. And our tribe aren't half fearsome when they want something.
KARREN BRADY, Birmingham City managing director, 2002.

The English stick their psychos in Broadmoor, while the Welsh put theirs in Ninian Park.
Fulham fanzine There's Only One F in Fulham, *awarding Cardiff City supporters 0 out of 10 in their Best Fans poll, 1995.*

Do they hate us? You go to take a corner at Elland Road and you've got 15,000 horrible skinheads in their end yelling murder at you.
RYAN GIGGS on Leeds fans, 1994.

The bloke next to me is reading *American Psycho*. It may well be the only book Leeds fans have ever read. This is how they think life is.
JOHN AIZLEWOOD, author of Playing At Home, *a travelogue of the 92 League grounds, 1999.*

I went over to take a kick where the Chelsea fans were and they started chucking things at me. Not the usual plastic cups and cans, but sticks of celery and sweetcorn. I don't know what that was about, but it made me laugh to think of them popping into greengrocers' shops on the way to Wembley.
RYAN GIGGS, after the FA Cup final; Manchester United v. Chelsea, 1994.

I made a two-finger gesture towards the fans to show that I'd scored twice, and that must have been misinterpretated.
PAUL PESCHISOLIDO, West Bromwich Albion striker, after confrontation with Port Vale supporters, 1997.

The Scotland fans' ability to smuggle drink into matches makes Papillon look like a learner.
Scottish Police Federation spokesman, 1981.

Communism *v.* Alcoholism
Scottish banner at Soviet Union v. Scotland, World Cup finals, 1982.

The kind of commitment Scots invest in football means there's less left for the more important concerns.
WILLIAM McILVANNEY, novelist and journalist, in feature on Scottish independence, reprinted in Surviving the Shipwreck, *1992.*

When Patrick Kluivert scored, it was the same feeling as when Mel Gibson got hung, drawn and quartered at the end of *Braveheart.*
DOMINIK DIAMOND, *broadcaster and Scotland fan, after a late Dutch goal* v. *England eliminated Scotland from the European Championship finals, 1996.*

Get intae them! Get intae them!
Chant by Scotland fans as Scotland kicked against no opposition after Estonia refused to agree to switch the kick-off time, 1996.

One team in Tallinn, there's only one team in Tallinn...
Song by Scotland fans when Estonia failed to turn up for match v. *Scotland, 1996.*

Most Scotland supporters have woken up to the fact that wearing the kilt is probably the easiest way in the world of attracting the opposite sex.
Haggis Supper, *Scotland fanzine, 1999.*

Who are the people? We arra people!
Rangers' fans' call-response chant, 1960s.

The Glaswegian definition of an atheist: a bloke who goes to Rangers-Celtic match to watch the football.
SANDY STRANG, *Rangers supporter, in Stephen Walsh, Voices of the Old Firm, 1995.*

After I joined Celtic I was walking down a street in Glasgow when someone shouted: 'Fenian bastard.' I had to look it up – Fenian, that is.
MICK McCARTHY, *Yorkshire-born Republic of Ireland manager, 1996.*

I'm a small, balding, ex-Communist, Celtic-supporting Catholic and Unionist. Therefore everyone seems to hate me.
DR JOHN REID MP, *Labour, Secretary of State for Northern Ireland, 2001.*

I would rather watch Celtic than be a bishop.
RODERICK WRIGHT *after relinquishing his post as Bishop of Argyll, 1996.*

I'm not a violent man but when you see the first flash of green or a Republic of Ireland jersey, something inside of you snaps.
Rangers supporter, interviewed on Channel 4 documentary Football, Faith and Flutes, *1995.*

They call themselves Protestants. But they say that just because they want to be different from Catholics. Most of them are atheists.
Celtic supporter on Football, Faith and Flutes, *as above, 1995.*

In Glasgow half the football fans hate you and the other half think they own you.
TOMMY BURNS, Celtic midfielder, 1987.

For a while I did unite Rangers and Celtic fans. There were people in both camps who hated me.
MO JOHNSTON on his spells on either side of Glasgow's great divide, 1994.

I hear that couples sometimes arrive at the Mersey derby together but wearing opposing colours. If you did that in Glasgow you'd get lynched.
JOHN COLLINS, Everton and former Celtic midfielder, 1998.

It angers me to see Rangers or Celtic fanatics getting all steamed up in the name of religion when most of them have never been near a church or a chapel in years.
DEREK JOHNSTONE, Rangers player, in Rangers: My Team, *1979.*

Do you want your share of the gate money, Jock, or shall we just return the empties?
BILL SHANKLY to opposing manager Jock Stein after visiting Scots threw bottles when Liverpool beat Celtic in the European Cup-Winners' Cup, 1966.

After the match against Inverness Caley [Celtic lost 3-2] I felt I was caught up in the Kosovo war, not a damaging football result. Some so-called fans covered my car in spit and shouted obscenities at me...It was stone-age stuff from reptiles.
IAN WRIGHT, Celtic and former Arsenal striker, 2000.

We were thrown to a veritable wild horde. It was a meeting of warriors where neither weakness nor nonchalance had a place. It was a test in the pure British tradition.
FABIEN BARTHEZ, Monaco goalkeeper, on the atmosphere at Rangers, 2000.

Sigmund Freud once described humour as being as incongruous as a buckled wheel, but he never played the old Glasgow Empire on a wet Monday night after both Rangers and Celtic had lost on the Saturday.
KEN DODD, comedian, 2002.

Joey ate the Frogs' legs
Made the Swiss roll
Now he's Munching Gladbach
Slogan on Liverpool fans' banner in praise of defender Joey Jones, European Cup final, 1977.

Jesus is a Wiganer
Slogan on Wigan Athletic fans' banner after Jesus Seba was signed from Zaragoza, 1996.

Brazil would pick Le Tiss
Slogan on Southampton fans' banner protesting against his

omission from the England squad v. Brazil, 1995.

Paul McGrath limps on water
Slogan on Derby fans' banner in praise of the injury-blighted defender, 1997.

Our husbands think we're shopping in Dublin
Slogan on Republic of Ireland fans' banner in Portugal, 1995.

Sex and Drugs and Oranje Goals
Banner at Dutch matches, Euro 2000.

Forget Ulrika – There's only one Good Johnsen
Slogan on Chelsea fans' banner in honour of Eidur Gudjohnsen, 2002.

The Silence of the Rams
Slogan on anti-Derby T-shirt sold outside Nottingham Forest ground, 1993.

I don't really think it's much fun when 50,000 spectators are singing: 'Posh Spice takes it up the a***' every weekend.
VICTORIA BECKHAM on the TV documentary Victoria's Secrets, 2000.

I thought I had seen it all when it comes to the fickleness of football folk. Then I heard the Spurs fans singing: 'There's only one Alan Sugar.'
MICK McCARTHY, Millwall manager, 1994.

We seem to be lumbered with the 'Inger-lund, Inger-lund, Inger-lund' chant. That may be boring but at least everyone knows the words.
HELEN JOSLIN, Football Supporters' Association official as England reached the semi-finals of the European Championship, 1996.

I wish there were 10,000 more in the ground chanting for my blood.
LEN WALKER, Aldershot manager, after demonstration against him by 50 fans, 1983.

Peter Shilton, Peter Shilton, does your missus know you're here?
Arsenal North Bank to the Nottingham Forest keeper after a tabloid revealed he had been caught in a compromising position in a car late at night, 1980.

We all agree, Emmerdale's better than Brookside.
Song by Halifax fans during FA Cup tie v. Marine on Merseyside, 1992.

We all agree, Asda is better than Harrods.
Song by Charlton fans at Mohamed Fayed-owned Fulham, 1999.

There's this staunch Stoke City fan who's getting some earache from his missus. 'You'd rather go and watch Stoke than take me out,' she complains. 'Correction,' he replies. 'I'd rather go and watch Port Vale than take you out.'
PETE CONWAY, Potteries comedian and father of singer Robbie Williams, 1991.

UNITED FANS: We want 10! We want 10!
IPSWICH FANS: We want one! We want one!
Chant and response in closing stages of Manchester United's 9-0 win, 1995.

It wasn't so much the death threats or the vandalism, but when you sit with your

family in the directors' box and hear a couple of thousand people chanting 'Gilbert Blades is a wanker', then you feel it's time to go.
GILBERT BLADES, on resigning as Lincoln chairman, in Anton Rippon's book Soccer: The Road to Crisis, *1982.*

I always answer letters from supporters. It's the death threats I object to.
REG BURR, Millwall chairman, 1990.

I understand and sympathise with their strong feelings, but I cannot accept their conservatism or parochialism.
ROBERT MAXWELL, Oxford chairman, on opposition from Oxford and Reading fans to his proposed merger of the clubs as Thames Valley Royals, 1983.

You can't force people to sit down, even if they have a seat. They want to sing, and unless you're Val Doonican you can't do that sitting down.
KEVIN KEEGAN, Newcastle manager, speaking against all-seated stadia, 1992.

In 10 years' time they will be sitting in the stand, watching the match, and their children will say: 'Daddy, did you really stand over there, in the wind and the rain? And did the man behind you urinate in your back pocket? And did you have a pie from that awful shop and a pint of beer thrust in your hand on a cold day?' The kids just will not understand.
SIR JOHN HALL, Newcastle chairman, 1995.

The World Cup in America was a throwback to the 1950s, in the way that 'rival' supporters enjoyed mixing with each other. The only trouble I saw was at a concert in the Dodgers Stadium.
RON ATKINSON, ITV pundit and Aston Villa manager, at the finals, 1994.

The atmosphere in the USA isn't right. The American public look at a game as a day out to eat hot-dogs and popcorn. In Europe the fans can't eat because their stomachs are tight with tension.
ANTONIO MATERRESE,

Italian FA president, at the World Cup finals in the United States, 1994.

The tension felt by football fans during penalty shoot-outs can trigger heart attacks and strokes in male spectators. The day Holland lost to France in Euro 96, deaths from heart attacks and strokes rose by 50 per cent.
DR MIRIAM STOPPARD, 2002.

It may have been an awful night, but the meat-and-potato pies were brill.
'Away Traveller', columnist in Crewe Alexandra supporters' newsletter after visit to Halifax, 1983.

My apologies to you all for supporting us through this trying season.
VINCE BARKER, Hartlepool chairman, in his final programme column, 1984.

It's bad enough having to go and watch Bristol City without having things stolen.
JUDGE DESMOND VOWDEN QC, sentencing a man who stole from a City fan's car, 1984.

I knew my days were numbered when I was warming up behind the goal at Parkhead and one of our fans shouted: 'Kinnaird, we like the Poll Tax more than we like you.'
PAUL KINNAIRD, Partick Thistle player, on his time with St Mirren, 1992.

Football fanzines are a case of successful cultural contestation in and through sport.
JOHN HORNE, Staffordshire Polytechnic lecturer and co-author of a paper on fanzines in Sociology Review, *1991.*

The worse the team, the better the fanzine.
JOHN HORNE, sociology lecturer, 1991.

Look Back in Amber
Hull City fanzine title, 1990s.

Dial M for Merthyr
Merthyr Tydfil fanzine title, 1990s.

Hyde! Hyde! What's the Score?
Preston fanzine title, 1990s. The name refers to North End's 26-0 win v. Hyde in 1887.

And Smith Must Score!
Brighton fanzine title, named after the TV commentary to Gordon Smith's last-minute miss in 1983 FA Cup final, 1988.

Sing When We're Fishing
Grimsby fanzine title, 1988.

City Till I Cry
Manchester City fanzine title, 1999.

The only time I turn my pager off is when I'm watching Burnley.
ALISTAIR CAMPBELL, press secretary to Prime Minister Tony Blair, 1999.

He has very broad musical taste, anything from Elgar and Bach to Genesis and Supertramp. He also supports Arsenal, but then nobody's perfect.
BRIAN PEARSON, secretary to the Archbishop of Canterbury, Dr George Carey, 1990.

I will die a Catholic. I will die an Arsenal fan. And I will die a Tory.
CHRIS PATTEN, former chairman of the Conservative party, 2000.

When we won the League in '89 it was the most cosmic thing that had ever happened. Better than any orgasm ever.
EMMA YOUNG, Arsenal fan, quoted in Tom Watt, The End: 90 Years of Life on Arsenal's North Bank, *1993.*

Fans are interested in their team being successful. If they wanted to see entertaining football rather than get results week in, week out, why don't all the Arsenal supporters follow Spurs or Chelsea?
DAVE BASSETT, Sheffield United manager, 1995.

I do hate Arsenal. With a passion. No money in the world would ever tempt me to play for them.
TEDDY SHERINGHAM, Tottenham player and fan, 1996.

Q: Which TV programme would you switch off?
A: Soaps and Luton on *Match of the Day.*
VINNIE JONES, childhood Watford fan, in Chelsea programme questionnaire, 1991.

I am a human being. I support Aston Villa, but I am still a human being.
JOHN TAYLOR, prospective Conservative candidate for Cheltenham, on being labelled a 'bloody nigger' by fellow Tories, 1990.

I still support the Villa but I don't like football as much as I did because the game has been tailored to the wine-bar fraternity. The culture has gradually been eradicated.
NIGEL KENNEDY, classical violinist, 1997.

You lose some, you draw some.
JASPER CARROTT on being a Birmingham City fan, 1979.

Any man who is paid to serve his country should never try to gain financially. That may seem an old-fashioned idea, but I am very patriotic at every level. I adore my county cricket team, Somerset, and my football team, because I support the greatest team in England, Bristol Rovers.
JEFFREY ARCHER, author and Tory politician, during the Spycatcher *case, 1987.*

You folks may be rightly proud of your title 'Football's Fairest Crowd', but for my part I would like to see a lot more partisanship in favour of Chelsea. All too many people come to Stamford Bridge to see a football match – instead of to cheer Chelsea.
TED DRAKE, Chelsea manager, in his programme column, 1952.

I collected Chelsea programmes for years, took them to New York with me when I moved there. But when I arrived and unpacked, I discovered they had all been stolen. It was very sad.
VIDAL SASSOON, hairdresser-millionaire, 1988.

[Fidel] Castro called the victory by the Cuban volleyball team over the US a 'sporting, psychological, patriotic and revolutionary triumph'. At Chelsea we're quite happy to settle for three points.
SEBASTIAN COE, former athlete, budding politician and Chelsea fan, 1990.

When I called Coventry
supporters a bunch of
wankers, it was the best 15
grand I ever spent.
*IAN WRIGHT, Arsenal striker,
recalling one of the fines he
incurred during his career, 1999.*

Adrian attends Bromley
Comprehensive and is a keen
goalkeeper. In his spare time
he likes listening to music
and playing computer games.
His favourite players have left
the club.
*CRYSTAL PALACE
programme on the mascot for
game v. Leicester, 1999.*

Fulham's support is an
enigma. I asked one woman
how she'd feel if we signed a
£2m player. She said: 'We
don't want £2m players here.'
*KEVIN KEEGAN, 'chief
operating officer' at Craven
Cottage, 1998.*

Mr Stanley Heathman,
married with five children,
said they had never been in
any doubt that they would be
liberated. It was just a matter
of how and when. He
astonished one soldier by
asking: 'Can you tell me –

have Leeds been relegated?'
*Pooled despatch by journalists
covering the Falklands War,
1982.*

It's often said that no club
have a divine right to be in
the First Division – well we
bloody have.
The Hanging Sheep, *Leeds
fanzine, 1988. Leeds had been in
the Second for six years.*

The accused claimed he was
the reincarnated brother of
Conan the Barbarian, that he
was turning into an elk and
had played for Leeds United.
A defence psychiatrist said he
was mad.
Court report, Daily Telegraph,
1988.

Man offers marriage proposal
to any woman with ticket for
Leeds *v.* Sheffield United
game. Must send photograph
(of ticket).
Advert in Yorkshire Evening
Post *as Second Division title race
came to the boil, 1990.*

I was in the Leeds fans' end,
chanting and going mad, and
the fans were saying: 'Hang
on, what's he doing here?'

NOEL WHELAN, Leeds-born Coventry striker, on continuing to follow his previous club when off duty, 1996.

I even judge people's characters according to whether they support Manchester United.
ARDAL O'HANLON, Leeds-supporting comedian, 2001. His father, the Irish politician Dr Rory O'Hanlon, is a Manchester United fan.

I don't expect people to change the team they support easily. I've supported Leeds United all my life and always will.
NASSER HUSSAIN, England and Essex cricket captain, on suggestions that British-based Asians should support England, 2001.

I told my lads that if they signed for Man United they would have to keep their shirts in their garage.
MARCUS WALMSLEY, Leeds fan, whose eight-year-old twins turned down United for Leeds, 1999.

I'd like to have been born Bob Latchford and then become Nye Bevan when I was too old to play football.
DEREK HATTON, Everton fan and former Labour councillor in Liverpool, 1988.

You always knew when it was derby week [on Merseyside]. The postman would say: 'We'll be ready for you.' Then the milkman would come round: 'You're in for it Saturday.' Then it would be the taxi driver. You never got away from it.
GORDON LEE, former Everton manager, in Brian Barwick and Gerald Sinstadt, The Great Derbies: Everton *v.* Liverpool, *1988.*

If I found out a candidate was a closet Man United supporter I would have to think very hard about voting for them.
ADRIAN HENRI, poet, painter and Liverpool fan, during General Election, 1992.

The fans keep waiting for something to go wrong. I call it City-itis. It's a rare disease whose symptoms are relegation twice every three years.

JOE ROYLE, Manchester City manager, as the club chased promotion, 2000.

I inherited two fatal flaws from my father: premature baldness and Manchester City, neither of which I can change.

HOWARD DAVIES, former deputy governor of the Bank of England, 1996.

I was in a bar in Manchester after watching City and these people wanted me to sign their programmes. One wanted me to put: 'You can bank on City for promotion.'

NICK LEESON, City fan and the trader who brought down Barings Bank, 1999.

I didn't watch the 1968 European Cup final. I never watch any match I think United might win.

Manchester City fan on the TV programme Manchester United Ruined My Life, *1998.*

Our new guitarist and bassist have to have nice taste in shoes and a good haircut, and not be

a Man United fan. If they can do that, they're sorted.

LIAM GALLAGHER, Manchester City-supporting singer with Oasis, 1999.

People are saying that Rupert Murdoch now owns Manchester United, but the fans own United and it's the same at Villa.

JOHN GREGORY, Aston Villa manager, 1999.

When we go away, there are all the supporters' coaches from places like Dover and Falmouth. I had never even heard of Falmouth. I like that passion. It seeps into you.

ALEX FERGUSON on Manchester United's nationwide following, 1995.

Fans can get very snooty about football. So a couple of ponces from Hampstead support Man United? Good luck to them.

PAUL WHITEHOUSE, comedian/actor and Welsh-born Tottenham fan, 1999.

The further you go from home, the more of the sad bastards there are. Kent is

full of them. Half the kids who go to my lad's school take their dinner in a Stretford Sam lunch box, tucked away in a Fred the Red rucksack.
Manchester City fanzine, King of the Kippax, *on United fans, 1999.*

I love Newcastle, I love that raw passion. I remember being there once and hearing newspaper vendors shouting: 'Sensation! Andy Cole Toe Injury!' Most people use the word 'sensation' for 'Major Resigns' or 'Aids Spreading Over Country'. It's unbelievable. Glasgow's like that.
ALEX FERGUSON, 1995.

With all those replica strips in the stands, coming to Newcastle is like playing in front of 40,000 baying zebras.
DAVID PLEAT, Sheffield Wednesday manager, 1997.

During the kerfuffle over Michael Heseltine's pit closures, Brian Clough led a march past my surgery, which is a short walk from the City Ground. Forest were heading for relegation at the time and I threatened to lead a counter-march past the ground.
KENNETH CLARKE MP, Conservative, Nottingham Forest fan, in Football and the Commons People, *1995.*

I've got this tattoo on my arm that says '100 per cent Blade'. When we were filming the steamy scenes in *Lady Chatterley's Lover*, Ken Russell used to hide it with a strategically placed fern.
SEAN BEAN, actor and Sheffield United supporter, 1996.

I did my grieving when I was kicked out of the band. Frankly, I'm more concerned about how Port Vale get on in the FA Cup tonight.
ROBBIE WILLIAMS as Take That broke up hours before Vale beat Everton, the Cup holders, 1996.

Supporting a second team in the Premier League is like Yasser Arafat saying he has a soft spot for Judaism.
NICK HANCOCK, TV presenter and Stoke City fan, 1997.

Can anything be done about entertaining us after the kick-off?
Stoke supporter during discussion of pre-match entertainment during the club's AGM, 1999.

It says on my birth certificate that I was born in the borough of West Bromwich, in the district of West Bromwich. I said all right, all right, I'll support the bloody Albion – no need to twist my arm.
FRANK SKINNER, comedian, 1995.

My great heroes are Sir Stanley Matthews and Dave Beasant.
JUNE WHITFIELD, comedy actress and Wimbledon supporter, 1988.

Q: What was the first gig you ever went to?
A: Wolves 2 Moscow Dynamo 1 on 9 November 1955.
ROBERT PLANT, former Led Zeppelin singer, interviewed in Q magazine, 1993.

As much as I love women and music, my first love will always be football.
ROD STEWART, pop singer, former Brentford trialist and Scotland fan, 1995.

Famous Carlisle United fans: Melvyn Bragg (unless he's in London, then he's an Arsenal supporter) and Hunter Davies (unless he's in London, then he's a Spurs fan).
Total Football *magazine, 1995.*

What a nightmare. I'm a Tottenham fan and I get cuffed to you.
TONY ADAMS, Arsenal captain, on what was said by the prisoner handcuffed to him following his arrest for drink-driving, 1998.

When socialists fall out, the Tories rejoice. When Sheffield Wednesday supporters fall out, the gods weep.
ROY HATTERSLEY, Wednesdayite and ex-deputy leader of the Labour party, 2000.

All that Sheffield has talked about for months is football. If there is a pit closure, or a factory goes down the pan, the MP has to get involved, so why shouldn't we use our

influence to try to save this club?
JOE ASHTON MP, Labour, Wednesday fan and former director, responding to accusations of interfering in the club's affairs by arguing that Danny Wilson should be relieved of the manager's job, 2000.

Anyone who has had to support the Labour party these past five years knows what it's like to be a West Ham fan. There is a great similarity in the 'Oh, fucking hell', head-in-hands response you have to what they do, the own goals and ridiculous defeats.
BILLY BRAGG, rock singer and socialist, 1991.

Not many people have to quit the BBC just to watch the Albion, but I did.
DES LYNAM, TV presenter, watching Brighton & Hove Albion on his first free Saturday after leaving Match of the Day, 1999.

Trying to explain why we hate Palace is like trying to explain why grass is green and vomit limp. We just do.

ATTILA THE STOCKBROKER, poet-ranter and Brighton fan, 1995.

Everyone talks about what people like David Beckham and Graeme Le Saux have to put up with. But I can assure you it's far worse in the First Division than the Premiership. When a visiting player gets a red card, it's the highlight of the day for some home supporters. They jump up and down with delight as though they have just won the game.
IAN WRIGHT, former England striker, on life with Burnley, 2000.

At the Worthington Cup final, when there was trouble on the pitch, with Robbie Savage involved, there was this guy behind me yelling: 'Savage, you cheating, long-haired, gypsy Welsh cunt.' I had to turn to him and say: 'Oi mate, less of the Welsh.'
PAUL WHITEHOUSE, comedian/actor and Welsh-born Tottenham fan, 1999.

It'll be a good day for the burglars and one when the sheep will be left in peace.

DICK CAMPBELL, *Brechin City manager, on the exodus of fans from the city (population 10,000) to Rangers for a Scottish Cup tie, 2001.*

The pub landlords in Walsall will be in the Bahamas in two weeks' time on the money they take tonight.
RAY GRAYDON, Walsall manager, after derby win at Wolves, 1999.

If it was one of our meat pies, it could have done more damage than a brick.
ANDY RITCHIE, Oldham manager, after food was thrown at the referee during FA Cup match v. Chelsea, 1999.

Q: What's the craziest request you have ever had from a fan?
A: Can you do your brother's autograph?
CARL HODDLE, Barnet midfielder and brother of Glenn, answering Sun *questionnaire, 1995.*

Did I get any enjoyment from my visit to Marston Road? As a matter of fact I did. Guessing the contents of the liquid which came out of the tea urn fired my imagination for some time.
Letter from disaffected Stafford Rangers fan to Staffordshire Newsletter, 1992.

When Saturday comes, a hell of a lot of lads go home with a hard-on.
JULIE BURCHILL, writer and critic, claiming a homo-erotic motivation for male football fans in her book Burchill on Beckham, *2001.*

Show me a man who loves football and nine times out of 10 you'll be pointing at a really bad shag.
BURCHILL in Burchill on Beckham, *2001.*

Diehard football fans are much more optimistic about their sex appeal after a victory.
DR MIRIAM STOPPARD claming football could induce hormonal change, 2002.

The bottom line is that I am English. I feel closer to England than to France. I love the fans in England. They are very passionate.
ERIC CANTONA, by now Barcelona-based, 2001.

I only hope that callers to *Six-O-Six* repeatedly ask David Mellor how he is on the off-chance that he will one day reply: 'Terminally ill.'
Letter to When Saturday Comes *magazine, 1999.*

You won't get me flicking on a [football] phone-in. I'd rather listen to a game of chess on the radio. Phone-ins are platforms for idiots.
JOE ROYLE, Manchester City manager, 2001.

There's a new breed of flash young executives who think they've got the right to call to account anyone in the world.
RON GREENWOOD, England manager, after the Wembley crowd booed his team v. Spain, 1981.

Football's getting too polished and nice and trendy now. You get media people in London saying: 'Football's the new rock 'n' roll.' For all us working class, football's a way of life, always has been.
SEAN BEAN, actor and Sheffield United fan, 1996.

I went with two friends to watch Forest's game at Barnsley. It cost over £60 to watch the football equivalent of what French farmers have been feeding their cattle.
Letter to Nottingham's Football Post, *1999.*

Same old story. Lost 5-0. Sometimes I wonder why I couldn't have been born in Liverpool.
RICHARD O. SMITH writing in Boston United fanzine Behind Your Fences *about a game at Cheltenham, 1990.*

Some people come to Old Trafford and I don't think they can spell football, let alone understand it. They have a few drinks and a prawn sandwich and don't realise what's going on out on the pitch.
ROY KEANE, Manchester United captain, on the club's corporate supporters, 2000.

The man in the street has been pushed aside for the corporate fan.
MARTIN O'NEILL, Leicester manager, 1999.

The average working lad can't understand or relate to the money involved in the game, but he'll go along with it if he believes it will make his team better.
ALEX FERGUSON, in interview with Racing Post, *1999.*

They sit and admire the stadium, waiting to be entertained as if they were at a musical. We have lots of visitors for whom it's a weekend holiday, and that's no use to me or the players.
ALEX FERGUSON on Manchester United's changing support, 1997.

There is an element of people coming to Old Trafford for the first time, looking around the place and forgetting there is a game on.
FERGUSON urging 'control' of corporate supporters, 1999.

Some fans would prefer we went back to Plough Lane and played Third Division football. They aren't true supporters. They'll end up buying a season ticket for Fulham.
CHARLES KOPPEL, Wimbledon chairman, arguing for the club to relocate to Milton Keynes, 2001.

If you listened to the fans you wouldn't have a club. I spend 40 per cent of my working life here for nothing. So I'm going to listen to someone who pays £15 on a Saturday? Leave it out.
BARRY HEARN, Leyton Orient chairman, 1999.

Why hasn't anyone taken me to a soccer game? There must be some English boy who wants to take me, for God's sake. I'll just have to cry and hope that someone will take me.
GWYNETH PALTROW, American actress, 2000.

11

BOARDROOM

Beware of the clever sharp men who are creeping into the game.
WILLIAM McGREGOR, founder of the Football League, in League Football and the Men Who Made It, 1909.

A man who gives himself up to football, body and soul, will take risks and get himself entangled in such a way as he would never consider in the conduct of his own business.
SIR FREDERICK WALL, FA secretary, in his book Fifty Years of Football, 1935.

We shall all be rich one day when we've got a Bupa hospital and a hotel on this ground.
ERNIE CLAY, Fulham chairman, 1979. He later claimed he had been joking.

I've still got my old school report. It says I was dyslexic, backward, mentally deficient and illiterate – all the qualifications you need to be a football club chairman.
GEORGE REYNOLDS, Darlington chairman, 2000.

The ideal board of directors should comprise three men – two dead and the other dying.
TOMMY DOCHERTY, manager with numerous clubs, 1977.

I'm drinking from a cup today. I'd like a mug but they're all in the boardroom.
DOCHERTY, 1988.

The biggest fans in the world are the chairmen, not the blokes on the terraces. Real fans? What does 'real' mean? A real fan is someone who works really hard for nothing, gives up all his time for nothing, worries all the time, and on top of that lot, puts in his own money.
BARRY HEARN, Leyton Orient chairman-owner, 2001.

I'd always thought of chairmen as tight bastards. Now I can only applaud them for the money they put in and the abuse they take.
BARRY FRY in praise of his Peterborough chairman, Peter Boizot, 2000.

I had hair when I became chairman. Not any longer.
PETER HILL, Hereford chairman, on using his toupée 'to wipe away my tears' after relegation from the League, 1997.

Nowadays chairmen seem to live in Spain. That bloke who was at Forest [Irving Scholar] lived in Monaco. I often wonder how people like that got into football. You can't love football and live abroad, because you miss the one thing you want to watch, your team.
BRIAN CLOUGH, former manager, 1999.

I have spoken to more than one chairman who has told me the quality they look for on a manager's CV is an ability to affect the share price.
HOWARD WILKINSON, FA technical director, 1999.

Football attracts a certain percentage of nobodies who want to be somebodies at a football club.
BRIAN CLOUGH, Nottingham Forest manager, 1979.

Football hooligans? Well. There are the 92 club chairmen for a start.
CLOUGH, 1980.

I've never been so insulted by anyone in football as this little upstart puppy.
DENIS HILL-WOOD, Arsenal chairman and Old Etonian, responding to Clough, 1980.

I am struck by the parallels between the disorder which characterises the approach of some football boardrooms and the disorderly behaviour of a minority of the game's followers.
NEIL MACFARLANE MP, Conservative, Minister for Sport, 1983.

Let club directors make a hash of the affairs of their own teams, but spare England the catastrophe of their attentions.
LEN SHACKLETON, journalist and former England player, on the committee of club directors who selected the national team, 1958.

Have you ever had an octogenarian English comedian at training before – apart from FA committee members?
NORMAN WISDOM, comic actor, to Sven-Goran Eriksson in Albania, 2001.

You have to be crackers to be a director of a football club. Who would pour money into football when you can earn 10 to 20 per cent with it?
ARTHUR WAIT, Crystal Palace chairman, 1971.

Soccer is run by second-rate con-men. Petit-bourgeois, frustrated small businessmen. It's a tragedy, because football is very important socially.
EAMON DUNPHY, Republic of Ireland midfielder, 1973.

Football chairmen are, almost to a man, butchers and sausage-meat manufacturers, pork-pie impresarios, industrial and property moguls.
DAVID TRIESMAN, sociologist, in Seven Days *socialist newspaper, 1973.*

We don't recognise any supporters' organisations...I never go to supporters' dinners; it only costs a fiver or so, but then they think they own you. I never accept money from supporters' organisations; they hand you a couple of cheques for a few thousand and the next thing you know they are demanding a seat on the board. My ambition is for the club to function completely without any money coming through the turnstiles at all. That is the road to Utopia.
BOB LORD, Burnley chairman and butcher in the town, 1974.

One wonders today what some businesses would be like if they were run on the same haphazard lines as most football clubs still are. The amateur director has been kicked out of most industrial and commercial boardrooms. But not in football.
DEREK DOUGAN, Wolves striker, in Football As a Profession, *1974.*

When I was a director of Sheffield United for six months, the chairman told

me normal business standards
didn't apply in football. It
was the most stupid advice
I ever had.
MIKE WATTERSON, Derby
chairman, 1982.

Normal business principles
don't apply in football.
LIONEL PICKERING,
publisher and Derby chairman-
owner, after investing £9m in the
club, 1992.

Industries go to the wall
every day...Football's a
business, it's no different,
and it is not going to be run
by the blazer brigade any
more. It needs to be run as a
business by businessmen.
SIR JOHN HALL, Newcastle
chairman and advocate of a
closed-shop, two-division Premier
League, 1995.

Football is an emotional
game and that's where it's
different from your average
major business.
DAVID SHEEPSHANKS,
Ipswich chairman, 2001.

I entered as just A.N.Other, a
member of the board, simply
to do a job, i.e. finance

director. No loyalty or love,
but a cold, clinical job. I
ended up falling in love like
the rest of you, which became
the most expensive love life a
man can imagine.
REG BREALEY, Sheffield
United chairman, in message to
supporters, 1990.

People tell me: 'You must
have better things to spend
your money on.' But I have
no desire for huge yachts in
Monte Carlo. I'm just a
homely boy from East
Northants who enjoys
doing what I do.
MAX GRIGGS, chairman of
Rushden & Diamonds and the
Doc Martens footwear empire, on
ploughing millions into the then
non-League club, 1995.

I went out to buy a car for the
missus and came back with a
football club that cost me
£5m just to clear the debts.
GEORGE REYNOLDS,
Darlington chairman, 1999.

Why have I bought
Birmingham City? Because
football is good for society.
DAVID SULLIVAN, Daily
Sport publisher, 1993.

When I used to watch Roy Rogers on his white horse, Trigger, he never lost. He always won because he was the good guy. The bloke on the black horse with the mask, the baddie who killed, raped and pillaged, always got beat. I want that to continue here.
DAVID GOLD, Birmingham chairman and Sullivan's co-owner, 2002.

Wolves, Derby, Blackburn: these fans with money pour it in, the club lights up, then it fizzles away. Doesn't work. End of story.
KEN BATES, Chelsea chairman, 1995.

Football clubs are great community institutions, to which supporters feel a huge sense of belonging. But the reality is that they are owned by private businessmen, using the clubs for their own purposes, who can ride roughshod over them. And the authorities are absolutely incapable of monitoring the game.
PETER KILFOYLE MP, Labour, on the ownership of Everton, 1999.

We're trying to get rid of the assumption that football clubs are the preserve of white, middle-class men in camel coats, sipping champagne and using the game as an extension of their own egos and virility.
DAVE HELLIWELL, leader of Calderdale Council, after it bought control of Halifax Town, 1990.

I've heard claims that I'm using Mafia money. Soccer clubs are in such a mess right now that you could buy them out of Brownie funds.
ANTON JOHNSON on becoming Rotherham chairman, 1983.

Football directors are nobody's friends except when there are Cup final tickets to give away.
ROY HATTERSLEY MP, Labour, Sheffield Wednesday supporter, in Goodbye To Yorkshire, 1976.

When I came to Manchester from the North-east aged 15, I didn't know what a director was or what he did. My dad

would have explained it as someone who didn't work.
BOBBY CHARLTON on joining the Manchester United board, 1985.

The Super League idea has about as much chance of getting through as there is of Arthur Scargill admitting he needs a wig.
ERNIE CLAY, Fulham chairman, a decade before the launch of the Premier League, 1982.

A few of us want to discuss super leagues but all the rest can talk about is the price of meat pies.
DAVID MURRAY, Rangers chairman, on his Scottish League counterparts, 1992.

Sir Harold Thompson, the chairman of the FA, treated me like an employee. These Arab sheikhs treat me like one of them.
DON REVIE, United Arab Emirates coach and former England manager, 1979.

I flew to Paris for the Real Madrid final with the Liverpool directors, and a more disagreeable bunch of people I've rarely encountered. I'd sooner take my chances with a bunch of so-called hooligans. They talked about players as if they were below-stairs staff. Their attitude towards them was so patronising it was almost Victorian.
JOHN PEEL, disc-jockey and Liverpool fan, 1987.

[The board] was full of furniture removers, insurance brokers and clueless fogies, living in a scotch-and-soda, curled-up-sandwiches world of self-congratulation.
ROBERT PLANT, former Led Zeppelin singer and Wolves fan, on why he resisted attempts in the 1980s to lure him on to the Molineux board, 2002.

You could put his knowledge of the game on a postage stamp. He wanted us to sign Salford Van Hire because he thought he was a Dutch international.
FRED EYRE, former assistant manager of Wigan Athletic, on a powerful director, 1981.

When I asked Michael [Jackson] to become a director, he said: 'Oh wow, do you realise I know nothing about sport?' I said: 'You don't have to.'
URI GELLER, spoon-bending psychic and joint chairman of Exeter City, on persuading the American pop singer to join his board, 2002.

The man who sacked me at Fulham was Sir Eric Miller, the property developer who shot himself. Shows how he reacted to pressure, doesn't it?
BOBBY ROBSON, Ipswich manager, 1981.

Even I could manage this lot.
SAM LONGSON, Derby chairman, after the final parting with Brian Clough, 1973.

Sacking a manager is as big an event in my life as drinking a glass of beer. I would hire 20 managers a year if I wanted to – 100 if necessary.
JESUS GIL, president of Atletico Madrid, 1989.

One chairman told me his club had only had 23 managers since the war. I said: 'Why man, the war's only been over four weeks.'
LAWRIE McMENEMY, England assistant manager, soon after Gulf War, 1992.

When I arrived here the board said there would be no money and they have kept their promise.
DAVE BASSETT, Sheffield United manager, 1994.

There just aren't enough raving lunatics out there with chequebooks.
MICHAEL KNIGHTON, Carlisle chairman-owner, on struggling to sell the club, 2000.

If anyone thinks we're going to give away a company that we've built up over six years at a personal loss in order to satisfy the whims of some Indian with a curry shop, they had better get real.
JIM OLIVER, Partick Thistle chairman, spurning takeover interest from a group of Asian businessmen, 1995.

We'll deal with anyone, whether they are Asian, Eskimo or a one-eyed black lesbian saxophone player.
OLIVER denying allegations of racism, 1995.

For years I've been saying that football should be run by football people. Then along came Franny Lee at Manchester City. Oh well, back to the drawing board.
JIMMY GREAVES, former England striker, in his Sun *column, 1995.*

I've played in the World Cup, sweated out multi-million pound business deals, I've trained some good horses and I'm a father. But 90 minutes at Maine Road can make me feel like an old dish-rag.
FRANCIS LEE, Manchester City chairman, 1997.

The chairman, Doug Ellis, said he was right behind me. I told him I'd sooner have him in front of me where I could see him.
TOMMY DOCHERTY after being fired as Aston Villa manager, 1970.

When Tommy [Docherty] does his rounds of after-dinner speaking, he uses me at every opportunity. Greavsie [Jimmy Greaves] calls me 'Deadly' and lads in the street shout: 'Oi, Deadly!' As long as Aston Villa's name is attached to it, I don't mind. If you operate at a high profile, you have to accept criticism.
DOUG ELLIS, Aston Villa chairman, 1991.

To be fair, although there's been 11 Villa managers in roughly 30 years, there's only been seven I've sacked.
ELLIS, 1999.

I'm just a frustrated would-be professional player who in the end wasn't good enough. Today you have prima donnas and they are highly paid. Their intelligence, across the board, is a lot higher than in my day. *Comic Cuts* was the typical newspaper of the dressing-room in my day whereas now it's the serious papers. We actually got complaints that there was only one public phone in the changing rooms because they

wanted to ring their stockbrokers after training.
ELLIS, 2000.

Aston Villa is the reason I get up every day and the day I'm not mentally able to hold my own with all the young whipper-snappers in this business is when I'll call it a day.
ELLIS at 77 years old, 2000.

This is my life. I kick every ball and sign every cheque.
ELLIS, 2000.

The trouble with our chairman is that he is living in a time warp.
JOHN GREGORY, Aston Villa manager, 2000. He later had to make a public apology to Ellis.

They're building another stand at Villa Park. They're going to call it 'The Other Doug Ellis Stand'.
KEN BATES, Chelsea chairman, in Jason Tomas' book Soccer Czars, *1996.*

With Ken Bates it's par for the course. He says derogatory things about a lot of people. It's sad that he has to be like that.

CHRIS SUTTON, shortly before leaving Chelsea for Celtic, 2000.

We see a lot of Ken Bates. He'll always have a laugh and a joke with you. At your expense, obviously.
GRAEME LE SAUX, Chelsea defender, 2000.

Ken Bates here. I understand you're richer than I am, so we'd better get together.
KEN BATES, Chelsea chairman, in call to wealthy supporter Matthew Harding, 1994. Harding put in £24m over the next two years.

The difference is that Bates appears to think Chelsea is his club, while Harding's attitude is that it's our club.
ROSS FRASER, chairman of Chelsea Independent Supporters' Association, as the Bates-Harding rift worsened, 1995.

So what? Ninety-nine per cent of Iraqis voted for Sadam Hussein.
BATES after a poll showed Chelsea fans wanted Harding to replace him, 1995.

When David Mellor is prepared to put money into the club – or even pay for his own tickets – he will be entitled to his opinion.
MATTHEW HARDING after Mellor, a Conservative MP, criticised him while hosting a radio phone-in, 1995.

I'm off to my 300-acre farm. You lot can bugger off to your council houses.
BATES to the press after Chelsea's relegation, 1988.

I'm not starstruck around players. How could I be? I'm the biggest star here.
BATES, 1997.

Has any chairman since Mao had more faith in his own opinions than Ken Bates? If laying down the law was an Olympic sport, the Chelsea chief would be staggering under the weight of gold medals.
ALEX FERGUSON in his autobiography, 2000.

Six months [after trying to buy Chelsea] he bought Fulham, having discovered that he was a lifelong Fulham supporter.
BATES on Mohamed Al Fayed buying control of Chelsea's neighbours, 2002.

The trouble with Fayed is that he doesn't understand British traditions and institutions. I mean, he took over Fulham and made them successful.
ANDY HAMILTON, panellist on Radio 4's News Quiz, 1999.

It's ironic that it's left to me to save the England team when no one will let me have a UK passport.
MOHAMED AL FAYED, Fulham owner, after agreeing to let Kevin Keegan coach England part-time, 1999.

I've survived two heart attacks and Stan Flashman. And Stan was the worst of the three.
BARRY FRY, Birmingham manager, recalling a turbulent relationship with his former chairman at Barnet, 1995.

Bill Bell: chairman and business entrepreneur, dedicated to making Port

Vale the No. 1 team in the Potteries. Bill also wants to find the lost city of Atlantis, be the first man to walk the Channel, and skateboard up Mount Everest.
The Oatcake, *Stoke City fanzine, derby-day edition, 1989.*

My mum rang up when she heard I wanted to take over the club and said: 'Oh son, don't.' Only an 11-year-old boy would want to get into something like this. You have to have that mixture of romantic and businessman. I know it's a risk, but I can't think of anything I'd risk more for.
BILL KENWRIGHT, theatre director, on his bid for control of Everton, 1998.

The lowest point of the year was hearing Nick Barmby had used the five worst words in the English language: 'I want to join Liverpool.'
KENWRIGHT after taking over at Everton, 2000.

Ron Noades is the Fidel Castro of football, an enlightened despot rather than a dictator.

STEVE COPPELL, Crystal Palace manager, on his chairman, 1992.

I'd rather die and have vultures eat my insides than merge with Crystal Palace.
SAM HAMMAM, Wimbledon chairman, on reports of a possible merger of the two Selhurst Park-based clubs, 1992.

I just hope I can grab the heart of this man [Kjell-Inge Rokke] and make him understand. The man lives in a world of accountants, not football. I must make him love us. We must show him our legs and cleavage to make him fancy us.
HAMMAM on Wimbledon's Norwegian co-owner, 1999.

We will serve sheep's testicles as a delicacy in the boardroom. There are plenty of sheep in Wales so it's right that they should make some representation at Ninian Park.
HAMMAM, having left Wimbledon and taken over at Cardiff City, 2000.

Alex Ferguson told me I was mad buying Cardiff City and gave me the address of a good psychiatrist.
HAMMAM, 2000.

Sometimes you need to employ someone who is a poacher turned gamekeeper. They know how the hooligans think.
HAMMAM after it was revealed that the Cardiff chairman's bodyguard was a convicted 'football' hooligan, 2002.

What entitles you to question Alex Ferguson on football matters?
Question to chief executive Martin Edwards at Manchester United plc meeting, 1999.

Manchester United have begun to think 'class' is something that comes with big office suites and flash cars. That great club is slowly being destroyed. And I blame one family for the ruin. The Edwards family, the master butchers of Manchester.
HARRY GREGG, former United goalkeeper, after his sacking as a coach at the club, 1981.

How can anyone praise Martin Edwards at Manchester United? He has twice tried to sell the club to the enemies of football, Robert Maxwell and Rupert Murdoch. How can he look anybody in the eye and say he loves the club when he has been trying to make 60 million quid selling it?
BRIAN CLOUGH, former manager, 1999.

Even the most brilliant manager could not deal with Manchester United as long as the club is run from the chairman's [Martin Edwards] office the way it is.
MICHAEL CRICK and DAVID SMITH, authors, Betrayal of a Legend, *1989.*

Peter Swales wore a wig, a blazer with an England badge on it and high-heeled shoes. As a man he really impressed me.
MALCOLM ALLISON, ex-Manchester City manager, on the club's former chairman in Jeremy Novick, In a League of Their Own: Football's Maverick Managers, *1995.*

Peter Swales likes publicity. He wears a card round his neck saying: 'In case of heart attack call a press conference.'
TOMMY DOCHERTY on the Manchester City chairman, 1982.

I gave up football the day I went back to Maine Road and saw the chairman [Peter Swales] signing autographs.
MIKE SUMMERBEE, former Manchester City winger, 1988.

The trouble was he had no repartee with the fans.
PETER SWALES, Manchester City chairman, after sacking Mel Machin as manager, 1989.

My chairman, Robert Maxwell, they ought to let him run football.
JIM SMITH, Oxford United manager, 1983.

I threatened to quit over the sale of Dean Saunders, but [Robert] Maxwell sacked me. He told me: 'No one resigns on the Maxwells.'
MARK LAWRENSON on his time as Oxford United manager, 1993.

[Robert] Maxwell has the posture and manners of the dominant male.
DR DESMOND MORRIS, author of The Naked Ape *and co-director of Maxwell's at Oxford, 1983.*

I have played football since I was a toddler. Left wing, as you would expect. I was very fast.
ROBERT MAXWELL, Oxford chairman, 1985.

If a supporter asked me about that [lending £1.1m to Tottenham to buy Gary Lineker], I'd tell him to get stuffed. What I do with my money is my business. Haven't I already done enough for Derby? They were in the knacker's yard when I was invited to help them.
MAXWELL, by now Derby chairman, on the club's 'transfer freeze', 1990.

There are still some things that baffle me about the bloke [Robert Maxwell]. Like why he loves seeing his mug across the back pages, because Robert Redford he ain't.

BRIAN CLOUGH,
Nottingham Forest manager,
1987.

Robert Maxwell has just
bought Brighton & Hove
Albion, and he's furious to
find out that it's only one club.
TOMMY DOCHERTY as
Maxwell tried to add to his
portfolio of clubs, 1988.

I like a challenge. If I'd been
a woman I would have been
pregnant all the time because
I can't say no.
ROBERT MAXWELL on his
interest in 'saving' hard-up
Tottenham, 1990.

Robert Maxwell's record is
exemplary...He has always
been prepared to invest
heavily in football at a time
when others are turning their
backs on the game. Some
people seem to doubt him,
but they don't know the man.
IRVING SCHOLAR,
Tottenham chairman, on
Maxwell's bid to take control,
1990.

I feel like the guy who shot
Bambi. I'm not an egotistical
loony.

ALAN SUGAR, Tottenham
chairman, on the fans' reaction
to his attempt to sack Terry
Venables as manager, 1993.

We will not be pushed around
by a bunch of north London
yobbos.
RUPERT LOWE, Southampton
chairman, as Tottenham courted
manager Glenn Hoddle, 2001.

When my son [Jonathan,
Wolves chairman] asks me
for more money to buy
another player, I tell him:
'This is blackmail.' He says:
'Do you want to get into the
Premiership?' I say yes.
Then he says: 'Do you want
to win the FA Cup?' I say yes.
Then I say: 'Oh, go and buy
him then.'
SIR JACK HAYWARD, Wolves
owner, 1995.

A friend has described me as
the village vicar of football-
club chairmen, which I rather
liked, but I've discovered
there are people in the game
who would slit your throat
for tuppence.
JONATHAN HAYWARD,
Wolves chairman and
Northumberland farmer, 1996.

I've never taken a penny out of Wolves and never want to. I only want an emotional return, not a financial one. If I go and stay with the team on a Friday night, I settle my own bill. When I eat in Sir Jack's [restaurant at the ground], I pay. I don't take a salary like some chairmen and I don't draw any expenses. That's why I was upset by this fan's remark, though I have to say that the letter he handed me was nicely typed and obviously thought out.
SIR JACK HAYWARD, Wolves owner and chairman, stung by a supporter's criticism, 2000.

I don't want Wolves fans to think I'm off my trolley, but Dermot Reeve [Warwickshire's cricket captain] is the kind of character I'm looking for as manager.
JONATHAN HAYWARD, Wolves chairman, 1995.

I only hope Tony Adams plays because he's the only name I know. All these Viallis, Vieiras and Viagras. I prefer old-fashioned names like Cullis and Wright.
SIR JACK HAYWARD before Wolves' FA Cup semi-final v. Arsenal, 1998.

They thought the Golden Tit – me – would go on forever.
SIR JACK HAYWARD on his £60m outlay on players and ground improvements, 1997.

My friends in America say I must love it [owning his home-town club] but unless we're 6-0 up with 15 minutes left I hate it.
SIR JACK HAYWARD after Wolves again failed to reach the Premiership, 2002.

Elton [John] and myself developed a relationship – it's a bit dangerous saying that about us, isn't it? For a period I was his reality.
GRAHAM TAYLOR, Watford manager, on his pop-star chairman, 2000.

I used to have to tour when I didn't really want to, to be able to afford to buy a centre-forward.
ELTON JOHN on his days of bankrolling Watford, 1995.

'Candle in the Wind' remains one of my favourite songs. But Elton [John] and I had this agreement that I would tell him nothing about music if he told me nothing about football, and it worked well.
GRAHAM TAYLOR on his relationship with the Watford chairman, 1991.

It has been the ultimate roller-coaster ride, but I hope that whoever takes this club over has as much success as I enjoyed in my first five years here. Obviously I wouldn't wish the last three on anybody.
MICHAEL KNIGHTON, Carlisle United chairman, on his plans to sell the club and their latest last-day escape from relegation out of the League, 2000.

From parks football to Carlisle to Milan, we all aspire to The Dream. Robert Maxwell dubbed me a Walter Mitty figure, but that's fine because this is the industry of dreams and I'm the greatest dreamer alive.
MICHAEL KNIGHTON, Carlisle chairman and ex-Manchester United director, 1995.

Q: How did you feel when Darlington got a wild-card entry back into the FA Cup?
A: I always felt we'd get it. I had a chat with Him upstairs the night before. Got through to him even though he's ex-directory.
GEORGE REYNOLDS, Darlington chairman, after the club were re-admitted to the Cup following Manchester United's withdrawal, 1999.

I'm a great believer in God. He has always been very kind to me. I say to him: 'Can you get your finger out and give us some help?'
REYNOLDS, 2000.

I won't turn my back on this club, and we will be successful, we will be profitable. I will turn it around. But I won't be travelling to Exeter to watch a pile of shite.
REYNOLDS after his wife criticised the Darlington players at a public meeting, prompting them to walk out, 2002.

At other clubs the directors probably get worried if things aren't going well, and they don't like people coming up to them criticising in pubs and at parties. That doesn't influence me at all. If people start telling me what's wrong with the team, I just say: 'Look, why don't you f— awff?'
PATRICK COBBOLD, Ipswich chairman, 1981.

You ask what constitutes a crisis here. Well, if we ran out of white wine in the boardroom.
COBBOLD, 1982.

If eventually I'm kicked out, I'll just go back to buying a season ticket.
PETER RIDSDALE, Leeds chairman, 2001.

A chairman's place is in the directors' box, not on the terraces.
DAVID WILLMAN, Merseyside police chief superintendent, after Peter Ridsdale left his seat at Everton to confront Leeds fans chanting against coach Brian Kidd, 2002.

If I fail, I'll stand up and be counted – no other idiot wants to come forward.
PETER HILL, Hereford chairman, after relegation to the Conference, 1997.

I've been chairman of a soccer club. I know how to lose.
ELTON JOHN before the Oscar ceremony, 1996.

Being part of this football club is the fullest experience you can have of being alive.
DELIA SMITH, TV chef and Norwich City director, 2002.

I came down last week to watch United play Port Vale. By the time I got home I was chairman again and looking for a new manager. My wife said: 'I'm taking you to the hospital to get your head examined.'
DEREK DOOLEY on his surprise return to the boardroom at Sheffield United, 1999.

12

REFEREES

Referees should arrive by the back door and leave the same way.
ALAN HARDAKER, Football League secretary, 1964.

The trouble with referees is that they know the rules but they don't know the game.
BILL SHANKLY, Liverpool manager, during referees' 'clampdown', 1971.

Next thing we'll be giving our handbags to the linesmen before we skip on to the field.
MIKE SUMMERBEE, Manchester City winger, 1971.

A good ref is one that doesn't chicken out; who'll give a penalty against Liverpool in front of the Kop.
DAVID CROSS, Coventry striker, 1975.

The basic training of referees is appalling. They tested my eyesight by getting me to stand at one end of a small room, facing a wall chart showing red, yellow and blue kits. Some guy pointed to one shirt and said: 'What colour's that?'

I replied 'Red' and he said 'You're in.'
GORDON HILL, Football League referee, in Give A Little Whistle, *1975.*

I got the impression that few toilets were used more than those in the referee's room.
JACK TAYLOR, World Cup referee, in World Soccer Review, *1976.*

Mr Martinez [the referee] was slow to realise that the Dutch invented the clog.
DAVID LACEY reporting in the Guardian *on the Netherlands* v. *Italy match, 1978.*

'Referee, what would you do if I called you a bastard?' one player inquired politely. 'I'd send you off,' I replied. 'What would you do if I thought you were a bastard?' was the next question. 'There's not a lot I could do,' I answered. 'In that case, ref. I think you're a bastard,' he said, turning smartly on his heel.
PAT PARTRIDGE, Football League referee, in Oh, Ref!, *1979.*

The referee must have felt like the President of the United States at the time of the Cuban missile crisis.
HOWARD WILKINSON, Leeds manager, after postponement of a crunch game v. Manchester United because of a waterlogged pitch, 1992.

It's getting to the stage where we hate referees and they dislike us.
KENNY SANSOM, Arsenal and England defender, 1983.

There's no rapport with referees these days. If you say anything you get booked. If you don't they send you off for dumb insolence.
JACK CHARLTON, Sheffield Wednesday manager, 1983.

People say we've got the best referees in the world. I shudder to think what the rest are like.
MARTIN BUCHAN, Manchester United defender, 1983.

We had a Mauritian referee against Paraguay. Mauritius is a lovely island, but they don't play football.
EVARISTO MACEDA, Iraq coach, World Cup finals, 1986.

There was a murderer on the pitch – the referee.
OMAR BARRAS, Uruguay manager, on the Italian official who sent off one of his players after 40 seconds against Scotland, World Cup finals, 1986.

Then my eyesight started to go and I took up refereeing.
NEIL MIDGLEY, FA Cup final referee, 1987.

We may be useless, but we are not cheats.
DAVID ELLERAY, referee, to Arsenal defender Tony Adams, who had called him a 'fucking cheat', 1989.

The referee is available for Christmas pantomime or cabaret.
KEITH VALLE, tannoy announcer, as Bristol Rovers and Wigan players left the pitch, 1989.

I have nothing against the visually handicapped as such, but I am surprised they are allowed to referee at this level.
The Soup, Kidderminster Harriers fanzine, 1989.

We are stage managers, not performers.
ALAN GUNN, FA Cup final referee, 1990.

I do it because I was a useless player.
JIM RUSHTON, Football League referee, 1991.

I'll have to stop that. I don't think the Italian referees appreciated being patted on the head or the bum.
PAUL GASCOIGNE, early in his Lazio career, 1991.

Thank God the referee and his linesmen are all out there together, otherwise they could have ruined three matches instead of one.
TOMMY DOCHERTY, working as a radio pundit at Old Trafford, 1992.

It takes some believing for a ref to mix up two players as different as we are. I'm 5ft 8in and white, he's 6ft 4in and black.
TONY SPEARING, Plymouth Argyle defender, after he was booked in mistake for Tony Witter's foul, 1992.

I'm 27 years old and yet the referee tells me I'm not allowed to swear.
VINNIE JONES, Wimbledon midfielder, after being dismissed for foul and abusive language, 1992.

The referee has got me the sack. Thank him for that.
GRAHAM TAYLOR to linesman and Fifa official as England lost to the Netherlands and failed to qualify for the World Cup finals, 1993.

The perfect referee does not exist. It's one man against 90,000 people and 22 actors, and a percentage of calls [decisions] will always be wrong.
GUIDO TOGNONI, Fifa spokesman, defending standards at the World Cup finals, 1994.

The official today was a Muppet.
IAN WRIGHT, Arsenal striker, after being booked at Norwich, 1994.

In fairness, the referee had a complete cerebral failure.
RICK HOLDEN, Oldham winger, after defeat at Southend, 1995.

My certain feeling is of being raped week in, week out, by referees and it just cannot go on.
SAM HAMMAM, Wimbledon owner, 1995.

I do swear a lot, but having played abroad I can do it in a language different from the referee's.
JURGEN KLINSMANN, Tottenham and Germany striker, 1995.

My wife, who was in the stand, told me that at one stage the entire row in front of her stood up and gave me the v sign. I asked her what she did and she said she didn't want them to know who she was so stood up and joined in.
NEIL MIDGLEY, retired referee, recalling his First Division debut in Derick Allsop, The Game of Their Lives, *1995.*

I've no objection to women referees provided they're good. My only concern is that a dishy referee will have players swarming round her and protesting against decisions.
JOHN RUDGE, Stoke City director of football, 2000.

I've been told off for smiling when I show the red card.
WENDY TOMS, first woman to referee at Conference level, 1996.

I saw someone eyeing me in the pub. I asked him: 'Do I know you?' He said: 'You should. You sent me off today.'
SONYA HOME, referee, 1995.

I played full-back in rugby union, wicketkeeper in cricket and goalkeeper in football. The positions in which you stand out. Refereeing is like that. We're very much loners.
PHILIP DON, Premier League referee, 1995.

Why should I allow a referee to do things which destroy my life? When managers make mistakes they get sacked. He [David Elleray] is probably going home in his car now thinking about where he's going to referee next week.
JOE KINNEAR, Wimbledon manager, 1995.

I've seen harder tackles in the half-time queue for meat pies than the ones punished in games.
GEORGE FULSTON, Falkirk chairman, 1995.

I have to hand it to Manchester United. They have the best players – and the best referees.
SAM HAMMAM, Wimbledon owner, 1995.

Most jobs get easier as you get more experienced. I've been a local-government officer for 20 years and it's getting easier. This [refereeing] is getting harder. The pressure has increased, the pace is greater. There's so much money involved, so much at stake.
STEPHEN LODGE, Premier League referee, 1995.

Can anyone tell me why they give referees a watch? It's certainly not for keeping the time.
ALEX FERGUSON after Graham Poll added 'only three minutes', Manchester United v. Everton, 1996.

In England the referees either shoot you down with a machine-gun or don't blow their whistle at all.
GIANLUCA VIALLI after his Premiership debut for Chelsea, 1996.

I do like Selhurst Park. There's a Sainsbury's next to the ground so it's an ideal chance to get some weekend shopping out of the way.
DAVID ELLERAY, Premier League referee, 1996.

I love my job. I get a buzz when I say 'Play on' and a goal results. I think: 'God, I made that.'
ALAN WILKIE, Premiership referee, 1998.

I made the gesture [punching the air] because the referee loves to see the ball in the net after he has played an advantage. It proves he was right.
MIKE REED, Premiership referee, after appearing to celebrate Patrik Berger's goal for Liverpool v. Leeds, 2000.

If we're going to have sponsored referees, maybe we could approach Optrex or the Royal National Institute for the Blind.
PAUL DURKIN, Premiership referee, 1998.

I understand that Walter Smith [Everton manager] described the ref as diabolical. I didn't think he was as good as that.
JIM SMITH, Derby manager, 1999.

There are occasions when you say to yourself: 'I need to give a yellow card here and re-establish my authority.' That's when it gets like teaching. When it gets a bit lively, you need a sacrificial lamb.
DAVID ELLERAY, Premiership referee and Harrow School housemaster, 1998.

This referee [Mike Reed] is so poor that I would have been booked just getting off the bus.
NORMAN HUNTER, Radio Leeds summariser and former Leeds and England defender, 1998.

Professional referees may help but it won't necessarily bring better positioning, better eyesight and more courage.
MARTIN O'NEILL, Leicester manager, 1998.

There's no point asking a referee for an explanation of his action. You get that in the report a couple of weeks later, when everyone has got the right story. The boys in black have time to organise a story, make sure it's right and then send it out. Yet I have to try to give instant explanations.
GORDON STRACHAN, Coventry manager, alleging conspiracy by match-officials after defeat at Liverpool, 1999.

I don't know why they don't have the bookings before the start so that we can get on with the game. You know they are coming.
DAVID O'LEARY, Leeds manager, complaining of over-zealous refereeing by Mike Reed at Tottenham, 1999.

I tried to have a word with him after the game but he wouldn't speak to me. He's untouchable. He should have been a policeman.
JOHN GREGORY, Aston Villa manager, on referee Jeff Winter after defeat at Leicester, 1999.

Referees act almost like policemen, and the fourth officials are becoming jobsworths. They are reporting managers up and down the country for stepping outside the technical area.
GREGORY, 1999.

It is a great profession being a referee. They are never wrong.
ARSENE WENGER, Arsenal manager, 1999.

The referee was bobbins. If you need that translating it means crap.
DAVE JONES, Southampton manager, 1999.

I don't think we should have shoot-outs. We should have a shoot-the-ref shoot-out. After that penalty, the referee should have been shot.

JOHN GREGORY, Aston Villa manager, after last-minute penalty awarded to West Ham, 1999.

Referees should be wired up to a couple of electrodes and they should be allowed to make three mistakes before you run 50,000 volts through their genitals.
GREGORY after David Elleray awarded a penalty against Villa at Sunderland, 1999.

The ref was a disgrace. He got three things right – the kick-off, half-time and full-time.
ANDY RITCHIE, Oldham manager, 1999.

It doesn't seem to matter how hard we try, we still get a slagging for trying to do the job as honestly as we can. It would be very interesting one Saturday if we decided not to turn up until 3.30pm.
PAUL DURKIN, Premiership referee, 1999.

The radio link will be a great help once we get used to it, but I'm still not sure where to put my microphone.

STEVE DUNN, Premiership referee, after a trial run with an earpiece and microphone, 1999.

Sometimes, privately, I say: 'The referee was crap today' but not publicly. Managers have a responsibility to protect the referee. You have to believe he gives his best. Good and bad decisions even themselves out.
ARSENE WENGER, 1999.

In the tunnel I say to [referee] David Elleray: 'You might as well book me now and get it over with.' He takes it pretty well but he still books me.
ROY KEANE, Manchester United captain, 2000.

They were like a pack of wolves. I've never seen so much hatred on players' faces. It looked as though they were trying to put pressure on Andy [D'Urso] so that he wouldn't send off Jaap Stam as well as giving the penalty decision.
KEITH COOPER, referees assessor and ex-referee, after United players pursued Andy D'Urso, 2000.

If the ref had stood still we wouldn't have had to chase him.
ROY KEANE, United captain, jokes about the D'Urso incident, 2000.

When linesmen come to check the nets when I'm warming up I'll usually say: 'I'm a referee too, so I know what you've got to put up with.' Referees could do with more help from us; players could sometimes be more honest with officials.
STEVE HARPER, Newcastle goalkeeper and referee in the Peterlee & District League, 2000.

The penalty decision put us back in the game. The player should have been sent off, but Mr Harris didn't know who the player was who had handled. The ref did get the minute's silence right before the game, though.
JOHN GREGORY, Aston Villa manager, after controversial game at Tottenham, 2000.

My players wouldn't take a throw-in for that sort of money.
GORDON STRACHAN,

Coventry manager, on learning
that Gerald Ashby's match fee
was £200, 1998.

I can't understand why the
ref wasn't more sympathetic.
After all, we used to go to
the same bookies.
STEVE CLARIDGE,
Portsmouth player-manager,
after his team incurred two red
cards v. Fulham, 2001.

[Elleray] went around with
his arms folded like a
schoolteacher. Which of
course he is.
SIMON JORDAN, Crystal
Palace chairman, 2001.

I've got no friends among the
players. You're doing a job of
work and so are they.
STEPHEN LODGE,
Premiership referee, 2001.

I'd like to smash the ball into
a referee at 200 miles an hour
and see if he can get out of
the way.
BOBBY ROBSON, Newcastle
manager, criticising Nolberto
Solano's dismissal for handling,
2001.

You cheated us. It was
impossible to miss that
handball. You deserve to go
and referee in Afghanistan. If
you made the same mistake
there, you'd get shot.
ROBERT NITA, Rapid
Bucharest player, picked up by the
TV microphones after match v.
Arges in which referee
Constantin Fratila denied his
team two penalties, 2001.

What makes a sane and
rational person subject
himself to such humiliation?
Why on earth does anyone
want to become a
Premiership referee?
LORD HATTERSLEY, Sheffield
Wednesday supporter, 2002.

I believe when the referees
are enjoying their recreation
on the sun-beds, or
swimming up and down the
pool and talking together in
their free time, there is an
agenda with Alan Smith.
They all have their little chats
and jump on him very, very
quickly.
DAVID O'LEARY, Leeds
manager, after Andy D'Urso
sent off Smith in FA Cup tie at
Cardiff, 2002.

This is what happens when you have village referees in the World Cup.

CHRISTIAN VIERI, Italy striker, after England's Graham Poll and his assistants denied the Azzurri two goals v. Croatia, World Cup finals, 2002.

We weren't lucky – it was the Irish who had a flower up their backsides. What the referee did makes you want to kill him. He crushed us. And as for the linesman, he's got a spring-loaded arm.

JOSE ANTONIO CAMACHO, Spain coach, on the Swedish referee after beating the Republic of Ireland on penalties, World Cup finals, 2002.

We were unlucky that we ran into a referee who ought to be thinking more about his diet than his refereeing.

ALESSANDRO NESTA, Italy defender, on the Ecuadorian referee for their defeat by South Korea, World Cup finals, 2002.

People say a good referee is one the fans don't notice but that's a myth. If a referee has to give three penalties in a match, then he is going to be noticed. That doesn't mean he's not a good referee.

PIERLUIGI COLLINA, Italian referee, shortly before officiating in the World Cup final, 2002.

13

WOMEN

Football is all very well as a game for rough girls, but it is hardly suitable for delicate boys.
OSCAR WILDE, 1890s.

Football reminds me of the Nuremberg Rally. It's so aggressive. Great men with bald heads, roaring and screaming. Why should anyone welcome that?
MICHELE HANSON, Guardian Women writer, in Match of the Day magazine, 1998.

Women should be in the kitchen, the discotheque and the boutique, but not in football.
RON ATKINSON, Sheffield Wednesday manager, 1989.

The future is feminine.
SEPP BLATTER, general secretary of Fifa, football's world governing body, after the Women's World Cup, 1995.

The Italians are a gayer set of lads, who love life and their girlfriends...They think the English boys are slightly mad putting sport before the ladies.

EDDIE FIRMANI on his move from Charlton to Sampdoria, in Football With the Millionaires, 1960.

Of course I didn't take my wife to watch Rochdale as an anniversary present. It was her birthday. Would I have got married during the football season? And anyway it wasn't Rochdale, it was Rochdale reserves.
BILL SHANKLY, Liverpool manager, 1966.

Basically, he [Bill Nicholson] doesn't think women have any place in football. I never saw him play for Spurs and I'm not allowed to go to see them now. I feel an outsider really, as if I was a member of the opposition.
GRACE NICHOLSON, wife of then Tottenham manager, in Hunter Davies' The Glory Game, 1972.

When I lose I've got to talk about it. I go home and relive it with the wife. She just nods and says yes or no.
NORMAN HUNTER, Leeds and England defender, 1973.

Q: Most dangerous opponent?
A: My ex-wife.
FRANK WORTHINGTON,
England striker, in magazine
questionnaire, 1975.

I used to stand up and glare around when fans were giving Geoff stick. Norman Hunter's mum used to lash out with her handbag when people booed her Norman.
JUDITH HURST, wife of Geoff Hurst, in Brian James' Journey To Wembley, *1977.*

Isn't one of the main features of football-match attendance still that it enables men to get away from nagging wives?
FRANK BURROWS,
Portsmouth manager, 1981.

I recently met Jimmy Hill, who argues for football as a family game. When I spoke to him, his reaction was polite but uninterested.
JILL TOWNSEND, girlfriend of the musician Alan Price, a co-director of Hill's at Fulham, 1981.

When I said that even my missus could save Derby from relegation, I was exaggerating.
PETER TAYLOR, Derby manager, 1982.

My wife knows more about football than any other woman I know...Many occasions I have said to her: 'Come on luv, I'll take you out for a meal,' and she'll look disappointed and say: 'You know that Wimbledon reserves are playing.'
ALEC STOCK, former manager, in A Little Thing Called Pride, *1982.*

My wife has been magic about it.
JOHN BOND when the story of his affair with a Manchester City employee broke following his resignation as manager, 1983.

John Bond has blackened my name with his insinuations about the private lives of football managers. Both my wives are upset.
MALCOLM ALLISON, Bond's predecessor as Manchester City manager, 1983.

We hope to revive the old tradition of the husband going to football on Christmas Day, while the wife cooks the turkey.
ERIC WHITE, Brentford official, 1983.

Only women and horses work for nothing.
DOUG ELLIS, Aston Villa chairman, 1983.

My idea of relaxation: going somewhere away from the wife.
TERRY FENWICK, QPR captain, in Match *magazine questionnaire, 1986.*

My wife says it would be better if there was another woman. At least then she would know what she's up against. But she says: 'How can I compete with football?'
DON MACKAY, Blackburn manager, 1988.

To score in front of 70,000 fans at San Siro is like finding a place in a woman's heart. No, it's better.
NICOLA BERTI, Inter Milan midfielder, 1988.

Blimey, you're the first bird I've met with an FA coaching badge.
RON ATKINSON to woman journalist who asked about Sheffield Wednesday's long-ball game under his predecessors, 1989.

If there really are men who prefer football to girls, I've never met any.
SHARON KNIGHT, 19-year-old Miss Stoke-on-Trent, 1990.

I know it sounds awful but it just hit me half-way through my stag night that I'd rather be going to the match with the lads than marrying Nicola.
KEVIN McCALL, Hereford fan, after cancelling his wedding to watch FA Cup tie at Aylesbury, 1991.

I hate football. I think most women do. It's not the sort of sport I'm interested in. I prefer the indoor sort of games.
CYNTHIA PAYNE, Streatham 'Madam', 1990.

The Old Firm are like two old girls in Sauchiehall Street raising their skirts to any league that walks past.
KEITH WYNESS, Aberdeen chief executive, on the possibility of Rangers and Celtic quitting the Scottish League, 2002.

If a woman suggested that the simplest way of brightening up football was by making the goals a bit bigger, they would say she didn't understand the game and why didn't she go off and practise her netball.
NIGELLA LAWSON in her Evening Standard *column after Fifa president Joao Havelange suggested widening the goals, 1990.*

They are nice people with a part to play but at the end of the day they are tea-ladies who do not understand the game.
TREVOR STEELE, Bradford Park Avenue chairman, resigning after two women directors were elected to the board, 1990.

The only place for women in football is making the tea at half-time.
RODNEY MARSH, former England player, 1997.

Doing well in football is like childbirth – it doesn't happen overnight.
BRIAN CLOUGH, Nottingham Forest manager, 1991.

Q: What has been your biggest thrill in life?
A: When my wife Norma told me she was pregnant and signing for Newcastle.
ALBERT CRAIG, Partick Thistle midfielder, in Sun *questionnaire, 1994.*

Why not treat the wife to a weekend in London and let her go shopping on Saturday afternoon while you go and watch the Latics play West Ham?
Oldham Athletic programme, 1991.

The reason I'm back is that the wife wants me out of the house.
KENNY DALGLISH on returning to management with Blackburn, 1991.

I've always believed in treating the ball like a woman. Give it a cuddle, caress it a wee bit, take your time, and you'll get the desired response.
JIM BAXTER, Rangers and Scotland player of the 1960s, 1991.

Leaving a club is like leaving a woman. When there's nothing left to say, you go.
ERIC CANTONA after leaving Leeds for Manchester United, 1992.

Footballers are the worst gossips – they're worse than women.
LEE CHAPMAN, Leeds striker, 1992.

We defended like women.
JOE ROYLE, Oldham manager, after 5-2 defeat by Wimbledon, 1992.

The strip was a bloody stupid colour. I think one of the directors' wives must have chosen it.
DAVID PLEAT, Luton manager, on the end of his club's tangerine-and-navy kit, 1992.

I married a girl who was very easily told: 'If you marry me you're marrying football.'
GRAHAM TAYLOR, England manager, 1992.

Women run everything. The only thing I've done within my house in the past 20 years is recognise Angola as an independent state.
BRIAN CLOUGH, 1992.

Every girl I ever went out with I took on the North Bank [terracing] at least once. They never wanted to go twice.
LAURENCE MARKS, comedy writer and Arsenal fan, in Tom Watt, The End: 80 Years of Life on Arsenal's North Bank, *1993.*

I loved football. I played in the morning and in the afternoon. Even when I went to bed with my wife I was training.
DIEGO MARADONA after his last match for Argentina, 1994.

Our last Prime Minister was a woman. The head of the Royal Family is a woman. And the head of Birmingham City is a woman.

KARREN BRADY,
Birmingham City managing
director, on why she believed men
and women 'receive equal
treatment in society', 1993.

I met much more [male]
chauvinism working for
the *Sport.* I've always had
the 'I bet she's shagging the
boss' remarks.
BRADY, 1995. Her 'boss' at the
Sport *and Birmingham was*
David Sullivan.

I know everybody thinks
I earned this job between
the sheets, but I'm not
bonking him.
BRADY on her relationship with
Sullivan, 1994.

I am probably more male
than most men. I was
brought up going to watch
boxing and football.
BRADY, 1995.

Q: At home, when was the
last time you ironed a shirt?
A: I pay my wife to do that.
MARK ROBINS, Leicester
striker, in programme Q&A,
1995.

I will tell you straight away,
before you ask me: I have
never slept with a footballer,
never gone to dinner with
one and never seen one naked
in the dressing-room. Okay.
Now we can start.
PAOLA FERRERA, Italian TV
football presenter, before being
interviewed, 1994.

I didn't get too many women
running after me. It was their
fucking husbands who'd be
after me.
CHARLIE GEORGE, former
Arsenal player, recalling his
1970s heyday, 1995.

Q: What's the craziest request
you've ever had from a fan?
A: A male fan once asked me
for my wife's phone number
and when my next away
match was.
FRANCIS BENALI,
Southampton player, in Sun
questionnaire, 1995.

Could you take Eric's sliding
tackle from behind? Football.
It's a girl's game.
Daily Star *advertisement, 1995.*

Q: Who's your dream
woman?
A: Jennifer Lopez with the
personality of Kathy Burke.
*JASON McATEER, Blackburn
midfielder, in newspaper
questionnaire, 2000.*

John Hollins was a mistake.
He has a very strong wife. It
might have been better if I
had made her manager.
*KEN BATES, Chelsea
chairman, 1995.*

You can tell how a team's
doing by the state of the wives.
Second Division wives always
need roots touching up.
*MRS MERTON, played by
Caroline Hook, on TV's The Mrs
Merton Show, 1995.*

If it wasn't for Tracy, I'd be
an 18-stone alcoholic playing
for Penicuik Athletic.
*ANDY GORAM, Rangers and
Scotland goalkeeper, paying
tribute to his second wife, 1995.*

After all, this is not a game
for little ladies.
*PLACIDO DOMINGO, opera
singer, defending Spain's rugged
tackling during the World Cup
finals, 1994.*

Men say things like: 'Oh,
they're just a bunch of
dykes.' I hate the fact that
there are girls who would
love to play but don't
ecause the image of women's
soccer is so bad.
*JULIE FOUDY, United States
captain, 1995.*

There's still the blinkered
view that all women
footballers have thighs like
joints of ham and make
rugby players look like
flake adverts.
*MARIANNE SPACEY, Arsenal
and England striker, 1995.*

Trollops on tour
*Sign on bus carrying Manchester
United ladies' team, 1996.*

The coach [Gaute Haugenes]
told me at half-time that he
was substituting me because
it was against the rules to
have 12 people on the pitch.
*KATIE CHAPMAN, Fulham
and England Ladies midfielder,
on how news of her pregnancy
was broken to team-mates, 2002.*

Some referees in women's
football are avuncular,
enthusiastic and fair. Some

use the game to prove that they can control women.
ALYSON RUDD, Leyton Orient Ladies striker and Times *columnist, 1994.*

The court said it was unusual for a husband to complain about his wife spending too much time on football.
WENDY TOMS, the first woman referee to reach the Football League's reserve list, after her divorce, 1991.

Stick to playing netball.
Chant by Kidderminster fans to Wendy Toms when she became the first woman to referee a senior match, 1999.

I am not sexist but...how can they make accurate decisions if they have never been tackled from behind by a 14-stone centre-half, or elbowed in the ribs or even caught offside?
JOE ROYLE, Manchester City manager, attacking the appointment of Wendy Toms as an official for the Worthington Cup final as 'politically correct', 2000.

I've played netball, but never football. I couldn't kick a ball to save my life.
AMY RAYNER, 21, on her rise from officiating in the Rugeley Boys League to being fourth official at First Division matches, 1999.

We just don't like the males and females playing together. Anyway, it's not natural.
TED CROKER, FA chief executive, 1988.

Women's football is a game that should only be played by consenting adults in private.
BRIAN GLANVILLE, journalist, 1990.

We are now getting PC decisions about promoting ladies. It does not matter whether they are ladies, men or Alsatian dogs. If they are not good enough to run the line then they should not get the job.
GORDON STRACHAN, Coventry manager, complaining about a female assistant referee, 1999.

Some of the girls can do things men would find very difficult to do. When I coached at the Centre of Excellence, one girl had a trick I'd never seen any professional do. I tried to work it out and gave up after 10 minutes. And they are physical when they want to be. They'll have a dig in and kick people – they're just the same [as the men].
KEVIN KEEGAN, England (men's) manager, 2000.

I don't care for women's football, especially when they distract me by running round in those tight shirts. I've watched it on TV and they're not suited to it. I like my women to be feminine, not sliding into tackles and covered in mud.
BRIAN CLOUGH, 2000.

I love women. I prefer their company to men's. Men are boring arseholes with nothing to talk about apart from football, and I don't like football.
LEMMY KILMINSTER of the rock group Motorhead, 1998.

Five minutes after a game, everything is all right. After the 1999 Champions' League final when Bayern lost to Manchester United, I had to comfort my girlfriend. She was much more upset than I was.
LOTHAR MATTHAUS, 2000.

Where's the girls, then? Where do we find them? Where's the shag?
STAN COLLYMORE in Leicester City's hotel at La Manga, as quoted by a businessman guest, 2000.

I love England, one reason being the magnificent breasts of English girls. Women are ultimately all that matters in life. Everything that we do is for them. We seek riches, power and glory, all in order to please them.
EMMANUEL PETIT, French midfielder, 1998.

I know women are stronger than we are. But I play the football, I make the money.
DAVID GINOLA, Tottenham winger, 2000.

I don't even understand offside so I'm not likely to understand a Manchester United contract.
VICTORIA BECKHAM as David renegotiated his deal with the club, 2002.

Whether or not we win against Germany, I will stay away from all of you for seven days. I have to sleep with my wife.
LUIZ FELIPE SCOLARI, Brazil coach, to the media on the eve of the World Cup final, 2002.

14

ARTS AND MEDIA

How can you lie back and
think of England
When you don't even know
who's in the team?
*BILLY BRAGG in his song
'Greetings To the New Brunette',
1986.*

It's coming home, it's coming
home
It's coming, football's coming
home.
*Opening of the England song
'Three Lions' by David Baddiel,
Frank Skinner and the
Lightning Seeds, 1996.*

Three lions on the shirt
Jules Rimet still gleaming
Thirty years of hurt
Never stopped me dreaming.
Chorus of 'Three Lions', 1996.

Ossie's going to Wembley
His knees have gone all
trembly.
*Tottenham FA Cup final song,
1981.*

He's football crazy
He's football mad
And the football it has
robbed him
Of the wee bit sense he had.
*Song by Scottish folk duo Robin
Hall and Jimmy MacGregor, 1960.*

Don't Come Home Too Soon
*Title of Scotland World Cup
song, by Del Amitri, 1998.*

We're representing Britain
We've got to do or die
England cannae do it
Cos they didnae qualify.
*ANDY CAMERON,
comedian/singer, on the World
Cup record 'Ally's Tartan
Army', 1978.*

O-li O-la
O-li O-la
We're gonna bring that
World Cup home from over
tha'.
*ROD STEWART song for
Scotland's World Cup campaign,
1978.*

We hate Jimmy Hill, he's a
poof, he's a poof.
*Song by Scotland fans, 1990s. As
a TV summariser, Hill had
dismissed David Narey's goal for
Scotland v. Brazil in the 1982
World Cup finals as a 'toe-poke'.*

I was aware that kids not
blessed with footballing
ability tended to kick with
the toe rather than with their
instep. I wasn't accusing
David [Narey] of that; I

merely believed he couldn't have reached the ball and shot so powerfully in any other way. Crestfallen, disappointed Scots [Brazil won 4-1] wanted to believe otherwise and have never let me forget it.
JIMMY HILL in The Jimmy Hill Story: My Autobiography, *1998.*

All I want for Christmas is a Dukla Prague away strip.
Title of song by Half Man Half Biscuit extolling joys of Subbuteo, 1986.

He looked into my eyes
Just as an airplane roared above
Said something about football
But he never mentioned love.
KIRSTY MacCOLL, pop singer, in song co-written with Jem Finer of The Pogues, 1991.

'But I don't see what football has got to do with being mayor.' She endeavoured to look like a serious politician. 'You are nothing but a cuckoo,' Denry pleasantly informed her. 'Football has got to do with everything.'

ARNOLD BENNETT in his novel The Card, *1911.*

To say that these men paid their shillings to watch 22 hirelings kick a ball is merely to say that a violin is wood and catgut, that *Hamlet* is so much paper and ink. For a shilling the Bruddersford United AFC offered you conflict and art.
J.B. PRIESTLEY in the novel The Good Companions, *1929.*

I'm a schizofanatic, sad burrits true
One half of me's red, and the other half's blue
I can't make up my mind which team to support
Whether to lean to starboard or port
I'd be bisexual if I had time for sex
Cos it's Goodison one week and Anfield the next.
ROGER McGOUGH in 'The Football Poem', 1975.

'Anything you say may be used in Everton against you.' said Harry. And it was.
JOHN LENNON in 'In His Own Write', 1964.

And that, boys, is how to take a penalty. Look one way and kick the other.
BRIAN GLOVER, playing the games teacher Sugden in the film Kes, *1969.*

I could have been a footballer but I had a paper round.
YOSSER HUGHES, played by Bernard Hill, in Alan Bleasdale's television drama series Boys From the Blackstuff, *1981.*

The sturdie ploughman,
    lustie, strong and bold
Overcometh the winter with
    driving the foote-ball
Forgetting labour and many a
    grievous fall.
ALEXANDER BARCLAY in 'Fifth Eclogue', 1508.

Am I so round with you as
    you with me
That like a football you do
    spurn me thus?
WILLIAM SHAKESPÈARE in Comedy of Errors, *1590.*

LEAR: My lady's father! my lord's knave! you whoreson dog! you slave! you cur!
OSWALD: I am none of these, my lord; I beseech your pardon.

LEAR: Do you bandy looks with me, you rascal! (Striking him)
OSWALD: I'll not be strucken, my lord.
KENT: Nor tripped either, you base football player.
WILLIAM SHAKESPEARE in King Lear, *1608.*

How the quoit
Wizz'd from the stripling's
    arm!
If touched by him
The inglorious football
    mounted to the pitch
Of the lark's flight, or shaped
    a rainbow curve
Aloft, in prospect of the
    shooting field.
WILLIAM WORDSWORTH in 'The Excursion', *1814.*

Then strip lads and to it,
    though sharp be the
    weather
And if, by mischance, you
    should happen to fall
There are worse things in life
    than a tumble in the
    heather
And life itself is but a game
    of football.
SIR WALTER SCOTT on the occasion of a match between Ettrick and Selkirk, 1815,

Then ye returned to your
trinkets;
Then ye contented you souls
With the flannelled fools at
the wicket
And the muddied oafs in the
goals.
RUDYARD KIPLING in 'The
Islanders', 1902.

I should rather like the *Match*
of the Day theme tune played
at my funeral.
CARDINAL BASIL HUME,
Newcastle fan, 1986.

It was when old ladies
who had been coming into
my shop for years started
talking about sweepers and
creating space that I really
understood the influence
of television.
JACK TAYLOR,
Wolverhampton butcher and
World Cup referee, 1974.

The governing body of
football: television.
MIKE INGHAM, BBC radio
football correspondent, 1991.

At the ITV Cup final my
enjoyment was considerably
impaired by an occasional
high-pitched whine on my

TV set. On ringing up to
complain I was told it was
Alan Ball.
SCOUSE BENNY, columnist, in
Foul! *magazine, 1975.*

It looks like a night of
disappointment for
Scotland, brought to you
live by ITV in association
with National Power.
BRIAN MOORE, ITV
commentator, during Brazil
v. *Scotland, World Cup finals,*
1990.

Poland *v.* England, 7pm
tonight, followed by Female
Orgasm, 10.50pm tomorrow.
Advert for Channel 5, 1999.

One old lady phoned to say
that the fireworks made her
cat bolt out of the door and
she hadn't seen it since.
BRIAN TRUSCOTT,
Southampton secretary, on
BSkyB's pre-match
extravaganza, 1992.

There are already millions of
camera angles showing
everything, and referees even
have things in their ears now.
Pretty soon they'll be going
out on to the pitch with a

satellite dish stuck up their arses.
IAN WRIGHT, former England striker and TV presenter, 1999.

Des Lynam on ITV? It's like David Ginola playing for Arsenal, Tony Benn voting Tory or George Clooney coming out.
BRIAN VINER, columnist, Independent on Sunday, *1999.*

For all my so-called obsession, I'm terribly conscious that football can start to eat you up a bit, and I try not to let it.
JOHN MOTSON, TV commentator, 2002.

Jimmy Hill is to football what King Herod was to babysitting.
TOMMY DOCHERTY, former manager, when Hill was a TV pundit, 1992.

There! He blew the whistle! Norway has beaten England 2-1 at football and we are the best in the world! England, the home of the giants! Lord Nelson! Lord Beaverbrook! Sir Winston Churchill! Sir

Anthony Eden! Clement Attlee! Henry Cooper! Lady Diana!
BJORGE LILLELIEN, Norwegian radio commentator, 1981.

Maggie Thatcher, can you hear me? I have a message for you in your campaigning. We have beaten England in the World Cup! As they say in the boxing bars around Madison Square Gardens in New York, your boys took a hell of a beating!
BJORGE LILLELIEN, 1981.

MICK CHANNON: We've got to get bodies in the box. The French do it, the Italians do it, the Brazilians do it.
BRIAN CLOUGH: Even educated bees do it.
Exchange on ITV World Cup panel, 1986.

These Iraqis don't take any prisoners.
RON ATKINSON for ITV at the World Cup as the Iran-Iraq war raged, 1986.

And the German stormtroopers are arriving at the far post.

BARRY DAVIES, BBC TV commentator, 1992.

Poland nil, England nil, although England are looking better value for their nil.
DAVIES, BBC TV, 1989.

2-0 is a cricket score in Italian football.
ALAN PARRY, ITV commentator, 1990.

Viv Anderson has pissed a fatness test.
JOHN HELM, ITV commentator, 1991.

Great striking partnerships come in pairs.
NIGEL SPACKMAN, Chelsea player, working as a Sky TV pundit, 1994.

He'll be the most famous Greek for years, even though he's Argentinian.
RON ATKINSON, ITV pundit, after Panathinaikos, managed by Juan Rocha, beat Ajax, 1994.

I would also like to think that the replay made it look worse than it actually was.
ATKINSON, 2000.

Shelbourne are obviously having trouble with Bohemians' five-man back four.
EAMONN GREGG, Irish TV analyst, 1995.

And that's a priceless goal, worth millions of pounds.
ALAN PARRY, ITV commentator, on European Cup final, 1995.

The Northampton striker went through Stoke's defence like a combine harvester on summer holiday.
BRIAN BEARD, Sky TV reporter, 2000.

And Hyypia rises like a giraffe to head the ball clear.
GEORGE HAMILTON, RTE (Dublin) commentator, 2001.

GARY LINEKER: Trevor Brooking is in the Sapporo Bowl. What's it like, Trevor?
TREVOR BROOKING: Well, it's a bowl-shape, Gary.
Exchange between Lineker and Brooking during BBC coverage of a World Cup match in Japan, 2002.

The Belgians will play like their fellow Scandinavians, Denmark and Sweden.
ANDY TOWNSEND, ITV pundit, World Cup finals, 2002.

You would think that if anybody could put up a decent wall it would be China.
TERRY VENABLES, ITV pundit, after Brazil scored from a free kick which passed through China's defensive wall, World Cup finals, 2002.

Germany benefited there from a last-gasp hand-job on the line.
DAVID PLEAT, ITV summariser, after Torsten Frings handled the ball v. United States, World Cup finals, 2002.

**PAUL GASCOIGNE: I've never heard of Senegal before.
DES LYNAM: I think you'll find they've been part of Africa for some time.**
Exchange on ITV after the Senegalese victory over France, World Cup finals, 2002.

**GARY LINEKER: Do you think he [Rio Ferdinand] is a natural defender?
DAVID O'LEARY: He could grow into one.**
Exchange during BBC TV's World Cup coverage, 2002.

England are sizzling in Shizouka and after this the sausages will be sizzling back home.
JOHN MOTSON, commentating on Brazil v. England, World Cup finals, 2002. Throughout the tournament Motson referred to what viewers might be having for breakfast.

**Q: What is your favourite TV programme?
A: Most nature programmes.**
VINNIE JONES in Chelsea programme questionnaire, 1991.

They [the Belgian press] are filth. They smell of shit as they torture themselves. Fortunately their criticism is erased by the praise of international connoisseurs Gary Lineker and Alan Hansen.
ROBERT WASEIGE, Belgium coach, during the World Cup finals, 2002.

George from Sligo has rung in to say that since most countries in Euro 2000 play in a colour that appears in their national flag, why is it that Italy play in blue? Well, George, I have to inform you that, as far as I know, the colours of the Italian flag are red, white and blue.
EAMON DUNPHY, media pundit and former Republic of Ireland player, hosting radio phone-in, 2000.

The good people of Suffolk will be looking forward to this.
BOBBY GOULD, Radio 5 Live summariser, before Norwich v. Bayern Munich, 1993.

Most players would give their right arm for his left foot.
MARK LAWRENSON, Radio 5 Live summariser, on Jason Wilcox, 1996.

And Vegard Heggem, my word, he must have a Honda down his shorts.
TERRY BUTCHER, Radio 5 Live summariser, on Liverpool's Norwegian defender, Euro 2000.

What a goal! One for the puritans.
Commentator on Capital Gold radio after Dennis Bergkamp scored for Arsenal v. Newcastle, 2002.

[Brian] Deane collapsed like the World Trade Centre, only less spectacularly.
GRAHAM RICHARDS, Radio Derby commentator, during Leicester v. Derby match three days after first anniversary of the attack on New York's twin towers, 2002.

What I said to them at half-time would be unprintable on radio.
GERRY FRANCIS, Tottenham manager, to Radio 5 Live after his team came from behind to beat West Ham, 1995.

We've got crash-bang-wallop journalism now where you're either the best in the world or the worst. You have letter pages, phone-ins, web sites and TV polls on football. Everyone thinks managing is fantasy football. They say: 'I'll take him off' or: 'I'll get him for £8m.'
JOE ROYLE, Manchester City manager, 2001.

For the press, you're either brilliant or you're crap. We didn't win so it was crap. That's how they work.
TEDDY SHERINGHAM, England striker, after 0-0 draw v. Croatia, 1996.

The shrewdest players never take any notice whatsoever of good press or bad press.
MALCOLM ALLISON, Manchester City coach, 1971.

A lot of people in football don't have much time for the press; they say they are amateurs. But I say: 'Noah built the Ark, but the Titanic was built by professionals.'
ALLISON, back as City manager, 1980.

Reporters can make or break footballers. The reverse can rarely be said.
MALCOLM MACDONALD, Newcastle player, 1974.

Mistrust of the press is a standard feature of any international footballer.
PETE DAVIES, author, All Played Out: The Full Story of Italia 90, 1990.

Theatre critics and film critics do know what the mechanics of a production are. Most football writers don't. So players tend to despise journalists. On the other hand players are flattered by their attention...So you have contempt and at the same time a slight awe at seeing your name in print.
EAMON DUNPHY in his book Only A Game?, 1976.

I have been let down so often, read so much that wasn't remotely true, that I now find it difficult to trust anyone who shows up with notebook and pen.
JOHN HOLLINS, Chelsea manager, 1988.

I have to making a living just like you. I happen to make mine in a nice way. You make yours in a nasty way.
SIR ALF RAMSEY to journalists, 1973.

Reporters want a quick answer to something I might want all Saturday night and all Sunday to get somewhere near.
HOWARD WILKINSON, Sheffield Wednesday manager, 1983.

I read the papers and they said we played badly last week. I thought we were fantastic, so it shows how much I know.
DAVID O'LEARY, Leeds manager, 1999.

The press in England make from a little mosquito a big elephant.
RUUD GULLIT at Chelsea, 1997.

Not only the cows are mad in England. The English press is also infected.
El Mundo Deportivo *newspaper after 'Spain-bashing' stories before the European Championship quarter-final, 1996.*

As it was the media who had tipped us to win, I thought one or two of their jobs might be in jeopardy. Not likely. It was me they were after.
BOBBY ROBSON, former England manager, recalling failure in the 1988 European Championship finals in Against All Odds, *1990.*

A very nice bunch of bastards.
GRAHAM TAYLOR, England manager, describing the English press pack in Norway, 1993.

During Scotland's 1974 World Cup in Frankfurt, my English colleagues –remember, 'Britain' didn't qualify for that one – labelled us 'fans with typewriters'. Here's an update: the English Brat Pack are hooligans with computers.
JIM BLAIR, columnist in Scotland's Daily Record, *after press vitriol aimed at Graham Taylor, 1992.*

I am ashamed of the [French] press. I am dealing with dishonest, incompetent yobs. I hope the public can figure that out.
AIME JACQUET, France coach, after criticism of him and his team en route to winning the World Cup, 1998.

It's nice to be stabbed in the front for a change.
TERRY VENABLES, Australia coach, on the open antipathy of the media Down Under, 1997.

You smell blood, don't you?
RUUD GULLIT to media
before defeat at Southampton
which provoked his dismissal by
Newcastle, 1999.

I never speak, according to
the newspapers. I just storm
and blast.
KEN BATES, Chelsea
chairman, 1990.

They were Rotherham feelers,
writing in a Rotherham paper
for other Rotherham feelers,
so bugger impartiality.
BILL GRUNDY, television
presenter, recalling his earlier
career as a football reporter,
1975.

Shame fills the heart of every
right-thinking Englishman.
How could our lads play like
that? How could they let us
down so badly?
Sun *leader column after*
England opened the World Cup
with draw v. *Republic of*
Ireland, 1990.

They couldn't play, sneered
the critics. They couldn't
string two passes together.
How wrong the world was.
Sun *leader column after*

England's semi-final exit v.
West Germany, 1990.

Swedes 2 Turnips 1
Headline in the Sun *after*
England lost to Sweden, 1992.

I'm beginning to wonder
what the bloody national
vegetable of Norway is.
GRAHAM TAYLOR, England
manager, before game in Oslo,
1992.

You lot got rid of [Neil]
Kinnock. You must be able to
do something about referees.
BOBBY GOULD, Coventry
manager, to the press after
match v. *Norwich, 1993.*

YES! WE'VE LOST!
Headline in Daily Mirror
after England lost at home to
Scotland but still qualified for
Euro 2000, 1999.

NORSE MANURE!
Headline in Scottish Sun
after Scotland drew 0-0 in
Norway, 1992.

Queen in brawl at Palace
Headline on match report in the
Guardian, *1970. Crystal Palace*
had a player called Gerry Queen.

I'll spill beans on Swindon
Headline in Today *newspaper*
about allegations of
corruption, 1990.

Yanks rate Arsenal as exciting
as a slice of cold pizza
Headline in Evening Standard
story on Arsenal's impact in
Miami tournament, 1989.

Super Caley Go Ballistic,
Celtic Are Atrocious
Headline in Scottish Sun *after*
Inverness Caledonian Thistle
won at Celtic, 2000.

United supporter to be next
Pope
Headline in Newcastle's
Evening Chronicle *on report*
that Cardinal Basil Hume
was likely to be elected to the
Vatican, 1981.

Next week Newton Heath
have to meet Burnley, and if
both play to their ordinary
style it will perhaps create an
extra run of business for the
undertakers.
Report in Birmingham Daily
Gazette, *1894. Newton Heath,*
soon to become Manchester
United, sued for libel and were
awarded a farthing in damages.

I kept wondering which side
had soiled their underpants
more with the fear of making
a mistake.
PAUL BREITNER, former West
Germany captain, reporting on
England 1 Germany 0, Bild
newspaper, at Euro 2000.

The patient's immune system
has collapsed. The patient
appears to have developed full-
blown AIDS (Alarming
Inability to Defend and Score).
TIMES OF ZAMBIA *report on*
Zambia's exit from the African
Nations Cup, 2000. One in five
Zambians aged 19-49 was HIV
positive at the time.

England star Rio Ferdinand
has admitted he has no idea
how he got his unusual
name. But today the *Daily*
Mirror can solve the mystery
once and for all. The Leeds
United centre-back is named
after a river – the Rio Grande
in Jamaica.
News section of the Daily Mirror,
11 June, 2002.

Rio Ferdinand has revealed
his ultimate World Cup
dream – a showdown with
Brazil. The England

defender, named after the Brazilian city, has been a fan since he saw Brazil in the 1986 World Cup.
Sports section of the Daily Mirror, *11 June, 2002.*

A mundane first half saw Everton nose in front thanks to a stunning strike from David Unsworth, whose swerving shot beat the despairing dive of keeper Patriot Fellatio.
Report in News of the World *on Derby* v. *Everton, 2002. The computer spell-check had corrupted the name of Patrick Filotti.*

Strictly off the record, no comment.
COLIN MURPHY, Lincoln manager, 1983.

15

FAMOUS LAST WORDS

Oh, it's okay, it's only Ray Parlour.
TIM LOVEJOY, Sky fanzone commentator and Chelsea supporter, seconds before Parlour's spectacular goal for Arsenal against his team, FA Cup final, 2002.

Rio Ferdinand is going nowhere. Where does he think he is going – into thin air?
PETER RIDSDALE, Leeds chairman, insisting they would never allow their captain to join Manchester United, 2002. Within days the £29.1m deal went through.

If someone wants to give you a bum steer on who we're after, then so be it. If you want to know, ask me because I have a list of players we want and Robbie Keane isn't on it.
GLENN HODDLE, Tottenham manager, shortly before paying Leeds £7m for Keane, 2002.

There is no limit to what this team can achieve. We will win the European Cup. European football is full of cowards and we will terrorise them with our power and attacking football.
MALCOLM ALLISON, Manchester City coach, 1968. City went out in the first round to unfancied Fenerbahce of Turkey.

Loyalty and respect seem old-fashioned words nowadays. But, as far as professional football is concerned, these are still the most important values of all in my view.
DON REVIE, England manager, in the FA Book of Soccer, 1975. Two years later he defected to Dubai.

Bobby, of course, was twice a contender for the Chelsea managership, a job he always wanted. But on the principle that you can't have friends in partnership, there's no chance that he will ever become manager of Chelsea.
KEN BATES, Chelsea chairman, in Chelsea: My Year, when Campbell was in charge of Portsmouth, 1984. Campbell eventually became manager at Stamford Bridge.

If anyone ever hears that Kevin Keegan is coming back to football full-time, they can laugh as much as I will. It will never happen. That is certain.
KEVIN KEEGAN leaving England to live in Marbella, 1985.

[Franz] Beckenbauer is like Humpty Dumpty, and the team are playing like a bunch of cucumbers.
ULLI STEIN, West Germany's third-choice goalkeeper, during the World Cup finals, 1986. Stein was duly sent home and the Germans reached the final.

I will wage my watch on Italy to beat France, and it's a gold Cartier. They will leave France by the wayside.
DIEGO MARADONA at the World Cup finals, 1986. France won 2-0.

Before City got their first we could have been 3-0 up. I turned to my physio and said: 'I think I'll have a cigar. If we keep this up we'll get double figures.'
MALCOLM MACDONALD, Huddersfield manager, after 10-1 defeat at Manchester City, 1987.

Arsenal and Spurs? No chance. The best two clubs in London are still Stringfellow's and the Hippodrome.
TERRY McDERMOTT, former Liverpool player, dismissing the capital's championship chances, 1988. Five months later Arsenal took the title – at Liverpool.

There's as much chance of [Frank] McAvennie moving as there is of Rangers beating us 5–1 tomorrow.
BILLY McNEILL, Celtic manager, 1988. Celtic duly lost 5-1 and McAvennie eventually left.

I might even agree to become Rangers' first Catholic if they paid me £1m and bought me Stirling Castle. Let me spell out where I stand. I am a Celtic man through and through and so I dislike Rangers because they are a force in Scottish football and therefore a threat to the club I love. But more than that I hate the religious policy they maintain.
MO JOHNSTON, then with Nantes, in Mo: An Autobiography, 1988. Within a year he had joined Rangers.

It's a complete fabrication. You can run that story for 10 years and it still wouldn't be true.
BILL McMURDO, agent to Mo Johnston, ridiculing reports that Rangers wanted to sign his client, 1989. Within days he had moved to Ibrox.

You can rest assured it will not happen again. Last year's defeat by Sutton United was our inoculation against that.
JOHN SILLETT, Coventry manager, the day before his team's FA Cup defeat by Fourth Division Northampton, 1990.

Good afternoon everyone, and yes, I am still here.
BRIAN TALBOT, West Bromwich Albion manager, in his programme column, December 1990. He was dismissed in January.

If that lad makes a First Division footballer, my name is Mao Tse Tung.
TOMMY DOCHERTY on Dwight Yorke while working as a radio pundit, 1991.

At least you know you're alive and not half-dead from all the emotion. Now that it has all come good, it's a lovely feeling. See you all next season.
JIM RYAN, Luton Town manager, after his team's escape from relegation, 1991. The next day he was sacked.

I must be barmy to think of leaving this club. I've got the best job in football. In the final analysis, I couldn't turn my back on people who have been so good to me.
RON ATKINSON, Sheffield Wednesday manager, after spurning Aston Villa's advances, 1991. Within a week he had joined Villa.

Let's kill off the rumours that Ossie Ardiles' job is on the line. If he ever leaves it will be of his own volition.
SIR JOHN HALL, Newcastle chairman, three days before dismissing the Argentinian and installing Kevin Keegan as manager, 1992.

We hope Peter Reid will see this club through to the next century.
PETER SWALES, Manchester

City chairman, after Reid signed a three-year contract, 1993. Within six months he had been sacked.

I like Nottingham. It's a bit like Ireland. My heart is with this club. My present contract has another three years to go, and I did have another one of three years in mind, but now I fancy something a bit longer.
ROY KEANE professing allegiance to Forest, 1993. Six months later he was with Manchester United.

You win nothing with kids.
ALAN HANSEN, Match of the Day pundit, after a youthful Manchester United lost 3-1 at Aston Villa on the season's opening day, 1995. United won the championship.

Touch wood, I've never scored an own goal in 10 years as a professional.
DAVID MILLER, Stockport defender, before scoring Derby's last-minute winner in the FA Cup, 1993.

If Alan Sugar thinks he can just walk in and take West Bromwich Albion's manager,

I'll be down that motorway in my car like an Exocet to blow up his bloody computers.
TREVOR SUMMERS, West Brom chairman, on Tottenham's interest in Ossie Ardiles, 1993. Ardiles duly became Spurs' manager.

I wish to make it clear I will not be the next manager of Aston Villa. I've had no approach from them and have no idea what my plans are. It's time to do something different with my life.
BRIAN LITTLE, resigning as Leicester manager four days before being unveiled at Villa, 1994.

I'm looking for a team that fights. No more nicey-nicey football.
STEVE McMAHON before being sent off on his debut as Swindon player-manager for elbowing an opponent, 1994.

I believe Big Ron to be one of the top three managers in the country.
DOUG ELLIS, Aston Villa chairman, three weeks before sacking Atkinson, 1994.

The players are under no pressure to get a result, so you never know what might happen.
TOMMY GEMMELL, Albion Rovers manager, before 11-0 drubbing by Partick Thistle, Scottish Cup, 1994.

I'm waiting for [Marcel] Desailly. I excel myself against blacks.
HRISTO STOICHKOV, Barcelona's Bulgarian striker, before European Cup final, 1994. Milan won 4-0 and Desailly scored.

Whatever the result, the players, directors, staff and of course the supporters of Kidderminster will have had a terrific day out.
Birmingham city programme welcome to Kidderminster Harriers, FA Cup tie, 1994. The non-League side won 2-1.

Carpenter's son Zeljko can be new City messiah!
Headline in Blue Army News, *Leicester City magazine, 1995. Goalkeeper Zeljko Kalac was dropped and offered to Wolves after two games.*

Rumours of my impending resignation have proved somewhat premature. After the Leicester game I was amazed to be asked whether I was going to resign on Monday...Anyway, that's another rumour squashed.
GEORGE GRAHAM in Arsenal programme column, published on the day he was dismissed as manager, 1995.

Good managers give in when they want to, not when other people tell them to.
HOWARD WILKINSON before what proved his last match in charge of Leeds, 1996.

We hope to surprise our Scottish friends on the playground.
MART TARMAK, Estonian FA vice-president, welcoming Scotland in the programme before 'the game that never was', 1996.

I've never stopped learning since I came to Inter. When I was young, I was a bit soft-headed, stupid sometimes. Having a family has settled me down. The older you get, the more you learn to take it. I feel more in control.

PAUL INCE in Inter Milan, 1996. He was sent off in his next match.

I think I've had only a couple of bookings in the last dozen games, which is good for me. I had better not say any more or I'll probably be sent off tonight.
ROY KEANE in Dublin's Evening Herald *before being dismissed playing for Republic of Ireland v. Russia, 1996.*

Ideally, I'd like to pop my clogs punching the air while celebrating Blues' winning goal at Wembley in the year 2130.
BARRY FRY, days before his sacking as manager of Birmingham, 1996.

I regard Aston Villa as my club. If some Villa fans are worried that I might be trouble, then I think they've got it wrong. The Liverpool experience has matured me.
STAN COLLYMORE starting a controversial spell with Villa, 1997.

I am a very happy man and every day I wake up with a smile because it is a thrill to go to work. I know one day I will be sacked. That is inevitable. But I won't cry – I'll just say I did my best and move on.
RUUD GULLIT shortly before his dismissal by Chelsea, which he disputed vehemently, 1997.

There's only one team that's going to win now and that's England. I hope I'm not tempting providence there.
KEVIN KEEGAN, working as an ITV summariser, moments before Dan Petrescu's winner for Romania, World Cup finals, 1998.

After tonight, England *v.* Argentina will be remembered for what a player did with his feet.
Advert by Adidas featuring David Beckham, who kicked Diego Simeone and was dismissed, World Cup finals, 1998.

George Graham will not go to Spurs. I spoke to him recently and he assured me he would not walk out on Leeds.
JOHN BARNWELL, chief

executive of the League
Managers' Association, days
before Graham moved to White
Hart Lane, 1998.

My old Manchester United
team-mate Mark Hughes has
now called me up for Wales,
and I am looking forward to
a long career with them.
*DAVID JOHNSON, Ipswich
striker, shortly before agreeing to
play for Scotland (although he
never did), 1999.*

Scotland are the West Ham of
world football – they never
quite live up to their potential.
*TONY BANKS MP, Labour,
the day before Scotland won
away to European champions
Germany, 1999.*

The future's bright, the
future's blue and white.
*Slogan on Blackburn Rovers'
credit card, bearing picture of
Brian Kidd in the week he was
sacked as manager, 1999.*

Now I'm a director, I can
give myself a vote of
confidence.
*STEVE BRUCE, Huddersfield
manager, 1999. He was sacked
the following year.*

All that stuff about the
foreigners and their superior
technique is a media myth as
far as I'm concerned. I was
playing for England 10 years
ago when were getting all
that, and we went to Spain
and beat them 4-2.
*TONY ADAMS, Arsenal
captain, on the eve of 4-2 defeat
by Barcelona, 1999.*

Go out there and drop
hand-grenades.
*KEVIN KEEGAN, England
manager, to Paul Scholes before
match v. Sweden, 1999. Scholes
was sent off.*

I don't think anyone can
put their finger on Tony
Parkes' success [as caretaker
manager] but he has got
us all playing for him.
We have team meetings
but we never talk about
the opposition.
*ALAN KELLY, Blackburn
goalkeeper, before 5-1 defeat at
Barnsley, 1999.*

That's it – I'm finished with
English football.
*EMMANUEL PETIT after his
third sending-off of the season,
1999. He left a year later for one*

season with Barcelona before
joining Chelsea.

I go to clubs. I'm a young lad, aren't I? I'm not going to live like a monk, as David O'Leary says. It's just natural but you have to know when to stop.
JONATHAN WOODGATE
shortly before the assault of
student Sarfraz Najeib which led
to his conviction for affray, 1999.

You have to be careful or you end up on the front page of the *Daily Record.*
DONALD FINDLAY QC,
Rangers vice-chairman, on
taking the stage at the Ibrox
social club to sing sectarian
songs, 1999. His behaviour was
exposed by the Daily Record,
forcing his resignation.

We don't need Viagra to stay up.
Banner by Charlton fans, a
month before their team were
relegated, 1999.

If we were getting murdered every week, I'd be panicking. As it is, I'm not anxious.
DANNY WILSON, Sheffield
Wednesday manager, before 8-0
defeat at Newcastle, 1999.

The bagpipes will scare the stupid bandana off David Beckham. I reckon there's one or two of their players that will crack under pressure. We've got more soul than England. They just take it for granted that they'll come up here, do the business and go away again. It's not like that for us.
JOHNNY MARR, Edinburgh
Tartan Army, before England's
2-0 win over Scotland at
Hampden Park, 1999.

If we lose [to Scotland], I'll emigrate. The simple fact is that we have better players.
EMLYN HUGHES, former
England player, before Scotland
won the second leg of their play-
off at Wembley but lost on
aggregate, 1999.

We'll probably get more fans than if we'd signed Ronaldo.
NEIL WARNOCK, Bury
manager, expecting a rush of
Asian spectators after signing
Indian international Baichung
Bhutia, 1999. His first
appearance drew 3,603.

Next year our ambition is to have a boring season.
GEOFFREY RICHMOND, Bradford City chairman, on his club's last-day escape from relegation to the First Division, 2000. They were relegated the following season.

I don't consider signing Stan a risk at all. He'll enhance the dressing-room spirit because he's a bright lad.
MARTIN O'NEILL, Leicester manager, a week before Collymore was prominent in the spraying of a Spanish hotel lobby with a fire-extinguisher, 2000.

My team just played like spoilt children who think they are great players for whom the victories will simply arrive...Today, if I was the president, I would dismiss the coach and line the players up against a wall and give them all a kick up the backside.
MARCELLO LIPPI, Inter Milan coach, after his team lost at home, 2000. He was sacked within 48 hours.

I would lie in front of a tank for the guy [Alex Ferguson]. Now that I'm here they will have to chase me out with wild animals.
MARK BOSNICH, Manchester United goalkeeper, 2000. Within months, Ferguson gave him a free transfer.

It's a question of me getting in and talking [to the media] about what's going on in the community, about the stadium, about disability. And about helping Paul Bracewell when you've got all these rumours that every manager in the world is taking his job, that they are all at Harrods having lunch with the chairman [Mohamed Al Fayed].
MAX CLIFFORD, public-relations consultant to Fulham, shortly before Fayed sacked Bracewell, 2000.

I'm not interested in the England job, so I hope no one has had a bet on me.
KEVIN KEEGAN a week before being named interim national coach, 1999.

If I am to lose this job they will have to take it away from me.
KEEGAN, weeks before resigning as England manager, 2000.

I want to reassure fans that Luis Figo, with all the certainty in the world, will be at Nou Camp on July 24 to start the season.
LUIS FIGO, Portugal captain, a fortnight before forsaking Barcelona for their bitter rivals Real Madrid, 2000.

Sven is staying until the end of the season. I shall not get tired of saying that.
SERGIO CRAGNOTTI, Lazio owner, gives a vote of confidence to the coach as the Italian champions struggled, 2000. Eriksson was named England manager within days.

Have you seen the size of the house he owns in Leicester? He owns half of Leicester and he's not going to want to leave that behind.
GORDON STRACHAN, Coventry manager, on why Gary McAllister would not be leaving the club, 2000. He soon joined Liverpool.

Peter Taylor needs three or four seasons with us, then he can become the next England manager.
JOHN ELSOM, Leicester chairman, 2000. He sacked Taylor within a year.

Ideally, I would like David O'Leary to be at this club for life.
PETER RIDSDALE, Leeds chairman, 2000. He sacked the Irishman as manager within two years.

There's only one way I will leave West Ham, and that is if the club kick me out. I feel the shirt like a second skin to my body.
PAOLO DI CANIO, 2001. The following year, when Manchester United tried to buy him, he declared his hope that the deal would like go through.

I congratulate the president for making the decision not to sack me.
LLORENC SERRA FERRER, Barcelona coach, after defeat by Liverpool in the Uefa Cup, 2001. Within 48 hours he had been fired.

They are just another
English club. It doesn't
make any difference if
we're playing Sheffield
United or Manchester
United. All English clubs
play the same way.
RONALD KOEMAN,
Barcelona and Netherlands
sweeper, before the European
Cup-Winners' Cup final v.
Manchester United, 1991.
United won 3-1.

This could be the most
boring cup final in history.
JOHAN CRUYFF, former
Netherlands captain, before
Liverpool beat Alaves of Spain
5-4 to win the Uefa Cup, 2001.

There's only one team
looking like scoring.
Scunthorpe have had all the
play. Burnley look very tired
all of a sudden. Hang on –
Burnley have scored.
ALAN MULLERY, Talk Radio
summariser, 2001.

Nikos the Greek [Burnley
goalkeeper Nikolaos
Michopoulos] is getting his
hands on everything. Except
that one – 1-1.
ALAN MULLERY, as above.

There's no chance of Sol
leaving for Arsenal. He's a
Spurs fan and there's not a
hope in hell of his playing in
an Arsenal shirt.
DAVID BUCHLER, Tottenham
chairman, weeks before Campbell
defected to Highbury, 2001.

It's hard to think of a
bigger and better club to play
for [than Manchester
United], especially as I have
no real desire to taste life in
Italy or Spain.
JAAP STAM in Head To Head,
published days before United sold
him to Lazio, 2001.

All the speculation
surrounding Birmingham has
been off-putting...I'm
extremely happy here. I want
to manage in the Premiership
and I'd love to take Crystal
Palace there. End of story.
STEVE BRUCE, Palace
manager, shortly before making
Birmingham his fifth club in
four years, 2001.

I have no doubts whatsoever
that Germany will thrash
England and qualify easily for
the World Cup. What could
possibly go wrong? The

English haven't beaten us in Munich for a hundred years. I'm convinced we're headed into another golden age of German soccer.
ULI HOENESS, former Germany player, on the eve of England's visit, 2001. England won 5-1.

In remembrance of arrogant, clinical, penalty-scoring and downright bloody irritating German football...Oliver Kahn's gloves will be cremated and the ashes taken to England.
The Mirror *after England's 5-1 win* v. *Germany, 2001. Ten months later Germany contested the World Cup final, England having gone out in the quarter-finals.*

I've never been tempted to walk away in frustration. It's a thing I would never do. I wouldn't turn my back on the players because they're still a fantastic bunch to work for. And I'm not interested in going to another club.
JOHN GREGORY, Aston Villa manager, weeks before resigning and joining Derby, 2002.

Zidane and Vieira? They're only names. I think we can win this game.
BERTI VOGTS in Paris before his debut as Scotland manager, 2002. France beat his side 5-0.

My view is that France are above everyone else. Their quality makes them super, super favourites.
ARSENE WENGER, French manager of Arsenal, before the World Cup finals, 2002.

My friends are coming over to Korea and Japan for the group stages but my family are not planning to visit until the final week of the tournament.
MARCEL DESAILLY, France defender, before his country's defence of the World Cup, 2002. France did not survive the first round.

Sometimes in such a Herculean struggle an outside body can influence the outcome. God, once again, will decide this match. And we will win it.
JUAN SEBASTIAN VERON, Argentina midfielder, before the meeting with England in the World Cup finals, 2002. England won.

Apart from [goalkeeper]
Oliver Kahn, if you put all
the players in a sack and
punched it, whoever you hit
would deserve it.
FRANZ BECKENBAUER,
former Germany captain and
coach, in the early stages of the
World Cup finals, 2002. Within
a fortnight Germany had
reached the final.

INDEX

Aberdeen 160, 283, 286, 287, 355
Adams, Tony 10, 11, 41, 50–1, 88, 130, 167, 193, 195, 196, 213, 240, 290, 315, 336, 341, 384
Adamson, Jimmy 102
Adamson, Tony 178
Agana, Tony 292
Agnelli, Gianni 20
Aitken, Roy 92
Aizlewood, John 302
Ajax 239, 369
Akinbiyi, Ade 257
Al Fayed, Mohamed 97, 306, 331, 386
Alaves 103, 388
Albarn, Damon 222
Albion Rovers 382
Aldershot 306
Aldridge, John 134, 205
Allen, Clive 66
Allen, Dave 265
Allison, George 88
Allison, Malcolm 53, 80, 142, 149, 175, 209, 227, 229, 333, 353, 372, 378
Allsop, Derick 343
Alwen, Roger 93
American Samoa 126
Amis, Martin 300
Anderson, Rachel 274
Anderson, Viv 369
Anderton, Darren 2, 276
Anelka, Didier 259
Anelka, Nicolas 2, 44, 254, 259, 273
Archer, Ian 137
Archer, Jeffrey 310
Archibald, Steve 232
Ardiles, Ossie 51, 74, 88, 116–17, 142, 212, 226, 380, 381
Arena, Bruce 244

Argentina 4, 10, 74, 126, 279, 356, 383, 389
Arges 348
Arif, Dogon 284
Armfield, Jimmy 76
Arsenal 2, 10–11, 14, 25–6, 28, 33–6, 38–41, 44–5, 50–1, 56, 58–9, 74–5, 79, 84, 88–9, 96, 98, 100, 117, 120, 129, 158, 160, 164, 166–7, 175–6, 178, 193, 195, 200, 208, 213–15, 227, 229, 233, 236–8, 240–1, 249, 251, 254, 261, 263, 265–6, 268, 270–1, 273, 276, 284, 288, 291, 294, 297–8, 304, 306, 309, 311, 315, 323, 336, 341–2, 346, 356–8, 371, 375, 378–9, 382, 384, 388–9
Ashby, Gerald 348
Ashton, Joe 315–16
Astle, Jeff 117
Aston, Ken 76
Aston Villa 12, 16, 22, 24–5, 27, 33–4, 43–4, 47, 52, 58, 61, 81, 89–90, 95, 168, 191, 193, 202–4, 206, 209, 212, 222, 227, 252, 262–3, 271–2, 274, 276, 280–2, 285–6, 288, 307, 310, 313, 329–30, 346–7, 354, 380–1, 383, 389
Atkins, Ian 215
Atkinson, Dalian 282
Atkinson, Margaret 142
Atkinson, Ron 39, 78, 81, 82, 84, 142–4, 152, 179, 186, 206, 212, 215, 224, 229, 235, 262, 280, 281, 307,

352, 354, 368, 369, 380, 381
Atletico Madrid 143, 288, 328
Attila the Stockbrocker 316
Auld, Bertie 92–3
Australia 126, 155
Azcue, Joe 242–3
Azzopardi, Tony 158

Babb, Phil 2, 135
Baddiel, David 169, 364
Baggio, Roberto 3
Bailey, Eddie 177
Bailey, John 19
Bailey, Mike 285
Baillie, Colin 146
Baker, Danny 21
Baldwin, Kevin 64
Ball, Alan 13, 51–2, 68, 104, 113, 144–5, 210, 232, 280, 284, 288
Ball, John 299
Baltacha, Sergei 262
Banks, Gordan 52, 129
Banks, Tony 21, 71, 94, 272, 384
Barcelona 35, 36, 90, 91–2, 95, 148, 191, 192, 219, 232, 239, 241, 274, 317, 382, 384, 387, 388
Barclay, Alexander 366
Barclay, Patrick 19
Barker, Paul 115
Barker, Vince 308
Barmby, Nick 3, 332
Barnes, John 52, 154, 240, 272, 274
Barnes, Ken 52
Barnet 90, 317, 331
Barnsley 211, 231, 384
Barnwell, John 200, 284, 383–4
Barras, Omar 341
Barrow 233

Barry, Gareth 290
Barthez, Fabien 3, 226, 241, 269, 305
Barton, Warren 3
Barwick, Brian 102, 312
Bassett, Dave 101, 119, 129, 145–6, 151, 203, 204, 257, 260, 261, 279, 280, 309, 328
Bastin, Cliff 84
Bastin, Joan 84
Bastock, Paul 249
Bates, Ken 34, 107, 161, 179–80, 219, 233, 240, 264, 326, 330, 331, 358, 374, 378
Bateson, Mike 294
Bath City 170
Batty, David 3–4, 57, 197, 237, 273
Baxter, Jim 52, 62, 129, 137, 262, 356
Baxter, John 52–3
Bayer Leverkusen 216, 253
Bayern Munich 16, 66, 94, 107, 148, 219, 266, 286, 360, 371
Bazar, Thereza 78
Bean, Sean 115, 314, 318
Beard, Brian 369
Beardsley, Peter 52, 53
Beasant, Dave 119, 144, 145, 315
Beaumont-Dark, Anthony 220
Beck, John 146, 285
Beckenbauer, Franz 16, 53, 132, 379, 390
Beckham, Brooklyn 7, 10, 271, 278
Beckham, David 4–11, 21–2, 24, 25, 76, 109, 162, 164, 256, 278, 283, 316, 361, 383, 385
Beckham, Victoria 4, 5, 6–7, 8, 9–10, 271, 278, 305, 361
Beelan, Johan 301
Beer, Eugen 9
Belgium 370

Bell, Bill 331–2
Bell, Colin 53, 175
Benali, Francis 357
Benarbia, Ali 11, 104–5
Benarrivo, Antonio 110
Benfica 240
Bennett, Arnold 365
Benny, Scouse 367
Bent, Marcus 227
Bergara, Danny 280, 284
Berger, Patrik 344
Bergkamp, Dennis 11, 88, 117, 240, 251, 371
Berkovic, Eyal 12, 25, 118
Bermuda 289
Berti, Nicola 354
Best, Alex 56
Best, George 5, 18, 19, 21, 30, 54–6, 59, 60, 71, 72, 76, 90, 109, 133, 222, 229, 237, 263
Beswick, Bill 240–1
Bevan, Bob 'The Cat' 50
Bevan, Nye 312
Bevers, Syd 297
Bhutia, Baichung 385
Bianchi, Carlos 215
Biggs, Ronnie 142
Billingham Synthonia 90–1
Bindel, Julie 8
Bingham, Billy 207
Birchenall, Alan 38
Bird, Tina 20
Birmingham City 91, 153, 165, 192, 207, 227, 248, 249, 264, 284, 298, 301, 310, 325, 326, 331, 356–7, 382, 383, 388
Birtles, Garry 105
Bizarri, Albano 207
Bjork 288
Blackburn Rovers 3, 12, 15, 18, 25, 32, 40, 42, 91, 94, 104, 153, 188–9, 206, 207, 237, 250, 252, 267, 273, 275, 285, 295, 297, 354, 355, 358, 384
Blackpool 76

Blades, Gilbert 306–7
Blair, Jim 373
Blair, Tony 10, 106, 111, 130, 160, 173, 252, 309
Blanc, Laurent 131
Blanchflower, Danny 54, 56, 59–60, 68, 75, 88, 133, 177, 215, 218, 230
Blatter, Sepp 218, 220, 352
Bleasdale, Alan 366
Blissett, Luther 117, 245, 266
Boateng, George 12, 22, 189
Bob, Lord 324
Bobroff, Paul 116
Boca Juniors 215
Boizot, Peter 322
Bolton 106, 207, 224, 254, 285
Bond, John 146, 153, 280, 353
Bonds, Billy 118, 278, 280
Booking, Trevor 182
Bosman, Jean-Marc 259
Bosnich, Mark 164, 386
Bossis, Maxime 291
Boston United 249, 318
Boswell, Thomas 243
Bothroyd, Jay 89
Bould, Steve 11, 50, 166
Bournemouth 54, 245, 298, 299
Bowden, Ray 75
Bowen, Dave 182
Bowles, Stan 56
Bowyer, Lee 12–13, 99, 100, 253
Bracewell, Paul 386
Bradbury, Lee 13
Bradford City 28, 35, 104, 113, 220, 262, 279, 386
Bradford Park Avenue 355
Brady, Karren 91, 248, 301, 356–7
Brady, Liam 51, 208

Bragg, Billy 316, 364
Bragg, Melvyn 315
Branfoot, Ian 97, 146, 220
Brazil 8, 11, 36, 37, 40, 52, 79, 126–7, 130, 159, 186, 215, 219, 220, 225, 226, 268, 286, 305, 364–5, 367, 370, 375–6
Brearley, Reg 325
Brechin City 317
Breitner, Paul 375
Bremner, Billy 46, 52, 56, 65, 98
Bremner, Rory 3
Brentford 354
Bridges, Michael 13
Bright, Mark 84–5
Brighton 149, 229, 281, 309, 316, 335
Brimson, Dougie 301
Brimson, Eddy 301
Brindley, Chris 262
Bristol City 308
Bristol Rovers 172, 201, 209, 341
Brolin, Tomas 167
Brooking, Trevor 31, 56, 84, 270, 369
Brown, Alan 219
Brown, Bob 147
Brown, Craig 137, 146–7, 177, 185, 214, 216, 240, 262, 280
Brown, Jock 147
Brown, John 17
Brown, Ken 270
Brown, Mary 155
Bruce, Steve 147, 161, 384, 388
Buchan, Martin 81, 341
Buchler, David 388
Bull, Steve 57, 124
Burchill, Julie 9, 267, 317
Burkinshaw, Keith 230
Burley, Craig 13
Burnige, Jeff 131
Burnley 91, 102, 221, 249, 272, 316, 324, 388

Burns, Tommy 304
Burr, Reg 307
Burridge, John 233
Burrows, Frank 353
Burton, Terry 38, 120, 267
Busby, Matt 54, 64, 64–5, 72, 147–8, 189
Bush, George W. 138
Butcher, Terry 13, 57, 185, 188, 208, 270, 274, 281, 371
Butt, Nicky 14
Byers, Stephen 107

Caine, Michael 21
Calderon, Marcus 136
Caldow, Eric 136
Camacho, Jose Antonio 282, 349
Cambridge United 285
Cameron, Andy 364
Cameroon 127–8
Campbell, Alistair 309
Campbell, Bobby 281, 378
Campbell, Dick 316–17
Campbell, Sol 14, 249, 388
Camus, Albert 224
Cannon, Tom 206
Cantona, Eric 57–9, 106, 109, 131, 197, 218, 219, 228, 238, 245, 275, 278, 298, 300, 317, 356
Capello, Fabio 193
Cardetti, Giorgio 223
Cardiff City 91–2, 302, 332, 333
Carey, George 309
Carey, Leanne 27
Carlisle United 92, 215, 219, 315, 328, 337
Carlos, Roberto 8, 25, 36–7
Carragher, Jamie 14
Carrott, Jasper 68, 69, 310
Carsons, Kit 253
Cartland, Dame Barbara 5

Cartwright, John 235
Cascarino, Tony 59, 179, 266
Cashmore, Ellis 300
Castro, Fidel 310, 332
Cattlin, Chris 281
Celtic 12, 13, 63, 69, 77, 78, 92, 92–3, 116, 136, 147, 154, 160, 179, 180, 189, 200, 267, 270, 279, 303, 304, 305, 330, 355, 375, 379
Chalmers, Judith 28
Channon, Mick 73, 368
Chapman, Herbert 88
Chapman, Katie 358
Chapman, Lee 59, 225, 269, 356
Chapple, Geoff 215
Charles, Gary 22
Charles, Glenda 60
Charles, John 59–60, 114, 251, 265–6
Charles, Prince of Wales 60, 288
Charlton Athletic 93, 206, 285, 306, 352, 385
Charlton, Bobby 60–1, 109, 114, 128, 129, 144, 161, 182, 250, 326–7
Charlton, Jack 17, 30, 60, 77, 129, 134, 135, 148–9, 156, 172–3, 182, 190, 219, 235, 237, 341
Chelsea 18, 31–4, 36, 44, 46, 48, 62, 67, 93–5, 107, 161, 164, 168–9, 180, 182, 193, 197, 201, 207, 212, 218–19, 222, 233, 236, 239–40, 244, 249, 262, 264, 266, 268, 271–2, 275, 281, 285–6, 288, 294, 299, 301–2, 305, 309–10, 317, 326, 330–1, 344, 358, 369, 373–4, 378, 383–4
Chester, Norman 209

Chesterfield 102
China 370
Chinaglia, Giorgio 230–1
Christian, Terry 106
Churchill, Winston 159, 291, 368
Clare, Anthony 7
Claridge, Steve 165, 348, 14
Clark, Frank 160, 211
Clarke, Alan 300
Clarke, Allan 299
Clarke, Kenneth 314
Clarke, Nicky 39, 53
Clay, Ernie 97, 322, 327
Clayton, Ronnie 250
Clemente, Javier 254
Clifford, Max 101, 112, 386
Clitheroe, Jimmy 52
Clough, Brian 8, 14, 27, 28, 29, 30, 39, 42, 56, 58, 61, 63, 68, 79, 81, 96, 108, 112, 116, 118, 146, 149–52, 162, 179, 180, 184, 188, 190, 196, 197, 203, 205, 209, 210, 213–14, 215, 227, 228–9, 235, 258, 299, 314, 323, 328, 333, 334–5, 355, 356, 360, 368
Clough, Nigel 14
Coates, Peter 76
Cobain, Kurt 221–2
Cobbold, Patrick 338
Cobh Ramblers 27
Coe, Sebastian 310
Cohen, George 61
Colchester 299
Cole, Andy 14–15, 41, 314
Cole, Joe 15
Collina, Pierluigi 349
Collins, Bobby 211
Collins, John 96, 304
Collins, Michael 30
Collymore, Stan 18, 61–2, 360, 383, 386
Colman, Eddie 61
Colquhoun, John 244, 261

Columbia 284
Conn, Alfie 116
Connolly, Billy 77, 112, 137
Conroy, Terry 65–6
Conway, Pete 306
Cooke, Charlie 62
Cooper, Keith 347
Coppell, Steve 84, 203–4, 212, 253, 276, 279, 281, 294, 332
Cork, Alan 119
Coventry City 27, 31, 34, 46, 69, 79, 82, 89, 95, 137, 144, 166, 189–90, 203–5, 208, 210–11, 254, 275, 281, 283–5, 289, 311–12, 340, 345, 348, 359, 374, 380, 387
Cowan, Tom 145
Cowdenbeath 95, 202
Cox, Arthur 19, 206
Cragnotti, Sergio 214, 286, 387
Craig, Albert 355
Craig, Norma 355
Crerand, Paddy 54, 147, 231
Crewe 56, 72, 204, 231, 235, 308
Crick, Michael 164, 333
Croatia 372
Croatia Zagreb 283
Croker, Ted 102, 359
Cross, David 340
Crossley, Mark 282
Cruyff, Estelle 168
Cruyff, Johan 95, 148, 239, 388
Crystal Palace 11, 34, 36, 43, 58, 84, 95, 97, 135, 142, 203, 208, 212, 253, 257, 278, 279, 281, 294, 311, 316, 324, 332, 348, 374, 388
Cullis, Stan 121, 152–3, 234
Cumbes, Jim 117
Curle, Keith 280
Currie, Tony 193

Dacourt, Olivier 45
Dailly, Christian 137–8
Daish, Liam 144
Dalglish, Kenny 40, 63, .102, 153–4, 159, 180, 207, 245, 355
Dani 288
Daniels, Robin 297
Darlington 96, 322, 325, 337
Davies, Barry 368, 369
Davies, H.D. 83
Davies, Howard 313
Davies, Hunter 50–1, 218, 223, 230, 256, 297, 315, 352
Davies, Pete 185, 372
Dawson, Jeff 182
De Boer, Frank 241
de Gaulle, Charles 151
De Silva, Desmond 12–13
Dean, Dixie 63
Deane, Brian 115, 271, 371
Deayton, Angus 269
Dein, David 2, 44, 196
Del Amitri 364
Del Bosque, Vincente 2
Dell'Olio, Nancy 158
Denmark 43, 44, 128, 268
Depford, Frank 243
Deportivo La Coruna 10
Derby County 19, 36, 45, 69, 96, 150, 151, 190, 191, 206, 213, 227, 231, 259, 305, 325, 328, 334, 345, 353, 371, 376, 381, 389
Desailly, Marcel 36, 130, 131, 219, 275, 382, 389
Dhalin, Martin 225
Di Canio, Paolo 15–16, 108, 118, 387
Di Stefano, Alfredo 64, 72, 114
Diamond, Dominik 303
Diana, Princess of Wales 288, 368

Dichio, Daniele 196
Dicks, Julian 64, 233
Dicks, Terry 220
Dijkstra, Eva 16
Dimbleby, Gordon 122
Diouf, El Hadji 15
Dixon, Lee 2, 114
Docherty, Tommy 64,
  69, 78, 82, 84, 103,
  105, 108, 121–2, 137,
  154–5, 200, 209, 211,
  221, 234, 288, 322,
  329, 334, 335, 342,
  368, 380
Dodd, Ken 305
Dokupil, Ernst 228
Dolan, Terry 279
Domingo, Placido 358
Don, Philip 343
Donald, Chris 67
Doncaster Belles 96
Dooley, Derek 338
Double, Steve 79
Dougan, Derek 89, 324
Downes, Wally 119, 145
Downing, Keith 122
Drake, Ted 310
Draper, Mark 271
Drew, Bryan 301
Drewery, Eileen 170
D'Souza, Christa 158
Duffard, Georges-Marie
  133–4
Duffy, Jim 72
Dugarry, Christophe 48
Dukla Prague 365
Dumitrescu, Ilie 116
Dundee United 281
Dunn, Steve 346–7
Dunnett, Jack 112
Dunphy, Eamon 66, 147,
  148–9, 182, 248, 324,
  371, 372
Durban, Alan 229
Durkin, Paul 345, 346
D'Urso, Andy 347, 348
Dury, Ian 170
Duscher, Aldo 10
Dusseldorf 219
Dyer, Kieron 16
Dynamo Kiev 262

Earle, Robbie 64
Edwards, Anne 65
Edwards, Duncan 64–5
Edwards, Martin 93, 333
Effenberg, Stefan 16
El-Mokadem, Ahmed
  134
Elizabeth II, Queen of
  England 21, 56, 173,
  229
Elleray, David 341, 343,
  344, 345, 346, 347,
  348
Elleray, Dorothy 162
Ellis, Doug 193, 329–30,
  354, 381
Elsom, John 38, 387
England 4, 6, 11, 13, 15,
  20–4, 28, 32–5, 39–41,
  43, 48, 50–3, 56, 60,
  68, 71, 73–5, 77–8,
  80–1, 83–4, 126–30,
  137, 151, 156–9, 161,
  165, 169–71, 173–4,
  176, 181–5, 187,
  190–4, 197, 200–3,
  205–6, 212–13,
  218–26, 228, 231–4,
  238–42, 248–50, 252,
  257–9, 261–2, 265,
  270–2, 274–6, 279–80,
  282–6, 288, 290, 292,
  297, 300–1, 305, 316,
  318, 323, 327–8, 331,
  341–2, 345, 349,
  352–3, 355–6, 358,
  360, 364, 367–70,
  372–5, 378–9, 383–9
England, Mike 134, 230
Eriksson, Sven-Goran 40,
  127, 130, 156–9, 164,
  200, 213, 214, 220,
  226, 240, 283, 324,
  387
Eriksson, Ulla 158, 164
Estonia 303, 382
Evans, Roy 96, 204
Everton 3, 17, 22, 24,
  37, 45, 47, 63, 66, 82,
  84, 96–7, 153, 174–5,
  201, 225, 226, 227,

  253, 282, 285, 312,
  314, 326, 332, 344,
  345, 376
Exeter City 328
Eyre, Fred 176, 327

Falkirk 344
Faroe Islands 148, 194
Fashanu, John 58, 65,
  120
Fashanu, Justin 150, 267
Faye, Amdy 138
Feltz, Vanessa 18
Fenwick, Terry 354
Ferdinand, Les 16, 274–5
Ferdinand, Rio 17, 18,
  33, 101, 109, 118,
  157, 183, 252, 271,
  275, 370, 375–6, 378
Ferguson, Alex 4, 7, 10,
  14, 22, 23, 26, 29, 34,
  39, 41, 44, 50, 58–9,
  61, 68, 71, 73, 88–9,
  103, 105–6, 108, 109,
  110, 118, 143, 146,
  148, 159–64, 168, 186,
  196, 202, 205, 209,
  219, 231, 239, 254,
  257, 263, 276, 282,
  283, 313, 314, 319,
  331, 333, 344, 386
Ferguson, Duncan 17
Ferguson, Ian 114
Ferguson, Martin 160
Ferguson, Ronald 95
Fernie, Willie 136
Ferrer, Llorenc Serra 387
Ferrera, Paola 357
Figo, Luis 387
Filotti, Patrick 376
Findlay, Donald 385
Finer, Jem 365
Finland 11, 36
Finn, Ralph 93
Finney, Tom 54, 65, 126,
  132
Fiorentina 210, 238
Firmani, Eddie 352
Fisher Athletic 284
Fjortoft, Jan Aage 115
Flashman, Stan 331

Flatts, Mark 276
Flitcroft, Garry 18
Fort Lauderdale Strikers 242
Foster, Jonathan 115
Foudy, Julie 358
Fowler, Robbie 18, 23, 64, 268
Fox, Ruel 289
France 48, 100, 130–1, 219, 220, 221, 222, 226, 237, 238, 239, 240, 264, 266, 268, 291, 370, 373, 379, 389
Francis, Gerry 117, 164–5, 201, 211, 371
Francis, Tony 167
Francis, Trevor 65, 91, 165, 257
Franklin, Neil 223
Fraser, Ross 330
Fratila, Constantin 348
Freud, Sigmund 195, 305
Frings, Torsten 370
Fry, Barry 55, 90, 91, 157, 165, 192, 201, 206, 322, 331, 383
Fry, C.B. 295
Fulham 38, 61, 97, 174, 214, 245, 250, 261, 298, 302, 306, 311, 322, 327, 328, 331, 348, 353, 358, 386
Fulston, George 344
Furnish, David 9
Fynn, Alex 251

Gahagan, John 294
Gallagher, Liam 313
Gallagher, Noel 7, 73
Gascoigne, Bamber 19
Gascoigne, Paul 18–23, 185, 188, 192, 244, 264, 269, 289, 292, 342, 370
Gascoigne, Sheryl 22
Gaspart, Joan 114
Geller, Uri 23, 328
Gemmell, Tommy 381
Gemmill, Archie 81

Gento, Francisco 80
George, Boy 6, 73
George, Charlie 357
George, Michael 75
Germany 8, 37, 43, 72, 74, 128, 131–2, 174, 194, 207, 255, 267, 282, 343, 361, 370, 375, 384, 388–9, 390
Gerrard, Steven 23, 28
Gibson, Alfred 116
Gibson, Garry 97–8
Gibson, Mel 303
Gibson, Steve 109
Gibson, Terry 289
Gidman, John 143
Giggs, Ryan 23–4, 27, 46, 55, 71, 162, 164, 269, 302
Gil, Jesus 288, 328
Giles, John 7, 65–6, 70, 148, 187
Gilfeather, Frank 164
Gillies, Ricky 154
Gillingham 97, 104
Gilzean, Alan 222–3
Ginola, David 24, 143, 154, 171, 360, 368
Given, Shay 227
Glanville, Brian 359
Gloster, Elizabeth 193
Glover, Brian 144, 366
Goater, Shaun 289
Godard, Jean-Luc 273
Gold, David 326
Goodall, John 222
Goram, Andy 24–5, 218, 358
Goram, Tracy 358
Gothenberg 281
Gough, Richard 227
Gould, Bobby 79, 95, 139, 165–6, 172, 210, 240, 258, 269, 285, 371, 374
Gradi, Dario 72, 231, 235
Graham, George 2, 58, 88, 117, 166–7, 175, 178, 195, 196, 209, 227, 228, 233, 256, 382, 383–4

Grantham Town 179
Gray, Andy 66, 201, 269, 271
Gray, Eddie 66
Gray, Ron 190
Graydon, Ray 204, 206, 317
Greaves, Jimmy 21, 66, 79, 98, 117, 137, 181, 182, 197, 262, 329
Greenwood, Ron 118, 151, 167, 176, 197, 221, 224, 231, 283, 318
Gregg, Eamonn 369
Gregg, Harry 61, 66, 72, 333
Gregory, John 24, 25, 27, 34, 44, 61–2, 90, 95, 168, 191, 204, 222, 227, 262, 263, 288, 313, 330, 346, 347, 389
Griffiths, Ed 249
Griggs, Max 325
Grimandi, Gilles 271
Grimsby Town 97, 309
Grobbelaar, Bruce 67
Grundy, Bill 374
Gudjohnsen, Eidur 305
Gullit, Ruud 39, 41, 66–7, 74, 94, 109, 133, 137, 168–9, 193, 196, 203, 206–7, 227, 232, 238–9, 271, 285, 373, 374, 383
Gunes, Senol 138
Gunn, Alan 342

Haaland, Alf-Inge 28, 29, 99
Hackett, Keith 188
Hadaker, Alan 250
Hagi, Gheorghe 67
Hajduk Split 287
Halifax 306, 308, 326
Hall, Douglas 111
Hall, Eric 46, 209, 259, 260–1
Hall, John 111, 218, 307, 325, 380

Hall Martin 152–3
Hall, Robin 364
Hamburg 286
Hamilton Academical 287
Hamilton, Andy 331
Hamilton, Billy 127
Hamilton, Bryan 280
Hamilton, George 369
Hammam, Sam 44, 70, 91–2, 120, 175, 178–9, 332–3, 343, 344
Hancock, Nick 53, 221, 314
Hand, Eoin 200
Hansen, Alan 4, 67, 83, 103, 138, 153, 251, 370, 381
Hanson, Michele 352
Hardaker, Alan 183, 340
Harding, Matthew 294, 330, 331
Hardman, H.P. 105
Harford, Ray 42, 169, 252, 285
Harper, Steve 347
Harris, 'Chopper' 237
Harris, Ron 31, 67
Hart, Graham 76
Harte, Ian 25
Hartlepool United 97–8, 149, 203, 204, 296, 308
Hartson, John 25, 71
Hasselbaink, Jimmy Floyd 95
Hateley, Mark 59
Hattersley, Roy 94, 315, 326, 348
Hatton, Derek 312
Hauge, Rune 166
Haugenes, Gaute 358
Havelange, Joao 355
Hay, David 136
Hayes, Dean 103
Haynes, Johnny 250, 251
Haynes, Richard 220
Hayward, Jack 229–30, 335, 336
Hayward, Jonathan 335, 336

Hearn, Barry 101, 319, 322
Heathman, Stanley 311
Hedman, Magnus 275
Heggem, Vegard 371
Heginbotham, Stafford 220
Heighway, Steve 33
Helliwell, Dave 326
Helm, John 369
Hemery, David 225
Henchoz, Stephane 91
Hendrie, Tom 286–7
Hendry, Colin 25
Henri, Adrian 312
Henry, Thierry 25, 237
Hereford United 211, 296, 323, 338, 354
Hertha Berlin 286
Heseltine, Michael 70, 314
Heskey, Emile 25–6, 171
Heyhoe-Flint, Rachel 122
Hibernian 72, 287
Hiddink, Guus 130, 139
Higuita, Rene 24
Hill, Bernard 366
Hill, Gordon (player) 340
Hill, Gordon (referee) 5, 231
Hill, Jimmy 68, 226, 249, 261, 353, 364–5, 368
Hill, Peter 323, 338
Hill-Wood, Denis 323
Hill-Wood, Peter 89
Hislop, Ian 33
Hobson, Gordon 291
Hoddle, Carl 317
Hoddle, Glenn 14–15, 34, 67, 68, 74, 169–70, 196, 212, 218, 225, 226, 238, 284, 288, 317, 335, 378
Hodge, Steve 116
Hodgkinson, Alan 228
Hodgson, Roy 170, 212
Hoeness, Uli 266, 286, 388–9
Holden, Rick 23, 342
Holdsworth, Dean 254
Holland 222
see also Netherlands

Holland, Julian 56
Hollins, John 358, 372
Holmes, Jon 202, 260
Home, Sonya 343
Hopcraft, Arthur 181, 222, 242, 296
Hornby, Nick 294
Horne, Barry 225
Horne, John 308
Horton, Brian 170, 210, 281
Houllier, Gerard 3, 34, 103, 171–2, 191, 236, 264, 283
Houston, Stewart 170
Howe, Don 166, 172, 206, 212
Howell, Denis 298
Huckerby, Darren 13
Huddersfield 75, 147, 379, 384
Hudson, Alan 6, 80, 165, 171, 187
Hughes, Charles 234
Hughes, Emlyn 102, 296, 385
Hughes, Mark 68, 384
Hull City 308
Hume, Cardinal Basil 367, 375
Hungary 132–3, 230, 234
Hunt, Roger 68, 182
Hunter, Norman 68, 183, 211, 225, 237, 345, 352, 353
Hurst, Geoff 68–9, 78, 181, 182, 201, 224, 231, 274, 353
Hurst, Judith 353
Hussain, Nasser 312
Hutchinson, Colin 32, 94, 168
Hutchison, Don 245
Hynd, Roger 211

I'Anson, Lisa 2
Icke, David 69
Ince, Paul 26, 171, 191, 225, 237, 382–3
Indriksons, Guntis 137

Ingham, Mike 367
Ingham, Roger 298
Inter Milan 26, 27, 37,
 58, 92, 170, 189,
 254–5, 354, 382–3,
 386
Inverness Caledonian
 Thistle 304, 375
Ipswich 47, 181, 184,
 227, 262, 269, 274,
 282, 306, 325, 338,
 384
Irwin, Denis 30
Italy 14, 48, 133, 135,
 149, 349

Jackson, Michael 77, 328
Jacquet, Aime 373
Jairzinho 126–7
Jamaica 64
James, Alex 51
James, Brian 69, 102,
 231, 274, 353
James, Clive 154
James, David 16, 26, 43
James, Leighton 69
Jansen, Matt 267
Jemson, Nigel 215
Jensen, Lisa 169
Jewell, Paul 35, 262
Jewhurst, Allen 252–3
John, Elton 9, 129,
 336–7, 338
Johnson, Anton 326
Johnson, David 384
Johnson, Jade 252
Johnston, Maurice (Mo)
 69, 304, 379, 380
Johnstone, Derek 304
Johnstone, Jimmy 69, 113
Jokanovic, Slavisa 275
Jones, Dave 124, 172,
 346
Jones, Joey 305
Jones, Steve 298
Jones, Vinnie 21, 43, 46,
 47, 66, 67, 69–71, 73,
 107, 139, 197, 203,
 229, 244, 259–60, 266,
 274, 287, 309, 342,
 370

Jonsson, Ulrika 157, 158,
 305
Jordan 48
Jordan, Simon 348
Joslin, Helen 306
Joy, Bernard 265
Juventus 20, 81, 114,
 223, 235, 251, 275,
 290

Kahn, Oliver 132, 389,
 390
Kalac, Zeljko 382
Kamara, Chris 115, 224
Kanoute, Frederic 290
Kanu, Nkwankwo 26,
 237
Katz, Delma 37
Keane, Robbie 27, 271,
 378
Keane, Roy 5, 27–30,
 36–7, 45, 82–3, 107,
 130, 135, 145, 149,
 162, 176, 253, 256,
 257, 265, 318, 347,
 381, 383
Keegan, Kevin 32, 33,
 35, 71–2, 79, 83, 110,
 129, 146, 161, 172–4,
 183, 187, 200, 205,
 208, 209, 245, 248,
 272, 279, 290, 307,
 311, 331, 360, 379,
 380, 383, 384, 386–7
Keen, Kevin 289
Keith, John 64, 135, 180
Keller, Kasey 110
Kelly, Alan 145, 384
Kelly, David 57
Kelly, Gary 30–1, 255
Kelly, Graham 41, 258
Kelly, Robert 92
Kendall, Howard 84,
 153, 174–5, 197
Kennedy, Nigel 310
Kennedy, Stewart 355
Kent, Keith 106
Kenwright, Bill 37, 332
Kenyon, Peter 284
Keown, Martin 31, 129
Kerr, Jim 270

Kershore, Albert 112
Kewell, Harry 31, 47
Keys, Richard 18
Kidd, Brian 338, 384
Kidderminster Harriers
 297, 341, 382
Kilfoyle, Peter 326
Kilminster, Lemmy 360
King, Andy 208
Kinnaird, Paul 308
Kinnear, Joe 120, 175,
 206, 257, 258, 287,
 343
Kinnock, Neil 374
Kipling, Rudyard 218,
 367
Klinsman, Jurgen 72,
 117, 132, 142, 343
Kluivert, Patrick 74, 303
Knight, Sharon 354
Knighton, Michael 92,
 219, 328, 337
Knowles, Cyril 297
Koeman, Ronald 388
Koppel, Charles 319
Koumas, Jason 118
Kulkov, Vassili 110
Kuper, Simon 222
Kuznetsov, Oleg 241

Labone, Brian 96
Lacey, David 3, 133, 340
Lambie, John 259, 289
Lampard, Frank 118
Lancaster, Dave 102
Latchford, Bob 312
Lattek, Udo 66
Laudrup, Brian 21
Laudrup, Michael 72
Law, Denis 72, 109, 128,
 241–2
Law, Nicky 284
Lawrence, Lennie 97
Lawrenson, Mark 12, 78,
 260, 261, 334, 371
Lawson, Nigella 355
Lawton, Tommy 75
Lazio 9, 20, 214, 257,
 286, 342, 387, 388
Le Pen, Jean-Marie 130,
 131

Le Roy, Claude 221
Le Saux, Graeme 3, 18, 25, 32–3, 40, 94, 272–3, 316, 330
Le Tissier, Matthew 72, 254, 265, 305
Leboeuf, Frank 31–2, 236, 237, 266, 268
Lee, Colin 62, 123
Lee, Francis 13, 47, 142, 175, 200, 329
Lee, Gordon 175, 205, 226, 282, 285, 312
Lee, Robert 3, 32, 169, 203, 256, 259
Leeds United 3, 4, 7, 12–13, 17–18, 25, 27, 30–1, 33, 45, 56–60, 65–6, 68, 70, 82, 96, 98–101, 107–9, 114–15, 148, 157, 167, 178, 183, 193, 196–7, 201, 204, 210, 212, 218, 228–9, 237, 245, 252–5, 270–1, 276, 278, 285, 287–9, 299–302, 311–12, 338, 341, 344–5, 348, 352, 356, 373, 378, 382–3, 387
Leeson, Nick 313
Leicester 14, 26, 38, 44, 90, 101, 160, 176, 191, 194, 204, 205, 215, 216, 264, 278, 318, 345, 346, 357, 360, 371, 381, 382, 386, 387
Lemerre, Roger 221
Lendl, Ivan 240
Lennon, John 365
Lennon, Neil 32
Lessing, Doris 9
Lethem, Jonathan 7
Levein, Craig 202, 255
Levin, Bernard 223
Lewelyn, Lawrence 169
Lewis, Lennox 29
Leyton Orient 101, 235, 319, 322, 359
Liberia 133, 283

Lightening Seeds 364
Lillelien, Bjorge 368
Limerick 200
Lincoln 190, 221, 290–1, 307, 376
Lineker, Gary 20, 60, 71, 72–3, 120, 131, 160, 201, 202, 204, 230, 279, 280, 282, 334, 369
Lippi, Marcello 386
Little, Brian 205, 285, 381
Liverpool 3, 14–15, 18, 23, 26, 28, 32, 34, 42, 46, 52, 61–4, 67–8, 78, 81, 85, 88, 96, 101–3, 119, 134, 151, 153–4, 159, 171–2, 180, 186–9, 191, 204, 207, 221, 223–4, 231–3, 236, 241, 251–2, 264, 267, 281, 283, 286, 289, 296, 304–5, 327, 332, 340, 344, 352, 379, 383, 387–8
Livingstone, Ken 219
Lizarazu, Bixente 48
Ljungberg, Freddie 33, 89, 267–8
Lloyd, Larry 151
Lochead, Andy 82
Lockley, Catherine 155
Lodge, Stephen 344
Lofthouse, Nat 204, 285
Logan, Gabby 35
Lomas, Steve 282
Lombardi, Vince 232
Longson, Sam 328
Lord, Bob 221, 249
Louis-Dreyfus, Robert 59
Lovejoy, Joe 159, 190
Lovejoy, Tim 378
Lowe, Rupert 335
Lukic, John 167
Luton 25, 81, 226, 356, 380
Lydon, John 9
Lynam, Desmond 3, 316, 368, 370
Lyons, Andy 133

Mabbutt, Gary 65
Mac, Johnny 258
McAllister, Gary 33, 387
McAnuff, Joel 121
Macari, Lou 206, 207, 255, 263
McAteer, Jason 30, 133, 195, 358
Macauley, Archie 216
McAvennie, Frank 379
McCall, Kevin 354
McCarthy, Mick 29, 30, 35–6, 110, 135, 176, 201, 207–8, 210, 228, 303, 306
McClair, Brian 38–9
McClaren, Steve 107
McClinton, Kenny 32
McCoist, Ally 21, 22, 77, 93, 129
MacColl, Kirsty 365
McCormick, Neil 15
McCracken, Bill 295
McDermott, Terry 286, 379
MacDonald, Malcolm 173, 372, 379
Maceda, Evaristo 341
McFarland, Roy 213, 227
Macfarlane, Neil 323
McGarry, Bill 240
McGaughey, Paul 21
McGee, Alan 77
McGhee, Mark 123, 160, 165, 176, 210, 213, 252, 257
McGinnity, Mike 95
McGlashan, Colin 289
McGough, Roger 365
McGrath, John 224
McGrath, Paul 77, 106, 276, 305
McGrath, Rory 5
McGraw, Alan 294
MacGregor, Jimmy 364
McGregor, William 113, 322
Machin, Mel 334
McIlroy, Jimmy 121
McIlvanney, Hugh 111, 189

McIlvanney, William 302
McIntyre, Donal 301
Mackay, Don 354
Mackay, Malky 13
McKenzie, Duncan 25,
   71, 98, 238
McLaughlin, Jim 227
McLean, Jim 281
McLean, Tommy 188
MacLeod, Ally 128, 136,
   176–7
MacLeod, Murdo 216
McLintock, Frank 51, 98,
   166, 178
McMahon, Steve 224,
   280, 381
McManaman, Steve 33,
   239, 268
McMenemy, Lawrie 20,
   67, 134, 328
McMurdo, Bill 380
McNeill, Billy 77, 92,
   136, 147, 228, 279,
   379
Macpherson, Archie 200
Macsporran, Alastair 53
McStay, John 17
McStay, Paul 77
Major, John 215
Malam, Colin 202
Maloney, Frank 113
Manchester City 11, 13,
   29, 53, 79–80, 83, 96,
   101, 103–5, 142,
   160–2, 164, 170, 174,
   176, 185, 200, 202,
   210, 228, 231, 233,
   256, 266, 279–80, 284,
   297, 302, 309, 312–14,
   318, 329, 333–4, 340,
   353, 356, 359, 371–2,
   378–81
Manchester United 3,
   6–7, 9–10, 14, 16–18,
   23–4, 26–30, 35, 39,
   41, 43–6, 50, 54–5, 57,
   60–1, 64–5, 72–3, 78,
   81–3, 89, 93, 99, 101,
   103–9, 118, 142–3,
   147–9, 154, 159–62,
   189, 196, 205–6, 216,

219, 224–5, 228, 231,
   235, 239, 241, 253–4,
   256–8, 263, 266, 269,
   276, 278, 282–4, 306,
   312–13, 318–19, 327,
   333, 337, 341, 344,
   347, 358, 360–1, 375,
   378, 381, 384, 386–8
Mandela, Nelson 150, 168
Manning, Bernard 155,
   297
Mansfield 208
Maradona, Diego
   Armando 10, 73–4, 80,
   90, 126, 196, 356, 379
Margaret, Princess 96
Marks, Laurence 195,
   356
Marr, Johnny 385
Marsh, Rodney 20, 104,
   117, 142, 174, 202,
   242, 248, 355
Marti, Rene 83
Martin, Caroline 269
Martinez, Jairo 189
Martinez, Mr (referee)
   133
Martyn, Nigel 270
Materrese, Antonio
   307–8
Matthaus, Lothar 8,
   74–5, 360
Matthews, Stanley 54, 58,
   65, 73, 75–6, 231, 251,
   315
Maude, Francis 248
Maxwell, Robert 223,
   307, 333, 334, 335,
   337
Mayo, Simon 24
Mee, Bertie 175, 251
Meek, Brian 187
Meek, David 54, 55, 68
Megson, Don 54
Megson, Gary 115, 118,
   175
Meijer, Erik 286
Mellor, David 168, 318,
   331
Mercer, Joe 51, 75, 101,
   175–6, 209, 229

Merson, Paul 22, 33, 90,
   252, 263, 284
Merthyr Tydfil 308
Merton, Mrs (Caroline
   Hook) 139, 358
Mexico 200
Michopoulos, Nikolaos
   388
Middlesbrough 22, 23,
   61, 109–10, 171, 185,
   202, 204, 237, 244,
   279, 294
Midgley, Neil 341, 343
Milan 35, 110, 175, 196,
   266, 283, 336, 382
Milburn, Jackie 181–2
Miljanic, Miljan 238
Milla, Roger 284
Miller, Alex 287
Miller, David 381
Miller, Eric 328
Miller, Karl 19
Milligan, Spike 223
Mills, Danny 33, 265
Mills, Lee 113
Millwall 110, 123, 176,
   201, 204, 210, 228,
   250, 298, 306, 307
Milne, Gordon 278, 280
Mirandinha 77
Mitchell, Reginald 76
Mitchell, Roger 112
Mogg, Dave 170
Molby, Jan 44
Monaco 226, 238, 305
Monroe, Michael 21
Moore, Bobby 15, 26,
   60, 77, 78, 128, 129
Moore, Brian 78, 367
Moreno, Byron 133
Morgan, Piers 32
Morgan, Rhodri 139
Morris, Desmond 334
Morris, Jody 34
Morrison, Clinton 34, 135
Morrison, Jim 57
Mortensen, Stan 78,
   296–7
Morton 294
Moscow Dynamo 223,
   315

Moses, Remi 78
Motherwell 211
Motson, John 72, 80, 114, 119, 368, 370
Muhren, Arnold 143
Muller, Gerd 263
Mullery, Alan 388
Munro, Iain 287
Murdoch, Bobby 77
Murdoch, Rupert 313, 333
Murphy, Colin 290–1, 376
Murphy, Eddie 244
Murphy, Jimmy 64–5
Murphy, Sheree 31
Murray, Bill 4
Murray, Bob 183
Murray, David 114, 327
Murray, Jim 242
Mussolini, Benito 15–16, 133
Mustoe, Robbie 23
Mykland, Erik 134

Najeib, Sarfraz 385
Napoli 286
Narey, David 364–5
Nayim 39
Neal, Phil 104, 207, 232
Neale, Phil 221
Necaxa 6
Neill, Terry 177
Nelson, Garry 275
Nesta, Alessandro 349
Netherlands 11, 74, 83, 133, 137, 190, 232, 239, 265, 342, 388
see also Holland
Netzer, Gunter 194, 255
Neville, Gary 34, 107, 161
Nevin, Pat 78
New York Cosmos 231, 243
Newcastle United 3, 14–16, 18–19, 24, 32, 40–2, 50, 77, 110–11, 120, 148, 154, 163, 173–4, 184–5, 203, 208–9, 218, 227, 256,

259, 268, 281, 286, 295, 307, 314, 325, 347–8, 355, 371–2, 374–5, 380, 385
Newman, Paul 158
Newman, Ron 242
Newport County 111
Nicholas, Charlie 78–9, 155, 263
Nicholas, Peter 225
Nicholson, Bill 42, 56, 177, 248, 352
Nicholson, Grace 352
Nicol, Steve 78
Nicol, Watt 173
Nielsen, Richard Moller 268
Nigeria 228, 268
Nish, David 227
Nita, Robert 348
Nixon, Pat 179
Noades, Ron 332
Northampton 369, 380
Northern Ireland 32, 54, 89, 127, 133, 207, 264, 280, 282, 295, 303
Norton, Graham 35
Norway 20, 99, 133–4, 177, 373, 374
Norwich 13, 111, 146, 216, 270, 282, 289, 338, 371, 374
Nottingham Forest 27, 42, 45, 56, 62, 81, 108, 112, 145, 150–2, 159–60, 179, 181, 191, 197, 205, 211, 214, 227, 235, 257, 274, 276, 299, 305–6, 314, 318, 323, 335, 355, 381
Notts County 112, 214, 227, 245, 284, 288, 291
Novick, Jeremy 333

O'Brien, Andrew 35
O'Connor, Des 129
O'Hanlon, Ardal 312
O'Hanlon, Rory 312

O'Keefe, Eamonn 60
Oldham 205, 248, 288, 290, 317, 342, 346, 355, 356
O'Leary, David 17, 18, 36, 47, 50, 99, 100, 107, 178–9, 183, 196, 345, 348, 370, 373, 385, 387
Oliver, Jim 328, 329
Olsen, Egil 177–8
O'Neill, Martin 25–6, 38, 44, 112, 179–80, 216, 318, 345, 386
O'Riordan, Marie 10
Ormond, William 65, 178
Orwell, George 70, 223
Overmars, Marc 34
Owen, Michael 15, 34–5, 103, 289
Oxford United 281, 307, 334

Pacheco, Antonio 239
Padfield, Emma 248
Paisley, Bob 63, 67, 102, 119, 151, 180, 231
Pallister, Gary 24, 160
Palmer, Carlton 180, 255
Palmer, Myles 196
Paltrow, Gwyneth 319
Panathinaikos 369
Paris Saint-Germain 2, 273
Parkes, Tony 384
Parkinson, Michael 273
Parlour, Ray 378
Parry, Alan 369
Partick Thistle 112, 216, 259, 289, 308, 328, 355, 382
Partizan Belgrade 279
Partridge, Pat 82, 340
Patten, Chris 309
Paul, Roy 265–6
Pawson, Tony 142, 182
Paxman, Jeremy 154
Payne, Cynthia 354
Peacock, Gavin 57
Pearce, Jimmy 230

Pearce, Stuart 45, 79, 236, 270–1, 276, 286
Pearson, Allison 70
Pearson, Bob 204
Pearson, Brian 309
Pearson, Harry 90–1, 294
Pearson, Keith 122
Pearson, Stuart 258
Peel, John 327
Pejic, Mick 83
Pele 20, 52, 61, 74, 79–80, 127, 129, 142, 218, 228, 244, 269, 289
Pereira, Luis 268
Perry, Chris 120
Perryman, Steve 65, 272
Peru 136
Peschisolido, Paul 302
Peterborough 55, 165, 201, 206, 260, 322
Peters, Martin 80, 127
Petit, Emmanuel 35, 195, 278, 360, 384
Petrescu, Dan 383
Phillips, Kevin 35, 269
Picken, Peter 297
Pickering, Lionel 325
Pickford, William 116
Pires, Robert 100, 238
Pistone, Alessandro 168
Plant, Robert 315, 327
Platini, Michel 220, 239–40
Platt, David 80, 181, 274
Pleat, David 81, 181, 200–1, 204, 215, 226, 285, 314, 356, 370
Plymouth 142
Poland 367, 369
Poll, Graham 344, 349
Port Vale 112–13, 116, 186, 203, 211, 224, 296, 302, 306, 314, 331–2, 338
Porto 264
Portsmouth 113, 145, 214, 232, 348, 353, 378
Portugal 47, 129, 239, 387

Powell, Lord Baden 295
Presley, Elvis 43, 84
Pressman, Kevin 298
Preston 64, 132, 155, 215, 288, 308
Price, Alan 353
Price, Paul 68–9
Priestley, J.B. 365
Puskas, Ferenc 73, 80, 132–3, 230, 233–4, 244

Queen, Gerry 374
Queen of the South 113
Queen's Park 113, 165, 211, 228, 275, 300
Quinn, Niall 35–6, 120, 170, 255, 256

Rae, Alex 298
Rafferty, John 92
Raith Rovers 17
Ramos, Tab 138
Ramsey, Alf 65, 74, 80, 126, 128, 136, 181–2, 233, 283, 296, 372
Rangers 17, 21–2, 57–8, 69, 72, 77, 82, 92–3, 97, 113–14, 116, 136, 160, 179, 185, 188, 218, 241, 255, 270, 303–5, 317, 327, 355–6, 358, 379–80, 385
Ranieri, Claudio 46, 182
Rapid Bucharest 348
Rapid Vienna 228
Ravanelli, Fabrizio 36
Rayner, Amy 359
Rayner, Claire 201
Read, Willie 235
Reading 250, 307
Reading, Dowager Marchioness of 300
Real Madrid 2, 8, 37, 64, 80, 114, 207, 210, 215, 238, 239, 244, 254, 256, 257, 273, 288, 327, 387
Recber, Rustu 37
Recorder Williams, Mr 192

Redford, Robert 334
Redknapp, Harry 12, 15, 144, 183, 203, 213, 214, 245, 288
Redknapp, Jamie 296
Reed, Arnie 69
Reed, Mike 344, 345
Reeve, Dermot 336
Regan, John 173
Regis, Cyrille 81
Reid, John 303
Reid, Peter 183, 195, 210, 281, 380–1
Republic of Ireland 20, 29–30, 36, 59, 66, 77, 130, 133–5, 148–50, 156, 176, 179, 182, 187, 200, 207–8, 235, 248, 255–6, 265, 303–5, 324, 349, 371, 374, 383
Revie, Don 66, 70, 82, 98, 99, 183–4, 327, 378
Revie, Duncan 184
Reynolds, George 96, 322, 325, 337
Richards, Graham 371
Richardson, Bryan 95
Richmond, Geoffrey 386
Ridley, Ian 128
Ridsdale, Peter 13, 47, 101, 301, 338, 378, 387
Rihilahti, Aki 11, 36
Rimbaud, Arthur 57, 278
Rimet, Jules 364
Rioch, Bruce 224, 270
Rippon, Anton 222, 307
Ritchie, Andy 290, 317, 346
Ritchie, John 261
Rivaldo 36, 127, 139, 220
Rivera, Gianni 242
Rober, Jurgen 152, 286
Roberts, Bobby 299
Roberts, John 72
Robertson, John 77, 81, 112, 179
Robins, Mark 357

Robinson, Paul 30–1
Robinson, Peter 102–3
Robson, Bobby 15, 42,
    61, 74, 120, 127–8,
    132, 163, 184–5, 197,
    206, 227, 268, 328,
    348, 373
Robson, Bryan 81,
    109–10, 185, 202, 225,
    261, 264, 282
Rocha, Juan 369
Rollin, Jack 243
Romania 383
Romario 37
Ronaldinho 40, 139
Ronaldo 10–11, 37, 74,
    108, 139, 268, 286
Rooney, Wayne 37
Rossi, Paoli 255
Rothenberg, Alan
    299–300
Rotherham 289, 326,
    374
Rowe, Arthur 105, 233
Rowell, Gary 294
Rowlandson, John 72,
    80, 114
Roxburgh, Andy 53, 67,
    172, 185, 207, 287
Royle, Joe 96, 104, 161,
    185, 200, 201, 205,
    225, 248–9, 256, 288,
    312–13, 318, 356, 359,
    371
Royle, John 17, 24
Ruberry, Barry 147
Rudd, Alyson 358–9
Ruddock, Neil 15, 18,
    38, 42, 45, 62, 84–5,
    275
Rudge, John 186, 203,
    343
Rush, Ian 81, 102, 235,
    290
Rushdie, Salman 19
Rushton, Jim 342
Russell, Ken 314
Russia 383
Ryan, Jim 380

Saha, Louis 38
St John, Ian 66
St Mirren 235, 287, 308
St Pauli 266
Salisbury Town 298
Sampdoria 352
San Marino 137
Sanchez, Lawrie 102
Sanderson, Tessa 94
Sansom, Kenny 341
Santamaria, Jose 114
Saporta, Don Raimondo
    257
Sassoon, Vidal 310
Saudi Arabia 208
Saunders, Dean 334
Saunders, Ron 186, 285
Savage, Robbie 38, 316
Scally, Paul 97
Scarborough 114–15,
    194
Scargill, Arthur 327
Schmeichel, Peter 38–9,
    43, 84
Scholar, Irving 323, 335
Scholes, Paul 39, 384
Schumacher, Harald 286
Schwarznegger, Arnold
    172
Scolari, Luiz Felipe 127,
    186, 226, 361
Scotland 48, 52–3, 62,
    65–7, 69, 77–8, 81, 84,
    128–9, 135–8, 146–7,
    150, 173, 177–8, 185,
    189, 194, 202, 207,
    214, 216, 218, 223,
    228, 231–2, 240,
    244–5, 255, 262–3,
    271, 280, 282, 287,
    290, 302–3, 356, 358,
    364–5, 367, 373–4,
    382, 384–5, 389
Scott, Sir Walter 366
Scunthorpe 279, 388
Seaman, David 33, 39–40
Seba, Jesus 305
Segers, Hans 70
Senegal 138, 370
Sexton, Dave 94, 224,
    228, 231

Seymour, Stan 18, 148
Shackleton, Len 110,
    111, 226, 232, 323
Shakespeare, William 366
Shamrock Rovers 227
Shankly, Bill 63, 64, 65,
    66, 68, 85, 88, 96,
    101–2, 135, 136, 150,
    151, 186–7, 189, 221,
    251, 258, 267, 289,
    304, 340, 352
Shankly, Nessie 187
Sharp, Alan 52–3
Sharp, Graeme 282
Sharpe, Lee 26, 167
Shearer, Alan 15, 40–2,
    50, 203, 248, 273
Shearer, Bobby 136
Sheepshanks, David 325
Sheffield United 115,
    129, 145, 151, 175,
    194, 203–5, 260–1,
    280–1, 292, 309, 311,
    314, 318, 324–5, 328,
    338
Sheffield Wednesday 115,
    181, 201, 204, 232,
    234, 265, 276, 285,
    298, 314–16, 326, 341,
    348, 352, 354, 372,
    380, 385
Shepherd, Freddy 40
Shepherdson, Harold 128
Sheringham, Teddy 42,
    309, 371
Sherwood, Tim 117
Shilton, Peter 187, 306
Shipperley, Neil 121
Shreeves, Peter 169, 225,
    283–4, 287
Shrewsbury 103
Sillett, John 211, 281,
    380
Silvestre, Mickael 160,
    266
Simeone, Diego 383
Simmons, Matthew 58
Sinatra, Frank 61, 143
Sinstadt, Gerald 102, 312
Sirrel, Jimmy 227, 245,
    288, 291

Sissons, Peter 172
Skinner, Frank 72, 192, 315, 364
Sklenarikova, Adriana 130
Skovdahl, Ebbe 244–5, 286
Slaven, Bernie 109, 279
Smith, Alan 34, 95, 97, 208, 348
Smith, Alex 283, 287
Smith, Colin 301
Smith, David 333
Smith, Delia 111, 221, 338
Smith, Denis 146
Smith, Gordon 309
Smith, Ian Duncan 159
Smith, Jim 45, 65, 110, 259, 334, 345
Smith, John 63
Smith, Martin 144–5
Smith, Michelle 158
Smith, Richard O. 318
Smith, Robert 278
Smith, Tommy 81, 236, 237
Smith, Walter 22, 47, 97, 187–8, 345
Snow, John 117
Socrates 220
Soderberg, Tommy 221
Solano, Nolberto 348
Solbakken, Stale 178
Solskjaer, Ole Gunnar 43
Sorensen, Thomas 43
Souness, Graeme 12, 63, 81–2, 84, 188–9, 206, 207, 241, 252, 264
South Korea 349
Southall, Neville 165–6, 253
Southampton 42, 67, 144, 146, 220, 254, 305, 335, 346, 357, 367, 374
Southgate, Barbara 43
Southgate, Gareth 12, 25, 43–4, 168, 271–2
Soviet Union 302
Spacey, Marianne 358
Spackman, Nigel 369

Spearing, Tony 342
Spencer, John 48, 280
Sprake, Gary 183
Sproson, Phil 116
Sproson, Roy 210–11
Stafford Rangers 317
Stam, Jaap 9, 14, 18, 35, 108, 162, 257, 347, 388
Stamp, Gavin 59
Staniforth, Mark 114–15
Stanley, Chantel 24
Stanton, Pat 159
Steele, Trevor 355
Stein, Edwin 249
Stein, Jock 63, 78, 92, 189, 200, 206, 304
Stein, Mark 275
Stein, Mel 22
Stein, Ulli 379
Sternmaker, Lars 159
Stewart, Kris 121
Stewart, Ray 279
Stewart, Rod 40, 315, 364
Stiles, Nobby 82, 182, 237
Still, Athole 159, 260
Stirling Albion 279
Stirling, Ray 170
Stock, Alec 230, 265, 298, 353
Stockport 180, 280, 284, 381
Stoichkov, Hristo 382
Stoke City 66, 75, 76, 83, 115, 145, 187, 209, 223, 229, 233, 237, 243, 261, 306, 315, 332, 343, 369
Stone, Steve 273–4
Stonewall 115, 233
Stoppard, Miriam 308, 317
Storey, Peter 261
Strachan, Gordon 31, 46, 82, 137, 143–4, 153, 161, 178, 189–90, 203, 204, 205, 245, 254, 278, 345, 347–8, 359, 387
Strang, Sandy 303

Stringer, Dave 216, 289
Stringfellow, Peter 55
Sugar, Alan 11, 111, 117, 167, 192, 258, 306, 335, 381
Suker, Davor 44
Sullivan, David 91, 264, 325, 357
Sullivan, Neil 44
Summerbee, Mike 104, 334, 340
Summerfield, Kevin 103
Summers, Trevor 381
Sunderland 41, 43, 110, 116, 183, 195, 208, 219, 255, 256, 269, 281, 294, 346
Sutch, Screaming Lord 213
Sutton, Chris 275, 288, 330
Swales, Peter 151, 333, 334, 380–1
Swansea 295
Sweden 221, 268, 374, 384
Swindon 142, 205, 255, 263, 280, 283, 284, 375, 381
Switzerland 212
Symons, Emily 265

Tagg, Ernie 56
Taggart, Gerry 44, 264
Talbot, Brian 380
Tanasijevic, Jovan 26
Tapie, Bernard 59, 254
Tarantino, Quentin 271
Tarmak, Mart 382
Taylor, Gordon 155, 157, 236–7
Taylor, Graham 41, 52, 122, 134, 174, 176, 190, 197, 201, 202, 203, 204, 213, 214, 227, 233, 234, 245, 258, 286, 292, 336, 337, 342, 356, 373, 374
Taylor, Ian 285
Taylor, Jack 242, 340, 367

Taylor, John 310
Taylor, Peter 38, 191, 387
Taylor, Peter 118, 150, 152, 190–1, 353
Taylor, Tom 173, 235
Telford 231, 284
Thames Valley Royals 307
Thatcher, Ben 116
Thatcher, Margaret 116, 151, 160, 172, 215, 219, 290, 368
Theerapunyo, Chan 8
Thomas, Clive 'The book' 63
Thomas, Mickey 82–3, 273
Thompson, Archie 126
Thompson, Harold 327
Thompson, Peter 88
Thompson, Phil 171, 191
Tigana, Jean 211
Tjernaas, Lars 177
Todd, Colin 227, 279
Tofting, Stig 44
Tognoni, Guido 148, 342
Tomas, Jason 330
Toms, Wendy 343, 359
Toppmoller, Klaus 216
Torquay 294
Toshack, John 207, 210, 287
Tossell, David 88, 98, 175
Tottenham 14–15, 19–21, 24, 39, 42, 44, 51, 56, 65–6, 68, 75, 85, 88, 98, 105, 111, 116–17, 119–20, 142, 154, 167, 169–70, 177, 192, 209, 212, 215, 218, 223, 225–6, 230, 233, 238, 248, 250, 256, 258, 272, 276, 283–4, 287, 297, 298, 306, 309, 313, 315–16, 334–5, 343, 345, 347, 352, 360, 364, 371, 378–9, 381, 383, 388
Totti, Francesco 289

Townsend, Andy 134, 266, 370
Townsend, Jill 353
Toye, Clive 243
Traill, Liz 14
Trapattoni, Giovanni 16, 210, 238
Trautmann, Bert 83
Triesman, David 324
Trinder, Tommy 250
Truscott, Brian 367
Turkey 37, 138, 220
Turner, Graham 57, 211
Turney, Simon 299
Tyldesley, Clive 144
Tyler, Martin 75
Tyson, Mike 6, 8, 70

United Arab Emirates 327
United States 137, 138, 370
Unsworth, David 376
Uruguay 138–9

Valencia 99
Valle, Keith 341
Van Basten, Marco 83
Venables, Terry 17, 20, 83, 109, 119, 131, 156–7, 191–3, 279, 280, 285, 335, 370, 373
Venables, Yvette 192
Venglos, Jo 193
Veron, Juan Sebastian 44, 389
VfB Stuttgart 289
Vialli, Gianluca 25, 193, 275, 344
Vialli, Luca 94
Vieira, Patrick 38, 44–5, 195, 389
Viera, Ondina 138–9
Vieri, Christian 254–5, 349
Viner, Brian 368
Vogts, Berti 23, 83, 128, 132, 194, 267, 389
Vowden, Judge Desmond 308

Waddell, Willie 113
Waddington, Tony 209, 237
Waddle, Chris 24, 59, 83, 91, 205
Wait, Arthur 324
Waite, Terry 223
Waldron, Colin 272
Wales 71, 82, 134, 139, 150, 165–6, 182, 225, 230, 235, 251, 253, 266, 384
Walford, Danny 301
Walker, David 57
Walker, Des 45
Walker, Len 305
Walker, Mike 120, 282
Wall, Frederick 322
Wallace, Dave 104
Wallace, Ian 150
Wallace, Jock 194
Walmsley, Marcus 312
Walsall 200, 204, 206, 317
Walsh, Bradley 4
Walsh, Stephen 303
Wanchope, Paulo 45
Ward, Andrew 222
Ward, Ashley 270, 272
Ward, Ken 270
Ward, Peter 150
Warhurst, Paul 288
Warnock, Neil 115, 151, 175, 194, 214, 281, 385
Waseige, Robert 370
Wassall, Darren 151
Watford 25, 41, 117, 201, 213, 214, 234, 245, 258, 266, 283–4, 301, 309, 336, 337
Watson, Dave 270
Watt, Tom 309, 356
Watterson, Mike 324–5
Weah, George 133, 272, 283
Webb, Neil 159
Welch, Racquel 82, 249
Wenders, Wim 228
Wenger, Arsene 2, 36, 38, 40, 45, 74–5, 89,

109, 130, 158, 160, 164, 195–6, 200, 208, 212, 213, 236, 254, 266, 284, 346, 347, 389

West Bromwich Albion 115, 117–18, 169, 175, 184, 215, 302, 315, 316, 380, 381

West Germany 53, 83, 218, 263, 286, 291, 374, 375, 379

West Ham United 12, 15, 16, 17, 25, 26, 56, 78, 98, 116, 118, 144, 183, 203, 206, 213, 214, 233, 245, 278, 280, 283, 288, 289, 290, 299, 316, 346, 355, 371, 384, 387

Westbrook, Daniella 248

Westerhof, Clemens 228, 268

Westerveld, Sander 46, 232

Westgarth, Fred 296

Westley, Terry 25

Wetzel, Jean Luc 263

Whelan, Noel 311–12

White, Eric 354

White, Noel 174

Whitehouse, Paul 313, 316

Whiteside, Norman 106

Whitfield, June 315

Whymark, Trevor 290

Widdecombe, Ann 53

Wigan 60, 305, 327, 341

Wiggins, Xavier 93

Wilcox, Jason 371

Wilde, Oscar 352

Wilkie, Alan 344

Wilkie, Ray 233

Wilkins, Ray 84, 196, 258, 284

Wilkinson, Howard 47, 57, 82, 98, 114, 115, 159, 196–7, 201, 204, 210, 211–12, 229, 232, 276, 287–8, 289, 299, 323, 341, 372, 382

Williams, Andy 290

Williams, Danny 283

Williams, Harold 60

Williams, John 218

Williams, Robbie 10–11, 24, 306, 314

Willis, Peter 28, 236

Willman, David 338

Wilnis, Fabien 269

Wilson, Bob 51

Wilson, Danny 316, 385

Wilson, Harold 290

Wilson, Ray 75

Wilson, Richard 161

Wimbledon 38, 43, 44, 46, 64, 65, 66, 70, 93, 102, 119–21, 145, 175, 177, 178, 206, 211, 234, 257, 258, 260, 267, 269, 279, 287, 315, 319, 332, 342, 343, 344, 353, 356

Windass, Dean 28

Winter, Jeff 43, 346

Winterbottom, Walter 197

Wire, Nicky 139

Wisdom, Norman 324

Wise, Dennis 46–7, 94, 188, 193, 266

Witschge, Richard 237

Witter, Tony 342

Wogan, Terry 19

Wolfsburg 16

Wolstenholme, Kenneth 76

Wolverhampton Wanderers 27, 30, 57, 62, 121–3, 152–3, 165, 172, 176, 204, 210, 213, 230, 234, 240, 252, 257, 315, 317, 324, 327, 335, 336, 382

Woodgate, Jonathan 17, 47, 99, 100, 252, 253, 289, 385

Woodhouse, Barbara 299

Wordsworth, William 366

Worthington, Frank 82, 84, 353

Wragg, Dick 183

Wrexham 273

Wright, Alan 47, 50

Wright, Billy 124

Wright, Ian 11, 14, 28, 52, 84–5, 178, 195, 226, 241, 304, 311, 316, 342, 367–8

Wright, Roderick 303

Wylie, Gill 96

Wyness, Keith 355

Xavier, Abel 47

Yeats, Ron 85, 119

Yeboah, Tony 47–8, 99, 237

Yorath, Terry 82, 225

Yorke, Dwight 6, 48, 256, 269, 380

Young, Big George 65

Young, Emma 309

Yugoslavia 26, 282

Yuran, Sergei 110

Zagallo, Mario 219

Zahavi, Pina 101

Zambia 375

Zaragoza 39, 256, 305

Zenga, Walter 269

Zico 225

Zidane, Zinedine 48, 389

Zola, Gianfranco 46, 48, 236–7